Fanon, Žižek, and the Violence of Resistance

ALSO AVAILABLE FROM BLOOMSBURY

Alienation and Freedom, Frantz Fanon
Žižek on Race, Zahi Zalloua
Freedom, Slavoj Žižek
The Political Writings from Alienation and Freedom, Frantz Fanon

Fanon, Žižek, and the Violence of Resistance

Zahi Zalloua

BLOOMSBURY ACADEMIC
LONDON • NEW YORK • OXFORD • NEW DELHI • SYDNEY

BLOOMSBURY ACADEMIC
Bloomsbury Publishing Plc, 50 Bedford Square, London, WC1B 3DP, UK
Bloomsbury Publishing Inc, 1385 Broadway, New York, NY 10018, USA
Bloomsbury Publishing Ireland, 29 Earlsfort Terrace, Dublin 2, D02 AY28, Ireland

BLOOMSBURY, BLOOMSBURY ACADEMIC and the Diana logo are trademarks of
Bloomsbury Publishing Plc

First published in Great Britain 2025

Copyright © Zahi Zalloua, 2025

Zahi Zalloua has asserted his right under the Copyright, Designs and Patents Act, 1988,
to be identified as Author of this work.

For legal purposes the Acknowledgments on p. viii constitute an extension of this
copyright page.

Cover image: *Map* (2006). Acrylic on Canvas, 100x100cm. Rafat Asad

All rights reserved. No part of this publication may be: i) reproduced or transmitted in any form, electronic or mechanical, including photocopying, recording or by means of any information storage or retrieval system without prior permission in writing from the publishers; or ii) used or reproduced in any way for the training, development or operation of artificial intelligence (AI) technologies, including generative AI technologies. The rights holders expressly reserve this publication from the text and data mining exception as per Article 4(3) of the Digital Single Market Directive (EU) 2019/790.

Bloomsbury Publishing Plc does not have any control over, or responsibility for, any third-party websites referred to or in this book. All internet addresses given in this book were correct at the time of going to press. The author and publisher regret any inconvenience caused if addresses have changed or sites have ceased to exist, but can accept no responsibility for any such changes.

A catalogue record for this book is available from the British Library.

A catalog record for this book is available from the Library of Congress.

ISBN: HB: 978-1-3505-1328-0
PB: 978-1-3505-1327-3
ePDF: 978-1-3505-1329-7
eBook: 978-1-3505-1330-3

Typeset by Deanta Global Publishing Services, Chennai, India
Printed and bound in Great Britain

To find out more about our authors and books visit www.bloomsbury.com and
sign up for our newsletters.

For Nicole

Contents

Acknowledgments viii

Introduction: Violent Ontologies 1

1 Being and Destitution 41

2 Disavowal in Crisis: The End of Liberalism 65

3 Decolonizing the Mind Under Occupation and Global Capitalism 97

4 Radical Others and Real Neighbors: The Politics of the Faceless 127

5 Against Exceptionalism 151

Conclusion 181

Afterword: A Small Note on a Great Book 187

Notes 191
Bibliography 255
Index 283

Acknowledgments

To write a book on violence and resistance—on the violence of resistance—is to welcome scrutiny and consternation. Talk of violent changes and ontological upheavals jars with liberal sensibilities. As a general principle, liberals prefer the slow path of reform over sudden shifts in the collective psyche. This book will undoubtedly disappoint readers inhospitable to intense transformations, but these are not the readers I have in mind. My fellow interlocutors are fed up with the scripts handed down to us by Western governments and parroted by profit-driven media outlets. They hunger for more and are tired of the depoliticizing spirit of the day. The book speaks to this generation, to a generation deeply marked by the movement for Black lives and outraged by the cruelty of Israel's genocidal campaign against the Palestinian people.

In these dark times, I find myself constantly turning and returning to the writings of Frantz Fanon and Slavoj Žižek, two thinkers often, and unproductively, pitted against one another. What Fanon and Žižek confirm for me is that the anti-colonial Left is indispensable for the universalist Left, and that, in the global struggle for justice, universality is not a luxury but a necessity. My book grew out of this commitment, in the face of a new McCarthyism that unconscionably criminalizes principled stances. The big Other says, "Don't write this"—so I write this. In my teaching at Whitman College, where classes serve as dialectical spaces to explore and test new ideas, I've been fortunate to encounter and engage with students who want to learn about anti-Blackness—not to feel good about their liberalism but to understand this insidious plague so as to better fight it—and whose passion for justice exceeded the confines of the classroom, spilling into teach-ins, encampments, and protests spearheaded by the intrepid students of the Whitman chapter of Students for Justice in Palestine.

Outside of Walla Walla, I'm always appreciative of my brother Mounir, whose steadfast support means the world to me. I want to thank the Arab Council for the Social Sciences for inviting me to contribute to their webinar "Critical Theory Encounters Palestine." For the countless exchanges at conferences and symposia that contributed generatively to the writing of this book, I thank Nadia Abu El-Haj, Linda Martín Alcoff, Bashir Bashir, Jake Blevins, Clint Burnham, Chad Cordova, Ben Davis, Jeffrey R. Di Leo, Amal Eqeiq, Al Frankowski, Carin Franzén, John Harfouch,

Jane Gallop, Amos Goldberg, Robin Goodman, David Gunkel, Agon Hamza, Peter Hitchcock, Derek Hook, Janine Jones, Leigh Johnson, Ilan Kapoor, Rick Lee, Geo Maher, Saree Makdisi, Michael Marder, Sophia McClennen, Paul Allen Miller, Dirk Moses, Oded Nir, Brian O'Keeffe, William M. Paris, Michael Principe, Mouin Rabbani, Arnab Roy, Frank Ruda, Ken Saltman, Khalil Saucier, Ben Schreier, Adam Stern, Rob Tally, Sjoerd van Tuinen, Cary Wolfe, George Yancy, Robert J. C. Young, and Alenka Zupančič. Special thanks go out to Rafat Asad and Joe Sacco for allowing me to use their powerful artwork in this book. I am very grateful to Liza Thompson at Bloomsbury for her unwavering commitment to this project. And I'd also like to express my appreciation to Slavoj for his uncompromising work and generosity in writing the Afterword to this study.

Colleagues at Whitman have been invaluable in helping me articulate and develop my ideas. I'm thankful to M Acuff, Susanne Beechey, Shampa Biswas, Matt Bost, Chetna Chopra, Tarik Elseewi, Robert Flahive, Giramata, Camilo Lund-Montaño, Gaurav Majumdar, Lydia McDermott, Libby Miller, Lauren Osborne, Kaitlyn Patia, Daniel Schultz, Andrea Sempértegui, Ozge Serin, Daniel Smith, Lisa Uddin, and Xiaobo Yuan. I also want to thank my amazing student research assistants Bex Heimbrock and Dante Filippetto for their collaboration on this project. And, as always, my deepest gratitude goes to Nicole, who grounds and inspires me like no other.

Portions of the Introduction appeared in "Framing Palestine," *Philosophical Salon* (May 6, 2024). Portions of Chapter 2 appeared in "Disavowal in Crisis: The Israeli Far Right and the End of Liberal Zionism," *Crisis and Critique* 11, no. 1 (2024): 210–235; "Reckoning with America's Anti-Blackness: From Repression to Disavowal—and Beyond," in *symplokē* 32, no. 1–2 (2024, forthcoming). Portions of Chapter 3 appeared in "Psychoanalysis as World Literature," in *Theory as World Literature*, ed. Jeffrey R. Di Leo (New York: Bloomsbury 2025, forthcoming). Portions of Chapter 4 appeared in "The Politics of the Faceless," in *symplokē* 32, no. 1–2 (2024, forthcoming). And portions of Chapter 5 appeared in "Against Exceptionalism," *Humanities* 13, no. 50 (2024): 1–23. This project was supported in part by a Louis B. Perry Summer Research Grant.

Introduction
Violent Ontologies

To paraphrase James Baldwin, not every ontology that is reckoned with can be changed; but no ontology can be changed until reckoned with.[1] This book argues that the efforts carried out by anti-colonial theorist Frantz Fanon and Marxist-Lacanian philosopher Slavoj Žižek to expose and scrutinize ontology's violent and ideological structures resonate with one another in productive and inventive ways. In pairing violence/resistance and ontology, I want to advance an anti-racist and universalist critique of ontology, attending to the processes by which ontology operates in a racial matrix to produce some human bodies that count and others (deemed not-quite human or nonhuman) that do not. For Fanon and Žižek, the violence of ontology must be met with another form of violence, a revolutionary violence that delegitimizes the logic of the symbolic order and troubles its collective fantasies, a violence that tears down the ideological veil of normalcy, exposing the ways in which bewitching, daily operations of life inflict an unbearable, numbing violence on society's wretched, on the world's surplus humanity. Whereas Fanon begins his challenge to ontology by exposing its historical linkages to Europe's destructive imperialist procedures, before proceeding to "stretch" Marxism, along with psychoanalysis and philosophy writ large, to account for the crushing colonial and neocolonial setting, Žižek premises his work on the refusal to accept the totality of ontology, unsettling the symbolic order's phantasmatic and ideological pretensions by gesturing to its immanent gap, incompleteness, and inconsistency. Because of these different points of intervention, Fanon and Žižek together offer a powerful and multifaceted assessment of the contemporary state of affairs. They help to invalidate not only the rise and proliferation of populist alt-right movements but also, and perhaps more importantly, the liberal anti-racist paradigm whose propensity for identity politics, easy wokeness, and aversion to antagonisms and class struggle silence the cry of the dispossessed and foreclose radical change. The liberal imperative is: *social coordinates are not to be transformed*. Avoiding contemporary tribalist or separatist temptations (decoloniality and Afropessimism), and breaking with a nonviolent, sentimentalist, liberal futurology that announces more of the same, cosmetically repackaged, Fanon and Žižek point in a different direction, one that considers the violence of the status quo as unacceptable while eschewing identitarian thoughts and positions in favor of a collective struggle for freedom and equality.

In this book, I explore Western ontology's complicity with racism, taking up, first, Fanon's disheartening claim in *Black Skin, White Masks* that "the black man has no ontological resistance in the eyes of the white man."[2] Ontology's relation to race and racism should not be ignored or underestimated. It is not enough to say that race is a social construct. The ontological effects of colonialization and racialization—on the colonized and the colonizer—must be given their full weight. Holding Western ontology to account, Fanon puts into relief the deep harms colonization does to people's minds and realities, the ways it touches society's marginalized and dispossessed bodies most drastically. Ontology is not neutral. Ontology is not destiny. The struggles against anti-Blackness and colonialism are struggles against/with/from ontology. I share Gautum Basu Thakur's belief that Fanon's critical engagement with colonialism and racist ideologies, more generally, has to do less with social justice—"as exclusively a matter of economic and/or political inequality"—and more with ontology.[3] A reckoning with domination portends ontological interruption and upheaval. Fanon decries the ways that white agents of ontology "turn man into a machine."[4] There is no account of Blackness or wretchedness that is not mediated if not overdetermined by a white metaphysics, by a "whiteness [that] burns me to a cinder."[5] Human existence as such is predicated on the violent reduction of Black folks to a mode of enslavement or thinghood, to their skin color or surface ontology (the phenomenon of epidermalization). Born damned, Black being is tethered to "an image, snaring him, imprisoning him as the eternal victim of his own essence, of a *visible appearance* for which he is not responsible."[6] Fanon laments the unremitting destruction of Blackness and implicitly sets the goal of forging a new ontology of (relating to) Blackness—a counter-ontology that violently upends the violence of the status quo, that undoes the self's, and the collective's, psychical attachment to the world, and that avoids the false colorblindness of abstract universalism (French republicanism) without at the same time ontologizing Blackness (as injury), reifying it anew, determining it as a static feature of Black existence.

Žižek echoes Fanon's call for counter-violence. As he puts it, sometimes an individual or a group can no longer tolerate their domination, their psychic and physical abuse, and can only react to their environment through some "irrational violent outburst."[7] At the same time, Žižek, like Fanon, is cognizant of the traps presented by impotent acts of violent rage and empty reversals, which reinstate a Manichean racial logic—us vs. them; good vs. evil—that locks individuals in their races and given positions, playing into the hands of a heartless system. In the contemporary scene, violence is increasingly taking on a one-dimensional face (as the expression of anger and frustration) while nonviolence—understood much too narrowly—is elevated in liberal circles to an unqualified good. This paints too simple a picture. In Fanonian fashion, Žižek exerts pressure on what he calls "the standard liberal motto" which maintains "that violence is never legitimate, even though it may sometimes be necessary to resort to it."[8] He reformulates the terms of the debate: "From a radical emancipatory perspective, this [liberal] formula should be reversed: for the oppressed, violence is always legitimate (since their very status is the result of the violence they are exposed to), but never necessary (it will always be a matter of strategy whether or not [to] use violence against the enemy)."[9] For Žižek, the choice of violence must be attentive to the situation:

> We effectively live in obscure times, and only a Leninist 'concrete analysis of concrete circumstances' can make clear what is the proper way to act in a given constellation—sometimes pragmatic measures aiming at particular problems are appropriate; sometimes, in a radical crisis, the transformation of the very fundamental structure of a society is the only way to solve its particular problems; sometimes, in a situation of *plus ça change, plus ça reste le même*, it is better to do nothing than to contribute to the reproduction of the existing order. (Not to mention the dialectical link between the particular and the universal, on account of which the very focus and insistence on an apparently particular problem can trigger a global transformation).[10]

Nonviolence cannot be imposed on the oppressed; it is not a privileged horizon of action, but neither is it a purely destructive physical violence. Though legitimate, to the extent that it is responding to an original but occluded violence, the violence of the oppressed disrupts the status quo but does not *necessarily* generate new possibilities or become world-forming. Worse, it almost guarantees a vicious backlash from your foe who instantly exploits your counter-violence and casts it as an "unprovoked."[11] The war on–Gaza launched in 2023 provides a striking example. For Western powers and mainstream media, this war began with Operation Al-Aqsa Flood (Hamas striking Israel, disrupting the supposed peace) and ended with Operation Iron Swords (Israel defending itself against Hamas and debilitating it, destroying its ability to strike again). I will keep returning to this convenient but deeply flawed narrative in the hope of making visible the type of crushing violence that Palestinians, and other racialized communities, have experienced on a daily basis but that rarely gets noticed by Western politicians and media. Facing this quotidian violence—bearing witness to the psychic and material reach of its life-draining tentacles—will clear the ground for imagining ways to jam or short-circuit violence's destructive operations.

Before striking at the enemy, however, both Fanon and Žižek enjoin us to consider or probe the self-violence that revolutionary change counter-intuitively requires of its subject. Effective violence against the existing system begins with a kind of self-violence, a self-critique; what is needed is "a violent reformation of the very substance of [the] subject's being."[12] Such self-invention opens to the reinvention of the Symbolic. Just as Fanon insists that "the real *leap* consists of introducing invention into life,"[13] Žižek frames resistant violence in terms of introducing a disruptive becoming at the heart of being, enacting a counter-violent "cut" in the symbolic field, and disclosing the world's fundamental chaos, its ontological incompleteness and inconsistency: the current system/the universe of meaning is, in Lacanian parlance, "not-all" (*pas-tout*). The symbolic order — which traffics in collective fantasies and illusions of completeness, deploying symbolic fictions to ideologically orient our approach to reality — does not exhaust the possibilities of racial expressions and subjectivities. For Fanon and Žižek, resistance to ontology is thus twofold, taking the form of a violent undoing/ decompletion that vigilantly guards against re-inscribing and naturalizing a new kingdom/order (the lie of a lost or regained social harmony), and an invention — the creation of new desires and new modalities of social existence.

The Politics of *No!*

For Fanon and Žižek, politics begins with a *No!* It strikes at the existing order, the status quo, at its insidious and invisible violence. But the existing order is also more than its positivity (what the status quo is) and includes a plethora of possible futures ideologically posited as immanent to it (what the status quo could be, once its impurities, lack, trauma, and so on have been corrected) that must be carefully unpacked and addressed:

> This is the key lesson to be learned by all authentic revolutionaries: the existing order is not just the positive order as such, it includes also the wealth of imagined alternatives that are part of the hegemonic ideological space. What this means is that the first gesture of a true revolutionary education is not just to oppose the existing social order, but to get rid of false dreams of overcoming it.[14]

Politics happens when you decomplete the social order, when you expose the contingency and inconsistency of the established order, when you reveal and avow what Lacan calls the *pas-tout*, "not-all" or "non-all" of symbolic reality, when you attend to the gap between what *is* and the ontological lack that sustains it. In Seminar XX, Lacan famously does this by laying out four formulas of sexuation.[15] On the masculine side, there are two: (1) there is at least one

X that says no to the phallic function, and (2) all Xs are subject to the phallic function. And on the feminine side, there are two more: (1) there is no X that says no to the phallic function, and (2) not all Xs are subject to the phallic function. Unlike the masculine side, there is no claim of universality rooted in exception here; woman (unlike Man) does not constitute a totality. If there is no exception that stands outside the social system, then the system as such is never whole or complete. And because there is nothing of woman *outside* the Law (no constitutive exception), woman is also "not-all," incomplete and imperfect, inside of the Symbolic.

Žižek critically reinterprets the Lacanian logic of the feminine "not-all" as referring to the ways a subject's enjoyment (*jouissance*) is structured and organized. The words "masculine" and "feminine" do not refer to anatomical differences but to a subject's relation to the phallus.[16] In other words, the masculine and feminine sides represent competing logics and different structures of enjoyment. It might be helpful to expand on this idea a bit. The masculine logic is first and foremost a logic of the exception: the exception that proves the rule, that closes the set. While all men are symbolically castrated due to their entry into the symbolic order, a masculine logic hangs on to the notion that there is always one "Man" who does not sacrifice his enjoyment, one Man who achieves plenitude, who must remain protected from the law of castration. For Lacan, the mythical primal father of Freud's *Totem and Taboo* incarnates such a figure. While the primal father—who enjoyed all women at will, "achieving complete satisfaction"[17]—had to be killed for the symbolic order to be erected, his exceptional subject position lives on in the cultural imaginary. The masculine logic dreams of perfection (from the Latin *perfectio*, meaning completion). Such a logic breeds nostalgia, always holding on to the phantasmatic promise or hope of returning to the prior, full plenitude of a pre-symbolic enjoyment.

In the feminine logic of the not-all, there is no claim of universality rooted in exception. So if there is no exception that stands outside the system, then the system as such is never whole or complete. And because there is nothing of woman outside the Law, "woman" is said to be "not-all" inside of the symbolic order. Again, there is always a risk of misreading Lacan/Žižek here. The feminine seems to evoke a biological register, but it actually denotes a logic and structure of enjoyment, and one that is available to all subjects. Whereas the masculine logic of exception posits a sovereign subject, a subject who has unlimited enjoyment, who stands outside the law of castration that governs social symbolic existence and whose self-presence is transparent, the feminine logic, by contrast, sees no exception to the law of castration. It declines the illusion of an uncastrated Man (and with it the possibility of absolute enjoyment), but at the same time takes castration to be "not-all," never complete or whole. This is why Žižek says, "*subjectivity as such . . . is feminine.*"[18] The question, of course, is whether or not individuals avow this ontological reality, the unsettling reality of "the void of the 'barred subject,'"[19] whether or not they decline their interpellation as a mystified, undivided, sovereign subject.

Žižek's Lacanian approach allows him to implicitly cast the subject not as an exception to tradition, to what lies outside its reach and governance, but as an unsettling source of de-completion. In other words, the not-all articulates the logic of the Real, pointing to what is irreducible to a society's symbolic representation of reality. The Real does not lie outside the Symbolic, external to its mechanisms; rather, "the Real is the Symbolic itself in the modality of non-All, lacking an external Limit/Exception."[20] The Real, Žižek insists, lacks a fixed ontology, "the very field of ontology, of the positive order of Being, emerges through the subtraction of the Real. The order of Being and the Real are mutually exclusive: The Real is the immanent blockage or impediment of the order of Being, what makes the order of Being inconsistent."[21] To embrace the not-all infects with doubt what passes for natural and stable in our social reality; it is to be skeptical of any culture's phantasmatic and ideological pretension of wholeness. The logic of the not-all enables Žižek to posit subjectivity and otherness, along with the signifying order, differently, underscoring the dynamism and mutability of ontology.

In a political register, this logic can be said to inform the "proletarian position," the position occupied by society's wretched subjects, its "parts of no-part," a notion Žižek freely borrows from Jacques Rancière.[22] The part of no-part stands for the abject others who are systematically excluded, racialized, and/or rendered vulnerable by society's laws and norms, falling outside the protection of the liberal and humanist umbrella. They are the "'supernumerary' elements" of their respective societies: "those who belong to a situation without having a specific 'place' in it; they are included but have no part to play in the social edifice."[23] As a given order's constitutive outsiders, they stand for "true universality,"[24] since their interests are not pre-determined by their subject positions. Indeed, when the parts of no-part seek to remedy wrongs, they are actually speaking to universal concerns (rather than to the particular interests of a group). Not attached to the status quo in the same libidinal and ideological way, the parts of no-part hold the promise of transformative change—of enacting politics as such.

To be sure, the masculine logic is also implicated in universal claims. An example can help shed some light on the fault lines between the logic of the exception and that of the not-all. Let's consider the universality of humanity along with its ambivalent relation to racism or anti-Blackness, more specifically. A masculine logic would read Black people as the remainders of a white supremacist-sanctioned humanity. That is to say, Black people stand outside the closed set of (white) humanity, dreaming of their inclusion one day in white civil society, of belonging to the "symbolic family" of humanity. A feminine logic, in contrast, would complicate this inside/outside opposition. The disruptive presence of Black subjects discloses the not-all of the Symbolic, of the American order of things. Take, for example, the anti-racist movement Black Lives Matter

(BLM). In their global protests, BLM activists are implicitly affirming that humanity is not-all—opening a space for thinking who or what might also count in or belong to this community, in what Achille Mbembe calls this "common world."[25] BLM is not after more rights or the full inclusion of Blacks into a ready-made humanity. It is at war with the social ontology of whiteness. The movement flatly rejects the ideological inclusivity of liberal democracy. What BLM is after is nothing short of a new humanity, what Fanon imagined as a new "species"[26] of humanity, a humanity that invariably threatens the centers of power. This humanity still to come is predicated on the modern political project to "redefine the very universality of what it means to be human"[27] (more on this later). The ontology of human is incomplete, not-all—and thus ripe for negation and reinvention.

In his works, Žižek often turns to the figure of the "unruly Jew,"[28] as exemplifying not only society's part of no-part but also philosophy's "constitutive 'homelessness,'"[29] its exilic underpinning and perpetual state of out-of-jointness. In "What Is Enlightenment?" Immanuel Kant argued that while individuals in an official capacity have to obey orders (in the domain of the "private use of reason"), individuals (as would-be philosophers) must not compromise on their "public use of reason," that is, they must not censure themselves and give up their right to address their views, to speak as *a scholar . . . before the entire public of the reading world.*"[30] As Žižek explains, the public use of reason, "in a kind of short-circuit, by-passing the mediation of the particular, directly participates in the universal," enabling the individual to be cosmopolitan, to break with the "communal-institutional order of one's particular identification."[31] This is precisely the position adopted by the cosmopolitan Jew, who maintains and nurtures a critical distance from the organic given, displaying an unwillingness to conform to the popular beliefs and suppositions of the day:

> The privileged role of Jews in the establishment of the sphere of the "public use of reason" hinges on their subtraction from every state power—this position of the "part of no-part" of every organic nation-state community, not the abstract-universal nature of their monotheism, makes them the immediate embodiment of universality. No wonder, then, that, with the establishment of the Jewish nation-state, a new figure of the Jew emerged: a Jew resisting identification with the State of Israel, refusing to accept the State of Israel as his true home, a Jew who "subtracts" himself from this state, and who includes the State of Israel among the states towards which he insists on maintaining a distance, living in their interstices.[32]

Occupying the position of the part of no-part, the cosmopolitan Jew stands for "the empty principle of universality."[33] What other figures stand today for this principle? Answering this question has everything to do with our understanding of violence and counter-violence, with our attunement to the workings of resistance and its antagonistic role in the struggle for freedom and universal justice.

Nonrecognition and Its Perils

A good place to begin is Fanon's critical engagement with G. W. F. Hegel's master–slave dialectic (or "lord–bondsman" dialectic) as the German philosopher imagines it in *Phenomenology of Spirit*. In this "fable of recognition,"[34] as Ato Sekyi-Otu puts it, two consciousnesses encounter one another in a struggle to the death for recognition. One of two consciousness (the slave) gives up, choosing life and submission, and recognizes the other (the master). The master's advantage is short-lived insofar as he becomes dependent on the slave for his recognition as an independent human being. The master's self-sufficiency is thus never fully secured. He finds himself at an impasse, his desire unsatisfied. Independence ironically comes to the slave, whose work simultaneously transforms things and himself, leading to his/our liberation. But for Fanon, matters unfold differently for the Black slave. What irremediably alters the development of an independent self-consciousness are the social relations under racial slavery and colonialism. Stressing the unbridgeable difference between Hegel's fabled slave and the historical Black slave, Fanon says, "For Hegel there is reciprocity; here the master scorns the consciousness of the slave. What he wants from the slave is not recognition but work."[35] And work for the former slave is by no means emancipatory; he is not able to change himself by changing the external world. Work indexes the master's brutal exploitation of the slave. In Fanon's account, ontological upgrades for the slave or the colonized through the labor of recognition are suspended. The structure of colonial domination fundamentally impedes the struggle for recognition. Mutual recognition is effectively ruled out as a possibility. The Black slave suffers an inferiority complex and sits outside of common history, thingified, alienated, reduced to a "suffocating reification,"[36] always exposed to a voracious white gaze:

> The white gaze, the only valid one, is already dissecting me. I am *fixed*. Once their microtomes are sharpened, the Whites objectively cut sections of my reality. I have been betrayed. I sense, I see in this white gaze that it's the arrival not of a new man, but of a new type of man, a new species. A Negro, in fact![37]

A reified and asphyxiated Fanon, a thing among other things, pleads his right, demanding human behavior from the white other: "I find myself one day in the world, and I acknowledge one right for myself: the right to demand human behavior from the other [*Je me découvre un jour dans le monde et je me reconnais un seul droit: celui d'exiger de l'autre un comportement humain*]."[38]

A "politics of recognition," as Charles Taylor articulates it, offers itself as a political remedy:

> Our identity is partly shaped by recognition or its absence, often by the misrecognition of others, and so a person or group of people can suffer real damage, real distortion, if the people or society around them mirror back to them a confining or demeaning or contemptible picture of themselves. Nonrecognition or misrecognition can inflict harm, can be a form of oppression, imprisoning someone in a false, distorted, and reduced mode of being.[39]

But colonial racism disables, amputating Fanon's being. What the Black slave receives is not recognition nor misrecognition (which can, in principle, be corrected through a politics of recognition), but a stagnant nonrecognition. Blackness as thinghood is afforded no relationality, a point that Afropessimists have made central in their work. The "recognition paradigm"[40] is no cure for coloniality's violent ontology. On this view, Taylor and others underestimate *negrophobia*'s ontological impact on the flesh of Black bodies. Blacks have no place in the established order of things. Their exclusion is not accidental but necessary; it is constitutive of the social order. To be Black is to not belong. Excluded from the potential rewards of dialectics, Black being, strictly speaking, does not occupy the position of an Other, but rather is relegated to the "zone of nonbeing,"[41] a position that Lewis Gordon describes as "below-Otherness."[42] *Contra* the Afropessimists, this holds as well for the settler-colonial scene. Palestinians and Blacks are nonrecognized. In the settler-Native aborted dialectic, the Zionist settler, for example, does not hunger for recognition. What he wants from the Palestinian Native is her land, resources, and disappearance (via physical death or forced migration). Mutual recognition is thus not only inapplicable, it violently distorts the realities of the enslaved, the colonized, and the displaced Native.

If Fanon decries the inapplicability of the master and slave dialectic to the colonial situation (in all of its various instantiations), Žižek rereads this dialectic with a focus on the violent process involved in reaching mutual recognition. It is not sufficient to affirm that I am a being constitutively tied to the Other, as does Judith Butler, he argues, when they take this—"I realize that I am bound to this other who is bound to me, and that my life is bound up with the other's life"[43]— to be Hegel's key insight. Recentering the human subject, Žižek retorts: "Yes, I am bound to the other who is bound to me, but it is only through destroying/ dominating that mutual recognition emerges: we arrive at mutual solidarity only through acting as solitary and suffering consequences. . . . In Hegel's thought, violence does not emerge as a possibility but as an ethical necessity, and remains there up to the end."[44] *How* we get to mutual dependence and mutual recognition is the point. Reinfusing Hegel's dialectics of recognition with friction and skepticism—"all there is is struggle, violence, domination, and the story of how it fails"[45]—Žižek points to the ways in which Hegel's thought can illuminate the tensions of colonialism and its impacts on self-consciousness, the human subject. If human relations are fraught, shot through with distrust, in any social context, a racial-colonial framework halts dialectical movement and renders the possibility of mutual recognition even more difficult to achieve. The master/colonizer/settler occupies the position of the human subject whereas the enslaved/colonized/Native occupies the position of the nonhuman object. Fanon tells us the Black subject—one of the exemplary figures of wretchedness then and now—"is not"[46] (*n'est pas*), thus inaugurating what Geo Maher calls "nonrecognition studies."[47] His being is barred, being eviscerated by an anti-Black gaze. Social death characterizes the condition of the wretched. At the same time, Fanon draws attention to the collective fantasy underpinning whiteness/pure humanity. The white subject lacks and is anxiously yearning for his white being to coincide fully with a phantasmatic humanity. A logic sets in: Blacks want to be whites and whites chase the "rank of man [*une condition d'homme*],"[48] Fanon observed.

Fanon takes stock of his human condition through Hegel's text (as interpreted by Alexandre Kojève, whose lecture on Hegel's *Phenomenology* at the École des Hautes Études attracted a number of French intellectuals, including Jacques Lacan, André Breton, and Maurice Merleau-Ponty, among others):

> I ask that I be taken into consideration on the basis of my desire. I am not only here-now, locked in thinghood. I desire somewhere else and something else. I demand that an account be taken of my contradictory activity insofar as I pursue something other than life, insofar as I am fighting for the birth of a human world, in other words, a world of reciprocal recognitions.[49]

Fanon wants to see himself in Hegel's narrative, having subscribed to the master–slave dialectic's "normative horizon."[50] But his "negating activity"[51] proves ineffective to the task. He finds himself stuck and condemned to "*bare existence*."[52] Speaking as a Black Martinican, Fanon laments the fact that he and his kin never fought for their freedom, and that currently "there is no open conflict between White and Black."[53] Through its 1848 decree of abolition, he explains, the French state simply informed the Black French of Martinique of their freedom:

> Historically, the black man, steeped in the inessentiality of servitude, was set free by the master. He did not fight for his freedom. . . . As master, the white man told the black man: "You are now free." But the black man does not know the price of freedom because he has never fought for it.[54]

The master cannot grant a freedom for-itself—such a freedom must involve struggle and thus can only be violently taken/earned from the white master.

As Fanon puts it in *The Wretched of the Earth*: "The colonized man liberates himself in and through violence."[55] Since the Black slave never imposed himself on the white master, the former was never recognized by the latter—whence the Black dilemma: "the former slave wants to *have himself recognized*."[56] Without recognition, Blacks are "locked in thinghood," deprived of the privileges of "human reality."[57]

Coloniality's racial matrix perverts social relations, trapping the colonized or racialized body in a suffocating Manichaeism. Fanon puts this in drastic terms in the first pages of *The Wretched of the Earth*: "The 'native' sector is not complementary to the European sector. The two confront each other, but not in the service of a higher unity. Governed by a purely Aristotelian logic, they follow the dictates of mutual exclusion: There is no conciliation possible, one of them is superfluous."[58] A metaphysical architecture divides the colonial world: "Looking at the immediacies of the colonial context, it is clear that what divides this world is first and foremost what species, what race one belongs to."[59] The zone inhabited by the colonizers must perish. Nothing of colonialism must remain, which by definition also involves the end of the zone of the colonized—*what is a colonized without his colonizer?* Echoing Fanon, Žižek writes: "To revolutionize a system is never equal to just eliminating one of its parts."[60] The identities of the racist settler as well as that of the Indigenous will have to endure "symbolic erasure."[61]

The oppressive colonial regime holds no dialectical futures. Decolonization is a counter-violent agenda of complete disorder for a reason. Removing one of its structural elements entails the dissolution of the whole system. But a dialectically oriented strain is not wholly absent from the new state of affairs; it is through destroying/dominating, through the absolute dismantling of the racial-colonial architectural order, that mutual dependence and mutual recognition can be achieved, where recognition among equals would gain a material reality as opposed to its abstract and formal character in contemporary Western societies marked by the afterlives of slavery and colonialism.

In this vein, Fanon quotes Hegel on the distinction between a recognition that acknowledges you as "a person" (freedom in-itself) and a recognition that elevates you to an "independent self-consciousness"[62] (freedom for-itself). Dependency plagues Black folks and other minoritized communities. The Black Martinican never attains the status of a being-for-itself and is never recognized as a fellow desiring subject. Legally, Black people were emancipated, transformed from "the animal-machine man to the supreme rank of *man*."[63] This alchemical change was clearly historically significant, but it remained an *ontical* transformation; *ontologically*, the Black individual remained (perceived and treated as) "the animal-machine man," oscillating between not-quite-human and nonhuman: "He went from one way of life to another, but not from one life to another."[64] Fanon craves a reckoning with whiteness, an opportunity to struggle for his recognition, and disclose to white people what his imputed difference actually signifies:

> When the black man happens to cast a savage look at the white man, the white man says to him: "Brother, there is no difference between us." But the black man *knows* there is a difference. He *wants* it. He would like the white man to suddenly say to him: "Dirty nigger." Then he would have that unique occasion—to "show them."
>
> But usually there is nothing, nothing but indifference or paternalistic curiosity.[65]

Once universal human rights are enshrined in the French Republic, whites can either bracket the question of race or ponder the oddity of its persistence: *Why are you still a problem?* Dissatisfied, Fanon continues, he itches for a violent encounter with whites, nostalgic for a lost opportunity and envious of his Black American counterparts:

> The former slave needs a challenge to his humanity, he wants a conflict, a riot. But it is too late: The French Negro is doomed to bite himself and just to bite. I say "the French Negro," for the American Negro is cast in a different play. In the United States, the Negro battles and is battled. There are laws that, little by little, are invalidated under the Constitution. There are other laws that forbid certain forms of discrimination. And we can be sure that nothing is going to be given free.[66]

Fanon here downplays or simply ignores Martinique's rich history of rebellion against French enslavement and colonialism.[67] Though, unlike Haiti, it did not realize national independence, Martinique had its share of revolts and struggles.[68] In America the Black combat against *negrophobia* is more explicit because the white display of anti-Blackness is more explicit.

Fanon adopts a two-pronged attitude to existence in an anti-Black world: "Yes to life. Yes to love. Yes to generosity. But man is also a no. No to scorn of man. No to degradation of man. No to exploitation of man. No to the butchery of what is most human in man: freedom."[69] Resistance to anti-Black violence will take a variety of forms, drawing on a multitude of emotions and ideals. Yes to relationality. No to amputation. Fanon ends the section on "Hegel and the Negro" with a commentary on Nietzsche's agitation for actional behavior, repeating the latter's warning against the lures of *ressentiment*:

> Man's behavior is not only reactional. And there is always resentment [*ressentiment*] in *reaction*. Nietzsche had already said it in *The Will to Power*.
>
> To induce man to be *actional*, by maintaining in his circularity the respect of the fundamental values that make the world human, that is the task of utmost urgency for he who, after careful reflection, prepares to act.[70]

Fanon repeats Nietzsche but also deviates from him, subjecting *ressentiment* to dialectic pressure. It is never a choice between actional and reactional behavior.

Counter-reactional behavior is an attempt to mobilize *ressentiment*'s negativity for an inventive political end: the abolition of coloniality's racial matrix. There is violence in *ressentiment*, but the proper counter-violence that it introduces in the world need not follow Nietzsche's damning script.

On *ressentiment*'s unsettling negativity, I follow Holocaust survivor and torture victim Jean Améry. Writing at a time when Germany was too eager to accelerate the healing process and collectively work through the trauma of the Shoah, Améry actively resisted social pressure to *forgive and forget* in the name of communal oneness, a dubious push to put the horrors of the past behind, "allow[ing] what happened to remain what it was."[71] He creatively rehabilitates Nietzsche's account of *ressentiment*, arguing for both its existential necessity and its productivity. *Ressentiment* is not a condition that we ought to overcome but something to cultivate and deploy socially. The impetus to turn the page, and celebrate a post-Nazi Germany, is nothing more than intellectual laziness. As Žižek observes, this strikingly un-Nietzschean account of *ressentiment* stands for a "refusal to 'normalise' the crime, to make it part of the ordinary/explicable/accountable flow of things, to integrate it into a consistent and meaningful life-narrative; after all possible explanations, it returns with its question: 'Yes, I got all this, but nevertheless, *how could you have done it? Your story about it doesn't make sense!*'"[72] This "authentic" *ressentiment* is not about leveraging one's pain for additional rights or privileges[73]; it is a public use of *ressentiment* that seeks to exert pressure on the system itself. Its demands cannot be met without a radical configuration of the status quo.

As I've argued elsewhere[74], in order to build on Améry's insights, rethink the internationalist Left, and advance an anti-racist politics of the human subject, we can redeploy Immanuel Kant's discussion of reason in "What Is Enlightenment?"[75] to distinguish between two types of *ressentiment*: the private and the public. The "private use of *ressentiment*" urges the privatization of grievances and thereby feeds a depoliticized politics of blame, envy, and victimhood, sealing the excluded in her rage and colonial desires. We can see, in *The Wretched of the Earth*, this form of *ressentiment* in the envy of the colonized for the life of the colonizer. *I resent you, I want to be you*:

> The gaze that the colonized subject casts at the colonist's sector is a look of lust, a look of envy. Dreams of possession. Every type of possession: of sitting at the colonist's table and sleeping in his bed, preferably with his wife. The colonized man is an envious man. The colonist is aware of this as he catches the furtive glance, and constantly on his guard, realizes bitterly that: "They want to take our place." And it's true there is not one colonized subject who at least once a day does not dream of taking the place of the colonist.[76]

Fanon understands the desire of the colonized and refuses to pathologize the latter's envy, to treat it as a sign of moral depravity and psychological defect. But Fanon also makes clear that this state or orientation further immobilizes the wretched, limiting their political imagination. Just substituting the colonizer for the colonized "leav[es] intact the oppressive colonial power structure and its complicity with metropolitan capital."[77]

In sharp contrast, the "public use of *ressentiment*" enjoins the excluded other to universalize her grievances, to denaturalize her ascribed identity, to disturb "existing group differentiations,"[78] to be counter-reactional, and to see her antagonism as cutting across societies (the genuine possibility of regroupments), turning personal trauma or slight into a common cause. Keeping in mind the private and public uses of *ressentiment*, we can further parse Fanon's evocation of *ressentiment*, where he places it alongside other problematic feelings and dispositions directed toward conquering settlers in the context of an anti-colonial war of liberation:

> Antiracist racism and the determination to defend one's skin, which is characteristic of the colonized's response to colonial oppression, clearly represent sufficient reasons to join the struggle. But one does not sustain a war, one does not endure massive repression or witness the disappearance of one's entire family in order for hatred or racism to triumph. Racism, hatred, *ressentiment*, and "the legitimate desire for revenge" alone cannot nurture a war of liberation.[79]

As with the possibility of a counter-reactional violence, a violence that insists on an originary violence and its undoing, a public use of *ressentiment* dislocates the "bad" affect from its Nietzschean context, universalizing it and making *ressentiment* serve as an endless source of resistance and dissensus. *Ressentiment* enacts "a dispute about what is given,"[80] as Rancière might put it. If a private use of *ressentiment* finds a home in the politics of recognition, which is primarily concerned with your and your group's demands (recognize me, include me in your system, take me back into the categorical fold of the human), a public use of *ressentiment* refuses this sanctioned form of resistance, a resistance that relies on fetishized identities and "counterfeit categories"[81] and operates within the confines of the system. A Fanonian *ressentiment* pushes us not only to transcend social boundaries delimiting identities but also to expand our horizons of resistance beyond the socially and biologically given. Practicing his public use of *ressentiment* in *Black Skin, White Masks*, Fanon both affirms the fact of Blackness—he avows that he has been rendered Black by an anti-Black world—and refuses to be sealed in his Blackness, to use his racial designation to lobby for additional rights.

A Fanonian subject refuses to give up her universalist aspirations and play the game of identity politics. When you bet on identity politics it is the liberal house that always wins. Multicultural liberal states, like the United States and Canada, deploy a private use of *ressentiment* precisely to shrink our horizons of resistance, masterfully trafficking in the rhetoric of inclusion and identity politics. In their dealings with Indigenous communities, for instance, they purport to be open to difference, to the recognition of society's excluded, but in fact, their various gestures of accommodation only masquerade as genuine recognition and engagement. Fake recognition—communicated or performed through vacuous statements about inclusion such as "I see you," "I hear you," "I acknowledge this land," "I want to lift up your concern," and so on—aims to pacify the wretched and their minoritized communities—along with those who refuse to normalize the crimes inflicted on the wretched, who are at the forefront of the struggle for the rights of the excluded. Multicultural liberal states interpellate the excluded in their own exclusion. A politics of recognition turns into "affect management," an effort to control the rage or anger of the wretched, contributing to a general sense of ideological numbness (Who are we fighting? What are we fighting for?), so that nothing actually changes, so that the violence of the status quo is left more or less unaffected, leading to the repetition of colonial injuries and the obfuscation of racial/economic divisions. In *Red Skin, White Masks*, Yellowknives Dene Glen Coulthard perspicuously attends to the fault lines separating an anti-colonial critique from a liberal politics of recognition:

> I argue that the expression of Indigenous anticolonial nationalism that emerged during this period forced colonial power to modify itself from a structure that was once primarily reinforced by policies, techniques, and ideologies explicitly oriented around the genocidal exclusion/assimilation double, to one that is now reproduced through a seemingly more conciliatory set of discourses and institutional practices that emphasize our *recognition* and *accommodation*. Regardless of this modification, however, the relationship between Indigenous peoples and the state has remained colonial to its foundation.[82]

Unlike the settlers of old who were preoccupied with the "genocidal exclusion/assimilation" of the Natives, the new settler-enemy of multiculturalism speaks the language of recognition and accommodation, inviting Indigenous input so long as it falls squarely within the limits of colonial reason alone—meaning, *no land back; no meaningful Indigenous sovereignty or power-sharing*.[83] Participating in the politics of recognition thus departs sharply from the tradition of anti-colonial critique that clearly articulated the contours of the enemy (state power's coercive practices). Recognition is a ruse, selling cosmetic changes as transformative ones. In a similar vein, Jodi Byrd, a citizen of the Chickasaw Nation, refuses to accept the liberal ideal of inclusion as an unqualified good: "The generally accepted theorizations of racialization in the United States have . . . tended to be sited along the axis of inclusion/exclusion. . . . When the remediation of the colonization of American Indians is framed through discourses of racialization that can be redressed by further inclusion into the nation-state, there is a significant failure to grapple with the fact that such discourses further reinscribe the original colonial injury."[84] The axis of inclusion/exclusion does not destabilize or contest but contributes to the settler's eliminationist project.

Rather than a politics of recognition and its correlate form of resistance, an Indigenous politics of refusal enacts a public use of *ressentiment*. A politics of refusal affirms its "right to *ressentiment*" (*Recht auf Ressentiment*), W. G. Sebald's apt description of Améry's deployment of the affect.[85] It does not forgive or forget the original and ongoing genocide of Indigenous people. Such a politics takes the struggle for racial justice to be irredeemably tied to questions of being, power, and sovereignty over land, not of the management of Indigenous anger. Moreover, an Indigenous politics of refusal declines to be pigeonholed (to limit its concerns to its own narrow predicament) and instead adopts a cross-racial and transnational posture; it stands with the movement for Black lives; it delegitimizes anti-Black state violence; its fight is to be waged from Turtle Island/North America to Palestine. It is an Indigenous rallying cry against "profit-driven logics of settler war, death and destruction."[86] A politics of refusal speaks truth to power. It declines the liberal blackmail: either you align your views with our values of toleration and reject what falls outside the scope of liberal propriety (we don't tolerate, for instance, a critique of Zionism or the chant "From the river to the sea, Palestine will be free") or you're banned as persona non grata (deemed too divisive, hostile to alternative views, or, in this particular example, anti-Semitic). The type of resistance that a public use of *ressentiment* fosters is inflected by this Indigenous sense of refusal, a refusal skeptical of the promises of a (post)politics of recognition. To paraphrase Fanon, *a universalist politics of refusal says Yes to Palestinian life. Yes to Black life. Yes to love. Yes to generosity. But Indigenous ressentiment is also a no. No to erasure of man. No to dispossession of man. No to displacement of man. No to the butchery of what is most human in us all: freedom and equality.*

When the politics of recognition is premised on an asymmetrical structure of power entrenched through reproduction over time, recognition in itself does nothing to challenge or alter society's existing configuration and distribution of value. Remedies can be dished out for your injuries, but only if it is done without making waves, "without disturbing the underlying framework that generates them."[87] Worse, these so-called remedies compound the problem; they further naturalize and legitimize the oppressive regime, since they actively involve you in your own marginalization or erasure. Liberals enjoy defending the unfortunate (again, within the limits of liberal reason alone)—getting a libidinal kick out of hating the haters, the Donald Trump and Marine Le Pen supporters of the world—without envisioning, or wanting to envision, a different configuration of things. In the anti-racist liberal imaginary, another world is precisely *not* possible.

We repeat Flavio Zenun Almada's observation about why we need Fanon today: "because our conditions have not improved since Fanon's time and in some cases have worsened."[88] Colonialism, in its many faces and afterlives, remains our problem. To entertain alternatives to the colonized and colonizing world is denounced as wild and, of course, violent. And we are told time and time again that violent musings can only lead to illiberal realities. I share Sekyi-Otu's lucid *ressentiment* toward a system that privileges a strict adherence to the pleasure principle, to what he characterizes as "the call to savage self-interest as the sovereign principle of human conduct."[89] Against the voracious few who actively abide by this "triumphal tenet"[90] and the many abandoned wretched who turn to it in despair, along with all those in between who opt to reap what fruits of the status quo they may rather than demanding more or rocking the boat of global capitalism, this book agitates for a vision of collective subjectivity that pushes beyond the appeals of self-interest and reinvests in an anti-colonial critique and an internationalist Left. Rejecting tribalistic identity politics, claims of/to exceptionalism, the lure of myopic victimhood, and phantastic returns to social harmony, we must recast resistance as an indispensable form of counter-violence to undo the narcissistic politics and reigning ontologies of the day.

Whither Violence?

Any inquiry into Fanon's and Žižek's accounts of resistance must attend closely to the concrete historical dynamics and political ontologies shaping the use and impacts of violence. For Fanon, violence pertains to "the last gesture of the hunted man."[91] Counter-violence becomes a genuine option when colonial domination reaches a state of cruel immobility—when existence takes the form of a "colonial prison"—unaffected by "the language of truth and of reason," of which the colonized are precisely denied any possession.[92] In order to effectively breach the colonial prison, critically engaging the specific types of violence enacted by settler colonialism is of paramount importance. The colonized/Native is on the receiving end of what Fanon describes as a "three-dimensional violence": "Violence in everyday behaviour, violence against the past that is emptied of all substance, violence against the future, for the colonial regime presents itself as necessarily eternal."[93] For the colonial regime, there is only colonial futurology. If there is "Manichean fervour," to take up an accusation drawn from Fanon's language and leveled at today's Gaza solidarity protests,[94] then it corresponds to the reversal of its colonial form. Nigel Gibson puts the matter clearly: "For Fanon, active resistance was the first stage toward self-discovery, and he was well aware that in its early stages anticolonial action was an inversion of colonial Manicheanism and remained within its framework."[95] For Fanon and the many activists/scholars that he inspires, an inverted Manicheanism as such is not a problem within a colonial situation. The problem lies in reifying this condition, in settling for the inversion of this binary vision—*we are now good and you're evil*. The goal for Fanon is ultimately to transcend Manichean logic, which entails dissolving not only the identity of the colonizer but also that of the colonized, something akin to proletarian class struggle, which "aims at abolishing class difference, eliminating not only the ruling class but also itself—the aim of proletarian struggle is to create conditions in which proletarians themselves would cease to exist."[96]

In the stage of the inversion of colonial Manicheanism, armed resistance as counter-violence will presumably play a significant role in abolishing colonial difference. But even under this condition, Fanon was cognizant of the limits and dangers of anti-colonial violence. On the one hand, it appears unavoidable and necessary. He tells us that "violence is a cleansing force."[97] The translation, however, does not fully capture Fanon's precise thinking. The revolutionary clinician writes, *la violence désintoxique*—violence detoxifies; it detoxifies the wretched, playing an instrumental role in enabling the colonized "to decipher social reality."[98] As Adam Shatz notes: "Fanon's more clinical word choice indicates the overcoming of a state of drunkenness, the stupor induced by colonial subjugation."[99] Violence sobers the colonized, offering the wretched political awareness or lucidity in relation to their oppressive condition. On the other hand, Fanon never celebrated unrestrained brutality. His great anti-colonial interlocutor Aimé Césaire appreciated Fanon's principled engagement with violence: "his was the violence of non-violence, by which I mean the violence of justice, purity, and intransigence. There is no paradox here. What must be understood is that his revolt was ethical, he acted from generosity. He was not simply taking up a cause. He gave of himself."[100] Fanon displayed this care by cautioning his Algerian comrades not to become like the French in their merciless use of violence:

> Because we want a democratic and renovated Algeria, because we believe one cannot rise and liberate oneself in one area and sink in another, we condemn with pain in our hearts, those brothers who have flung themselves into revolutionary action with the almost physiological brutality that centuries of oppression give rise to and feed.[101]

Undisciplined violence is not an end in itself, nor does it dismantle the settler's Manichean logic of self and other. Fanon never gave up on the idea of mutual recognition: "At the end of this book [*Black Skin*] we would like the reader to feel with us the open dimension of every consciousness."[102] Having said that, there seems to be an irresistible desire among critics to rescue Fanon (*contra* Sartre's "Preface"[103] to *The Wretched of the Earth*) and simply jump to the stage where Manicheanism is no longer needed, when violence recedes into the background. The problem is that you don't get to this position unless you take to heart the colonial regime and the specificities of its various instantiations. Comparing the Zionist settler state in the case of Palestine to the French colonial regime in Algeria shows how this matters. It is fair to ask what similarities obtain between the two. Drawing on the Algerian example, Fanon writes: "colonialism is not a machine capable of thinking, a body endowed with reason. It is naked violence and only gives in when confronted with greater violence."[104] Mark LeVine views Zionism as dissimilar: "Zionist settler colonialism—is very much a 'thinking machine' with very powerful and longstanding logic and rationalities that are the key to its success."[105] I agree, but would go further. Zionism functions not only as a complex ideology, legitimizing a crushing apartheid regime, a chauvinist and expansionist settler movement, but also subtends Israel's libidinal economy or collective unconscious. Zionism as a mode of desire helps to explain its almost magical psychic hold on Jews in Israel and abroad. Zionism, incarnated in the state of Israel, interpellates Jews as the sole authority and final arbiter over Jewish matters, over Jewish desires. It resides in the racial collective fantasies of Israeli Jews, teaching them what and who to desire, hate, identify with, and, most importantly, what makes them as Jews desirable and what makes Palestinians/Arabs beyond the pale. Zionism inaugurates a generalized Palestinophobia: the Palestinian is to be feared and despised by Jews. The Zionist big Other (the order of laws and rules of Jewish society) thus orients the lives of Jews as well as mediates and structures their social reality. An Israel minus Zionism is an unrecognizable Israel.

Moreover, LeVine adds: "Palestine today is not Algeria in 1956, which was Fanon's most important reference point. Nor is Israel France, with a metropole to which settlers can return (unless we consider Tel Aviv the metropole)."[106] And then, commenting on Fanon's reference to a "greater violence," LeVine expresses his skepticism:

> Because of this, considering what "a greater violence" would look like and how it can be measured, never mind achieved, is a crucial task for those analysing and fighting colonial violence alike. I have yet to see any plausible scenarios in which Palestinians acquire the means to deploy "far greater violence" vis-a-vis Israel/the Zionist entity for any length of time in any conceivable geostrategic balance of power. Even if Iran (the only major power that supports Palestine in any meaningful way), for example, wanted to deliver heavier weapons to Palestinians, Israel's control over access points, as well as Egypt's and Jordan's, will prevent that from happening. Palestine is not Ukraine, supported by major powers and able to utilise land, water and air corridors to obtain an unending stream of weapons deliveries to fight a much larger and better-armed adversary. Quite the opposite, in fact.[107]

LeVine's observation is valid but also misses a key point in Fanon's analysis. Palestinians will not defeat Israel in a military assault. However, what Fanon helps us understand is the impact of colonialism, as well as violent resistance, on the Native's psyche and social existence. The reason why Fanon resonates with us when we're watching a genocide streamed live is that Fanon offers a grammar that sheds light on the thinking and actions of the subjugated colonized. Material conditions matter. We must speak here of the longue durée of this violence against Palestinians, beginning with British colonialism. The Great Arab revolt of 1936–9 saw Palestinians engaging in counter-violence and massive strikes against Britain's colonial presence. The mighty British Empire eventually crushed the Palestinian uprising—killing, injuring, imprisoning, or sending into exile a sixth of the adult male population.[108] A defeated and demoralized Palestinian people were still reeling from the collective trauma of 1936–9, unprepared to fully deal with the eruption of the Nakba. Colonialism mutated into settler colonialism. Colonial violence never disappeared. Zionist violence, in fact, prolonged British violence. As Rashid Khalidi notes, "The Zionists were taught every underhanded colonial technique by counterinsurgency experts . . . and other specialists in torture and murder."[109] Zionism is the colonial offspring of the British Empire. As with Algerian violence, Palestinian violence is the fruit of an originary and ongoing violence, that of the Israeli occupiers and the British forces that created the conditions for Zionist usurpation of Palestinian land.[110] As with Algerian violence, Palestinian violence is the fruit of an originary and ongoing violence, that of the Israeli occupiers. Fanon would have warned, as Nicki Kattoura and Geo Maher explain, that "colonial violence" has been "pumped mercilessly into Gaza for decades. At some point, like a balloon, it can only explode."[111] In its raid into southern Israel, Hamas sought to match the criminality of Israel's habitual terror. To borrow Israel's genocidal metaphor, Hamas undertook to "mow the lawn" on the other side of the fence. Israel's outrage that Hamas's attack was unprovoked is a flat lie: How can you not expect resistance from a caged Indigenous population?[112] Early Zionist leaders expected resistance from the Natives of the land. They anticipated reciprocal violence and perceived Palestinian resistance as "understandable, inevitable—and anticolonial."[113] For example, Vladimir "Ze'ev" Jabotinsky, speaking in 1923 from the position of a conquering settler pioneer, noted that "every native population in the world resists colonists as long as it has the slightest hope of being able to rid itself of the danger of being colonised. That is what the Arabs in Palestine are doing, and what they will persist in doing as long as there remains a solitary spark of hope that they will be able to prevent the transformation of 'Palestine' into the 'Land of Israel.'"[114] Jabotinsky even compared the Arab Palestinians to the Aztecs and Sioux: "they feel at least the same instinctive jealous love of Palestine, as the old Aztecs felt for ancient Mexico, and their Sioux for their rolling Prairies."[115] What shocked the Israeli government on October 7 is that Palestinians were capable of striking back, sufficiently skilled in breaching their enemy's territory with such brazen disregard for Israeli life. But Israel's response to Hamas's uprising was sadly all too predictable.[116] It is the response of all colonial powers when they are dealt a taste of their own medicine. As Dirk Moses pointedly avers,

> Mass state violence against civilians is not a glitch in the international system; it is baked into statehood itself. The natural right of self-defense plays a foundational role in the self-conception of Western states in particular, the formation of which is inseparable from imperial expansion. Since the Spanish conquest of the Americas starting in the sixteenth century, settlers justified their reprisals against indigenous resistance as defensive "self-preservation." If they felt their survival was imperiled, colonizers engaged in massive retaliation against "native" peoples, including noncombatants. The "doctrine of double effect" assured them that killing innocents was permissible as a side effect of carrying out a moral end, like self-defense. They understood their presence in far-off lands as legitimate, based on civilizational and racial hierarchies. "Native" resistance was framed as illegitimate and terroristic. . . . More recently, this colonial ideology has manifested itself in the project of "bringing democracy to the Arab world," with Israel designated as the "the only democracy in the Middle East," the proverbial "villa in the jungle."[117]

Colonial ideology, as long as it is supported by Western powers, will immunize Israel from facing justice for war crimes, crimes against humanity, and the "crime of all crimes"[118] — genocide.

Student protestors today are insisting, however, that *another understanding of Palestine is possible*. Most of them are part of the BLM generation. Their concern for racial justice didn't originate on October 7, 2023. BLM did a lot to show how Blacks and Palestinians have common cause, reigniting Black-Palestinian solidarity, much to the annoyance of the Democratic Party establishment and liberal elite. Numerous BLM chapters renewed their commitment to Palestine after October 7, and the Black for Palestine collective reiterated in no ambiguous terms their support for Palestinian struggle.[119] A generational shift is clearly taking place. The Palestinian struggle taps into students' sense of justice. The 2020 murder of George Floyd disclosed a new reality. The US police — subjects-supposed-to-protect-and-serve — transformed into agents of injustice. The movement to "defund the police," to which I will return in Chapter 2, was an attempt to capture this unsettled social reality.

I am tempted here to extend Žižek's musings on "structural necessity" to the relation between the 2020 protests against anti-Blackness (crystallized in the call "to defund the police") and the protests beginning in 2023 against Palestinian genocide (crystallized in the call "from the river to the sea, Palestine will be free"):

> When Napoleon lost for the first time in 1813, it looked like just bad luck; when he lost the second time at Waterloo, it was clear that his time was over. And

does the same not hold for the ongoing financial crisis? When it first hit the markets in September 2008, it looked like an accident to be corrected through better regulation, and so on; now that signs of a repeated financial meltdown are gathering, it is clear that we are dealing with a structural necessity.[120]

The acts of racialization and animalization that we're witnessing in the United States and Palestine are not instances of bad apples, evil prime ministers, or isolated, complicit presidents. They are not bugs but features of the system: racial violence is a structural necessity for the function of the world order, which is ultimately a colonialist order. Palestine reminds us—and the protesting students are making sure that we remember—that settler colonialism and slavery are not past chapters, but persist, in different forms, in the present; the recent student encampments remind us that a logic that distinguishes who matters from who doesn't is still operative and is baked into the status quo. As Franco Berardi recently observed, students in the United States and beyond are identifying with Palestinian despair.[121] They see their own precarity reflected in the destructive assault in Gaza. They're blaming Western leaders for their inaction in protecting Palestinian lives and their unwillingness to confront impending catastrophes. This identification is fueling their courageous refusal to accept their state's narrative. The explanation that *Palestinian violence provokes Israeli self-defense* rings hollow. No, they are rejecting the hegemony of this narrative, in and outside of the United States.

Soyons sérieux, demandons l'impossible

In an interview with Michael Smerconish on CNN, Thomas Friedman—liberals' favorite "subject-supposed-to-moralize/depoliticize," a reassuring, authoritative voice on the Middle East and pundit invested in America's leadership in the world—implicitly recognizes the threat to the status quo that the student protests represent when he attempts to reimpose a liberal order by lecturing his audience on what a "serious" position on Palestine/Israel looks like:

> FRIEDMAN: Well, you know, Michael, if you're only condemning Israeli violence against Palestinians and you're ignoring what Hamas did on October 7, you're not morally serious. If you're for a ceasefire now, and not for a return of hostages now, you're not morally serious, it seems to me. And if you're not talking about a two state solution but you're talking about a Palestinian state from the river to the sea, you're not morally serious. OK?
>
> There's only one solution here. And that is two states for two indigenous people between the Jordan River and the Mediterranean. And if you're not for that, if you're not for ending the violence, and for a hostage release, if you're

only condemning one side and not the other, you're not morally serious. And you're not going to be at all productive and helpful, because there's only one way out, two states for two people.[122]

Friedman is the paternal figure who is intended to bring university students back to common sense and moral rectitude, putting an end to their erring and flirtation with the Palestinian question. Intoxicated by the pathos of suffering, students don't see straight; their moral compass incapacitated, Friedman steps in to restore their liberal vision. Friedman appears oblivious to the fact that common sense and invocations of a two-state solution have been murderous for Palestinians. The students' response to Friedman and his liberal ilk should be *Soyons sérieux, demandons l'impossible*. This modification of the '68 slogan *Soyons réalistes, demandons l'impossible* (Let's be realistic, let's demand the impossible) preserves the emancipatory and aspirational force of the original but returns "serious" to liberals in a dislocated form. This is why the chants "defund the police" and "from the river to the sea, Palestine will be free" are erroneously and cynically read as absolutist ("appealing in its absolutism"[123]) meaning unbending, not open to different perspectives, or what Friedman calls "not serious." But absolutism here stands precisely for seriousness, an unwillingness to compromise on justice for Palestine. This sense of seriousness relates to Žižek's reflections on the difference in seeing "the situation [as] catastrophic, but not serious."[124] Students are objecting because their government and media treat the situation as catastrophic (we know about the devastation; we report the Gazan casualties daily; we know about the famine), but are not serious about dealing with that reality. Knowledge of the Palestinian catastrophe is contained, its horror diffused, never taking on a sense of emergency (Biden's "red lines" are ridiculous but tragic). Being serious means refusing Friedman's, and many others', nostalgia for October 6 or it means nothing at all. Tired of empty promises from their elected representatives and college presidents, students want an end to Palestinian suffering and a start to Palestinian liberation. Palestinian lives matter connects the anti-colonial struggle of Palestinians to the struggle of Blacks in the United States and beyond, crystallized in movement for Black lives, synecdochally manifested by BLM.

The matter of absolutism is also closely related to the students' alleged "Manichean fervour," meaning how their *parti pris* for the Palestinian cause is distorting their vision and understanding of what is actually happening in Gaza. Again, "Manichean" is a loaded term. It evokes an absolute dualism between good and evil that is ripe for abuse and an overblown sense of righteousness. But Manicheanism in a colonial context means something more precise. It first describes the colonial mentality and its division of the world in zoological terms. "The colonized world is a world divided in two," writes Fanon.[125] Native peoples are rendered as other species: "When the colonist speaks of the colonized he uses zoological terms. Allusion is made to the slithery movements of the yellow race, the odors from the 'native' quarters, to the hordes, the stink, the swarming, the seething, and the gesticulations."[126] What the students are expressing is a profound discontent with the hypocrisy of their political leaders, who are playing a cynical game, appealing to international law (the integrity of borders) in one instance—Ukraine's response to the 2022 Russian invasion—and suspending it in another: Hamas's response to Israel's 75-year-old invasion. Their encampments symbolize a desire to reclaim the language of justice away from those in power who wielded it purely for *savage national interest—the sovereign principle of conduct among Western nations*, to adopt Sekyi-Otu's formulation.[127]

Anatomy of Violence in a World in Crisis

What we have here is a fundamental division in the way we look at a world in crisis. Bruno Maçães distinguishes between the hermeneutic orientations of "Westernists" and "universalists."[128] The first back Ukraine and Israel for geopolitical reasons; the second stand with Ukraine and Palestine for principled reasons. For the Westernists, international laws are conditional, relevant only when they adequately serve national interests. For universalists, there is a deep investment in the "common pattern holding the views on the two conflicts together"; international laws must be applied consistently (what applies to Ukraine applies to Palestine and vice-versa) to preserve a minimum degree of legitimacy in the eyes of the rest of the world, especially in the Global South where Russia and the United States are practically indifferentiable in their unilateralist decision-making (as when they abuse their veto power on the UN security council, making a "mockery" of international law[129]). As a universalist, Žižek argues that "Ukraine is Palestine" rather than "Ukraine is Israel," as Ukrainian president Volodymyr Zelensky stated to the Knesset on March 20, 2022, and repeated many times since then. Zelensky presented himself as an ally of the Westernists. The cost is a betrayal of global solidarity. He failed to universalize Ukrainian grievances, to turn national trauma into a common cause against global thugs, to see his struggle against a colonizer bent on domination and dispossession as cutting across societies. Unlike Zelensky's dubious identification of Ukraine with Israel, 200 Ukrainian researchers, artists, political and labor activists, and members of civil society expressed their support for Palestine. The signatories acknowledge what Zelensky had occluded.

> We . . . stand in solidarity with the people of Palestine who for 75 years have been subjected and resisted Israeli military occupation, separation, settler colonial violence, ethnic cleansing, land dispossession and apartheid. We write this letter as people to people. The dominant discourse on the

governmental level and even among solidarity groups that support the struggles of Ukrainians and Palestinians often creates separation. With this letter we reject these divisions, and affirm our solidarity with everyone who is oppressed and struggling for freedom.[130]

Neither tribalistic nor opportunistic, they embrace Palestinian resistance with all its backlashes. The language of the signatories is strikingly reminiscent of Fanon's: "Every time a man has brought victory to the dignity of the spirit, every time a man has said no to an attempt to enslave his fellow man, I have felt a sense of solidarity with his act."[131] Palestinians are saying no to Israel's attempt to subjugate them—this act alone sparks solidarity with Palestine and positions you as a revolutionary.[132] If Westernists recognize that the situation in Palestine is catastrophic, but not serious, a Manichean fervor resists the Westernists' hegemony. It finds the playbook of Western powers morally and politically bankrupt. For the universalists, another image of justice is possible.

Realizing another world requires grappling with our current grammar of violence, which works to obfuscate the settler-colonial situation faced by so many around the world. To stay with the example of Palestine as an elucidating case study, we might ask, What did violence look like before October 7? I want to think through this question and the workings of our grammar by turning to Žižek's key distinction between "subjective violence" and "objective violence." Žižek calls subjective violence the violence that is "performed by a clearly identifiable agent . . . [and] . . . is seen as a perturbation of the 'normal,' peaceful state of things."[133] Žižek supplements this common understanding of violence with objective violence, which he then divides into, first, "symbolic violence" (the violence of language as the hegemonic imposition of a given universe of meaning) and, second, "systemic violence" (such as the violence done by capitalism, which becomes a naturalized, smooth-functioning background force, covering over its oppressive exacerbation of inequalities). "Objective violence is invisible," Žižek avers, "since it sustains the very zero-level standard against which we perceive something as subjectively violent."[134] In the context of Palestine/Israel, subjective violence happens when the Israeli Defense Forces (IDF) disrupts the "normal," peaceful state of Palestinian existence (let's say the Occupation on October 6). Unlike subjective violence, objective violence is indiscernible; when war in Palestine is not the object of media attention or political deliberation, Palestine is not on any Western agenda.[135] Writing in 1974, Fawaz Turki similarly described objective violence as a series of "private terrors," reserved for those consigned to that "encapsulated world of non-being," a place considered by the West bereft of innocent people.[136] This is a violence that the average Western individual never grasps, since the violence has been purely naturalized. And this is the type of violence that Žižek enjoins us to consider when we imagine and consider quotidian Palestinian life:

What goes on in the Middle East when *nothing goes on there* at the direct politico-military level (i.e. when there are no tensions, attacks, negotiations)? What goes on is the incessant slow work of taking the land from the Palestinians on the West Bank, the gradual strangling of the Palestinian economy, the parceling of their land, the building of new settlements, the pressure on Palestinian farmers to make them abandon their land (which goes from crop burning and religious desecration up to individual killings)—all this supported by a Kafkaesque network of legal regulations.[137]

In Gaza, objective violence is perhaps best captured by what Sara Roy calls "de-development." Prior to October 7, Israel's "policies of separation, isolation, and closure . . . deliberately aimed to weaken, undermine, and hollow out Gaza's economy over time."[138] De-development is precisely what happens in Gaza when *nothing happens there* at the direct politico-military level (when the IDF are not mowing the lawn). De-development does not preoccupy the Western world. Occupation on cruise control is "manageable."

After October 7, Israel's destruction of any infrastructure capable of supporting life increased exponentially:

> The total siege of Gaza that was imposed following the horrifying murders of Israelis by Hamas militants on October 7, 2023, was part of that same policy continuum of separation and closure—clearly, its most extreme and pernicious form characterized by the destruction of Gaza's infrastructure (especially housing) and the denial of food, water, electricity, and fuel to its population.[139]

Econocide—"the wholesale destruction of an economy and its constituent parts"—is de-development on steroids, accelerating the entry of large swaths of Palestinians into the zone of nonbeing.

At the same time, the type of violence taking place in Palestine is not always clearly discernible. For example, Israel's deadly bombing of a World Central Kitchen convoy on April 1, 2024, appeared to collapse the two registers of violence. The targeting of this convoy, containing seven aid workers from Australia, Britain, Poland, the United States, Canada, and Palestine, provoked outrage—or at least the performance of outrage—among political leaders in the Global North. Biden, we're told by his staff, was disturbed.[140] His call to Netanyahu compelled the prime minister to allow more aid, briefly, into Gaza, and Biden warned him that Israel's military tactics need to change or there would be consequences. Months later, we have seen no changes from Israel and no consequences from the United States. The loss of lives of these aid workers is undeniably tragic, but let's not forget that 177 Palestinian UN staff had already been killed prior to this incident. It is not hard to conclude that the bodies of Westerners count more than those of faceless Palestinians. When Israel kills Palestinian aid workers, Western officials look the other way. But when Israeli violence is visited on Western bodies, Israel must be held accountable for its criminal actions—or, at the very least, Western leaders have to give the appearance that they care about pro-Palestinian Western bodies involved in the distribution of humanitarian aid.[141]

While subjective violence, in principle, can provoke empathy through a captivating image of the victim[142] (an image which, Žižek maintains, contributes to the invisibilization of objective violence), subjective violence in Gaza appears to follow a different logic. The deaths of Western aid workers are clear instances of Israel's subjective violence: Israel is the perpetrator and the Western aid workers its victims. But clearly discernible acts of violence committed against Palestinian non-combatants by Israeli snipers, drone strikes, and extra-judicial killings in hospitals, for example, do *not* register as subjective violence. They remain invisible, experienced as if the violence were objective violence, as if it was a natural occurrence and part of the daily fabric of Palestinian life. Death tolls are reported, and the obscenity of the number clearly impacts the pro-Palestinian public. And yet the outrage that it produces is contained and neutralized at the politico-military level. Its impact on Western policies is blunted. *How* Western mainstream media frame Palestine involves symbolic violence. Žižek rightly notes the excessive bias in reporting, which obfuscates even the clearest instances of subjective violence suffered by Palestinians: "While Israelis are killed in a 'massacre,' Palestinians are merely 'found dead.' These forms of 'soft' censorship pervade public discourse."[143] Palestinians are abject casualties but without a named perpetrator (if anyone is named or blamed, it is Hamas, for its use of "human shields") whereas Palestinians are effortlessly cast as the victimizers, even when they are defending themselves against Israeli soldiers and unhinged settlers. Achille Mbembe alerts us to the pivotal role of language in the enactment of symbolic violence. He observes, "the act of violation [*le viol*] often begins with language."[144] *Viol*, in French, means violation in multiple senses, including "rape"; the violence that begins with language, in Mbembe's formulation, can thus be symbolic, psychic, and physical. Invisibilizing the violence in Gaza facilitates its repetition and diffusion.

The challenge, as I see it, however, is not to "democratize" subjective violence so that political leaders and mainstream reporters can empathize with Palestinians as well as Western aid workers. Empathy is not a political agenda. The challenge is to harness the fleeting outrage over the subjective violence visited on the international aid workers by linking it to the objective violence of the Occupation, of settler reality, of colonial time. As I'll discuss in more detail in Chapter 4, empathy is useful when talking about Palestine only if it opens to a decolonizing agenda.

Israel will undoubtedly survive any setback with the United States and the other Western nations, and push through the world's visceral reaction to the devastation of Gaza. Israel seems to have made the calculation that it does not really matter how many more Palestinians it murders. What the Israeli government and its supporters fear more and more, however, is the growing dissatisfaction with Israel among a younger generation of Western citizens. And the blame for this development lies not with Hamas but with the anti-colonial Left, the Left that names, ridicules, and shames the refusal of Western leaders to describe Israel's actions as genocide. The cartoonist Joe Sacco captures these moral and political failures well when he coins the term "genocidal self-defense"[145] (see Figure 1) and when, countering Western obfuscation of the matter, he gives a stark visual illustration of what the right of genocidal existence actually means.

What throws a wrench in the Zionist framing of Palestinians is again an insistence on the violence of settler colonialism. But who's afraid of settler colonialism? I don't believe that it is the warmongering, far-right or messianic Zionists who are really afraid of settler colonialism. They are not at all ambivalent about Israel's founding violence; in fact, they are calling for a second and final Nakba, the Arabic word for catastrophe. Writing on social media after Hamas's bloody incursion, the right-wing member of the Israeli Knesset Ariel Kallner backed an immediate genocide: "Right now, one goal: Nakba! A Nakba that will overshadow the Nakba of 48. Nakba in Gaza and Nakba to anyone who dares to join!"[146] The Israeli government did not disappoint, launching a vengeful onslaught on the Gaza Strip. "Israel's religious settler vanguard," Joshua Leifer writes, "has greeted the intensity of this assault with a kind of messianic ecstasy."[147] The new Right in Israel waxes nostalgic for the ethnic cleansing of old. It is the liberal camp who fears the settler-colonial framework. As Raz Segal points out, settler colonialism is a "Pandora's box for the West."[148] If the settler-colonial framework gets traction outside the spheres of activists and academics, the United States could find itself next in the crossfire of public opinion. It is no longer the "Red Scare" that terrifies Western elites; their fear is *fear of an anti-colonial nation*.[149] In this light, there is no appetite in American leadership to come to terms with its own settler-colonial history/reality, which explains the nation's aversion to calling what Israel is doing settler-colonial genocide.

If the US political establishment neuters its original sins—chattel slavery and Indigenous genocide—by relegating them to the dustbin of the past, some academics move to discredit settler-colonial studies by challenging its accuracy and utility. They argue that the evocation of "settler colonialism" is off-putting, too aggressive—not respectful of one's right not to be disturbed or harassed. As the argument goes, talk of settler colonialism is divisive, when we should be looking for connections that bring us together. Seyla Benhabib exemplifies this tendency. Already in her review of Judith Butler's 2012 *Parting Ways: Jewishness and the Critique of Zionism*, Benhabib writes: "I do not believe that we will get

Figure 1 "The War on Gaza," in *The Comics Journal*, January 26, 2024.

very far by repeating the formula that 'Zionism is a form of settler colonialism.'"[150] And in response to the open letter "Philosophy for Palestine," which objected to a palpable "reckless indifference"[151] to history in the prevailing discussions of Hamas's attack on October 7 and Israel's retaliation, Benhabib denounces the reduction of the "conflict" to settler colonialism and argues that both the peoples involved have evolved and that Zionism is not a form of racism:

> By construing the Israel-Palestine conflict through the lens of settler-colonialism, you elide the historical evolution of both peoples. Zionism is not a form of racism, though the actions and institutions of the State of Israel towards the Palestinian people of the occupied West Bank, the refugee camps and, of course, Gaza, are discriminatory on the basis of nationality, not color, and reflect the continuing state of emergency that exists between Israel and its neighbors.[152]

Though "Philosophy for Palestine" never refers to settler colonialism directly, Benhabib is not wrong in singling out that framework, but she is quite wrong in her analysis of it. Her opposition between settler colonialism and "the historical evolution of both peoples" reveals her failure to understand how settler colonialism functions: Zionist invasion, as Patrick Wolfe famously put it, is a "structure not an event."[153] Claiming that the original settler underwent change is nothing more than an instance of what Eve Tuck and K. Wayne Yang call a "settler move to innocence."[154] Benhabib is both channeling settler anxiety about guilt and responsibility and putting on full display her own fetishist disavowal: *I know very well that Palestinians are mistreated by the Israeli state, but all the same I don't believe that "Zionism is a form of racism" captures the complex situation.*

Benhabib's presumptuousness, in the guise of a measured intervention, not only reveals the truism that nobody likes to be called a racist—a racist settler, in this case—but also demonstrates a greater concern for the well-being of the occupier, the invader. Like Butler, I refuse to sugarcoat objections to Israeli violence. For the Palestinian question to be heard, a critique of Israel's systemic violence against Palestinians must be direct and fearless. Benhabib obfuscates. She is more interested in understanding the collective psyche of the oppressor than attending to the condition of the subjugated. She faults Butler for their ungenerous reading of Israeli Jews and for failing to understand their predicament: "As psychoanalytically astute as Butler is, she seems to turn a blind eye to the lingering collective psychosis of many Jews, whether in Israel or not, namely, their fear of annihilation in the hands of a hostile world. The tragedy of Israel is that the stronger Israel has become militarily, the more paranoid and bullyish it has become."[155] Israeli paranoia is both explained and explained away as a reaction to past trauma and legitimate security concerns. Consequently, the objective violence of the colonial situation is effectively minimized. Israeli paranoia is abated or even excusable, a manifestation of both historical vulnerability and absolute victimhood, and has nothing to do with Zionism's racial matrix and management of Jewish supremacy over the Palestinians. So, I am still inclined to say the opposite. *I do not believe that we will get very far unless we repeat the formula that "Zionism is a form of settler colonialism."*[156] We are not dealing with a conflict but an antagonism. A conflict is resolvable without jeopardizing the functioning of the system and power structure. This is not a land dispute with two parties having legitimate but competing claims to the land. What we have here, in the words of Rashid Khalidi, is "a colonial war waged against the indigenous population, by a variety of parties, to force them to relinquish their homeland to another people against their will."[157] A settler-colonial framework names the antagonism: Native vs. invader. This binarism—which is typically dismissed, ignored, or disavowed—must serve as the basis for any reconciliation between Palestinians and Israelis.

Settler colonialism reminds Israel that it "hasn't yet obliterated the 'founding violence' of its 'illegitimate' origins," as Žižek avers. Palestinian *ressentiment* refuses to let Israel repress its unsavory origins into a "timeless past."[158] Žižek then draws the larger point: "In this sense, what the state of Israel confronts us with is merely the obliterated past of every state power."[159] Yes, all nations want to naturalize their founding-violence, but settler states in particular are constantly deploying a logic of elimination (through integration, forced removal, or genocide) to achieve that end. The Native remains anathema to the settler.

Benhabib's resistance to settler colonialism is symptomatic rather than unique. Talk of settler colonialism is a killjoy for liberal Zionists and liberals, like Benhabib, more generally. It strips them of their alibi: *I don't support Netanyahu and his fascist coalition; I belong to the Peace Camp; I believe in the two-states solution; Palestine is a '67 problem; the settlers are not who we are*, and so on. Exposing Israel as a settler-colonial formation pulls the rug out from under the feet of liberals. They must choose between the status quo (an Israel that no longer hides its aspirations for a Greater Israel) or Palestine/Israel as a place where equality and freedom are shared by all (binationalism or/as a just one-state solution).

A Greater Violence

The response to "naked violence" is not a "greater violence" in the style of colonial retaliation, as in dreaming of a revenge attack that is even more effective than October 7. No, if a greater violence is needed to compel colonial powers to give in, that violence must be pursued in the counter-violence of resistance that aims to delegitimize and demythologize such states. The example of the Boycott, Divest, and Sanctions (BDS) movement, launched in 2005 by Palestinian civil society groups, shows us what the frontline of this struggle looks like. Israel fears BDS. Why? Because BDS is more violent than Hamas.[160] Its nonviolent violence is more effective in convincing a younger generation of students that Israel is an illiberal state, that it is an apartheid state from the river to the sea, as the Israeli human rights group B'Tselem concluded. As a movement, BDS is interrupting the basic hermeneutic framework that uncritically paints Israel as a Jewish and democratic state. BDS recasts Israel without its fake veneer of liberalism. And it is for this reason that "the Palestinians are winning,"[161] to repeat the first line from Ali Abunimah's 2014 *The Battle for Justice in Palestine*.

Students in the encampments are combatants of the imaginary, supporting Palestinians and calling out Israel's pounding of Gaza into a desolate wasteland. These *ressentimental* students refuse to normalize Israel's crimes and their government's ugly complicity with the genocidaires of Gaza. They meet Israel's naked violence with a greater violence: they dismantle the Westernist grammar that shields Israel from legitimate criticism, the grammar that exceptionalizes Israel (how can we be guilty of any crimes when we possess the world's "most moral army"?) and makes liberals feel that they need to stand with Israel—*I'm not an anti-Semite, so I stand with Israel*. The language of settler colonialism terrifies Israel and its supporters. It puts front and center the stark realities of Israeli coloniality, giving the lie to propagandistic claims: How can a most moral army appear on the United Nations' "blacklist" of countries who harm children in conflict, joining the grim ranks of Saudi Arabia, Afghanistan, the Democratic Republic of Congo, Sudan, and Syria, among others?[162] As if there were any doubt about the gratuitous and sadistic violence of the most moral army, consider the testimony of Israeli soldiers who described "the near-total absence of firing regulations in the Gaza war, with troops shooting as they please, setting homes ablaze, and leaving corpses on the streets—all with their commanders' permission."[163] Apparently, the enjoyment of shooting at Palestinians breaks the boredom of carrying out genocide. Israeli soldiers numbed by the objective violence of the daily carnage want to experience Operation Iron Swords through the lenses of subjective violence (as victimizers, of course): "the ability to shoot without restrictions gave soldiers a way to blow off steam or relieve the dullness of their daily routine. 'People want to experience the event [fully].'"[164] In Gaza, IDF soldiers "'kill on site/sight'"[165] as a form of obscene enjoyment.

The grammar of settler colonialism is slowly transforming how we think and talk about Palestine/Israel, providing activists, students, and academics with the language to articulate their critique of Israel's subjugation of Palestinians. To be crystal clear, this is not an instance of woke liberalism or a cancel culture that silences Jewish voices. "What permeates 'cancel culture,'" Žižek writes, "is a 'no-debate-stance': a person or position is not only excluded—what is excluded is the very debate, the confrontation of arguments, for or against this exclusion."[166] As I've witnessed first-hand with my own students at Whitman College, pro-

Palestinian supporters welcome debates, holding frequent teach-ins, urging their peers to look at Zionism from the standpoint of its Palestinian and Jewish victims (as Edward Said and Ella Shohat taught us and them), and challenging long-held beliefs in Israel's liberalism, multiculturalism, and democratic ethos.

These students are not delegitimizing Israel because they want to put Jewish lives at risk. A Jewish life is worth as much as a Palestinian life—and that's the point. Among the pro-Palestine protestors, Jewish students are spearheading the call to revisit what constitutes anti-Semitism, contesting Israel's self-appointed authority to speak for them. Students who protest are delegitimizing Israel not because they want to eliminate Jews,[167] but because Israel is starving Palestinian civilians; because it is murdering children, journalists, and healthcare workers at an unprecedented rate; because it acts as a racist state; because its basic power structure works to dispossess and marginalize Palestinians inside and outside the Green Line.[168] It is Israel and its Western backers (ranging from the liberal establishment to the far Right, from Joe Biden to Marine Le Pen) who are engaged in the worst aspects of cancel culture—not only removing Israel's policies and settler crimes from debate but demonizing/criminalizing anyone for even raising the Palestinian question: *You are evil/anti-Semitic for standing for Palestinian rights, for being in solidarity with Palestine*. But students are steadfastly refusing this perverse logic. "By thinking with/through/from Palestine," as Maryam Kashani puts it, a hysterical questioning is taking hold: *Why are the Palestinians what you are telling us that they are? Again, why should we listen to war criminals and their accomplices/ enablers?*[169]

Just as the US police appear as agents of injustice in their mistreatment of the internally colonized, rather than agents who serve and protect (their stated purpose), the IDF, for Palestinians and their supporters, cannot but appear as a misnomer in its subjugation of Palestinians.[170] Žižek notes this parallel: "In US slums and ghettos, police effectively functions more and more as a force of occupation, something akin to Israeli patrols entering the Palestinian territories on the West Bank."[171] For many Palestinians and Blacks, daily living is living under military occupation.[172]

Haim Bresheeth-Zabner has meticulously tracked the transformation of the IDF over the last decades, particularly since the Oslo Accords of 1993. He writes: "These changes in the nature, size, and character of the IDF were driven by the shifting challenges since 1967, when the IDF started functioning as an army of occupation. The last time the IDF faced a foreign army in major combat was in 1973."[173] After signing peace agreements with Egypt and Jordan and neutralizing Lebanon and Syria, the IDF could concentrate on its primary task: "fighting a Palestinian population of (then) over two million civilians, without an organized or functional leadership, army, or any other civic or national government. The IDF became the Israel Occupation Forces."[174] The Israeli forces are indeed better understood and designated as IOF, Israeli Occupation Forces: they are not agents of defense but agents of state terror: How else do you describe a mighty military force whose main task is to dominate a mostly civilian population? US agents of injustice and Israeli agents of state terror meet: *Is it then a surprise that a number of US police forces are being trained by Israel's military?*[175] Naming *the IDF as IOF* reminds us the act of resistance often begins with language as well.

The pro-Palestinian students and proponents of BDS are not exceptionalizing Palestinian lives (I return to the question of exceptionalism in Chapter 5). In their struggle against Palestinophobia, they are taking up a universalist position. This is not a choice between universality and racial difference. Turning to Hegel's notion of concrete universality, Žižek explains:

> The properly Hegelian paradox is that, in today's concrete situation in the US, the only way really to make the universal claim "All lives matter" is to say "Black lives matter," since the oppression of blacks is today the symptomatic point, the exemplary case, of the universal oppression. The moment one says "But why only black lives? All lives matter!," such a leveling cuts off the edge of the universal oppression. In a similar way, if, in Hitler's Germany, one were to say "But why such a focus on anti-Semitism? Other races are also oppressed!," one would have obfuscated the true horror of the Nazi racism, which is exemplified in anti-Semitism. And, one should add here, the same goes for today's Israel with regard to how it relates to Palestinians: the only way in Israel today to be really anti-racist is to admit that the way the State of Israel is treating Palestinians is racist."[176]

Sadly, the opposite is happening in Israel today. Far-right Zionists are turning to Adolf Hitler for inspiration and wording in order to better articulate their genocidal sentiments toward Palestinians. Former Israeli MK Moshe Feiglin, speaking to Channel 12 news, said, "As Hitler said, 'I cannot live if one Jew is left,' we can't live here if one 'Islamo-Nazi' remains in Gaza." Feiglin further added, Jews "are not guests in our own land, it is entirely ours"—whence his murderous desire to "turn Gaza Hebrew."[177]

Whereas Palestinophobia is engulfing almost all of Israel, "philosemitic McCarthyism"[178] pervades many US campuses with the same tenacity, distorting or exaggerating violent incidents of anti-Semitism (students being disturbed by the chant "free Palestine" is not an instance of anti-Semitism) while ignoring the aggressive "Zionist anti-Semitism"[179] targeting Jews who stand with Palestine. In American society, Zionist anti-Semitism is not really legible, not visible as a racist discourse. There is a willful disregard for its operations: how it polices and punishes Jews, greasing the wheels of objective violence, the normalization of the ideological lie that Israel speaks for all Jews. Philosemitic McCarthyism couches its inquiry as driven by a concern for Jews, but it seeks to demonize, bully, and eradicate all voices that refuse to submit to a pro-Israel agenda, sparing no one in its way.

What is even more infuriating for liberal elites and the political class in the United States is that the language for the support of justice in Palestine does not follow the American identity politics script. Not unlike the feminist slogan "Women's rights are human rights," the chant "Palestinian rights are human rights" echoes loudly and clearly at marches. A universalist orientation does not stop at the redistribution of rights, at rendering more democratic an existing framework. Commenting on the universalist character of modern feminism, Žižek with good reason underscores the larger ontological stakes in thinking of an emancipatory movement in universalist terms:

> In this sense I claim that you [women] must aim at universality. This is what you must be conscious of, that when you fight for your position, you at the same time fight for the universal frame of how your position will be perceived within this universal frame. This is for me, as every good feminist will tell you, the greatness of modern feminism. It's not just we women want more. It's we women want *to redefine the very universality of what it means to be human*. This is for me this modern notion of political struggle.[180]

We can further read the universalist underpinnings of feminism through the language of the part of no-part. Who are the women who are systematically abjected from the existing social order? They are society's marginalized women of color. To read from below, "to read up the ladder of privilege," as Chandra Talpade Mohanty put it in her interpretive challenge to Western feminists, is to put subaltern voices front and center.[181] To advance universality, we must begin with society's least privileged, at the bottom of the ladder. Poor women of color are "the 'nothing,' not counted in the order"[182]; they stand for social justice and for universality as such because, through their positioning, they have an intimate understanding of the workings of power and its exclusions: "If we pay attention to and think from the space of some of the most disenfranchised communities of women in the world, we are most likely to envision a just and democratic society capable of treating all its citizens fairly."[183] Black and Indigenous Feminists have disclosed time and time again that knowledge of the human is *not-all*, not because there is something foreign or unintelligible that evades it, but precisely *because* there is nothing that evades it. "For this very reason it cannot be totalized,"[184] whence the ontological possibility for redefinition and reinvention of the human against racist regimes. Fanon's cry that "the last shall be first"[185] is not about substituting the colonized for the colonizer. Empty reversals have never advanced emancipatory projects. Olúfẹ́mi Táíwò correctly discloses the universalist underpinnings of Fanon's expression: "Fanon is not demanding the subjugation of the coloniser; instead, he is calling for the restoration of the equality all humans share by virtue of their humanity itself."[186] I would stress, though, that this humanity is more invented than restored. This humanity emerges out of the ashes of the reigning humanity. The "genre of the human," what constitutes the human as such, is captured and hoarded by whiteness—a position occupied in Palestine/Israel by Ashkenazi, or European-descended, Jews—which, as Sylvia Wynter might put it, "overrepresents itself as if it were the human itself."[187] Overrepresentation is in the ideological business of totalizing knowledge. The investment in "one mode of being human"[188] cannot but foster an apartheid logic, a segregationist orientation. Central to the dismantling of this logic and matrix, to this ontological upheaval of/in the human, is global solidarity.

Likewise, the students are not simply celebrating Palestinian difference. They are aligning with Palestinians and the movement for Black lives precisely because they want *to redefine the very universality of what it means to be human*. A crucial part of redefining what it means to be human, of keeping the question open, involves reckoning with our unrecognized unfreedom: "We 'feel free' because we lack the very language to articulate our unfreedom."[189] The labor of resistance resides in carefully disclosing the processes responsible for our "unfreedom." Freedom here lies in the public use of reason: the ability to adopt a transnational position, to unplug and distance yourself of your given organic society and the ideological ways it libidinally and cognitively maps social reality for you. The public use of *ressentiment*, likewise, positions you as unwilling to go along with the smooth operation of your social order; it blocks your (neo)colonial interpellation "to join in the ranks marching against one or another approved enemy," as Edward Said put it.[190] The force of the students' *ressentiment* is found in its refusal to accept Palestinians as the "approved enemy," or the Ziofascist Israeli as the "approved friend." They refuse a world translated for them in zoological terms. They refuse to forgive and forget the Biden-Harris administration (and the Democratic Party in general) for the United States' unwavering support of Israel's genocidal campaign, for supplying the settler state with 2,000-pound bombs and Hellfire missiles that turned what was already the largest open-air prison into the largest "open-air graveyard."[191]

The tide is changing, and there is a growing realization among this younger generation that we (the general public) feel that Israel is liberal only because we lack the very grammar to articulate Israel's illiberalism. An effective blow to Jewish supremacy is to challenge Zionism's authoritarian monopoly on defining what constitutes anti-Semitism, Jewishness, and Jewish identity/value. This is what anti-Zionist Jewish students are doing when they disidentify with the Israeli apartheid regime, when they call out settler-state terrorism masquerading as defense, and when they shout, "Not in our name," "Never again for anyone," and so on. The Palestinian cause also generates a boomerang effect: a critique of Israel indicts the rest of the West, in genocidal complicity and moral bankruptcy.

Redefining the very universality of what it means to be human is a herculean and endless task that my resisting protagonists can be seen undertaking in this book. Of course, the list is not exhaustive. Fanon and Žižek serve as my interlocutors in this project, which is squarely oriented toward Palestine/Israel and the United States, two geographical sites of systemic and spectacular violence that continue to arouse, around the world, sentiments of hope and despair, anger and solidarity, and many entangled feelings in between.

In Chapter 1, "Being and Destitution," I explore the contours and consequences of philosophy's investment in the human subject. I draw here on Žižek's radical reappropriation of Cartesian subjectivity, which recasts the *cogito* as an endless source of negativity, capable of interrupting the everyday flow of things and becoming, in turn, a precondition for thinking the subject and social identity *otherwise*. Still, a Fanonian retort to Žižek might be *Don't forget about race/racism and the (neo)colonial situation*. Are we really all Cartesian subjects positioned in the same way? If self-destitution can be experienced by some as an encounter with the Lacanian Real—a masochistic form of radical *jouissance* for queer white, male bodies, for instance—for others, such a destitution marks instead the numbing effects of a naturalized form of social violence. Simply put, how does attending to the (neo)colonial apparatus and the racial situation qualify this *cogito* and caution us against romanticizing desubjectivization and the heroic resistance of the *cogito*? Is it possible to break with an anti-Black futurology, upend the "afterlife of slavery,"[192] as Saidiya Hartman calls it, and annul the ontological death sentence of indefinitely dwelling in the zone of nonbeing with no prospects of flight in sight? I take up these questions by looking at Toni Morrison's 1987 novel *Beloved* and Boots Riley's 2018 film *Sorry to Bother You*, which stages Black identity at the interstices of being and nothingness, humanity and animality. Recounting the story of Sethe's infanticide in the times of slavery, *Beloved* summons us to think and imagine the impossible, to unsettle the underground of our cultural imaginary. Set in a dystopian capitalist world, *Sorry to Bother You* draws us into scenes of subjective destitution, scenes both tragically/courageously willed by their protagonists and forcefully imposed on them, spurring us to consider the stakes of living in conformity with—or, conversely, resisting and altering—the social coordinates of being Black in an anti-Black world.

Chapter 2, "Disavowal in Crisis: The End of Liberalism," examines the cognitive mapping and political force (or the lack thereof) of the liberal position toward the legacy of slavery and settler colonialism and its negation by far Right and conservative politicians in the United States and Israel. I first draw on the psychoanalytic distinction between repression and disavowal, referring to two distinct ways American ideology and Zionism deny or neutralize unpleasant knowledge about the past. Historically, repression has characterized America's general approach to racial slavery and Israel's relation to ethnic cleansing, though in more recent years, a fetishist disavowal, fostered by the liberal Left and liberal Zionism in the United States and Israel, is starting to exemplify these nations' engagements with their traumatic pasts. I then discuss how the far Right in both nations is moving beyond the existing models of repression and disavowal by imposing their own phantasmatic visions on the racial past/present. I trace political Zionism's overwhelming of its "liberal" twin, attending to the ways it has sabotaged the fetishist disavowal that kept liberal Zionists and Western powers more or less content with the status quo. In the United States, the far Right's fight against "wokeness" provides an ideological cover for whitewashing legacies of slavery and settler colonialism. Finally, I consider what an actual reckoning with ontological and racial systems (epitomized in Palestine and Turtle Island by settler colonialism's zoological reason) and anti-Blackness (epitomized in the United States with police violence) might actually entail. For Fanon and Žižek, there is no justice without an engagement with society's antagonisms, as opposed to ideological talks of conflicts or pseudo-struggles.

Chapter 3, "Decolonizing the Mind Under Occupation and Global Capitalism," adopts and adapts Fanon's injunction to "stretch" Marxism in *The Wretched of the Earth* in order to stretch psychoanalysis, making it more hospitable to non-European voices and attentive to the colonial situation, such as Palestinian lives under Occupation. First, I focus on the ways decolonization of the mind opens to an intervention that resonates with psychoanalysis' reflections on identity and resistance. I critically address Eve Tuck and K. Wayne Yang's desire to reign in the force of this anti-colonial imperative, overstating their case in demoting the Fanonian injunction, reducing it to a "first step" among more important ones (claims to resources and land sovereignty) in the project of decolonization. Next, I address Žižek's call to move beyond decolonialization in order to confront the Left's true enemy: global capitalism. Like Huey P. Newton, a cofounder of the Black Panther Party, Žižek decries the anachronism of decolonization, since global capitalism is no longer hindered in the least by local (national) resistance to its circulation and expansion. Lastly, as a Fanonian rejoinder to Žižek (and Newton), I consider whether their dismissal of decolonization is too hasty. If Newton elaborates on Fanon's concerns beyond the pitfalls of national consciousness (the dangers of neocolonialism), factoring in the voracious expansion of the US Empire, Žižek rules out the project of decolonization in its current decoloniality-inspired form. To decolonize in the Fanonian sense is precisely not to become what the colonized formerly were, returning, as it were, to an ontologized pristine time before the colonial encounter absent any internalized subaltern oppression or racism. Decolonizing the mind takes a dialectical form, forcing the mind/subject to confront and move beyond the morbid and unsustainable reality of the present (for the colonizer/settler as well as for the internally colonized/Native);

it entails a counter-violence, a libidinal divestment, a self-violence, a painful but necessary experience of revolutionary suicide.

In Chapter 4, "Radical Others and Real Neighbors: The Politics of the Faceless," I address the question of facelessness and how this concern might contribute to our thinking about resistance and politics. First, I turn to Saidiya Hartman's formulation of the "position of the unthought," tracking the challenges involved in imagining the unimaginable—Black abjection. Next, I put Hartman's notion of Black abjection in dialogue with the position of the Palestinians, exploring the ethics and politics of the faceless through a critical reading of Emmanuel Levinas's infamous interview after the 1982 massacres of hundreds in the Sabra and Shatila refugee camps. Levinas's answer to his interlocutor's question—*Isn't the Palestinian the other of the Israeli?*—falters, disclosing the limits of a Levinasian ethics. If Levinas avoids an engagement with the face of the Palestinian, Fanon and Žižek pursue what we might call a "politics of the neighbor" by adopting and adapting the biblical figure of the neighbor—the "neighbor" of the injunction to "love your neighbor as you love yourself"—opening, in turn, alternative routes for rethinking the face and facelessness of the Palestinian. Lastly, I consider the ontological and political ramifications of thinking the faceless Palestinian and Black, the human without a face, of European modernity. A politics of the neighbor centers facelessness, not so much a condition to overcome but a reorientation away from the mystifying lure of dyadic ethics toward an emancipatory universal politics, of humans and beyond, a path/void opened up by the paradoxical figure of the "real" neighbor.

In Chapter 5, "Against Exceptionalism," I question the logic informing paradigms of trauma that essentialize violent events such as the Shoah and the Maafa, rendering them unique, incomparable exceptions that thematize the violence of Western modernity while standing outside and above the order they inaugurate. Such paradigms are prone to identity politics and block multidirectional, comparative approaches to history, invalidating the solidarity movements required to dismantle the racial colonialist and capitalist structures that continue to destroy lives today. Models of the Shoah and Maafa that ontologize anti-Semitism and anti-Blackness work against one another by de-historicizing these differing forms of violence, transforming them into quasi-eternal foundations that shape political possibilities. In an effort to avoid the temptation to rank that follows from such ontologization, with competing charges of "relativizing" when critics dare to compare and contextualize, I mobilize the appeal to the universal undergirding the labor of Žižek and that of Fanon. Unlike partisans invested in the exceptionality of the Shoah or the Maafa, Fanon and Žižek decline to reify suffering, which seals injured bodies in their victimhood. In their anti-racist politics, they welcome comparison of traumas, choosing to de-ontologize the "pure" victim.

Chapter 1
Being and Destitution

Psychic investments in ontology abound. Philosophers crave ontology to the point that they can be said to behave, as François Laruelle once remarked, like "junkies of Being," "drug addicts of metaphysics."[1] Philosophy dreams of a complete sovereign who has actualized the phantasmatic desire for self-identity. To explore the contours and consequences of this fantasy more closely, I begin by foregrounding the vexed place of identity in Western philosophy's cultural imaginary, relating it especially to its twin concept of the subject. What constitutes the difference between the two? Is identity more available for libidinal attachments? If identity suggests a penchant for rootedness, the subject—particularly in its Lacanian psychoanalytic-inflection—assumes a less stable and anchored reality. Consider Žižek's radical reappropriation of Cartesian subjectivity. It is primarily the emptiness of the Cartesian subject, its out-of-jointness—and not the positivity of the *cogito* (the thinking substance)—that captures Žižek's interest. Indeed, as he stresses, the Cartesian subject is paradoxically "*a subject bereft of subjectivity*,"[2] or we might say that it is a subjectivity bereft of positive identity. Psychoanalysis' anti-identitarian orientation puts front and center the undoing of the subject's being. "The ultimate aim of psychoanalytic treatment," Žižek writes, "is for the subject to undo the ultimate 'passionate attachment' that guarantees the consistency of his/her being, and thus to undergo what Lacan calls 'subjective destitution.'"[3] What happens to "being" in this psychoanalytic moment of subjective destitution? Is destitution a sign that we have freed ourselves from the hegemony of identity? Are moments of destitution to be sought and celebrated? Lee Edelman, for instance, aligns self-destitution with an encounter with the Lacanian Real, which Žižek glosses as the experience of "the immanent blockage or impediment of the order of Being, what makes the order of Being inconsistent."[4] As a masochistic form of radical *jouissance*—the unsettling enjoyment in "the loss of identity and coherence"[5]—self-destitution names queer resistance to heteronormative futurity. Contrary to typical, well-meaning liberals responding to homophobes in power, Edelman does not attempt to win over a homophobic audience with rhetorical or imaginary appeals to sameness (of the sort: queer people are like everyone else, good, bourgeois citizens invested in the common good and well-being of society; their values are the same as ours, they aspire to marry, adopt, serve in the military, and so on). Quite the contrary, Edelman's brand of queer oppositionality accepts the right-winger's accusation and boldly affirms it: "rather than rejecting, with liberal discourse, this ascription of negativity to the queer, we might . . . do better to consider accepting and even embracing it."[6]

But such traumatophilic proclivities also raise questions of racial inequities and white privilege.[7] Do they not reflect a desire to celebrate self-abnegation without coming to terms with destitution as the consequence of a racist distribution of precarity?[8] Beginning with this racial matrix, Fanon locates ontological destitution within the zone of nonbeing rather than in the *jouissance* of desubjectivization. Associating destitution with social death, Fanon marks the numbing effects of a naturalized form of social violence. Here, destitution is something done to you by an external social force. In this respect, we can ask, How does Fanon's zone of nonbeing—a site that denotes the existence of those racialized, colonized, or blackened bodies, whose very ontology has been discredited and hollowed out—impact our understanding of the Žižekian *cogito*? Simply put, how does attending to the racial situation qualify this *cogito* and caution us against romanticizing desubjectivization and/as resistance?

I tackle these questions in the following pages by turning to works of fiction, Toni Morrison's 1987 novel *Beloved* and Boots Riley's 2018 film *Sorry to Bother You*, whose creative mode of intervention I explore via a dialogue with Žižek, Fanon, and the Afropessimists. Afropessimism, arguably the most vocal and iconoclastic wing of the field of Critical Black Studies, challenges the often-accepted view that the hegemony of whiteness is *the* problem confronting all racialized communities. The movement turns its attention instead to the singularity of anti-Blackness. Afropessimism is best understood as an "ensemble of questions"[9] oriented toward "Black positionality" and emanating from theorists who "share Fanon's insistence, that though Blacks are sentient, the structure of the entire world's semantic field . . . is sutured by anti-black solidarity."[10] Afropessimists draw our attention to white civil society's libidinal economy— the collective unconscious which regulates desires and fears, governing our sense of who affectively matters, belongs, counts, and who doesn't. In this anti-Black libidinal economy, an abhorrent image of the Black imago, a Blackness construed "out of a thousand details, anecdotes, and stories," writes Fanon, circulates effortlessly.[11] Black being/imago stands for the absence of humanity, and embodies external terror itself: "The Negro is not a human being that is simply mistreated," writes Calvin Warren, "but is, instead, an invention designed to embody a certain terror for the world."[12] For Frank B. Wilderson III, the Black subject's own gaze is seemingly powerless, unable to alter and restore his blackened image to the world: "My gaze, a blackened gaze, cannot reposition me, restore me to a paradigm whose coherence—that is the integrity of Humanity at every scale: the national, the civic, the domestic, the corporeal—is predicated on the production and reproduction of my non-being."[13] This is an echo of Fanon's devastating realization that "the black man has no ontological resistance in the eyes of the white man."[14]

If Blackness circulates as a phobic object, a source of horror and anxiety for whites *ab initio* ("The children know that innocence is not black"[15]), Black people are not spared from its madness, enduring the phantasmic image's corrosive reach. "*All sentient beings*, Humans and Blacks, bond over the imago of the Black phobic object, that we might form a psychic 'community' even though we cannot form political community," says Wilderson.[16] On this view, Blacks are at birth dispossessed of their psyches. As Wilderson observes: "there's always an intrusion at the lowest level of abstraction in our unconscious, which means that we are always fighting the Black imago, and desiring the white ideal to be a part of ourselves."[17] To be Black entails a double threat, a double struggle: one against the white terror emanating from the outside (white people *are* the police) and one against the self-image emanating from within: "Existence might be a daily struggle for us all, but for the black his being is the effect of a war fought on at least two fronts. He must enter into combat not only with the presentiments and premonitions of a world condemning him to nonexistence, he must also enter the lists against his own image."[18] A storehouse of ruined ontology, the Black imago further ties those rendered Black to the zone of nonbeing, to the site of existential erasure.

Given the bleakness of this situation, what resources are available to exit this hellish zone, find refuge from ontological deterioration, and break with the predominant libidinal economy? Is a cut in the white symbolic order, underpinned by an anti-Black libidinal economy, even a possibility? I believe it is. White civil society's libidinal economy is not immune to critique or change, as Žižek argues in adopting and adapting Virgil's saying (which also serves as the epigraph to the first edition of Freud's *The Interpretation of Dreams*): "I will move the infernal regions. Dare to disturb the underground of the unspoken underpinnings of our everyday lives."[19] Žižek undertakes this inventive task by critically reframing the relation of fantasy to reality:

> Even if reality is "more real" than fantasy, it still needs fantasy to retain its consistency: if we subtract fantasy, the fantasmatic frame, from reality, reality itself loses its consistency and disintegrates. The lesson is thus that the very alternative of "either accept reality or choose fantasy" is a false one: what Lacan calls *la traverse du fantasme* has nothing to do with dispelling illusions and accepting reality the way it is. This is why, precisely when we are shown someone doing just that—renouncing all illusions and embracing miserable

reality—we should focus on identifying the minimal fantasmatic contours of this reality. If we really want to change or escape from our social reality, the first thing to do is to change the fantasies tailored to make us fit this reality.[20]

Against the forced choice of accepting reality or opting for fantasy, we must instead alter how our fantasies work in order to change being and dislodge identity from its sedimentation in social reality. Todd McGowan highlights the primacy of fantasy in both understanding and combatting unconscious bias:

> Unconscious bias denotes racism that persons have without knowledge, not the part of racism that resists knowledge, which is the effect of the unconscious. The unconscious isn't simply a lack of knowledge. It is what one does without being able to know it prior to acting. The unconscious acts ahead of our knowledge. Taking this understanding of the unconscious as our point of departure, we must reverse the relationship between racism and knowledge. Racism is not the result of a bias in our knowing, but rather we have a bias in our knowing because of racism. To find the root of racism we must look not at mistakes in knowing but at successes in enjoying. These successes occur through fantasy.[21]

An anti-racist discourse invested exclusively in demystification (in the notion that knowledge will set you free) will reach its limit. Fantasy, and its circulation in the cultural imaginary, demands more critical attention. There is no transformation of reality without moving the underground of our racist fantasies.[22] To disturb the underground of the unspoken underpinnings of our everyday anti-Black lives— the obscene underside of white America—is to labor to dislocate the Black imago and derail the smooth workings of race-fantasies, which structure or support white reality. I believe that literature and cinema are apt venues for enacting such changes insofar as their interventions and inventions are experienced by readers and viewers at the level of the cultural imaginary. Authors and directors become, in the words of Patrick Chamoiseau, *guerriers de l'imaginaire*,[23] warriors of the imaginary who, through their aesthetic practice, reach down into their society's libidinal economy in order to wreak havoc on the self and society's coherence, to block or disrupt their suffocating hold on minds and desires.

Still, we can anticipate an Afropessimist reproach: Isn't the language of "warrior of the imaginary," a combatant of the libidinal economy, if you will, too attached to the metaphysical idea of the human along with its agential grammar? Isn't this evidence of a lingering humanist belief in the subject's powers to change worldly matters, to alter what humans have brought into being?[24] Is it possible to break with an anti-Black futurology, upend the still-active past of slavery, and annul the ontological death sentence of indefinitely dwelling in the zone of nonbeing with no prospects of flight in sight? I take up these questions through Morrison's *Beloved* and Riley's *Sorry to Bother You* precisely for the way they stage Black identity at the interstices of being and nothingness, humanity and animality. Morrison invites us to "defend the dead"[25] and reckon with the unimaginable violent realities of chattel slavery, where Black flesh indexes the site of annihilation and bare life, and, at the same time, gestures to what must be returned to—and reclaimed and enjoyed—in the face of unyielding white terror. Riley throws us into the dystopian capitalist world of Power Callers and *equi-sapiens*, where racialized surplus humanity abounds and slavery is absurdly made to appear as a "rational" life option that meets the various challenges of the day (where to eat, where to sleep). *Sorry to Bother You* draws us into scenes of subjective destitution, scenes both tragically/courageously willed by their protagonists and forcefully imposed on them, spurring us to consider the stakes of living in conformity with—or, conversely, resisting and altering—the social coordinates of being Black in an anti-Black world.

The Žižekian *Cogito*

The first thing to say about Žižek's reading of the Cartesian moment or "event" in philosophy is that it is no standard Cartesianism. As Ernesto Laclau observes, "this is a *most* peculiar way of being a Cartesian."[26] Indeed, the Žižekian *cogito* couldn't be more at odds with the traumatophobic protocols René Descartes himself outlined in *The Passions of the Soul*. Assessing philosophy's epistemic norms, Descartes pathologizes an excess of wonder (the English translation of the French *admiration*); too much wonder paralyzes the subject of philosophy, resulting in debilitating astonishment (*étonnement*), a dreadful malady of the soul. "Astonishment is an excess of wonder which can never be anything but bad," Descartes writes.[27] A healthy *cogito* must be measured and must avoid the unsettling effects of astonishment by successfully translating the new into the familiar, into a body of knowledge, thus delivering on the mind's epistemic investment.

If the Cartesian *cogito* of *The Passions of the Soul* seeks a trauma-free approach to certainty, to knowledge production, the Žižekian *cogito* dwells instead in negativity, insisting on its trauma-inducing radical separation from the world. While both introduce a gap between the subject and the symbolic ego, the *cogito* of *The Passions* takes the form of a foundational substance, the Žižekian *cogito* that of a disturbing void. Modern philosophy, as we know, was to aggressively pursue the traumatophobic path laid out by Descartes, producing evermore Enlightened (i.e., masculinist) subjects, the template of human knowers as "masters and possessors of nature," as Descartes puts it in *Discourse on Method*.[28] Psychoanalysis, however, proceeded differently, derailing the all-too-confident march of humanist philosophy. This detour was in no small part sparked by the "narcissistic wound" Freud dealt to philosophy's humanist subject, which exposed and insisted on the ego's radical ontological demotion. As Freud affirms: *"the ego is not the master in its own house."*[29] The discovery of the Freudian unconscious violently disrupts the identification of the subject with the ego. The full ramifications of the Freudian split subject take up much of Lacan's hermeneutic energy. In "The Instance of the Letter in the Unconscious, or Reason since Freud," the early Lacan flatly rewrites Descartes's "I think therefore I am" as "I am thinking where I am not, therefore I am where I am not thinking."[30] The unconscious fractures the fantasy of the Cartesian *cogito*, revealing that being and thinking fail to overlap. Unlike its Cartesian counterpart, the Žižekian *cogito* is not embarrassed by the presence of the unconscious. On the contrary, it avows the unconscious. Žižek often credits, and clearly is inspired by, the late Lacan's own return to the *cogito*, to the unsovereign *cogito* dominated by signifiers and led back to its "signifying dependence."[31] Lacan's "minimal cogito," as Ed Pluth points out, is "a subject without qualities."[32] Like Lacan, Žižek declines to identify the *cogito* with "the pacifying image of the transparent Self"[33]—the site of full positivity that Martin Heidegger would decry as substance ontology. Instead, he repeats Lacan's counter-intuitive claim that the "*cogito* IS the subject of the unconscious—the gap/cut in the order of Being in which the real of *jouissance* breaks in."[34]

According to Žižek, Descartes's error lies in his "ontologization of the *cogito*,"[35] his conception of the *cogito* as a substance. The *cogito* is not a *res cogitans*; rather, "this *cogito* is the *cogito* 'in becoming,'"[36] a non-substantial subjectivity. Žižek laments the neglect of the *cogito* and its deleterious effects on thinking as such, and recasts Descartes's modernity, associating the birth of the *cogito* with what he calls "psychotic withdrawal,"[37] a suspension and questioning of the positive order of reality. Žižek returns to the "evental *cogito*,"[38] to the *cogito*'s promise. Without the *cogito*, without the chance to "start with a clean slate," "to erase the entirety of reality,"[39] to withdraw from your own substantive identity, the subject would be reducible to the socially given, enclosed in its organic community, and condemned to the private use of reason, a reason that serves and is "constrained in advance by state and other institutions."[40] The virtues of the *cogito* thus lie not in its masculinist drive for mastery and domination of nature, or its claims to self-sufficiency and self-transparency, but in its relativizing of particularity, in its capacity to adopt a properly multiculturalist perspective (to escape the prison-house of customs, and see one's tradition alongside, and not above, other traditions) and performance of hyperbolic doubt, the ways in which the *cogito* effects "a crack in the great chain of being," disclosing the "abyss of subjectivity," a void, or what Hegel dubs the "night of the world":

> One of Hegel's names for this abyss of subjectivity that he takes from the mystic tradition is the "night of the world," the withdrawal of the Self from

the world of entities into the void that "is" the core of the Self, and it is crucial to notice how in this gesture of self-withdrawal (in clinical terms: the disintegration of all "world," of all universe of meaning), extreme closure and extreme openness, extreme passivity and extreme activity, overlap.[41]

Hyperbolic doubt is a mode of questioning that violently withdraws the subject from the world and its common sense and received wisdom, interrupting "the normal flow of things"[42] and introducing another dimension into the world. As a locus of negativity, the *cogito* becomes a precondition for thinking the subject, identity, and attachments *otherwise*.

The *Cogito* and/in the Zone of Nonbeing

If, for Žižek, the *cogito* depicts subjectivity reduced to its zero-level, Fanon pointedly reminds us, through his formulation of the zone of nonbeing—a region where social egos come undone—that such a reduction has racial implications:

> There is a zone of nonbeing, an extraordinarily sterile and arid region, an incline stripped bare of every essential, from which a genuine new departure can emerge. In most cases, the black man cannot take advantage of this descent into a veritable hell.[43]

While the *cogito*'s capacity to unplug from the organic community, to practice what Kant calls the "public use of reason," [44] casts the subject in its immanent universality, the zone of nonbeing enables as it disables—the dissolution of the ego discloses the subject in her universality but only up to a point. In most cases, the subject rendered Black is plagued by existential precarity, deprived both of a stable social identity and of the prospect of refashioning the self. When the zone of nonbeing gains a quasi-permanent reality, Black being becomes effectively Black ~~being~~. The Black *cogito*'s ontological makeup is by extension compromised. This is, we might say, Fanon's version of W. E. B. Du Bois's formulation of "How does it feel to be a problem?"[45] How does it feel to be trapped in the zone of nonbeing?

The *cogito*'s ontological capacity to "start with a clean slate" does not appear to transfer to Black individuals; it is as if a more originary political ontology shackles the Black *cogito*, denying the racialized subject the human/white privileges of transcendence. At the same time, we should not forget that Fanon never claimed that all individuals racialized as Black are incapable of removing themselves from the zone of nonbeing. Still, "in most cases" is a significant qualifier. How does Fanon explain this incapacity, and how does it relate to

Žižek's understanding of the *cogito*? It might help to compare Fanon's framing of the Black condition with Simone de Beauvoir's formulation of the feminine condition in *The Second Sex*.[46] Both Fanon and Beauvoir are repeating and dislocating the Sartrean existentialist account of transcendence. In *America Day by Day*, published in 1948, one year before *The Second Sex*, Beauvoir describes the Black condition as one of absolute inferiority. She states "the fact" that "blacks *are* inferior to whites"[47]; they are "dirty" and "uncultured."[48] The evidence: "You only have to travel through America to be convinced of it."[49] Beauvoir is not, however, trafficking in white supremacist tropes as it might at first glance appear; her point is to register the ontological devastation of anti-Blackness. She draws attention to the verb "to be" in the statement "Blacks *are* inferior to whites," unpacking its interpretive force: "But what does the verb 'to be' mean? Does it define an immutable substance, like oxygen? Or does it describe a moment in a situation that has evolved, like every human situation? That is the question. And to fresh eyes it's clear that the second meaning is the correct one."[50] Beauvoir's observation is thus not an attempt at naturalizing this inferiority, but rather the opposite: her claim is that Black inferiority is a worldly matter, the effect of social processes. *You are not born an inferior, you become one*. In *The Second Sex*, Beauvoir makes the same point vis-à-vis the condition of women; they are likewise *produced* as the "second sex," as inferior beings: "When an individual or a group of individuals is kept in a situation of inferiority, the fact is that he or they *are* inferior. But the scope of the verb *to be* must be understood; bad faith means giving it a substantive value, when in fact it has the sense of the Hegelian dynamic: *to be* is to have become, to have been made as one manifests oneself."[51]

It is safe to say that Beauvoir's musings about the inferiority of Blacks and women jar with a liberal sensibility. A liberal feminist and anti-racist scholar would insist on distinguishing between the misogynist or anti-Black representation of women or Blacks and how they really *are*.[52] Beauvoir refuses to do this for a reason. Misogyny and anti-Blackness, so deeply enmeshed in material practices, affect the very being of Blacks and women; they operate at the ontological level—the struggle against them must be waged on the same plane. The label of inferiority is not merely a subjective judgment on the part of the sexist or racist that liberals can negate simply by asserting its falsity, that Blacks and women, in fact, are equal to white men. Resistance to symbolic violence fails if the fight is exhausted at the level of ideas. Demystifying racist and misogynist ideas is, of course, necessary, but it is not sufficient. Like Beauvoir, Fanon is not satisfied with an easy opposition between the ontological and the ontical: Blacks are (ontologically) equal to whites but (ontically) inferiorized under the yoke of white supremacy.[53] Such a framing obfuscates the ontological violence of anti-Blackness. Anti-Black ideology impacts Black identity at its core, drains it of its vitality, produces collective psychopathologies, and pushes Blacks further and further into the zone of nonbeing. Anti-Blackness wields a "performative efficiency."[54] It is more than an interpretation of what Blacks *are*; anti-Blackness is "an interpretation that determines the very being and social existence of the interpreted subjects"[55]; anti-Blackness targets the "socio-symbolic identity" of Black folks and thus inferiorizes them. Beauvoir follows her quote above by gesturing to what the next step might look like: "Yes, women in general *are* today inferior to men; that is, their situation provides them with fewer possibilities: the question is whether this state of affairs must be perpetuated."[56] The surest way to remain sealed in the position of inferiority (Blacks locked in their Blackness) is to psychically attach your self to Black identity.

Transcendence for Blacks is wanting: but without it, the zone of nonbeing is experienced as destiny. Here again, Beauvoir's analysis of the feminine condition proves useful. In formulating her feminist existentialist standpoint, Beauvoir reveals the constitutive role played by the material conditions of social existence:

> The perspective we have adopted is one of existentialist morality. Every subject posits itself as a transcendence concretely, through projects; it accomplishes its freedom only by perpetual surpassing toward other freedoms; there is no other justification for present existence than its expansion toward an indefinitely open future. Every time transcendence lapses into immanence, there is degradation of existence into "in-itself," of freedom into facticity; this fall is a moral fault if the subject consents to it.[57]

Here we have an account of bad faith as the ultimate moral fault. At this point, Beauvoir is expressing the party line of existentialist thought: freedom is absolute; there is no compromise. Freedom defines who we are as human beings; this is why Jean-Paul Sartre can make the claim that "the slave in chains is as free as his master."[58] But then she adds the following: "if this fall is inflicted on the subject, it takes the form of frustration and oppression; in both cases it is an absolute evil."[59] Frustration and oppression fester in the zone of nonbeing. But inferiority is not destiny. Destitution is not all. Again, *what disables enables*. True, the situation of Black people provides them with fewer possibilities: the question is whether this anti-Black state of affairs must be perpetuated *by us*.

Attentive to the force of this question, Alenka Zupančič comments on the Afropessimist critique of answers that fail to bear witness to the cry for justice, translating "Black agendas"[60] back into the familiar human rights discourse:

> When blacks are given this or that "right" and insist that "that's not it," it's not simply because more rights could and should be given, or because they are never satisfied and don't understand that this is all about an endless progress toward full equality etc. If you read afropessimism authors, they reply: you completely miss the point; it is not that we want more rights or different rights,

we *want to be*, and that is impossible in this world; our being is excluded from the world such as it is, regardless of its progress in terms of rights and political correctness.[61]

"To be," on this view, is precisely what an anti-Black world denies its Black bodies, depriving them of being, endlessly repeating the trauma of the Maafa—a Swahili term meaning "great disaster," "calamity," or "terrible occurrence"—the "metaphysical holocaust," as Frank Wilderson provocatively put it,[62] visited on Africans during the Middle Passage.

Being Impossible

For Wilderson, the world of the human is not the world of the slave/Black. He turns to Toni Morrison's *Beloved* to convey the bare life of the enslaved. Sethe, Morrison's protagonist, stands for the negation of the human; she is the product of slavery, an effect of this "ontological cataclysm."[63] Ethics, politics, and law fall short in accounting for Sethe's infanticide, which saves her child from a life of racial bondage. Did Sethe have a right to kill her child? Wilderson quotes the author's paradoxical answer: "'It was the right thing to do,' Morrison said, 'but she had no right to do it.'"[64] Wilderson adds that *Beloved*'s characters are utterly "void of relationality," deworlded, drowned/drowning in the zone of nonbeing, where "death is a synonym for sanctuary."[65] In *The Fragile Absolute*, Žižek analyzes the force and implications of Sethe's infanticide:

> As is well known, *Beloved* focuses on the traumatic desperate act of the heroine, Sethe: after she has escaped slavery with her four children, and enjoyed a month of calm recuperation with her mother-in-law in Cincinnati, the cruel overseer of the plantation from which she escaped attempts to capture her by appeal to the Fugitive Slave Law. Finding herself in this hopeless situation, without any prospect of escaping a return to slavery, Sethe resorts to a radical measure in order to spare her children a return to bondage: she cuts the throat of her eldest daughter, tries to kill her two sons, and threatens to dash out the brains of her infant daughter—in short, she commits a Medean *act* of trying to exterminate what is most precious to her, her progeny.[66]

Žižek considers Sethe's killing "an exemplary case of the properly *modern* ethical act."[67] For Žižek, Sethe's sacrifice does not follow the traditional logic of sacrificing, where one sacrifices X for the greater Y. Faced with the prospect of a return to slavery—and with the even worse proposition of a life of slavery for her children—Sethe acted in a way that "did *not* compromise her desire, but fully assumed the impossible-traumatic act of 'taking a shot at herself,' at what was most precious to herself."[68] She sacrificed her "best thing"[69]—her object-cause of desire (her *objet petit a*)[70]—her child. For Žižek, Sethe's *No!* alters the social coordinates of her being, radically undermining and exceeding the terms of her oppressors: their interpellation and cognitive mapping of the situation.

Žižek is of course not oblivious to the "cruel irony" of Sethe's position, since her act of (self-)violence and subjective destitution merely confirms racist ideology, the view of Blacks as animals. Indeed, the overseer Schoolteacher uses Sethe's infanticide as a pedagogical moment for his nephew by drawing such an analogy: "what would your own horse do if you beat it to beyond the point of education . . . you just can't mishandle creatures and expect success."[71] Still, Žižek insists on the radicality of Sethe's act, on the ways she sustains its monstrosity by refusing to qualify it upon her return to the community:

> What makes Sethe so monstrous is not her act as such, but the way she refuses to "relativize" it, to shed her responsibility for it, to concede that she acted in an unforgivable fit of despair or madness—instead of compromising her desire by assuming a distance towards her act, qualifying it as something "pathological" (in the Kantian sense of the term), she insists on the radically ethical status of her monstrous deed.[72]

By stressing the non-pathological character of Sethe's *No!*, Žižek wants to highlight the freedom underpinning her act, an act that can appear only as monstruous, outside of the order of things, for all those involved, including the readers. As Todd McGowan observes:

> Morrison creates a narrative designed to deliver a traumatic shock to the reader, and this trauma resides in the eruption of the impossible as possible. When confronted with returning to the horror of slavery, Sethe makes an impossible choice: killing her daughter. Morrison's novel shows the appropriateness of this act, and its positive depiction in the novel forces the reader to confront the possibility of the impossible act in the contemporary world.[73]

Morrison's novel disturbs and immobilizes, but it also shakes our ethical, political, and hermeneutic bearings. To borrow from Christina Sharpe, *Beloved* incites us to be relentless in "the continued imagining of the unimaginable."[74] How do we react to Sethe's act of subjective destitution, this sacrifice that undoes her own identity? We may, in fact, take our interpretive cue from Baby Suggs, Sethe's mother-in-law and witness to the traumatic event, who forges a new, (im)possible language in order to relate, and relate to, Sethe and her act. Baby Suggs is, in principle, ideally situated to understand Sethe's devastation, since it was her teaching—Baby Suggs is described as "an unchurched preacher"[75]—that rejuvenates Sethe's spiritual being. Baby Suggs called upon the people of her community to cultivate their bodies, to reaffirm a healthier relation to self: "Here . . . in this here place, we flesh; flesh that weeps, laughs; flesh that dances on bare feet in grass. Love it. Love it hard. Yonder they do not love your flesh. They despise it."[76] But the text makes clear that her ethics of love has been severely disrupted by whites: "Those white things have taken all I had or dreamed. . . . There is no bad luck in the world but whitefolks."[77] In her description of Sethe's act, Baby Suggs suspends moral judgment: "she could not approve or condemn Sethe's rough choice."[78]

Beloved stages many Afropessimist insights. Gratuitous violence follows Black people. Believing you're free can get you murdered. Baby Suggs's dream is precisely the *fantasy* of human dignity, the belief that a runaway slave could become again a desiring subject, that she could relate to her body and children as something other than alienated objects, things to be violated with impunity. The arrival of Schoolteacher shatters the reality of Baby Suggs and Sethe, their fantasy of personal security, communal safety, Black sociality, and love. Schoolteacher's traumatizing presence discloses the ideological gap between their celebration of universal self-worth and America as a racist society, between social reality and the Real. Though Baby Suggs and Sethe share a great deal, their differing legal status—one is legally freed while the other has "illegally" escaped slavery—is significant, but can be overstated. Under the Fugitive Slave Law of 1850, slaveholders could track runaway slaves across free states and claim them as their property. This formal legal protection is significant insofar as it protected Baby Suggs from capture, but anti-Blackness as constitutive of a white libidinal economy persists unabated. Schoolteacher lives. He is the agent behind every act of gratuitous violence visited on Black people then and now. The "and more" in Morrison's dedication of the novel to the *Sixty Million and more* might be seen as indexing the unended and unending devastation of Black lives at the hands of the Schoolteachers of the world.

For Afropessimism, slavery never ended ontologically. The Black stands for the nonhuman, not the degraded or not-quite human. The excluded or racially marginalized non-Blacks—including Palestinians, Native Americans, undocumented immigrants, refugees, and queers—are still deemed relatively human and extended (at least some of) the privileges of humanity. Wilderson describes non-Blacks disparagingly as "junior partners of civil society."[79] They may not have all the privileges of white men, but they still benefit from living in an anti-Black world; their humanity, even if aspirational, is premised on not being a slave, that is, Black. Non-Black people have recourse, a mechanism—albeit imperfect—through which they can voice their grievances and make appeals. Wilderson writes:

> In its critique of social movements, Afro-Pessimism argues that Blacks do not function as political subjects; instead, our flesh and energies are

instrumentalized for postcolonial, immigrant, feminist, LGBT, and workers' agendas. These so-called allies are never *authorized* by Black agendas predicated on Black ethical dilemmas. A Black radical agenda is terrifying to most people on the Left because it emanates from a condition of suffering for which there is no imaginable strategy for redress—no narrative of redemption.[80]

The "essential antagonism" does not lie "between the workers and the bosses, not between settler and the Native, not between the queer and the straight, but between the living and the dead."[81] Jared Sexton makes a similar point: "the social life of the hegemonic contest among the 'free' (workers, immigrants, white women, even indigenous peoples, insofar as resistance to colonial genocide is constituted as a matter of *sovereignty*) relies on the social death of the slave."[82] Anti-Black violence is of another breed:

> Unlike violence against the working class, which secures an economic order, or violence against non-Black women, which secures a patriarchal order, or violence against Native Americans, which secures a colonial order, the jouissance that constitutes the violence of anti-Blackness secures the order of life itself; sadism in service to the prolongation of life.[83]

The counter-violence to anti-Black violence would have to disturb the underground of our "order of life." Anything less, the Afropessimist deems sadistic in its complicity with anti-Blackness.

The stakes are significant. Afropessimism is not only raising concerns about the feasibility of cross-racial solidarity, it is also pointing to the ways non-Black liberation movements are premised on anti-Blackness. What gives chattel slavery its incomparability is the *ungeneralizability* of social death, which, as Sexton puts it, "is indexed to slavery and it does not travel."[84] White civil society is predicated on the demise of the Black body: "death of the black body is . . . foundational to the life of American civil society."[85] What is at stake here is white civil society's collective unconscious, its anti-Black libidinal economy: the implicit rules and principles regulating desires and fears, the production, circulation, and consumption of anti-Blackness. Because Blackness has become inimical to being "human," an actual recognition of Blackness would be traumatic for non-Black people; it would unsettle the core of what it means to be human—whence the resistance to Black agendas.

Though Fanon and Afropessimists both call for the destruction of this white world, Fanon is not a separatist in his revolutionary thinking. When it comes to revolutionary struggles, Fanon adopts a de-Manichean posture; always alert to the dynamism of circumstances, he keeps his eye on the antagonisms shaping political reality. After gaining national independence, the formerly colonized,

Fanon suggests, may have to reckon with their own: "The people who in the early days of the struggle had adopted the primitive Manichaeanism of the colonizer—Black versus White, Arab versus Infidel—realize en route that some blacks can be whiter than the whites."[86] Blackness and whiteness were never understood as fixed ontologies. Essentializing them can only lead to political dead-ends.

Unbecoming Human

Sorry to Bother You enacts just such a reimagining and one that foregrounds liberatory imagining as a necessarily collective project. The film centers on an underemployed telemarketer, Cassius "Cash" Green (Lakeith Stanfield), struggling to cope in a racist-capitalist society where resistance often appears futile and slavery persists in the guise of a "free" contract, as workers sign themselves over to lifetime labor commitments in exchange for room and board. Initially, Cash struggles to make sales, though he follows the script given to him (the company's motto is "S.T.T.S.= Stick To The Script!"), his calls are systematically met with indifference or rudeness. His "luck" changes, however, when Langston (Danny Glover), his more seasoned Black coworker, shares with him the secret to telemarketing: one has to use one's "white voice." "White voice" is more than standard English[87]; for Langston this model is not reached by caricaturizing how whites speak nor by imitating their grammar ("Well, you don't talk white enough. I'm not talkin about Will Smith white. That ain't white, that's just proper"), but rather by conveying ease, confidence, and a sense that one has no cares in the world. The secret obviously applies to non-white workers but not exclusively so. Since white people themselves have to cultivate their "white voice," their whiteness is performed as well.[88] In psychoanalytic terms, the "white voice" refers to the "ideal ego," standing for the idealized self-image of whiteness: the privileged white person I would like to be, and more importantly, that I would like others to see me as.[89]

"White voice" is a tool of survival. When one is unable to deploy white voice, one encounters the phenomenon that Sylvia Wynter has powerfully critiqued, that of "N.H.I.," or "No Humans Involved," a shorthand used mainly to designate young Black men. Following the 1992 acquittal of the police officers charged with beating Rodney King, a report on the LA Police Department's practices observed that the police and "public officials of the judicial system of Los Angeles routinely used the acronym N.H.I. to refer to any case involving a breach of the rights of young, jobless, black males living in the inner city ghetto."[90] "N.H.I." is a symptom of an anti-Black world, a world whose "classificatory schemas" normalize and naturalize the violence visited on white America's surplus humanity. This world operates according to the "present conception of the human being" as "Man" (white, male, ableist). Strictly speaking, you are not born human; you become one, and some never do: "Being human can therefore not pre-exist the cultural systems and institutional mechanisms, including the institution of knowledge, by means of which we are socialized to be human," writes Wynter.[91] Since Blackness emerges as overdetermined from the outside, epidermalized, thingified, worldless, white voice expresses, or rather manufactures (for a hostile white gaze), an interiority, a humanness, beyond the surface ontology that governs white perception of Blacks. Tapping into this imaginary whiteness is, at its basic level, a defensive practice for the unprivileged and racialized (mastering the white voice can also be lucrative, but at its core, it functions to combat a racist and inegalitarian world). Langston reminds Cash that it is actually a familiar tool, for white voice is used any time a Black person is "pulled over by the police." White voice conveys a plea: *don't negate my humanity, undo your negation of my being*. And here Afropessimism reminds us that beyond its official officers, the police is constituted by white folks in general, as Wilderson argues: "White people are not simply 'protected' by the police, they *are* the police."[92] White people as a whole function like the social phenomenon represented by the figure of the Karen or Karenning, a term from digital culture "referencing a specific type of middle-class white woman, who exhibits behaviours that stem from privilege."[93] To Karen is to harness privilege in order to police social space and exercise power over racial minorities, particularly Black people. In this respect, we might say that white voice works as a Karen-blocker, a lifesaver for Black people caught up in a world where Black death could come from seemingly endless sources, any non-Black, including non-Black people of color, who, as "junior partners," are as complicit as white folks in the demise of Blacks: "George Floyd was murdered by the white state . . . but I would say that George Floyd was also murdered by [non-Black] people of color who are oppressed by white supremacy and who, simultaneously, secure their status as humans (however much degraded) by anti-Blackness."[94] In an anti-Black world, Blacks are bodies that "magnetize bullets."[95] They are a security risk and must not only put on a white mask but also cultivate and channel their white voice: tactics meant to lessen or temper allegedly "immanent" negrophobic qualities by recoding/reconfiguring your Blackness as white-like. Whiteness is a fleeting idea/I, a collective fantasy preoccupying anyone—though by no means equally—involved in this tortured dance of recognition. As Fanon observes, Blacks want to be white and whites themselves never coincide with an unadulterated whiteness/humanity: "the black man wants to be white. The white man is desperately trying to achieve the rank of man [*Le Noir veut être Blanc. Le Blanc s'acharne à réaliser une condition d'homme*]."[96] Whites lack; the plenitude of whiteness, or what is promised by whiteness (a life of plenitude), remains unfulfilled, a collective fantasy, something white people anxiously yearn for.

    With his cultivated white voice, Cash magically becomes "human," civilized—to the people who hear him on the other side of the phone call and to his supervisors who now see him as a valuable economic asset. And this newfound humanness is intimately linked to his promotion to the WorryFree account, marking his ascendency (he literally takes the elevator) to humanity. The inference in the film is clear: capitalism meets racism. A libidinal economy underpins a political economy. Cash's Blackness—manifested in his "urban" voice—was getting in the way of economic success, or more accurately, undermining his chances of meeting his basic economic needs for food and shelter (at the RegalView corporation, telemarketers get paid on commission, not salary). Cash's talent for projecting a white voice (dubbed by David Cross) dramatically increases his sales. The ability to pass for white among clients—and to pass as supportive of whiteness among one's bosses—is a necessary condition for capitalist success. Cash's promotion to the prestigious position of "Power Caller" reflects not simply his sales numbers, but also the establishment's need to conscript him to its project, which they accomplish for a time by turning his precariousness against him, promising him a significant pay bump in exchange for distancing himself from his unionizing coworkers and agreeing to cross their picket line. Cash is torn between loyalty to his artist-activist girlfriend Detroit and his coworkers on the one hand, and the enjoyment of being good at something and being recognized by his bosses as an excellent worker on the other. Last but not least, there is the enjoyment of the white voice itself, of experiencing himself phantasmatically as human (through the desire of the Other), as an embodiment of culture and civilization.

Cash's willingness to play this game is tested when he learns what his new task will be: selling WorryFree manpower (voluntary servitude) and firepower (militarism) to wealthy customers:

> We sell power. Fire power. Man power. When U.S. weapons manufacturers sell arms to other countries, who do you think makes that call at the precisely perfect time which is during dinner? We do. Before a drone drops a bomb on an apartment building in Pakistan, who drops the bomb-ass sales pitch over the phone? We do.

Surplus humanity multiplies: from the economically decimated (those prepped for voluntary servitude) to the War on Terror (those Pakistanis prepped for destruction). Cash as Power Caller is in the business of instrumentalizing and destroying human life. In WorryFree, humans are involved in selling slavery (N.H.I.) and military weapons (targeting places where, likewise, no "humans" are involved). The film introduces viewers to WorryFree first through the company's aggressive marketing campaign advertising comfort and satiety in exchange for lifetime employment. Neoliberalism's increasingly disenfranchised and destitute subjects are promised security and predictability. WorryFree is basically inculcating in its viewers—its would-be employees—a belief in voluntary servitude. This profitable company interpellates its audience as neoliberal subjects, transforming human beings into subjects ready "to turn [their life] into viable merchandise and put it up for sale."[97] Though a Senate committee has cleared WorryFree of slavery charges, the accusations persist, leading the company's CEO Steve Lift (Armie Hammer) to swiftly denounce them in an interview with Oprah that doubles as a sales pitch for another of his products: "The comparison to slavery is just ludicrous and offensive. . . . We're saving lives. It's all highlighted in my book." Voluntary servitude allegedly saves lives, like the life of Cash's uncle and landlord, who is facing repossession of his home.

Servitude is made in this campaign to represent a wise economic choice, a calculated move on the part of free, rational citizens to maximize their economic well-being. Why live with economic uncertainty, when WorryFree can guarantee food and shelter, protecting you from the vicissitudes of market forces? This is a new form of slavery—slavery 2.0—that purports to help people: Why suffer if you don't have too? To paraphrase Žižek, I would say that WorryFree is offering *slavery with a human* face.[98] Being human and being slave are no longer mutually exclusive. Or to put it more pointedly, your current humanness does not guarantee your immunity from slaveness. WorryFree's labor force consists of being-objects—accumulable and fungible—to be used indiscriminately and exchanged as a commodity. This moral catastrophe prompts what appears at first to viewers as a stunning, disconcerting remark from Langston, in the course of explaining to Cash that ordinary telemarketers and Power Callers operate at radically incommensurable levels. Thinking he understands, Cash ventures, "So I guess that comparing what we're doing to what they're doing is like apples to *oranges*." But Langston corrects the analogy: "More like apples and the *Holocaust*." WorryFree, this character suggests, operates a *metaphysical* holocaust; it disfigures the ontological being of humans, transforming them into pliant instruments, into living-dead tools to be milked for every ounce of productivity they can provide.

The economic cruelty of this labor system is matched by the popularization of brutality as entertainment in the cultural realm, where contestants on the wildly successful game show *I Got the Shit Kicked Out of Me* allow themselves to be beaten and dunked in fecal matter in exchange for money and fleeting fame. In this hyper-consumerist society, human dignity is readily commodified and bought (and destroyed) for ceaseless fun, acquiescing to the superego's excessive demand to enjoy, which further attaches the viewers libidinally to the social order. In *Sorry to Bother You*, commercials for WorryFree and *I Got the Shit Kicked Out of Me* often run back to back on television, cementing their ideological affinities in the minds of the audience.

The film does, then, lend support on one level to an Afropessimist reading of political ontology. Anti-Blackness still structures the universe of *Sorry to Bother You*, whose financial and libidinal economies revolve around enslavement, as the legalized exploitation of labor and as a driving force that structures civil society's enjoyment. But the film is better described as Fanonian in the way it generates insights into both destitution—the descent into the zone of nonbeing—and the possibility of exit, tightly connected to class struggle, a possibility that remains open and central to the film's arc. Against the Afropessimist view, the worker and the enslaved are not irremediably separate and distinct; the order of life is entangled with the economic order, the libidinal economy enmeshed with political economy.[99]

The film's dual focus on devastation—which touches all, Black people and others, at varying levels of intensity—and resistance is manifested particularly well in the film's staging of enclosure, which, for Cash, signifies at once an idealized (and ultimately unattainable) stability and an intolerable entrapment. A number of scenes show Cash longing to enter closed spaces in which he hopes to find meaning, purpose, and happiness, from the banal example of a secret VIP room at a bar he frequents, to RegalView's mysterious gilded elevator, a symbol of financial power and peace of mind (class ascension/hegemony, a vertical and individualistic exit from the zone of nonbeing), to WorryFree CEO Lift's inner sanctum, located at the end of a corridor of closed rooms, behind a magenta door. An early scene captures the dynamics of Cash's anxiety and longing well: lying in bed with Detroit, he worries about the meaning of his existence and the eventual explosion of the sun; just as Detroit pulls him back into the comforting sensuality of their present connection, the bedroom is revealed to be a garage whose door pops open, exposing the couple and underscoring Cash's exposure and vulnerability. None of these enclosed spaces delivers the "good stuff" he seeks (a desire humorously questioned, moreover, in a scene portraying a bartender delivering to Langston a tiny whiskey bottle hidden behind a small door in another standard-size, top-shelf bottle[100]). Nor do they remain closed; rather, they are revealed to be alcoves, semi-enclosed dead-ends that force a decision of some sort. The garage is an unstable refuge exposed to the harsh light of day; the VIP room is crowded and uncomfortable. The gilded elevator, protected by an impossibly long and tedious security code, takes Cash to a luxury that proves precarious, that of a Power Caller whose job must be carried out under the scrutiny of others—both that of his bosses and coworkers, and that of Cash's own conscience. This latter is poignantly externalized in the photograph he carries with him into his work spaces, a portrait of a man who goes unnamed but who appears to be a lost father figure or moral role model, and whose changing expressions show disapproval for Cash's complicity in exploitation, and joy at his eventual resistance.

But the space that proves most unsettling for Cash and for viewers alike is a dingy bathroom in Steve Lift's basement, where, behind yet another door, Cash accidentally discovers a monstrous truth: Lift has been injecting his slave-workers with "the new miracle," a formula that turns them into stronger, more vigorous, and productive horse-human hybrids, or *equi-sapiens*. Interestingly for the Afropessimist subtext, the film suggests that the first batch of slave-workers-cum-*equi-sapiens* are Black. It reminds us that a "'Black Human' remains an oxymoron."[101] Blacks were always already other than human, produced as "no-bodies," writes Ferreira da Silva.[102] Though he is producing a more profitable workforce (a move that "democratizes" slavery), Lift expects resistance from his new workers and fears that the *equi-sapiens* will be asking for more; room and board for lifetime labor may not be sufficient to pacify these new slaves. Lift concocts a nefarious plan to contain future acts of rebellion by infiltrating the *equi-sapiens*, deploying Cash as a fake Martin Luther King, Jr. figure to depoliticize and crush a new *equi-sapiens* civil rights movement. After accomplishing his mission of trickery, Lift promises, Cash will receive a formula returning him to his "human" form. Cash will make $100 million, and to seal the deal—recycling the stereotype of the hyper-sexualized male Black body—a self-assured Lift tells him he will get to keep his "horse cock."

A horrified Cash declines Lift's offer. Part of his horror lies in the unshakable unsettlement produced by his initial encounter with an *equi-sapiens*, which allows him to visualize the raw brutality and animalization of enslavement. Seeing this *equi-sapiens* writhing naked on the floor, in chains and begging him for help, his first reaction is to flee. In humanist fashion, he is appalled, repulsed, and profoundly disoriented by this uncanny embodiment of an abjection he can no longer ignore. The image of the *equi-sapiens* stands for the human minus its symbolic gentrification. With this eruption of the Real, Cash momentarily loses his humanist bearings. He sees the *equi-sapiens* as fundamentally other, ontologically altered, as faceless and worldless others. He is threatened and repulsed by them. The extra-humanity of the *equi-sapiens* destabilizes his investment in the imago of the human: the self as not-animal. The *equi-sapiens* appear to Cash as uncanny, crisis-inducing. The *equi-sapiens* are unbearable neighbors—nonbeings with whom no relation, "no symmetrical dialogue, mediated by the symbolic Order, is possible."[103] They are abject beings whose altered human features affectively and cognitively overwhelm him. Cash's humanist sensibilities register a horror: who or what did he just encounter? This reaction is understandable, for what causes him to fear the *equi-sapiens* is ingrained in the very fabric of civil society, in its libidinal economy along with its humanist and racist social scripts. It is at this moment of the encounter that he feels the full weight of the Black imago—a projected image of Blackness that phantasmatically identifies it with animality, ugliness, and moral depravity[104]— whose presence and demands he has up to this point managed to dismiss as insignificant, even as he has been called upon to perform its various facets, from donning his white voice to rapping on command for a bored audience of mostly white partygoers at Lift's mansion.

Earlier at the party, Lift tells Cash to suspend his use of "white voice." Why? Lift wants raw "Blackness" (i.e., what he imagines and projects Blackness to be). Lift wants to hear Cash rap, since he believes that rap is a "natural" and "effortless" expression of Black being. But Cash is incapable of rapping, and yet despite his lyrical deficiencies, Cash lands on a simple, repeated line, "Nigga shit, Nigga shit, Nigga nigga nigga shit," which proves to be a big hit with the mostly white audience. Before asking him to rap, Lift wants to hear stories about Cash's "Black culture," fantasizing about his employee's gangster life in Oakland (asking him if he "ever had to bust a cap in somebody's ass"), transforming, in turn, white fear of Black violence into an opportunity for white entertainment. What Lift and white civil society really desire is decaffeinated Blackness.

The only two Black people at the party are Cash and Mr._____ (Omari Hardwick). Robin D. G. Kelley paints an incisive portrait of Mr._____:

> He is a quiet, mysterious, powerfully built black man with a patch over his left eye—symbolizing his blindness to the truth, necessary for the only other black person allowed in the realm of the power callers. Mr. _____ is every manservant: the trusted doorman, the loyal slave promoted to driver, the eunuch. He consistently uses his white voice. He runs interference for Cash as they break through the picket line. He has authority but no power.[105]

Mr._____ serves an ideological function in racial capitalism. He is a member of the Black elite, one of the "Black faces in high places" as Keeanga-Yamahtta Taylor formulates it, repeating Amiri Baraka.[106] The successful Mr._____ and the promising Cash are the exceptions that proves the rule white discourse holds up as true: Black people in general are unsuccessful (because lazy and criminal, as the images of the "welfare queen" and "gang member" continue to circulate in the white cultural imaginary). In the liberal capitalist world, Black people are either relegated to the zone of nonbeing (the majority), exposed to racism and economic hardship, or exempt from the most cruel aspects of anti-Blackness within the limits of white reason: you can have authority—especially to enact an anti-Black agenda—but no power. Cash's new privileges can be stripped away at any time. Cash may be useful, and even praiseworthy for the sales he brings RegalView and WorryFree, but he will never be more than a "cunning racoon" for Lift.[107] Mr._____ is Cash's future unless the latter traverses his fantasy of neoliberal meritocracy and personal economic autonomy (what WorryFree offers him). Cash rejects this forced choice, resists his "decaffeination," and seeks another way out from the zone of nonbeing.

The encounter with the *equi-sapiens* clears the grounds for his transformation. Cash's affective shock eventually produces a major change in him and a rededication to justice: Cash shifts loyalties back to Detroit and his striking coworkers, who help him rejoin the labor movement, release the *equi-sapiens* from bondage, and, with the assistance of the hybrids, successfully repel the police battalions called in to break the RegalView picket line. That Cash witnesses the climax of this battle—the arrival of the powerful *equi-sapiens* in a fog of chaos and teargas—through a small window in a police van where he has been contained and chained is suggestive of the subjective transformation he is undergoing. In risking his safety for the cause, he has been rendered physically helpless, a spectator at the mercy of others, but has regained the connection of solidarity and sense of purpose that had eluded him. Enclosure features here not as an ideal, but as a dangerous entrapment, and while exposure brings vulnerability, it is also the condition of possibility for change and resistance. The police wagon door is torn away, Cash is liberated, and the successful revolt leads RegalView to modify its compensation structure. Squeeze (Stephen Yeun), Cash's comrade in class struggle, captures a fleeting moment of solidarity, saying "same struggle, same fight" to these latest figures of wretchedness.

The film's subsequent return to the space of Cash's newly renovated garage-bedroom suggests a conventional happy ending. There is progress. Antagonisms recede to the background. It may take baby steps, but *the arc of the moral universe bends toward justice*. The strikers have unionized and won gains; Cash and his family are no longer in danger of eviction, and he has reconciled with Detroit and the friends he had let down. Their disposability has materially decreased. But this moment of re-equilibrium is short-lived. In the final scenes of the film, the garage door again delivers a reality check: when Cash bangs his head against it, we learn that Lift has tricked him into ingesting the formula, for he is transformed before our eyes into an *equi-sapiens*.[108] The film appears momentarily to conclude with this tragic scene, unsettling the illusion of a progress achievable from within the racial-capitalist system, the progress of reform without revolution, which gives way to the enduring horror of exploitation and violation. Lift has the last laugh. Capitalism triumphs—union negotiations are an acceptable substitute for a revolutionary redistribution of wealth.[109]

Yet the film does not end here. Rather, Cash returns with the other *equi-sapiens* to sack Lift's mansion, their counter-violence overwhelming the capitalist order's invisible systemic violence. His profound transformation marks at once the height of his destitution and his exit from it. As such, this ending can be read as qualifying Afropessimism's conclusions. *Sorry to Bother You* invites us to read WorryFree's neoliberalism through the lens of racial capitalism, staging for us the imbrication of exploitation and domination under this system. WorryFree clearly embodies and practices a politics of enslavability. It brings to light capitalism's irresistible compulsion to extract and commodify, "the compulsion to put things in order as a precondition for extracting their inner value. It is the compulsion to categorize, to separate, to measure and to name, to classify and to establish equivalences between things and between things and persons, persons and animals, animals and the so-called natural, mineral, and organic world."[110] Yet under a borderless global neoliberalism, the drive to animalize and instrumentalize becomes a generalizable condition. Mbembe describes this process as the *"Becoming Black of the world."*[111] N.H.I. is a marketing pitch for shareholders of WorryFree. Humans are involved, but not for long. WorryFree harnesses all bodies in its dream of optimization. The becoming *equi-sapiens* of the world reflects Lift's desire to transform his labor force from slaves into animals, epitomizing the phantasmatic desires of global capitalism: a workforce that has the endurance of beasts of burden (capable of working long hours, thus increasing profit margins) and the skills of humans (able to adapt to new environments and follow complex sets of rules).

The marriage of democracy and free-market capitalism is dissolving. The struggle for human rights and the expansion of capital stand in an antagonistic relation. The liberal promise that "the rest of the world was destined to converge on the model pioneered by the West," as Grace Blakeley puts it, has failed to come true.[112] Capitalism's voracious appetite returns home. "Without excess profits extracted from the rest of the world to keep this conflict under wraps," Blakeley argues, "there was only one choice for the ruling class: all-out war on workers."[113] Even when Cash exposes WorryFree's nefarious plans by leaking a video displaying Lift's abuse of the *equi-sapiens*, the video fails to produce outrage or public shame or financial damage to the corporation. On the contrary, the market reacts quite positively to "the new miracle." WorryFree's shareholders make even more money and the media dubs Lift the latest tech genius. *Sorry to Bother You* discloses capitalism's obscene underside, a reality minus liberal sentimentalism (of the sort: *this is not who we are, we should take better care of our workers; they are our family and so on*). What ultimately matters is *profit, profit, profit*. The film harnesses the rage of capitalism's blackened workers. We find an implicit response to, or commentary on, capitalism's violence, earlier in the film, in the earrings that Detroit is sporting. They visualize the words "Murder/Kill": the words can be read as a reference to the systemic violence of racial capitalism (a system that murders/kills its workers in plain sight) and to the *equi-sapiens*'s counter-violence (the latest image of capitalism's grave diggers).[114] As Kelley observes, Detroit's earrings serve as a visual commentary, a counter-violence of sorts, to "the phallic and masculine character of power."[115] Against an exploitive capitalist world in which misogynoir flourishes, Detroit figures herself as the continent of Africa in her solo art performance, summoning us to recall that from its beginning, the capitalist project was racial and masculinist. Her body transfigures the site of capitalism's despoiling, its historical and ongoing violence. After condemning the West's mining of coltan (a mineral used for smartphones and other lightweight electronics) in the Congo, Detroit, switching to her own "white voice" (featuring the British accent of Lily James), calls on her mostly white bourgeois art-enthusiast audience to fling bullet casings, cell phones, and goat blood at her almost bare and exposed body, repeating the primal scene of racial subjugation, mimicking capitalism's rape of Black bodies and extraction of African minerals. To be sure, Detroit's own art performance is not immune to the logic of commodification, nor protected from the white/male voyeurism and enjoyment of violated Black goods. Still, the reflexivity of the scene troubles a triumphalist capitalist reading: *yes, everything is for sale, even Black being*. We're not Detroit's audience—we're Riley's. *Sorry to Bother You* doesn't romanticize resistance. The upshot is that scenes of ontological upheaval don't need to originate from the ranks of "Beautiful Souls," from subjects in possession of a pure and uncompromised soul, who refuse to get their hands dirty, a stance that makes any Beautiful Soul "an accomplice in the disorder of the world it bemoans."[116]

In addressing the question of modern-day slavery, Riley does so in a way that avoids ideological liberal traps that dull the film's "critical edge"; his approach is not a "decaffeinated" one, as Žižek would say.[117] "Communitarian corsets"[118] are loosened; identities (of the worker, the enslaved, the human, the posthuman, etc.) are reconfigured. A warrior of the imaginary, Riley declines to neutralize the world's disorder, "to press it into a tidy narrative arc."[119] Refusing to turn the struggle against exploitation and domination into a feel-good story—refusing to deprive it of its jolt, of the film's encounter with racial capitalism—*Sorry to Bother You*'s conclusion returns us to the zone of nonbeing and the question of its permanence/dynamism.

Must we become *equi-sapiens* before we can engage in revolutionary violence? It is only when Cash hits rock bottom and has nothing to lose that he violently strikes at his boss. The film implicitly asks us to consider here two versions of subjective destitution: the first is forced on Cash by Lift (he tricks him into snorting the formula), but the second becomes visible only when viewers ask themselves, *do I have to undergo ontological transformation (by an external force) to act?* If so, revolutionary acts will be rare. *Sorry to Bother You* answers this in the negative. The film takes us to the zero-level of subjectivity, placing us in the position of the becoming *cogito*. Reform is not the solution insofar as it reinforces attachments rather than dissolving them, thereby keeping you unfree and tethered to the life-draining zone of nonbeing. Reform bewitches. It covers over "white ferocity" and entices you to operate within the limits of the possible, neutralizing your desire for more.[120] You are reduced to who you *are*. The private use of reason defines your world. Not all attachments are, of course, of equal value. Cash's attachments to Detroit and to the ethical cause of liberation from the Lifts of the world do not feed a narcissistic identity (or a narcissistic dissolution of identity à la Edelman) but open to a collective we, a political *jouissance* stemming from a break with capitalist futurology. As an *equi-sapiens révolté*, Cash maintains "a foothold in the Symbolic"[121] and refuses the choices implicitly imposed on him: flee with the other *equi-sapiens* and live on the margins of society or accept his barred human identity, his official status as N.H.I. (perhaps with the hope that *equi-sapiens* can incrementally get more rights if an authentic MLK emerges from their rank, and ignite a civil rights movement for *equi-sapiens*). Rather, Cash finds his liberation by coming to terms with the fact that he has no place, could not have a place, and wants no place in Lift's ontological partition of the world. His descent into the veritable hell of racial capitalism triggers his revolutionary will. *The way down is also the way up*. The final word Cash the *equi-sapiens* addresses to Lift from the gate intercom of his mansion is a sarcastic "sorry to bother you"—followed by an inhuman growl, announcing the violent de-gentrification of Lift's mansion and *Lebenswelt*—which echoes a Fanonian sorry paraphrased well by Alenka Zupančič: "Sorry, but *that's not it*, you are bombarding us with such offers just to retain your basic social position of superiority!" Sorry, but I'm not sticking to your racist script; I refuse to play your capitalist WorryFree game. I have no role to play in the present socio-symbolic formation. We want *equi-sapiens* worldliness. Riley offers us "strong and real coffee . . . [and] real politics."[122]

Revolutionary change as self-destitution involves something like the "'madness' of decision,"[123] a psychotic withdrawal from symbolic reality—an act of freedom that paradoxically unravels the self, unsettling its attachments to any form of identity. Reminiscent of the Derridean aporetic, this revolutionary decision does not originate from a "calculating machine"[124]; the decision determined by one's narrow self-interest. The decision is always "heterogeneous to knowledge,"[125] in excess of knowledge. Even when Cash hits rock bottom and has objectively and humanistically nothing to lose, the force or madness of the decision persists. Cash the *equi-sapiens* decides to act in a way that breaks with the pleasure principle, that which ensures the continuity of the social coordinates of his existence (WorryFree would make the transition from human slave to *equi-sapiens* as smooth as possible, insofar as we are dealing with a very accommodating racial capitalist system—if the market response to Lift's "new miracle" is an indicator), abandoning his pursuit of self-preservation (fleeing harm). He affirms/enjoys his self-destitution. Cash risks his life. *So can we*. The *cogito* is a kind of permanent compound drug generated from within, inhospitable to scripts of all kinds, ready to unleash mutations upon the world; akin to the death drive, it is always immanent to my identity, to my being, enabling me "to start with a clean slate," "to erase the entirety of [capitalist/anti-Black] reality."[126] In Lacanian parlance, the symbolic order is not-all, but forever incomplete and inconsistent. The *cogito*'s very negativity opens up a space to forge new desires, to abolish *collectively* the existing state of affairs, and imagine a radical reordering of the world beyond the values of the marketplace. The alchemical *cogito* undoes identity while gesturing to its potential reinvention and repoliticization. It points simultaneously to our entry and exit from the zone of nonbeing.

Chapter 2
Disavowal in Crisis
The End of Liberalism

Prime Minister Benjamin Netanyahu's religio-nationalist government is redefining the Right at home and abroad. Unleashed, it is no longer giving the appearance of playing by the rules that one would expect liberal democracies to adhere to. The Israeli government bucks national and international laws. From its judicial coup within Israel to its terror-inducing raids in the Occupied West Bank to its genocidal campaign in Gaza, Netanyahu's coalition is not only making its Western supporters uncomfortable, it is also, and more importantly, exposing the illiberal and eliminationist core of Israeli politics that the perceived opposition between political Zionism and liberal Zionism tends to obfuscate. This chapter traces political Zionism's cannibalization of its "liberal" twin, looking at the ways it has rendered inoperative the fetishist disavowal that kept liberal Zionists and Western powers more or less content with the status quo, that is, with the Occupation on cruise control. Fetishist disavowal, as Octave Mannoni defines it, follows the pattern, "*Je sais bien, mais quand même;* I know very well, but all the same . . ." This logic accounts for the way in which "a belief can be abandoned and preserved at the same time."[1] As Žižek observes, "fetishist disavowal" is an attempt to deal with anxiety; in the cases we will take up here, this takes the form more specifically of white anxiety and Zionist/settler anxiety. Fetishist disavowal splits the ego between knowing and not knowing; new information has been admitted into consciousness but its symbolic impact has been minimized and "not really integrated into the subject's symbolic universe."[2] There is a willful ignorance in fetishist disavowal: "'I know, but I don't want to know that I know, so I don't know.' I know it, but I refuse to fully assume the consequences of this knowledge, so that I can continue acting as if I don't know."[3] In the case of Palestine/Israel, the logic of fetishist disavowal paints a soothing picture: *We know very well that Israel must reach a compromise with the Palestinians, that it must not be seen as an apartheid state, but all the same, we believe in the Zionist cause, in Israel's unique claim to be at once democratic and Jewish.* Yet the Netanyahu government's stark brutality has thrown Euro-American disavowal into crisis, for Israel is openly engaging in the type of overwhelming colonial violence that international law was created to prevent.[4] This gross violence so blatantly violates international norms and human rights protections that it can no longer be so easily disavowed; the fetish is losing its power to dull the urgency of intervening to enact change. Israel's anachronistic violence—Western nations are now expected not to act cruelly like this any longer, at least not in plain daylight— invites a Fanonian intervention, which puts front and center the colonial situation in the deployment and unraveling of the fetishist disavowal.

Attending to the crisis of fetishist disavowal also tells us more. The American government's unconditional support of Israel—along with the internal fractures and reactionary entrenchments this is provoking—tells us something about its racial politics at home, about America's failure to reckon with the Indigenous genocides and chattel slavery on which it is founded, and whose afterlives continue to shape life in the nation. What we are seeing in Israel—a hyper-racialized existence lived under occupation (racialized *because* it is lived under occupation)—echoes what we see in the United States because both nations have emerged from similar, though distinct, settler-colonial histories. The United States' unconditional military and political support for Israeli carnage in Gaza tells us something about the colonial core of America's politics, a core orientation, I would add, that does not come as a surprise for the Global South or for North America's internally colonized and segregated communities. Not unlike Israel's faltering fetishist disavowal, liberal America's fetishist disavowal—*I know very well that structural racism exists, but all the same I believe in the American dream, in America's manifest destiny, that we can follow our better angels,* and so on—is facing a challenge of its own from the far Right.

A post on X from the progressive Jewish organization IfNotNow brings the global racial politics of the United States and Palestine/Israel into sharp dialogue. The statement captures the porous fault lines separating liberal Democrats from their far-right counterparts, highlighting the political motivation behind the oppositions to Critical Race Theory (CRT) and the BDS movement: "The fanatical anti-CRT and anti-BDS movements are one and the same: a desperate attempt to hide historical and current reality, to police free speech when it threatens nationalism."[5] Both CRT and BDS trouble a collective psychic investment in the existing nationalist and racist order of things. Many racially sensitive liberals are happy to publicly decry the anti-CRT legislation emerging across the nation, but are tacitly willing to join the same guardians of white supremacy in supporting anti-BDS bills. Donald Trump's slogan, "Make America Great Again" (MAGA), gets a chilly reception from the liberal Left, but the implicit charge, "Keep America anti-Palestinian," finds a more receptive ear.[6] Among the liberal elite, there is little appetite to revisit the Palestine exception, what Pro-Palestinian activists have long decried as "Progressives Except for Palestine" (PEP).[7] Liberals in the United States back CRT, but block BDS by actively supporting anti-BDS legislation aiming to delegitimize and criminalize the pro-Palestinian movement. I believe that we need to read the generalized liberal hostility toward BDS not as ignorance about the subject matter (though the Palestinian narrative still lacks visibility in Western corporate media) but rather as evidence of liberal complicity and collusion with an anti-Black world, casting doubt on the actual liberal support of and commitment to CRT, to the Movement for Black Lives. Woke white liberals favor cosmetic changes. You can talk about Black suffering, celebrate and honor Black history as much as you want, but don't ask America to give up on the white American dream and its claim to exceptionalism, to confront police brutality and the mass incarceration of Black and Brown bodies (in the end, liberals are by no means hostile to the racialized "law and order" narrative)—in short, don't ask us white Americans to give up our privilege or priority.[8] Presidents like Joe Biden can talk about introducing new economic policies allegedly targeting Black people, but they fall short in facing "the gaping wounds of racial economic injustice."[9] Why? For the liberal Left, America, not unlike Israel, is *not* a racist state or project.

A "structural necessity," as Žižek might put it, ties the 2020 protests against anti-Blackness and the 2023–4 protests against Palestinian genocide together. The answer proposed to the first global disruption has been better regulation, more funding, and training of police. The national and worldwide protests over Gaza stem from the systemic problems that gave rise to the outpouring of support for BLM and point to a lingering deep anger at America's political class and its Western counterparts.[10] The world system does not need tuning—it needs an overhaul. The chant "Palestinian Lives Matter" signals, repeats, and harnesses the universalist cry of "Black Lives Matter," foregrounding race as "the site of inequality."[11] What the protests are saying is that Blacks or Palestinians are not the "problem"—you are; it is the West's racist core. When the liberal elite join the far Right in condemning the mostly groundless and fantasized hatred underpinning solidarity with Palestine, we see their investments in what Sebastian Althoff calls "a securitization of the status quo."[12] One of the most effective ways to defend what *is*, the current order of things, is to naturalize and pathologize any negative reaction to it, to state as self-evident, for example, that "those on the inside of democracy will naturally agree that hate needs to be condemned."[13] Conversely, Zionist feelings are "courageously" taken up by the gatekeepers of the status quo to curb any form of resistance. Zionist feelings become the stuff to be defended, functioning as a synecdoche of the status quo. How we feel about anti-Zionism (the triggering effects of the chant "Free Palestine") comes to displace the reality of Palestinian genocide, which cannot be addressed without overturning or severely impeding the operations of the status quo.[14] Consequently, those "on the outs" with democracy—Israel's and the United States' parts of no-part—will have their affect dismissed as irrational, excessive, violent, and a threat to democracy/civilization.

This chapter examines the psychic life of liberalism in the wake of anti-racist and anti-colonial disruptions of the status quo through recent examples of liberal attempts to recuperate the fetish, to stave off the collapse of disavowal and the reckoning that such an upheaval politically demands. What does the cognitive mapping and political force of the liberal position look like once its fetishist disavowal misfires or is no longer operative? The crisis in fetishist disavowal, I argue, opens up an opportunity for universalists to embrace an anti-colonial, anti-racist leftist politics. It clears the ground for what Fanon agitated for all his political life: the creation of a "new human"—what might emerge out of the ruins of settler colonialism and the dismantling of anti-Blackness. But, as Žižek reminds us, the life of fetishist disavowal is tenacious and long, while the perpetuation of liberalism's fantasies continues to dull resistance and feed the power of an ultranationalist and racist far Right that liberalism ostensibly abhors and opposes. The liberal Left, no less than the far Right, covers over society's antagonisms, preferring to frame matters as "conflicts" that can be incrementally resolved, and thus invisibilizing further the workings of objective violence. For Fanon and Žižek, no justice will be had unless we face society's antagonisms and punch through ideological talks of conflicts or pseudo-struggles.

Repression and the American Unconscious

In trying to make sense of the crises liberalism is traversing, I draw on the psychoanalytic distinction between repression and disavowal, referring to two distinct ways that people deny or neutralize unpleasant knowledge. Historically, repression has characterized America's general approach to racial slavery, though in more recent years a fetishist disavowal, fostered by the liberal Left, is starting to exemplify the nation's engagement with its traumatic past. The far Right, however, is moving beyond the existing models of repression and disavowal by imposing its own phantasmatic vision of the racial past. Their tantalizing fight against "wokeness" provides an ideological cover for whitewashing the legacy of slavery. *There is no denial, nothing to see. God bless America!*

"The essence of repression," Freud tells us, "lies simply in turning something away, and keeping it at a distance, from the conscious."[15] In repression, memories are expelled from consciousness and relegated to the unconscious. When the topic of racial slavery is systematically repressed, what we get is "national amnesia," which is the way Toni Morrison described the American context in

1989 after writing *Beloved*, which is itself a powerful tale of repression and hauntings. As Morrison says, *Beloved* is "about something that the characters don't want to remember, I don't want to remember, black people don't want to remember, white people don't want to remember."[16] The trauma of America's past is too much to absorb, too painful to confront. But when the practice of repression is no longer effective, when censorship falters, which is always a possibility insofar as the repressed material is never destroyed, we witness "the return of the repressed," its return in a symptom or distorted form. If the material or fact of chattel slavery, the unadulterated expression of anti-Blackness, is repressed, it comes to reside in the American unconscious.

When there is no outlet to articulate and address America's ongoing anti-Blackness, under the "New Jim Crow," as Michelle Alexander dubbed it, Black rage festers. In Alexander's powerful indictment, America today is a caste system; racial segregation is a feature, not a bug of American society. We might be tempted to say that racial apartheid is experiencing a renaissance of sorts, except that the point is really to stress the crushing continuity of anti-Blackness, the thriving "afterlife of slavery."[17] It is under this condition of naturalized anti-Blackness that the BLM movement exploded. To briefly recall: On July 13, 2013, George Zimmerman was acquitted for the shooting death of an unarmed Black teenager, Trayvon Martin. Black, queer activists Alicia Garza, Patrisse Cullors, and Opal Tometi introduced the life-altering and world-forming #BlackLivesMatter, infusing new forms of signification into America's thinking and public discussion of racism and anti-Blackness. What is equally important to stress, as Cornel West does, is that BLM burst onto the national scene under a Black president, a Black attorney general, and a Black secretary of homeland security. West chillingly described President Barack Obama as "a global George Zimmerman."[18] Ideologically speaking, liberal America, delighted in its racial progress, was enjoying its postraciality—but BLM confronted America with its political unconscious, a return of the repressed, the uncanny or "strangely familiar" scene of a Black man killed with impunity. The Movement for Black Lives (M4BL)—which describes itself as an "ecosystem and hundreds of allied organizations and individuals,"[19] with BLM falling under its banner—couched the eruption of Black consciousness in decidedly leftist terms—not in the familiar language of identity politics but rather in a different return of the repressed, the repressed language of class struggle:

> The interlinked systems of white supremacy, imperialism, capitalism and patriarchy shape the violence we face. As oppressed people living in the US, the belly of global empire, we are in a critical position to build the necessary connections for a global liberation movement. Until we are able to overturn US imperialism, capitalism and white supremacy, our brothers and sisters around the world will continue to live in chains. Our struggle is strengthened

by our connections to the resistance of peoples around the world fighting for their liberation. The Black radical tradition has always been rooted in igniting connection across the global south under the recognition that our liberation is intrinsically tied to the liberation of Black and Brown people around the world.[20]

On one hand, BLM is a *symptom* of America's foundational anti-Blackness. America's failure to confront its past and ongoing violence brought the movement into being. Black rage was unleashed on the streets. On the other, BLM can be seen as enacting the return of the repressed Black radical tradition—an anti-racist and anti-capitalist tradition that never sat well with the liberal establishment. In their public discourse, liberal democrats prefer to decouple race and class whenever possible, wanting to block any pathway to the return of the repressed (class struggle). Black rage they can manage; Black rage with an anti-capitalist orientation proves more difficult to handle.

At the same time, the return of the repressed is subjected to internal pressure. BLM's eruption risked compromise, containment, and co-optation from its beginning. Since its emergence in 2013, BLM has experienced internal conflicts, which reached their tipping point in 2021 when a number of chapters broke with the BLM Global Network. BLM Inland Empire, for instance, aimed to return the movement to its focus on racial and economic justice, which pits the Democratic establishment as a foe rather than a friend, an ally in the struggle for freedom and equality[21]:

> The issue of greatest concern for us is the relationship between the Global Network and the Democratic Party. This is hypocritical at best, as the Democratic Party has historically rejected and ignored BLM's demands and has made it clear that they are pro-police, pro-prison, and committed to capitalism. . . . This is a party that is a threat both here and internationally. To ally with them is to ally against ourselves.[22]

"To ally against ourselves" should be understood here to mean to ally with our political vision of liberation rather than conforming to the self-interests of one's ethnic identity. To ally with the Democratic Party is to obfuscate the fundamental antagonism, the "new forms of social apartheid—new walls and slums," sprawling in the United States and abroad. To ally with the Democratic Party is to conform to the liberal playbook of identity politics and to settle for *band-aid solutions*.[23] Let's not forget that in 2015, BLM activists flatly declined the Democratic National Committee's endorsement and transactional overtures. Displaying Bartlebian sensibility, BLM—like Herman Melville's Bartleby, who answers every demand of his superior with "I would prefer not to"—declines the offer to be involved in the Democratic Party. Doing nothing is always a dangerous proposition. But, as

Žižek clarifies, involvement with/in the system has a way of depoliticizing your resistance. By refusing the Democratic Party's interpellation, BLM drew attention to the dubious gesture of inclusion and introduced clarity about anti-Blackness and the political situation: "The first truly critical ('aggressive,' violent) step is to withdraw into passivity, to refuse to participate—Bartleby's 'I would prefer not to' is the necessary first step which, as it were, clears the ground, opens up the place, for true activity, for an act that will actually change the coordinates of the constellation."[24] BLM activists *preferred not* to endorse then presidential candidate Hillary Clinton. Why should they endorse a hawkish, Wall Street Democrat whose fingerprints were all over the 1994 Crime Bill, which targeted Black youth and contributed to the rise in mass incarceration?[25] Nor did BLM activists want to be pigeonholed into a domestic agenda (solidifying the commitment of the "Black vote" to the Democratic Party is not what they're after). BLM's agenda, from the start, had a cross-racial and internationalist dimension. Black interests were not limited to the interests of Black people. Black struggle exceeded the US borders.[26] To the chagrin of the Democratic establishment, they *violently* aligned the Black cause with the Palestinian cause, denouncing Israel (and by extension the US government for its unconditional support of Israel) as an apartheid state and an ally of imperial powers. A common struggle was reignited. It is not surprising that the same hysteria around the teaching of CRT echoes the hostile reactions to the BDS movement. IfNotNow captured well the links between the anti-CRT and anti-BDS legislations, exposing the ideological overlap between liberal Democrats and far-right demagogues. Whereas IfNotNow worries about this overlap, Conservative activist Christopher Rufo embraces it and sees linking the Palestinian cause (as articulated by BDS) to BLM as a wedge issue to divide the mostly impotent/post-political liberal Left: "Conservatives need to create a strong association between Hamas, BLM, DSA, and academic 'decolonization' in the public mind. Connect the dots, then attack, delegitimize, and discredit. Make the center-left disavow them. Make them political untouchables."[27] Rufo's pitch: Make the anti-colonial and anti-racist Left radioactive. Cancel them from within and without. Return to the lessons of McCarthyism.

By exploring Palestine and racism in the classroom, activists for Black and Palestinian lives are accused of fomenting hate of country (the United States and Israel), stoking anti-Semitism, and creating unsafe conditions for students in public schools and universities. During the Virginia governor race in 2021, Republican candidate Glenn Youngkin (who ended up winning the race) ran a symptomatic ad taking up the topic of safety, featuring a white mother upset that her son, a high school senior, had been made to read Morrison's *Beloved* and was left distraught by this unsettling encounter with a narrative about the brutality of slavery. The injunction to protect students is weaponized to preclude exposure to accounts of anti-Blackness. The same logic is also being applied to pro-Palestinian speech when perceived as tantamount to hate speech.

The Youngkin example signals another return of the repressed: white populism. The Obama years and the BLM protests in Ferguson, Missouri, spurred by the 2014 high-profile killing of another Black man, Michael Brown, further hystericized the Right—which was already reeling from the liberal war on coal and the opioid epidemic in red states.[28] BLM and its fantasized criminality only fueled white panic, intensifying *negrophobia* in a significant segment of the population. Trump, a savvy trader in shame and the repressed, translated white America's anxiety about their diminishing white privilege/priority into love of country, alchemically transforming anti-Blackness into white victimhood.[29] "Make America Great Again" affectively signified "Make America White Again." This return of the repressed took the form of a culture backlash, or a "whitelash," as CNN commentator Van Jones justly dubbed it after Trump's election in 2016.[30]

Fetishist Disavowal, Anti-Blackness, and the Liberal Attitude

If a collective repression of racial slavery created national amnesia—an entrenched desire to forget the past or for "selective memory"[31]—after M4BL, a different operation of denial started to take hold: a shift from repression to fetishist disavowal. Fetishist disavowal is marked by a willful turning away. So libidinally enthralled are we by the comforts and security of our white social order that we are unwilling to make any significant changes to our lives. Fetishist disavowal characterizes best the liberal attitude toward anti-Blackness, setting the stage for an ineffectual reckoning, a non-reckoning. Liberals know very well about racial slavery and the ongoing systemic racism visited on Black communities, but all the same, they believe in America's capacity to correct itself (the ideal of "a more perfect union"), that the arc of history bends toward justice and so on. Fetishist disavowal offers the liberal subject not only the enjoyment of being anti-racist but the surplus enjoyment of hating the haters.[32] Liberal outrage at anti-Blackness feeds a woke identity without ever prompting a reckoning with America's afterlife of slavery—the unbearable truth of anti-Blackness. *I know, but I don't want to know that I know, so I don't know*. I know very well about the exclusion of Black people, but all the same, I still believe in the greatness of the United States; I refuse to assume the knowledge that America is a racist project—since such an avowal would entail an undoing of my white/bourgeois privilege, an acknowledgment that the victimization of Blacks is of an ontological order, and a radical change to my social coordinates and perception of reality. This dynamic explains why anti-Blackness is not merely a lingering national problem, but a permanent facet of American society, its "racial realism," as Derrick Bell called it.[33]

Fetishist disavowal casts our culture wars in a new light. Neither side of the culture wars is really willing to reckon with anti-Blackness. Right-wing conservatives tend to minimize its structural relevance, placing anti-Blackness firmly in the past, its lingering traces ending with the Civil Rights Movement. On the whole, they adopt a colorblind ideology. The Right loves to claim Martin Luther King, Jr.'s legacy, a legacy which, of course, has been rendered toothless. It is not the MLK fighting for workers' rights nor the anti-militarism MLK who lives in the Right's cultural imaginary.[34] Rather, it is a decontextualized MLK, reduced to his aspirational vision of a future where children "will not be judged by the color of their skin but by the content of their character," a phrase that the Right repeats *ad nauseam*.[35] Even worse, MLK's inspiring statement perversely comes to justify a supremacist mindset underpinned by the slogan "All Lives Matter." The fake universality of the slogan abstracts and distorts, covering over the power imbalances and racial inequalities in America. Liberals strike a more conciliatory tone with the traumatic past of slavery, and their MLK is primarily about nonviolence and tolerance. Generally speaking, the liberal Left is less prone to downplaying the shameful episodes of America's past. Neither the Democrats nor the Republicans are interested, however, in taking up the challenges posed by M4BL. The liberal Left's attitude toward the demand to defund the police reveals its deep affinity with the conservative Right. After the death of George Floyd in Minneapolis, liberals initially appeared open to radical change, but they ultimately sided with the "law and order" narrative over the much-needed reinvention of police enforcement. This is true at the level of voters (the liberal public) and political leadership (the Democratic Presidency and Congress).

A 2021 vote in the Democratic city of Minneapolis serves as a cautionary reminder of the status quo's resilience. The bill to remove the Minneapolis Police Department from the city charter and to replace it with a "public-health oriented" Department of Public Safety was rejected by many Democratic voters. Defunding the police is a catchy rallying slogan for white liberal Americans, but they don't really want to implement it; they don't want to actually change the structures of policing. They prefer to talk about the dismantling of white privilege without it actually impacting the operations of their white privilege.[36] And if there was any doubt about a backlash to BLM's call to "Defund the Police," witness President Biden's 2022 State of the Union address, in which he confidently asserted, "We should all agree. The answer is not to defund the police. It's to fund the police. Fund them. Fund them. Fund them with resources and training. Resources and training they need to protect their communities."[37] Two weeks earlier, then House Speaker Nancy Pelosi, D-Calif., told ABC's George Stephanopoulos that defunding the police, contrary to the will of the progressive wing of the party (the Squad), "is not the position of the Democratic Party."[38]

The unprincipled wager in this political calculation is that acknowledging white fear of crime garners more votes than insisting on the struggle against anti-Blackness. Even the stalled "George Floyd Justice in Policing Act" does not change the landscape of policing. M4BL opposes the bill, faulting it for its reformist vision and strategies. Giving the police more funding for training, more body cameras, for instance, has been tried and has failed to introduce any significant changes. Such proposals ultimately compound rather than fix the problem. M4BL proposes instead the "BREATHE Act," which "addresses fundamental causes of police violence by scaling back the bloated and ineffective mechanisms of policing and incarceration and makes investments in non-punitive, non-carceral approaches to community care, healing, and safety."[39] Any transformative bill that reckons with anti-Blackness must fully avow and take into consideration the police's well-documented anti-Black origins. The police were never meant to protect "law and order" for all. As Robin D. G. Kelley puts it, the creation of the police served an ideological function: the preservation of "bourgeois class rule *and* white supremacy."[40] It should be no surprise that the modern US police operates as "an occupying force," enacting "the coercive arm of the state," imposing their ruthless presence in "America's impoverished ghettoes, barrios, reservations, on the Southwest border, and in any territory with high concentrations of subjugated communities."[41] The "BREATHE Act" points in a different direction; it not only advocates rolling back the resources that fueled the New Jim Crow, that "have gone to underwriting mass incarceration in our criminal legal system," but actively encourages localities through incentives to pursue non-carceral and nonpunitive approaches, such as eliminating the money bail paradigm (which penalizes Black people, especially Black women) or investing in affordable housing and mental health programs for low-income individuals.[42] In the "BREATHE Act," Black people, and other historically disenfranchised people, are posited as an object of care rather than a phobic object that is *ab initio* guilty. Unless Blackness stops appearing as an ontological menace—where the Black imago triggers an allergic reaction in the eyes of the police[43]—anti-Blackness will persist unhindered by new regulations.

Anti-Woke Enjoyment

If white liberals enjoy the effects of their fetishist disavowal, conservative Republicans after Trump are not simply trying to bury or ban the past, repressing the fact of anti-Blackness. Trump's "Make America Great Again" campaign reinfused whiteness with energy and pride. We can draw a parallel with the far Right in Israel for whom the Nakba (the Arabic word for catastrophe, marking the displacement and dispossession of the Indigenous Palestinians during the 1948 Israeli war of independence) is not something to repress—by making its commemoration illegal, for instance—but to repeat and complete, to realize the Zionist project of a total eradication of the Palestinian people.[44] Exposing Israel as a genocidal settler-colonial regime—narrating the Palestinian side[45]—no longer provokes consternation among religio-nationalist Israelis. The image of wild settlers setting Palestinian villages ablaze captures the full enjoyment of the right-wingers who relish full sovereignty over the contested land. To be sure, the United States is not quite there. But the rhetoric emerging from the far Right about chattel slavery is inching in that direction. If Israel's right-wingers are in part reacting to liberal Zionists, who vaguely belong to the "Peace Camp," endorse a two-state solution, and hope that a multicultural Israel can better accommodate Palestinian citizens of Israel (labeled Arab Israelis by the Israeli government), America's right-wingers are reacting against the liberal Left's hegemonic political correctness and wokeness.

In the United States, the liberal enjoyment in hating the haters is being matched if not overwhelmed by the Right's anti-woke enjoyment. The Right's rejoinder is to deny that racism in the form of colorism exists today while at the same time explicitly embracing the national project of eradicating "backwards" and "anti-patriotic" cultures and character traits, as well as anyone who opposes this vision of American greatness and progress. Such a position leads proponents to assert, on the one hand, that CRT is divisively inventing the problem of racial antagonism (whites vs. Blacks) rather than promoting national unity (Ron DeSantis' proposal for a "patriotic education" further weaponized Trump's slogan, "Make America Great Again"[46]), and, on the other hand, that slavery on balance was not only an unfortunate but necessary evil, but actually a necessary *good* for the slaves themselves (as witnessed in the state of Florida's new 2023 history education standards proclaiming that slaves learned useful skills—falsely implying both that enslaved labor was largely comprised of skilled work and that Africans had not already developed such skilled industries[47]). This new right-wing orientation is not responding to anti-Blackness by either repression or disavowal. Instead, the extreme Right is doubling down on America's "greatness" and turning the cultural wars over race into a referendum on the nation's preeminence. For far-right political leaders, the question now becomes, *Is America a racist project or not?* And the Right's wager is that flag-waving Americans are unlikely to answer in the affirmative. "Make America Great Again" resonated, and continues to resonate, with a disenchanted white America at large (including many who dislike the man who utters it). "Law and order" is a message that still carries much affective force among the white liberal bourgeoisie; it taps into an anti-Black libidinal economy, the unconscious mechanisms at work in the racialization of Blacks through their identification with criminality or barbarity.

As I see it, going beyond repression and disavowal, in the context of a national reckoning with anti-Blackness, can take at least two paths: anti-wokeness and defunding the police. The first, anti-wokeness, crudely transcends the problem by delegitimizing the cry of the afflicted (as articulated by CRT and enacted on the streets by BLM and other activists): CRT is labeled hateful and anti-American. You move past anti-Blackness (assuming the Right acknowledges its existence, without ever encountering its history and afterlives) through a reinvestment in institutions of public and higher education that promote patriotism. The second exerts pressure on the split attitude of white liberals who know about anti-Blackness (and enjoy canceling racists from the Right) but are not willing to assume the consequences of that knowledge (a redistribution of priority and power). New information about police brutality and the killing of Black people has been admitted into their consciousness (liberals, we know, actively promote the teaching of racial inequality in public schools), but its symbolic impact has been defanged, minimized, so that liberals can, on one hand, continue to criticize Trump and his ilk, and, on the other, ignore their own complicity in the production and reproduction of an anti-Black world. To break, or at least weaken, the hold of fetishist disavowal requires integrating the fact of anti-Blackness into the symbolic universe of liberal white America. Remaining comfortably stuck in this fetishist disavowal is, in the long term, far more harmful to an anti-racist politics than a patriotic education agenda insofar as, in the latter, the fault lines are clearly drawn. The far Right is nostalgic for white times,[48] for an America comfortable in its claims of white priority (in the short term, Trump and his progeny are unquestionably the bigger risk to even the semblance of American democracy). The liberal Left, for its part, is invested in prolonging the status quo of a multicultural America. Liberal ambivalence (*I know but I don't want to know, so I don't know about anti-Blackness*) creates a convenient enemy (the extremists on the Right) who can be called out whenever they overstep or transgress liberal public sensibilities, but this stance—opting to mildly reckon with MAGA's anti-Blackness rather than America's—only masks liberals' own complicity with the capitalist and racist system. The "direct reign of Rightist populism"[49] guarantees disasters; the hypocrisy of the center or liberal Left guarantees frustration. The former is explicit in its crudeness and viciousness, the latter traffics in ideals (such as human rights) that it never fully implements. The way forward is to flatly reject the populist Right's nostalgic desire for a return to white times and take to task the liberal Left for "not living up to their proclaimed principles." You say, "Black lives matter"—prove it! Start with dismantling the prison-industrial complex, putting an end to the school-to-prison pipeline. You say, "the life of Palestinian civilians matter"—prove it! Close the US Embassy in Jerusalem, adhere to the Leahy Law and suspend the delivery of weapons to Israel, officially endorse BDS, and impose impactful sanctions in order to de-exceptionalize Israel and force it to abide by international law.[50]

Who's Afraid of Context? Or Disavowing Zionist Settler Colonialism

For most liberal Zionists, Benjamin Netanyahu is a national scandal, a political embarrassment. Liberal Zionists want peace, a resolution to the troubles inaugurated by '67, which is viewed as *the* fundamental problem facing the nation. Liberals distinguish between a Zionist Israel and a Ziofascist[51] Israel. The former is Jewish and democratic, whereas the latter is illiberal and theocratic. Liberal Zionists welcome a critique of Israel, but typically only within the limits of Zionist/colonial reason.

For these reasons, in forging a parliamentary coalition with extreme-right parties, Netanyahu has drawn severe critiques from citizens across the center-left spectrum in Israel, who are alarmed by the sharp turn toward illiberalism manifest in the coalition's political agenda, most visibly in its attempts to reduce the power of the judiciary. Eva Illouz, who publishes fairly frequently in the center-left *Haaretz*, has pushed this critique farther than most by extending it to the Occupation itself. In a 2014 article titled "47 Years a Slave: A New Perspective on the Occupation," Illouz writes, "What started as a national and military conflict has morphed into a form of domination of Palestinians that now increasingly borders on conditions of slavery."[52] Likening Israel's treatment of Palestinians to chattel slavery is a powerful analogy and a disconcerting one for liberal Zionists in particular, who are committed to democratic norms and universal human rights. In this piece, Illouz attempts to unsettle the social coordinates of her fellow Israelis so that the *knowledge* of the inhuman(e) Occupation is not contained and rendered toothless, but might become life- or world-altering.

After October 7, one might have expected Illouz to pursue this analogy further, in the vein of Norman Finkelstein, who compared Hamas's attacks to a "slave revolt" of the type exemplified by the enslaved Nat Turner, who, in Southampton, Virginia, in 1831, "killed a lot of white people, civilians in a rampage."[53] The point here, of course, is not to celebrate violence for the sake of violence, but to keep in mind the Fanonian insight that butchery has historically been met with butchery (and this butchery has in turn been met again with even greater butchery). But Illouz does not follow Finkelstein; in a series of articles she takes the opposite tack and unleashes ire on the global Left for daring to contextualize and explain Hamas's violence, which she views as minimizing or relativizing the attacks. Like many center-left Israelis, Illouz has "sobered up."[54] Disillusioned by the scale and intensity of Hamas's incursion, she makes axiomatic that the evil of Hamas has no context and undertakes to save the universalist Left from what she characterizes as its "postcolonial" hijacking. Delving into this reaction helps us understand what is at stake for liberal Zionists and how disavowal functions in response to crises that threaten to upend its stabilizing mechanisms.

Liberal-leftist Zionists in Israel are dismayed, perplexed, hurt, and enraged, struggling to process not only the stunning brutality of Hamas's October 7th attacks but also what they perceive as an ungenerous, indifferent, or even malicious response by the global Left. For Illouz, the global Left's failure to take a stronger stance against Hamas shows that its scrutiny of the Jewish state stems from a "carefully formulated ideology, and part of a far broader alliance between religious Islam and the 'postcolonial' left."[55] On Illouz's reading, Islam, as the object of Western powers' demonization, finds an ally and a receptive hearing from the Left; the latter, suspicious of Western hegemony, is all too eager to defend the former's cause to the rest of the world. But much of Illouz's argument against the global Left relies on a familiar pattern of objections leveled at pro-Palestinian activists,[56] who are frequently accused of incarnating and proliferating a "new anti-Semitism."[57] Illouz objects, for example, to the singling out of Israel for its nationalism (the Why-are-you-picking-on-Zionism? argument) and the Left's failure to stand up to Islam's abuses (the Why-are-you-defending-the-indefensible? argument). The Hamas attack and its purported support among leftist circles crystallized, for Illouz, what she calls the Left's "moral and intellectual bankruptcy."[58] Why? Because the global Left failed to stand with Israel. Leftists unforgivably turned their back on Jews and channeled their care toward the "Arabs," the Palestinian population. The titles of Illouz's articles take on an increasingly alarmist and accusatory form: from "The Global Left's Reaction to October 7 Threatens the Fight Against the Occupation" (November 11, 2023) to "How the Left Became a Politics of Hatred Against Jews" (February 3, 2024). In these *Haaretz* articles, Illouz seeks to delegitimize the global Left, first, by charging its champions (including Butler and Žižek) with a hatred of Jews, and, second, by undertaking to de-postcolonize the Left, that is, to expose its anti-Semitic proclivities, to dismiss its reductive explanatory framework, and to expunge its interpretive biases when it comes to Palestine/Israel.

Illouz indicates her disdain for postcolonial studies by putting quotation marks around the "postcolonial" in the phrase "'postcolonial' left."[59] This Left, we're told, is promoting and nurturing a "nihilist art of paranoia and exclusion,"[60] relishing in dividing the world crudely into two sides, victims and victimizers (with Jews now permanently occupying the position of the victimizer). Illouz relies on Aviad Kleinberg to take down postcolonial theory. Kleinberg's article "Are All Israelis 'Colonialists' Who Deserve to Die?" echoes the moralizing and contemptuous tone of Illouz's writings. For Kleinberg, postcolonial theory has bewitched today's readers; its excessive skepticism negates all the gains of a more nuanced account of received knowledge. According to Kleinberg's vision—which, I must admit, veers on the caricatural—postcolonial skepticism has given way to a self-righteous dogmatism, where a Manichean logic prevails: "the West is the victimizer and everyone else its victim."[61] Such "selective vision,"[62] Kleinberg warns, simplifies global matters. Kleinberg's manufacturing of outrage falls flat. Let's consider some remarks by Edward Said and Gayatri Chakravorty Spivak, two founding figures of postcolonial theory. Said constantly argued against a "politics of blame" that turns your own status as victim into a weapon and instead insisted that the heart of any solidarity movement must be animated by a critical impulse—"never solidarity before criticism," as he put it.[63] And Spivak likewise warned against the Western self's impulse to fetishize the non-European other and to arrogate to itself the problems of complexity. By this Western logic, Spivak explains, "the person who knows has all of the problems of selfhood. The person who is known, somehow seems not to have a problematic self. These days . . . only the dominant self can be problematic; the self of the Other is authentic without problem. . . . This is frightening."[64] Rather than endorsing a rhetoric of authenticity or pure celebration of the non-Western difference, postcolonial theory underscores that such gestures come at a political and hermeneutic cost.

While viewing herself as a defender of Enlightenment values invested in forging a "just peace" between Palestinians and Israelis, Illouz was nevertheless distraught by the Left's insistence that Hamas's attacks did not materialize out of thin air. The belief that Hamas's brutal assault "did not occur in a vacuum" was itself read as an anti-Semitic observation insofar as the condemnation of Hamas was qualified by the impulse to understand the attacks and cast the Palestinian condition in a different light. Offended by this line of argumentation, Illouz intervenes in an attempt to shame the global Left and set straight its path, which, again, has been derailed by anti-colonial thought, by postcolonial theory and its morally dubious historicizations:

> If we use "context" as an analytical tool to explain and understand, how far should context go? Should we, for example, invoke the context of murderous antisemitism, which has given rise to Zionism, thereby making it drastically different from all forms of settler colonialism? Should we include in our contextualization the fact that the Jerusalem mufti Amin Al-Husseini supported the Nazis and their Final Solution and that, as such, losing Palestine was a part of the redrawing of maps after World War II?[65]

It is not clear where Illouz stands on these specific examples. Are they alternative frames for understanding context (i.e., Do they supplement postcolonial reasoning and thereby reshape the conclusions the analyst should draw)? Or are they exaggerations to be dismissed, pointing to the futility of contextualizing itself? Illouz's first alternative contextual example has merit and should be introduced in any discussion of Palestine/Israel. The fact that many Jews turned to Zionism as a way to escape anti-Semitism in Europe is deeply important for understanding the settler-colonial context. Like Said, I believe that it is ethically and politically paramount for Palestinians to *understand* the libidinal and material appeal of Israel (which includes a recognition of Jewish suffering). For Zionists, Israel symbolized and continues to symbolize a place of belonging where their safety would not be contingent on the whims of majoritarian rule.

Zionism's origins as a liberation movement for Jews cannot be forgotten. Without grasping the passion for Zion, as Jacqueline Rose might put it, understanding (the actions of) your oppressor will always be unnecessarily incomplete.[66] But this line of argumentation has its limits. The history of anti-Semitism cannot justify the Zionist dispossession of the Indigenous population and mass ethnic cleansing of their villages. When Zionism becomes an exclusive attachment to historic Palestine (the dream of a Greater Israel, or Eretz Israel)—so that from the river to the sea, all that you will see is Jewish sovereignty—Zionism morphs into an unabashed racism, a supremacist program. For Fayez Sayegh, Zionism's racist proclivities were present from the get-go, set on a collision course with the "inferior" native Palestinians: "Zionist *racial identification* produces three corollaries: *racial self-segregation*, *racial exclusiveness*, and *racial supremacy*. These principles constitute the core of the Zionist ideology."[67]

So, you can (and must) acknowledge Jewish suffering, while still situating Hamas's attack in the context of settler colonialism, where Zionism operates as an ideology and collective fantasy that fuels the settler-colonial project. This project has taken to weaponizing the horrors of the Shoah to silence critics of Israel, and has reached absurd realities: even using the word "Occupation" to describe Israel's relation to the Palestinian people supposedly "gives credence to the modern blood libel that fuels a growing anti-Jewish hatred around the world, in the United States, and in Hollywood"[68] (as stated in an open letter from over 450 Jewish creatives and professionals responding to Jonathan Glazer's condemnation of the Occupation in his acceptance speech after winning an Oscar for his Holocaust film, *Zone of Interest*).[69]

Illouz's second alternative contextual example is ridiculous. It takes the form of an argument that spoils of war go to the winners. Except that the Palestinians, at the time British colonial subjects, were not defeated in World War II, nor were they responsible for the Nazi murders of six million Jews. Illouz concocts a scenario in which Palestinians could be held responsible for their own dispossession. The claim that *some Palestinians are worse than Hitler and that's why their claim to the land is forfeited* is not by any stretch a credible context for understanding the present situation. Rather, it colludes with the Israeli Right's demonization of Palestinians (Palestinians are worse than Nazis). As Illouz is aware, Netanyahu made just such an inflammatory statement in 2015, trafficking in racist fabulations and claiming that a Palestinian, Haj Amin al-Husseini, the Grand Mufti of Jerusalem, was responsible for giving Hitler the idea to exterminate the Jews, when Hitler merely wanted to relocate them.[70]

I want to linger a bit more on the question of suffering and the ways in which contextual layers must be seen not simply as oppositional but rather as interlocking or enmeshed with each other. The fact of suffering (the fact that a people has suffered) does not transform a group or its members into ethical subjects (the International Court of Justice's ruling that the Israeli state is plausibly committing genocide gives the lie to the Israeli military's claim to be "the most moral army in the world"). Rashid Khalidi comments on the cruel irony of tragic victims becoming the vicious victimizers of others, and this insight applies to Jews as well as to Palestinians: "many of [the Israelis] descended from victims of persecution, pogroms, and concentration camps, have themselves been mistreating another people. We thus find that the sins done to the fathers have morally desensitized the sons to their sins toward others, and have even sometimes been used to justify these sins. (Many Lebanese would bitterly say the same thing about the behavior of the PLO in Lebanon between the late 1960s and 1982)."[71]

Context is no excuse. Context is not straightforward causation. The turn to context represents a concern with understanding, not justification. To disavow the material conditions of the Occupation, to assert that there is no context to the Hamas attacks, leads to the Nazification of Palestinians and genocidal consequences: evil must be annihilated. In Orientalist fashion, it is to confirm, as Odeh Bisharat notes, that "the Palestinians were simply born bloodthirsty beasts, and that the 56-year-old occupation and the state of perpetual, suffocating refugeehood had no connection to or impact on their behavior."[72] It is to confirm that Palestinian psychology is "perverse,"[73] that Palestinians exist outside of history, that they are and will always be the same, and that there can thus be no encounter with them other than a violent one. Isn't this the ideological lie that Netanyahu and his far-right cabinet sold to a sympathetic world, horrified by the events of October 7? The desire to bracket context stems from a deep-seated unwillingness to confront the uncivilizing forces of settler colonialism, from a failure to reckon with Zionism's inextricable link to a settler supremacist mindset. In *Discourse on Colonialism*, Aimé Césaire drew attention to the ontological ill-effects of colonization on the colonizers' moral fabric: "We must study how colonization works to *decivilize* the colonizer, to *brutalize* him in the true sense of the word, to degrade him, to awaken him to buried instincts, to covetousness, violence, race hatred, and moral relativism."[74] Israelis cannot see that Palestinians are not born angry; their anger is a *response*, as Audre Lorde would put it, to anti-Palestinian racism, to the Zionist settler's motto of "*racial elimination*,"[75] to the Occupation, to the caging and genocide of Gazans, and so on.

The call for context disconcerts liberal Zionists. Why? Is the worry that when we contextualize and examine the situation, the question "Do you condemn Hamas?" will lose its rhetorical efficiency? Currently, the accusatory question

"Do you condemn Hamas?" is fully naturalized in mainstream media in the West. To be a legitimate interlocutor—to be on the side of "humans," not "human animals"[76]—you have to begin by firmly responding *"Yes"* to the question. If you hesitate or refuse to answer, you are deemed an anti-Semite, a cheerleader for Hamas, or worse than Hitler.[77] Here, Palestinian citizen of Israel Tamer Nafar puts his finger on the ideological trap set by the question: "I have no difficulty expressing empathy to anyone who's been hurt; the problem is with political statements, since in order to embrace this terrible pain, one has to line up behind Western leaders and global media outlets, which embrace Israel emotionally and politically, as well as sponsoring its army. These are the same bodies that ignore our pain and which have always funded its erasure."[78] This is the double bind: to be against the suffering of innocent civilians in Israel *and* to refuse to ignore the Jewish state's "organized inhumanity"[79] in Gaza, to refuse to align oneself with the same forces that contribute to the systematic demonization and suffocation of the Palestinian people.

When Judith Butler similarly attempts to reorient the discussion to the colonial situation so that a more generative exchange can be had, they are bitterly criticized and dismissed.[80] Declining to label Hamas a terrorist group, Butler, during a panel discussion in France on anti-Semitism, its instrumentalization, and revolutionary peace in Palestine, sought to understand the group's attacks as instances of anti-colonial resistance: "I think it is more honest and historically correct to say that the uprising of October 7 was an act of resistance. It is not a terrorist attack and it is not an antisemitic attack. It was an attack against Israelis."[81] To see only, or primarily, anti-Semitism in the deadly assault is a flagrant disavowal of the settler-colonial context. Butler is, in some ways, reiterating Sayegh's *cri de guerre*, "rights undefended are rights surrendered."[82] Hamas is defending the rights of the Palestinians against an eliminationist Zionist settler regime. And for this reason, Hamas fighters are misrepresented as bloodthirsty terrorists. Seeing Palestinian violence as a counter-violence against an occupying Zionist state whose constitutive violence is often left unacknowledged or distorted by claims that Israel is defending itself might help to shift the public discourse on Palestine/Israel.

If a Zionist hermeneutic dehistoricizes and converts all uprisings into instances of anti-Semitism, another attack on Jews because of their Jewishness—and thus draws a straight line from the Third Reich to Hamas—Butler dispels Zionism's phantasmatic machinery by situating Hamas's violence firmly in the context of the Occupation, in the struggle for freedom and dignity. The uprising marks a preexisting or originary violence; it "comes from a state of subjugation, and against a violent state apparatus."[83] To better understand Hamas's attacks—if for no other reason than to prevent future ones—we need to examine "the political structure and the violence structure from which that uprising emerged."[84] If we bracket these structures from critical purview, all we see, and project, is a timeless or ontological hatred of Jews; we never understand Palestinian *actions* as *responses*, or instances of counter-violence, to the Occupation. Again, unless you believe that Palestinians who join Hamas are "simply born bloodthirsty beasts" (to be summarily eliminated), you have to look at their actions, and their psychic states, in a broader political context, in the stultifying and humiliating reality of the Occupation. Moreover, acknowledging Hamas as a movement committed to armed struggle against a colonial occupier does not in and of itself constitute an endorsement of the *form* that those actions take (such as the tactic of targeting civilians). But it does enable a different debate to unfold, which historicizes the shifting identities of Israelis and Palestinians as they relate to the ebb and flow of the Occupation: "Let's at least call it armed resistance and then we can have a debate on whether it's right or did they do the right thing."[85] Armed resistance indexes an invader and reorients an interpretive gaze modeled and manufactured by Western power and mainstream media. The message is simple: our gaze cannot solely be engulfed by Hamas's actions.

Another Political Constellation Is Possible

On multiple occasions, Butler has explicitly condemned the violence of Hamas's attacks. Seeing Hamas as engaged in armed resistance "neither romanticizes their atrocities nor justifies their actions."[86] Butler stresses that "we can, and must, disagree with the tactics of such a movement," and adds, "my view is that the atrocities committed then, and the genocidal actions of the State of Israel, are both to be opposed."[87] Still, it is easier to distort and cry foul. There is a sadistic enjoyment and virtue signaling in going after anti-Zionist Jewish intellectuals who actively disidentify with the state of Israel and work to reconfigure the interpretive scene and political landscape. For instance, Cary Nelson, in his typically belligerent fashion, indicts Butler for their anti-colonial reasoning, denouncing it as "irredeemably antisemitic."[88] All resistance to Israeli state violence, including peaceful protests (with a very strong vocal Jewish presence among the activists), become instances of "genocidal intention,"[89] even transforming a call for ceasefire into a call for the destruction of Jewish lives. Despite Butler's stated preference for the nonviolent BDS movement, they do not foreclose the question of armed struggle. Rather, as they state,

> it is important to ask those who defend Hamas as a movement of armed resistance how they situate this armed resistance within a history of armed struggles, and what, if any, conditions would have to be met for the laying down of arms. One obvious answer is that Israeli state violence would have to end. If Israeli state violence is the condition of possibility for armed resistance,

then the cessation of that violence would doubtless produce another political constellation.[90]

It is that other "political constellation" that fetishist disavowal wants to eclipse and keep at bay: *I know very well that the Israeli government is committing state violence, but all the same, I don't believe that we need another political configuration; Israel in its current form can accommodate the Palestinian desire for self-determination; reconciliation is possible; after Netanyahu, we can resume the peace process and talks of a two-state solution.* By never assuming the consequences of the knowledge of state violence (that the Israeli government in its default mode is committing a slow genocide), liberal Zionists are not able to imagine nor agitate for an alternative political constellation. Netanyahu and his band of fascists function as a fetish for liberals of all shades, enabling "the Western liberal to contain what is wrong with Israel to a minority of fundamentalist fanatics who spoil the innocent Zionist project, i.e., to avoid confronting the much more unsettling fact that the notion of Israel from the river to the sea is inscribed into the basic Zionist problem (today, over 80% of Jews in Israel support it)."[91]

Israeli politics has normalized apartheid, selling it to its citizens and the Global North as a security measure. Žižek decries that "Israel is practicing a politics of apartheid that reduces Palestinians to second-class citizens."[92] Yes, but matters are actually worse. Israel is constantly driving Palestinian otherness further and further in the zone of nonbeing. Racialized Palestinians are nowhere close to being "second-class citizens." Let's not forget that Israel's racial matrix not only targets Palestinians, but also its own. At the top of the hierarchy sit Ashkenazi Jews, European Jews who forged their image of Israel in a European settler-colonial mold. Israel's other Jews—Mizrahi Jews (Arab Jews, that is, Jews of Middle Eastern or North African origin), Sephardi Jews (descendants of Jews from Spain), and Ethiopian Jews—are subjected to discrimination and neglect, the last appallingly so (though they are still better off than any Palestinians according to the Zionist ontology of humanity).[93] And then comes the Palestinians who constitute the bottom of the hierarchy, though we can see them oscillating between not-quite-human (Palestinian citizens of Israel, as long as they are "good Arabs" who prove the rule that Arabs are bad; along with some West Bankers and Jerusalemites) and nonhuman (Gazans, refugees in exile), the latter undeserving of *human*itarian aid.

Jewish privilege is what is at stake here. The privilege to mourn and the privilege to subjugate implicate one another. Under a Zionist/Western horizon, normative ontology elevates the Israeli Jew but degrades the native Palestinian. The former, especially in its Ashkenazi/white form, embodies/overrepresents the "Human"[94] while the latter is pathologized, reified, and ascribed a "wholly human Other status," as Sylvia Wynter might put it.[95] When the grievability of Israelis is premised on the ungrievability of Palestinians turned into "depthless savages,"[96] when Palestinian life as such is not experienced or seen as grievable—it is a life lacking ~~human~~ rights—but rather as corrupt and disposable by Israelis and the Global North at large, what are Palestinians and activists defending Palestine to do? A concern for history remains unwelcome in the aftermath of October 7. Nor is there an appetite for imagining the existing political constellation otherwise. There is no daylight between center-left Zionists and far-right Zionists when it comes to reckoning with settler colonialism. The latter is far more belligerent in its opposition, but the former is catching up. One disavows the need for decolonization; the other transforms it into an anti-Semitic slur.

Aligning a group, movement, or cause with terrorism is a sure way to cancel it.[97] But here there seems to be a willful amnesia vis-à-vis Zionism's own brushes with terrorism. Menachem Begin, father of the right-wing Likud party who was elected prime minister in 1977, had, during the Mandate period, led the Zionist paramilitary organization Irgun, which targeted British installations and personnel, including kidnapping and executing soldiers (out of impatience with the British timetable for independence) and Arab civilians, including shootings and bombings of pedestrians, cafes, and buses (in an effort to clear non-Jews from the contested land). "No one who stands athwart the path of Zionism is immune from Zionist vengeance," writes Sayegh.[98] And as Gilles Deleuze reminds us, terrorism was constitutive of Zionist nationalism under the British Mandate: "Zionist terrorism was not only directed against the British, but against the Arab villages that had to be erased."[99] Interestingly, for our purposes, here, Begin objected to the British's labelling of Irgun as a terrorist group, rhetorically asking: "what has a struggle for the dignity of man, against oppression and subjugation, to do with 'terrorism'?"[100] Begin waxes poetic on terror, opposing it to the noble Zionist fight for freedom, the desire to drive out "tyrannous rulers" and their reign of fear:

> The historical and linguistic origins of the political term "terror" prove that it cannot be applied to a revolutionary war of liberation. . . . A revolution, or a revolutionary war, does not aim at instilling fear. Its object is to overthrow a regime and to set up a new regime in its place. In a revolutionary war both sides use force. Tyranny is armed. Otherwise it would be liquidated overnight. Fighters for freedom must arm; otherwise they would be crushed overnight. Certainly the use of force also wakens fear. Tyrannous rulers begin to fear for their positions, or their lives, or both. And consequently they try to sow fear among those they rule. But the instilling of fear is not an aim in itself. The sole aim on the one side is the overthrow of armed tyranny; on the other side it is the perpetuation of that tyranny. The underground fighters of the Irgun arose to overthrow and replace a regime. We used physical force because we were faced by physical force. But physical force was neither our aim nor our creed.

We believed in the supremacy of moral forces. It was our enemy who mocked at them.[101]

Both agents of terrorism and freedom fighters traffic in fear, but whereas the former deploys it to pacify those they subjugate, the latter makes use of it to bring about a new order of things, freed of tyranny. If, today, Britain and the rest of the Global North have embraced Begin's view, accepting Israel's brand of state terrorism as a legitimate use of violence (though they never call it state terrorism), the label of Zionist terrorism more accurately captures what is happening from the standpoint of Zionism's Palestinian victims.[102]

So, when Butler asks us to pause, to question the language we use and how we frame the problem (since bad formulations often lead to worse solutions), they are not obfuscating or muddying the interpretive waters. Quite the contrary, they are pushing us to think: Isn't Hamas introducing fear in the occupiers' lifeworld, in "their positions, or their lives, or both," in order to bring about a "new regime"? If the question has any plausibility, which I believe that it does, then the October 7th uprising, as Butler observes, is better understood as an act of armed resistance.[103] When liberal Zionists bemoan Butler and others for elevating Hamas's actions, they perhaps don't realize that they are recycling the discourse of the far Right. Journalist Etan Nechin, for instance, claims to attend to the complexity of the situation: "Butler's method glosses over the personal impacts of the conflict, and instead generalizes the situation into broad, unchanging categories of oppressor versus oppressed. Butler's approach fails to acknowledge the complex realities on the ground, where the lines between oppressor and oppressed blur and challenge these simplistic distinctions."[104] This is a perfect example of deploying "complexity" as an ideological ruse, distracting us from a confrontation with the real Israel, marked by the objective violence of the Occupation.

A settler-colonial framework does not crudely simplify matters, but it does point lucidly to an antagonism at the heart of Palestine/Israel: the opposition between Native and settler. Saying the situation is "complex" constitutes what Eve Tuck and K. Wayne Yang call "settler moves to innocence": "those strategies or positionings that attempt to relieve the settler of feelings of guilt or responsibility without giving up land or power or privilege, without having to change much at all."[105] As Patrick Wolfe argues, the impulse to deny the Native/settler binary reflects a "settler perspective."[106] It neglects to see that the Zionist invasion is precisely a "structure not an event,"[107] not something that can be fixed and relegated to a tumultuous Israeli past. Bizarrely, Nechin even accuses Butler of an accidental Orientalism: "Butler inadvertently adopts an Orientalist stance, too. By casting Palestinians, Arabs, and people of color in a perpetually conflictual role, Butler's narrative brands these groups as inherently confrontational."[108] It is not a question of "casting Palestinians, Arabs, and people of color in a perpetually conflictual role" but of bearing witness to their refusal to accept the existing reality (the Occupation, New Jim Crow, Apartheid). And if the colonized desire for freedom from the yoke of Zionist colonialism is deemed Orientalist, would Nechin extend this observation to Menachem Begin and the Jewish revolt against British imperialism?

Illouz, Nechin, and others, who are equally worried about the shrinking Israeli Left, swiftly dismiss a line of thinking coming from "lazy left intellectuals" for its too-easy adoption of a settler-colonial framework, for uncritically putting front and center the colonial situation in their engagement with the Hamas attacks (which itself seems to feed the perception that this engagement constitutes an unqualified defense). Here we can contrast Illouz's move to innocence— Israeli Jews are not simply settlers but victims as well, and not really settlers at all, since "there has been an uninterrupted Jewish presence in Palestine since antiquity"[109]—with the perspective of Indigenous activists and scholars from Turtle Island (North America). From the standpoint of the Red Nation, a collective committed to the liberation of Indigenous peoples from capitalism and colonialism, the affinity between the Palestinian condition and their own is striking. Shortly after October 7, they issued an open letter stressing their support of and commitment to Palestinian resistance:

> The settler states that dispossess and occupy our lands support Israel in dispossessing and occupying Palestine. We see and feel the strength of Palestinian families in the face of the quotidian violence of the Israeli apartheid regime. Colonized peoples have the right to defend themselves and to resist colonial violence. We support Palestinian liberation and their right as an oppressed people to resist colonialism and genocide.[110]

Resistance against the occupier and the desire for freedom are not to be pathologized.[111] Indigenous solidarity has everything to do with context, that is, with the material realities imposed by settler regimes. It does not mean that their condition is identical, only that they share in their struggle against an eliminatory logic that seeks their erasure by whatever means necessary (siege, starvation, transfer, etc.). If Israel falls, the United States is next. If Israel is indicted, the United States is next . . .

In addition to exceptionalizing Israel (Israeli settler reality/history is unlike any other settler states), Illouz believes that we can decouple Zionism from "Jewish fascism," from its corrosive religious-messianic excesses.[112] A secular Zionism would duly underscore Zionism's origins as a movement of liberation and legitimize the existence of Israel as a place of security for all Jews around the world while still treating its Palestinian population with dignity. And if Jews are currently unsafe in Israel (and abroad), the blame lies not in Zionism's intrinsic aggressivity but in its capture by religious fanatics who are currently in political control (and the global Left is not helping by its attempts to delegitimize the idea of Israel). If Zionism is not essentially characterized as a racist ideology or a tyrannical collective fantasy of subjugation that rationalized the colonization of historic Palestine, Illouz can paint a less compromised image of the Israeli state.

Illouz is by no means alone in making such arguments. Howard Jacobson also dismisses the charge that Israel is a colonial/racist project. And he equally frames the question of settler colonialism around the Left and Jewish hatred. He distinguishes between a Palestinian anti-Semitism and a leftist anti-Semitism, and finds the latter more offensive: "That many Palestinians have been indoctrinated into the grossest forms of Jew hate is—let us say, so as not to have a fight—understandable. That students at elite Western universities should submit without a whimper to the same indoctrination is not."[113] In one swoop, Jacobson naturalizes Palestinian anti-Semitism, hinting that they can't know any better (acknowledgment of Palestinian hatred comes at the expense of their agency), but Western students should. The title of the article, "The Founding of Israel Wasn't a Colonial Act—a Refugee Isn't a Colonist," announces the wrongheadedness of this intervention. We're told the author is "furious," "afraid," and "defiled"—the Palestinians and their leftist supporters display only hateful rage since, presumably, the reality of anti-Semitism does not temper but instead encourages their anger at Israel and its settlers. Jacobson dismisses the charge that Israel is a colonial/racist project. As he smugly affirms, "Fleeing from pogroms isn't colonizing."[114] Yes, fleeing for your life doesn't make you a colonist, but it does if you, tacitly or actively, found and support a state that sought and seeks the dispossession of an Indigenous population. It is an inconvenient truth if we turn to Zionism's founding architects. The Zionist leader Vladimir Jabotinsky, speaking as an invading sovereign settler, says:

> My readers have a general idea of the history of colonisation in other countries. I suggest that they consider all the precedents with which they are acquainted, and see whether there is one solitary instance of any colonisation being carried on with the consent of the native population. There is no such precedent.
> *The native populations, civilised or uncivilised, have always stubbornly resisted the colonists, irrespective of whether they were civilised or savage . . .*
> Every native population, civilised or not, regards its lands as its national home, of which it is the sole master, and it wants to retain that mastery always; it will refuse to admit not only new masters but, even new partners or collaborators.[115]

Likewise, Israel's first prime minister David Ben-Gurion, in a letter to his son Amos, articulates this very settler-colonial plan: "A Jewish state on only part of the land is not the end but the beginning. . . . The establishment of a state, even if only on a portion of the land, is the maximal reinforcement of our strength at the present time and a powerful boost to our historical endeavors to liberate the entire country."[116] Though Ben-Gurion recognizes Indigenous resistance to the partition of historic Palestine ("If I were an Arab I would have been very indignant"[117]), Jewish dominion over the land is the goal: "Palestine is grossly under populated. It contains vast colonization potential which the Arabs neither need nor are qualified (because of their lack of need) to exploit."[118] Even Jabotinsky's colonizing Zionism imagined a continued presence of Palestinians in historic Palestine. He acknowledges the impossibility of their erasure:

> I am reputed to be an enemy of the Arabs, who wants to have them ejected from Palestine, and so forth. It is not true. Emotionally, my attitude to the Arabs is the same as to all other nations—polite indifference. Politically, my attitude is determined by two principles. First of all, I consider it utterly impossible to eject the Arabs from Palestine. There will always be *two* nations in Palestine—which is good enough for me, provided the Jews become the majority.[119]

For later Zionist right-wingers like Netanyahu following in the footsteps of Jabotinsky—"the radical heirs of Jabotinsky," as Seth Ackerman puts it—two nations in Palestine was no longer good enough.[120] The Right's attitude has changed. A Greater Israel—the fascist one-state solution—now constitutes the Israeli political horizon.[121] For the Israeli far Right, ejecting Palestinians, for the purposes of territorial expansion, is now both militarily possible and highly desirable.

And let's not forget the work of Israeli historians, like Ilan Pappé, who have convincingly shown that Zionist leaders, from the beginning, were planning to erase Palestinians from the contested land. As Pappé points out, Zionist leaders, in 1948, adopted Plan D (Dalet in Hebrew), a military blueprint for ethnic cleansing. The Dalet Plan emerged as

> both the inevitable product of the Zionist ideological impulse to have an exclusively Jewish presence in Palestine, and a response to developments on the ground once the British cabinet had decided to end the mandate. Clashes with local Palestinian militias provided the perfect context and pretext for implementing the ideological vision of an ethnically cleansed Palestine. The Zionist policy was first based on retaliation against Palestinian attacks in February 1947, and it transformed into an initiative to ethnically cleanse the country as a whole in March 1948. . . . When it [the mission] was over, more than half of Palestine's native population, close to 800,000 people, had been uprooted, 531 villages had been destroyed, and eleven urban neighbourhoods emptied of their inhabitants.[122]

Pappé does not mince words; the Dalet plan constituted a full-blown agenda of physical removal of Palestinians from their homeland, a premeditated uprooting, a "clear-cut case of an ethnic cleansing operation, regarded under international law today as a crime against humanity."[123]

If the argument that people fleeing pogroms are not colonialists is less than convincing, Jacobson draws a distinction between Israel and its settler excess. Jacobson can then proceed to make inconsequential statements like "the building of settlements on the West Bank is indefensible,"[124] which he, in turn, qualifies immediately by claiming that the Palestinians are to blame for their displacement and suffering, because their violent actions have hardened the hearts of Israeli Jews: "If something hard entered the Israeli soul, it was not unconnected to the seeming promise of an eternal war with a Palestinian people for whom co-existence with Jews appeared all but unthinkable. Hateful as they are, the settlements were not written into the small print of Zionism. They belong to history, not principle."[125] Aside from blaming the victims, I agree: today's Zionism is not the consequence of a necessity. Zionism is not by definition a hateful machine. In Saidian terms, Zionism, like any other "ism," is a worldly matter, subjected to the struggle for meaning. But in its recurring historical manifestations, it comes to gain a material force and an inexorable logic of its own; in this respect, we can speak here of historical residue, colonial time, or a Zionist futurology.[126] We can extrapolate an Israeli aggrandizing sovereignty, a merciless drive for territorial expansion, working its way toward a Greater Israel or a historic Palestine without Palestinians.[127] In other words, I see continuity between the early Zionists, the Dalet Plan of 1948, and the current Settler Movement constituting the core of the Israeli far Right.

Liberal Zionists might object that this is not their narrative of Zionism, that among their ranks stand people who actively seek to challenge the march of the Right's cruel Zionism. Alon Schwarz's 2022 documentary *Tantura* might serve as a case in point. Though it dares to engage the taboo topic of the Nakba, bucking the official historiography in Israel and returning to the destruction of the Palestinian village Tantura, the documentary treats the problem of ethnic cleansing as one of acknowledgment or recognition rather than accountability[128]:

> We must do this [acknowledge the past] while seeking ways that will allow for a reconciliation and an end to the conflict. Acknowledgment is the basis of everything. Without acknowledgment, the war will continue. We need to come up with new ideas. Zionism must upgrade its operating system if it wants to survive. Taking responsibility doesn't mean returning the refugees to Tantura and deporting the kibbutzniks of Nahsholim—which now stands on the site of the village. There are other ways.[129]

Undoubtedly, but what, more precisely, are these other ways? Reparations, retribution, the decolonization of Israel . . . ? No, it is again an alarmist attempt to resurrect the two-state solution. Indeed, the two-state solution as "reconciliation" has everything to do with "rescuing settler normalcy," "rescuing a settler future."[130] What Schwarz fears is an unjust one-state solution which would erode Zionism at its core: "Zionism today is destroying itself in a rush to a single binational state from the river to the sea. The Jewish state has no future if the oppressive rule over the Palestinians continues and if the land will not be divided to form two states."[131] My riposte to Schwarz: the Tantura massacre, and the settler violence that marks it, is not an aberration or exception to the Zionist dream, but constitutive of it, part and parcel of its "operative structure."[132] Zionism is inextricable from its colonial reason. If Schwarz urges his fellow Zionists not to repress the factual truth of the Tantura massacre, there is no suggestion that knowledge of it will alter the social coordinates of Israeli lives in any significant way. Schwarz is asking his fellow Israelis to "upgrade [Zionism's] operating system," not erase its racist programming. No politics follows this acknowledgment. Guilt, maybe, but hardly any sense of responsibility. Zionists are not being asked to curtail, let alone dismantle, their Jewish privilege or priority. Israel can still be in the business of destroying Palestinian worlds and dreams. No concrete actions are in fact required of Israeli Jews. You can still be a Zionist, you just have to recognize that Israel's founding involved crimes against humanity. And since the founding violence of nations is not unique to Israel, an acknowledgment of it does not in itself threaten Israel's place among Western nations. By extension, those who keep insisting on Israel's original violence/sin must be anti-Semitic.

Again, what worries Schwarz's liberal Zionism the most is not the Right's repression of Zionism's dark chapters and myths. What it desperately seeks to exclude from the realm of possibilities is a *just* one-state solution from the river to the sea. A just one-state solution might be the only political constellation capable of dissolving or transcending the Native/settler binary. But there is no new political constellation without a reckoning with settler colonialism. This is why the common impulse to quickly dismiss settler colonialism and its "application" to Palestine/Israel must be staunchly resisted. In "Restoring the Past Won't Liberate Palestine," Lydia Polgreen exemplifies this trend, appealing to the liberal and moderate sensibilities of *New York Times* readers. Reminiscent of Illouz's and Kleinberg's objections, Polgreen juxtaposes a caricatured media discourse, reduced to a simplistic postcolonial binarism—"in this analysis, there are two kinds of people: those who are native to a land and those who settle it, displacing the original inhabitants. Those identities are fixed, essential, eternal"[133]—with a desire to be forward looking, moving beyond the vicissitudes of decolonization. Polgreen turns to Fanon and Edward Said for conceptual support, and ends her article with the observation: "Liberation requires invention, not restoration. If history tells us anything, it is this: Time moves in one direction, forward."[134] Yes, I agree that "liberation requires invention," but there is no liberation without decolonization, which is precisely Fanon's point. Fanon's "we must invent and we must make discoveries"[135] are both premised on *we must decolonize*. Unless you want to turn Fanon into a "toothless revolutionary," decolonization is a precondition, a "tabula rasa," for ontological upheaval and creative invention, as in the creation of a "new man."[136] There is no liberation of the "human" without decolonization: "The 'thing' colonized becomes a man through the very process of liberation."[137] Fanonian decolonization is clearly not interested in the recovery of a pristine past, in a time prior to the colonial encounter. Decolonialization is an "agenda for total disorder,"[138] and, in the context of Palestine/Israel, the disorder will most likely take the form, at least in part, of armed resistance against the settler-colonial order of things (as already mentioned, the BDS movement may contribute to this disorder, casting Israel as a pariah state—for its theft of land, systemic subjugation of Palestinians, and, yes, genocide—to the global community). Likewise, Said's vision of a just one-state solution must be set against the failures of the peace process between Palestinians and Israelis, which yielded the Oslo Accords. The absence of a reckoning with settler colonialism transformed the Oslo Accords into "an instrument of Palestinian surrender, a Palestinian Versailles."[139] Urging a move beyond the settler/Native binary leaves intact the asymmetrical structure between Palestinians and Israel. Neither Fanon nor Said wanted to end with that binary, but they both recognized that there is no liberation without facing the bewitching wickedness of coloniality. Indeed, it is hard to imagine a just peace between Palestinians and Israelis without the latter confronting the state's displacement and dispossession of Palestinians *and* expressing a commitment to changing the colonial situation (before coexistence comes co-resistance), to decolonizing Palestine/Israel (along with the collective psyche of both peoples—whence the necessity of decolonizing the minds of the Native and settler in order to transcend the Manichean logic operative in settler colonialism).

The idea of a *just* one-state solution unsettles liberal Zionists because it casts them as accomplices to an openly supremacist regime, implicated in a national romance of racial elimination. Schwarz pursues the path of an introspective and sensitive Zionism,[140] and, in this respect, he can have his cake and eat it too. Schwarz can acknowledge Israel's vicious chapters (and thus gain the moral high ground vis-à-vis political Zionists who are aggressively phobic about the Nakba) and he can proceed with his life without any existential crisis or major disruption. No need for reparation nor redistribution. Israel remains Jewish and democratic. With Schwarz's self-reflexive Zionism, we can observe a shift from the "shoot and weep" genre of Israeli cinema to "acknowledge and weep": acknowledge the ethnic cleansing and feel bad about it. The remorse happens only belatedly when it doesn't really matter, when there is opportunity not for accountability but for some surplus-enjoyment in righteousness, that is, in feeling good about feeling bad. Some liberal Zionists "care" about the Nakba but it is a care devoid of responsibility and political commitment. As Nadia Abu El-Haj pointedly notes, "the Nakba has ethical force in the hands of liberal Zionists as a practice of liberal self-fashioning."[141] Liberal self-fashioning feeds and sculpts Zionist identity rather than questioning it in any fundamental way.

In their own distinct ways, Illouz, Jacobson, and Schwarz seek, in the words of Lara Sheehi and Stephen Sheehi, "to recuperate and validate the legitimacy of sovereignty of a settler state."[142] There is no need for another political constellation. Each dreams of an Israel capable of reigning in the state's fascistic and expansionist tendencies. Jacobson and Illouz are more ferocious in demonizing the leftist critics of Israel. Jacobson can even claim that it takes more "moral courage" to castigate Palestinians, since "right now it takes none to castigate Jews"[143]—a surprising statement given the Zionist-inflected McCarthyism reverberating across university campuses in the Global North.[144] Schwarz, for his part, wants "change without change," as Žižek might put it; he wants a self-reflexive Zionism that acknowledges its past wrongs but without any real accountability, without any gestures toward decolonizing Palestine/Israel. The three exhibit "settler moves to innocence." What we get in Illouz, Jacobson, and Schwarz is obfuscation at its best: *Israel is not really a settler-colonial state; plus, our own origins begin in trauma and anti-Semitism; yes, we are mistreating Palestinians (how do you respond to a terrorist group like Hamas?) but we are not committing genocide.*[145] *Yes, we did terrible things in the past (ethnic cleansing in 1948) and in the present (the expansion of illegal settlements in the West Bank; Netanyahu's mismanagement of the Gaza War), but Zionism can be redeemed and brought back to align with the ideals of the European Enlightenment.* Or, formulated in the language of fetishist disavowal: *We know about Israel's past and present violence done to Palestinians, but all the same we don't believe the facticity of Israel, including Jewish fascism, exhausts or overrides Zionism's ethical core and thus what Israel could be.* Another constellation is off the table.

The Bigger Elephant in the Room

Illouz, in particular, ironically ends up in Netanyahu's camp.[146] The anti-colonial Left is an anti-Semitic Left. The possibility of engaging with the Palestinian question, of getting her liberal Israeli audience to think more critically about "the elephant in the room,"[147] that is, the Occupation, is foreclosed. Worse, Illouz suspends critical thinking in the name of bearing witness to the suffering of Jews: *don't hijack the event, blame Israel, theorize about the situation, and rob me of my/people's pain*. For Illouz, "the true left, the only one, is the one that recognizes the intractability of certain conflicts because it refuses to privilege the rights of one people to the detriment of another."[148] I find this vision of the Left distorted, lacking attention to antagonism. Žižek reorients our interpretive gaze back to the antagonistic struggle at play in the genocidal Gaza War: "Hamas is the last thing a Zionist sees before confronting the actual antagonism that underlies the Israel-Palestinian conflict."[149] Hamas becomes the new political fetish of center-leftist Zionists, a phantasmatic image of the enemy whose purpose is to secure their self-identity while covering over the true antagonism: Native vs. settler.[150] What makes the Palestine/Israel "conflict" intractable stems from the wrongheaded belief that we are dealing with a conflict—and not an antagonism—that is resolvable within the existing Zionist (and Western) order of things. There is nothing leftist in failing to deal with the "bigger elephant" in the room: settler colonialism.

All of Illouz's notable work in making Palestinian duress and misery visible to Israelis crumbles; what ultimately matters is not Palestinian lives (collateral deaths). October 7 is about Jewish life and death, and only about Jewish life and death. Anti-colonial reason, in its hunger to understand the colonial situation (Fanon's enduring lesson), in its refusal to accept the image of Palestinians as intrinsically anti-Semitic and barbaric, betrayed the Jewish people. I see this reaction to the anti-colonial Left as marking a cultural shift. A fetishist disavowal no longer seems to be operational in it. What once operated in the form *I know very well about Palestinian misery, but all the same I believe in Israel's universalist aspirations, I believe in an Israel after Netanyahu* now becomes *I know very well about Palestinian misery, that the Occupation is grotesque, but all the same I don't care.*[151] *In this moment, when it comes to trauma, my kin come first.*

Illouz keeps insisting on the universalism of her Zionist position, but it is an anxious universalism, a universalism in crisis worried that Israel as such (and not only its right-wing governments) will lose credibility and be deemed an enemy of universal thought. She feels betrayed, blames this leftist abandonment on the Left's paranoid hermeneutic, that is, on its reflexive anti-Zionism and simplistic binarism originating in the anti-colonial thinking of Fanon and his heirs. Her strike at the anti-colonial Left is an attempt to reset the moral high ground, which had been slipping well before October 7 due in no small part to the successes of BDS. This is a nostalgic universalism that effortlessly opens to a Zionist muscular nationalism or, as Odeh Bisharat put it, to the "warm (and suffocating) embrace of ultranationalism."[152] Ultranationalism is a form of tribalism and does nothing to challenge Israel's anti-Palestinian collective psyche.

The Shoah and October 7 trump the Nakba and the Occupation—as if it was a matter of choosing. The ultranationalism nurtured and weaponized by the Israeli far Right does not need fetishist disavowal to sustain its operation. Ultranationalist logic is explicit: *we know very well about the 1948 Nakba, we don't find this piece of knowledge disruptive in the least,* and *we now want to complete it in the annihilation of Gaza.* Their anti-peace plan is total and permanent security through merciless conquest. Normalizing colonial subjugation is its business. Liberal Zionism, on the other hand, desperately needs fetishist disavowal to sustain its life, its settler innocence, to maintain the unbearable realities/atrocities of genocide at a distance. Sobering up (the eclipsing of the peace-loving Israeli liberals) moves you as far as possible from politics, from its demands to make the "unthinkable thinkable," as Žižek puts it.[153] Liberal Zionism's formal commitment to peace could always have been dangerously actualized—producing actual *change with change* (in which case decolonization is not a metaphor), but now liberal Zionism is spinning its wheels. It is caught in a paradox of its making. Support for Palestinian rights, which, in principle, separates liberals from their fascist counterparts, can never take place within the limits of Zionist reason alone, which, in practice, keeps rendering the *unthinkable unthinkable*.

The global Left should welcome the now visible convergence between the two positions, which can prompt a reframing. The false choice between political/religious Zionism and liberal/cultural Zionism was always a bogus opposition, an ideological ruse that makes liberals feel good about their support of a settler state and obscures their collusion with a genocidal state. For many Palestinians and their anti-colonial supporters, the choice has always clearly been between a muscular and expansionist Zionism on the one hand and an anti-colonial struggle on the other. It is up to the rest of the world now to take their stand.

Chapter 3
Decolonizing the Mind Under Occupation and Global Capitalism

Psychoanalysis is frequently viewed with suspicion. It is accused of being too Eurocentric, conservative, hegemonic, and inattentive to non-European cultures and histories. At best, psychoanalysis requires a thorough decolonization; at worst, it is determined to be complicit with Western domination and thus irredeemable. This chapter complicates both assessments, beginning with the flat indictment of psychoanalysis. Many critics adopting this line of argument fail to appreciate the discipline's transformation in recent decades and the expansion of its planetary reach, to which no other social theorist has more strongly contributed than Žižek. Far from deeming psychoanalysis an unquestioned interpretive authority, Žižek foregrounds its negativity, describing it as a kind of anti-hermeneutic. It is a skeptical practice that stresses the opacity of the signifier, the untranslatability of the patient's message into the analyst's preexisting interpretive horizon. The authority of the analyst is at stake. In the analytic session, the "subject supposed to know" does not stand for the analyst as such but rather marks his function in the treatment, indexing the patient's perception of the analyst as a figuration of absolute certainty who possesses knowledge of the patient's secret meaning or unconscious desire (disclosing and ceasing what had been concealed, what lay behind the patient's speech): the analyst "is supposed to know that from which no one can escape, as soon as he formulates it—quite simply, signification."[1] Without the idea of the "subject supposed to know," transference would be impossible, for it is predicated on the patient's (mis)identification of the analyst as a "subject supposed to know." Endowed with "a certain infallibility,"[2] the analyst, in the eyes of the patient, is capable of probing their unconscious desire at will, deciphering the meaning of the latter's hidden secrets and symptoms. In stark contrast, the aim of the analytic session is to *de-suppose* the analyst, to strip the analyst of that phantasmatic status. The analyst declines the power attributed to them by the transference: "he is not God for his patient."[3] Rather, the task of the analyst is to guide the patient, through free association, to discover, or rather to come to terms with the fact that *there is no ultimate authority; there is no big Other who knows*. "The whole psychoanalytic operation," Jason Glynos argues, "is aimed at deflating the analyst's own status as Subject-Supposed-to-Know by making the patient him- or herself do the work, only intervening so as to facilitate the subject's confrontation with his or her truth, namely, that there is no universal symbolic Guarantee."[4]

Still, concerns about merely translating the colonial situation into European psychoanalytic terms remain justified. To adapt Fanon's statement on Marxism from *The Wretched of the Earth*, we can say that psychoanalytic analysis should always be *slightly stretched* when it comes to addressing colonization. Not unlike the way Fanon stretches existentialism with the zone of nonbeing insofar as Blacks experience this zone as a quasi-permanent condition rather than a momentary existential crisis, as an *ontocide* or a destruction of their being in an anti-Black world, we must stretch psychoanalysis and "dislocate" the analytic scene in a way that makes it hospitable to non-European voices/concerns and attentive to the (neo)colonial situation.

To do so, this chapter takes up Fanon's crucial injunction to "decolonize the mind," teasing out its psychoanalytic, ontological, and political force, and potential limitations, in the pursuit of liberation. I focus here on the ways decolonizing the mind opens to an intervention that resonates with psychoanalysis' reflections on symbolic identity and the abyss of subjectivity. Decolonizing the mind worlds psychoanalysis, turning its historically Eurocentric concerns into planetary ones.

Decolonizing the mind indexes the degree to which colonial objective violence degrades the *ontology* of Indigenous peoples, the wretched of the earth. At the same time, we might ask with Eve Tuck and K. Wayne Yang how decolonizing the mind actually relates back to the project of decolonization. In their now classic "Decolonization Is Not a Metaphor," Tuck and Yang downplay the political priority of the Fanonian injunction: "Fanon told us . . . that decolonizing the mind is the first step, not the only step toward overthrowing colonial regimes. . . . Until stolen land is relinquished, critical consciousness does not translate into action that disrupts settler colonialism."[5] This is obviously true: critical consciousness might be necessary, but it is not enough; it is, in and of itself, *insufficient* to dismantle the machinery of settler colonialism. And yet, Tuck and Yang overstate their case in demoting the Fanonian injunction, reducing it to a "first step" among more important ones (claims to resources and land sovereignty) in the project of decolonization. It is not at all clear that decolonizing the mind is merely a metaphor. Or if it is a metaphor, it is a metaphor that discloses something about the dynamism of language and registers the limits of a liberal anti-racist critique that restricts its intervention at the level of representation—believing that words affect *thinking*, but not *being* itself. In the struggle against racial domination, racist *words* do ontological damage and thus must be given their full material and psychoanalytic weight. Words infiltrate bodies; they generate psycho-affective complexes and abject monsters. In Césaire's *A Tempest*, decolonizing the mind begins with purging Caliban's body, with forcibly removing all the venom of colonialism and all the traces of Prospero's discourse: "I'd spit you out, all your works and pomps! Your 'white' magic!"[6] Reversing a common saying, Hortense Spillers pointedly remarks, "Sticks and bricks *might* break our bones, but words will most certainly *kill* us."[7] This is why warriors of the imaginary constitute a counter-violence to the violence legislated by the colonial big Other, colonial society's symbolic rules and demands.

Decolonizing the mind, this chapter argues, must be understood as a materialist project. Excising the colonizer's collective fantasies from the colonized's mind/being involves the dialectical and arduous task of undoing what has been done *to* the colonized. Decolonizing the mind is an act of self-violence addressed to the colonized and colonizer; it is tantamount to symbolic suicide, a "self-beating"[8] of sorts, as Žižek puts it, which begins with a disruption of the subject's affective investments in her own identity. As it relates to the colonizer, it involves a process of de-decivilizing his identity, counterbalancing the colonizer's sense of murderous superiority. As it relates to the colonized, it proceeds first to overturn what has been produced by the internalization of the colonizer's discourse, and, second, it serves as a critical check on an imagined restored identity in an ideologically projected decolonial future.

But does decolonization's agenda—the introduction of complete disorder in the colonial world—still have purchase on the world, especially in a world where capitalism's tentacles touch us all? Žižek repeats Fanon's theorization that changes in the being of the colonized and colonizer entail an internal upheaval, an "ethical violence," a mutation in one's mode of being, but he also follows Huey P. Newton, a cofounder of the Black Panther Party, in his critique of decolonization. For Newton and Žižek, talk of decolonization distracts us from reckoning with the true enemy: global capitalism. This was the case in the early seventies for Newton and is even more true for Žižek today. But I think this break with decolonization is premature. Decolonization must itself be dislocated and reimagined in light of today's antagonisms.

To this end, this chapter explores the entanglement of settler colonialism and global capitalism, looking at Palestine/Israel as a site for decolonizing the mind under occupation and global capitalism. I argue that reading Fanon and Žižek together, stretching each one's work through that of the other, allows us to advance a vision of decolonization that returns to its anti-colonial kernel (and its emancipatory promises) and avoids its decolonial reappropriation. Decolonizing the mind under occupation means confronting a variety of necropolitical processes: *onticide*, *epistemicide*, *econocide*, among others. The racial matrix of the human, the erasure of Indigenous modes of knowing and living, along with infrastructural starvation, all weigh heavily on the prospects of decolonizing the mind. Is decoloniality an exit from the stale and stalled condition of decolonization? Is decolonizing the mind tantamount to delinking from coloniality and relinking to precolonial ways of thinking and living? If not, what role, if any, does culture play in the decolonization of the mind? Though I have strong reservations about decoloniality's political vision, I do believe that culture can serve as a form of resistance, a refusal to submit to coloniality's orders, and an answer to the colonist's underlying question, "Why don't you die or disappear?" *Existence is resistance*. Your existence—your culture's existence—is an affront to the colonizer and settler, a reminder and remainder of the state's colonial crimes and failures to eradicate the Indigenous population. Culture, for example, can, and often does, nurture the Palestinian right of *ressentiment*. *I will not forgive and forget about the Nakba (the catastrophe of 1948) and the Naksa (the setback of 1967); I will not forgive and forget Operation Iron Swords; I will not forget and forgive your carnage. The sight of body-parts and the smell of rotting flesh are seared in my memory. I will not be made an instrument in my own cultural and ontological erasure: peace talks Israeli/Western style.*

"One cannot divorce the combat for culture from the people's struggle for liberation," writes Fanon.[9] Culture matters. It is a source of psychic and material strength. But its elevation and defense are, I believe, only part of the picture. A Fanon-inflected decolonization of the mind adopts a skeptical and hysterical pose toward the authority of the master/settler/colonizer—*Why are we what you are telling us that we are?* Fanon writes: "Because it is a systematized negation of the other, a frenzied determination to deny the other any attribute of humanity, colonialism forces the colonized to constantly ask the question: 'Who am I in reality?'"[10]

Such an approach also interrogates all modes of resistance to domination. Decolonizing the mind centers on the existence of antagonisms within and without; there is no harmonious state to retreat to. Dialectically speaking, decolonizing the mind summons both the colonized and the colonizer to confront and move beyond the morbid and untenable reality of the present. It demands a libidinal divestment in given identitarian boundaries, a self-violence to meet the violent racial formation of the Zionist colonial regime. But as Fanon and Žižek stress, to revolutionize a system involves an agenda of complete disorder. Neither Palestinian particularity nor Israeli particularity will be left untouched.[11] The new human that emerges from the debris of coloniality will not be recovered but invented.

Stretching Psychoanalysis

Working from a decolonial perspective, Walter Mignolo voices a critique of psychoanalysis, encapsulating key concerns about the discipline's Western orientation and inability to address the needs of the colonized. Psychoanalysis' limitations are rooted, first, in its focus on the bourgeois family and its structures of trauma and, second, in its pretensions to universal validity and its failure to recognize its own cultural specificity. Psychoanalysis is not only unhelpful for the colonized and the non-European; it is imperialist in its orientation, assuming that the Western context is everyone's. On Mignolo's reading, decolonizing the mind would necessitate a rupture with psychoanalysis: "When I say . . . that psychoanalysis is irrelevant to healing colonial wounds, I am not making a critique of Freud and psychoanalysis. I am underscoring the consequences of assuming universal totality of knowledge, which is the politics of Eurocentric knowing."[12] Eurocentric knowing is premised on *epistemicide*: silencing non-Europeans, denying their agency, and barring their participation in any interpretive projects and official knowledge production.[13] What Mignolo terms the Colonial Matrix of Power (CMP) must be addressed instead through "decolonial analytics": "While psychoanalytic investigations foster a therapeutic cure, decolonial investigations invite decolonial healing. Psychoanalysis deals with traumas, decoloniality with colonial wounds."[14]

Beginning with this distinction between Western and colonized social structures and needs, Mignolo advocates delinking from the CMP by withdrawing and relinking to decolonial ways of thinking and ways of living. This decolonial project of healing is informed by Fanon's clinical experiences in Algeria. For Mignolo, Fanon discloses the irrelevance of psychoanalysis when it comes to decolonial struggles: "I am saying only that in many contexts psychoanalysis is out of place because the 'individual' is not the center and the communal is not the Western social. When Fanon perceived the limits of psychoanalysis for the Berber and Arab population . . . he was well acquainted—as a psychologist—with psychoanalysis, and he embodied the colonial wound of his own Black Caribbean experience in France."[15] Psychoanalysis is cast here as singly preoccupied with the Western bourgeois individual and her cure.[16] While psychoanalysis cares about curing the ego of the Western individual, Mignolo's decoloniality adopts a geopolitical focus, calling for delinking "from the paradigm of European modernity/rationality that engenders the wound in the same society it creates."[17] At best, psychoanalysis—which stands for European modern discourse broadly—is irrelevant; at worst, it is not the cure but the disease. Psychoanalysis is a bourgeois discipline invested in a decaying and repulsive bourgeois world, "a closed society where it's not good to be alive, where the air is rotten and ideas and people are putrefying."[18] The web of psychoanalysis further traps the non-European, tying her to coloniality's devastating ways: "Healing colonial wounds cannot be achieved without delinking from CMP because individual healing cannot happen in the same epistemic frame of CMP that inflicts colonial wounds. Psychoanalysis operates within the same frame that provokes the trauma in the individual."[19] For Mignolo, the concerns of psychoanalysis are not worldly as it purports but Western through and through; psychoanalysis foregrounds the analytic cure in its dealings with neurosis.[20] For this reason, Mignolo repeatedly insists that "colonial wounds could hardly be 'cured' by psychoanalysis, as Fanon clearly witnessed in Algeria. Colonial wounds had to be *healed* (not cured) by the wounded herself/himself in communal work, not in isolation."[21] Psychoanalysis is *of* the Western system whereas decoloniality seeks to extricate the non-European from it.

Decoloniality advocates a clean break with anything Western (since it always embodies the "universal totality of knowledge"). This is true of Marxism as well, though Mignolo's interest in a statement Fanon makes in *The Wretched of the Earth*—"Marxist analysis should always be slightly stretched when it comes to colonial issues"—suggests a different path, the possibility that oppositional discourses that emerge within Western thought can in fact be extended and made useful to colonized peoples. But while Mignolo adopts the language of stretching—"And I would add here, along with Fanon, James, and Wynter, that it [Marxist analysis] should always be stretched *when addressing the colonial matrix of power*"[22]—he also observes that "Marxism doesn't have a monopoly on critiques of capitalism or on visions of the future."[23] In effect, what matters more here is not so much the suppleness of Marxist analysis, but rather the need to devalue and displace Marxism as a master discourse, to open up space for a break, for other, non-Western critiques and approaches. The need for such a break is even clearer for Mignolo in the case of psychoanalysis, for what he is basically saying is that psychoanalysis not only ignores the colonial situation, but that its fundamental assumptions and procedures dictate that it *must* do so.

However, rather than rejecting psychoanalytic inquiry, Fanon himself centered it in *Black Skin, White Masks*, stating on the contrary that such an approach is indispensable:

> We believe, in fact, that only a psychoanalytic interpretation of the black problem can reveal the affective disorders responsible for this network of complexes. We are aiming for a complete lysis of this morbid universe.
>
> As a psychoanalyst I must help my patient to "*consciousnessize*" his unconscious, to no longer be tempted by a hallucinatory lactification, but also to act along the lines of a change in social structure.[24]

And because "we are in completely different worlds," Fanon insists that what is needed for the colonial situation is: "Psychoanalytic interpretation of the black man's lived experience" and "psychoanalytic interpretation of the black myth."[25] Though meditating on the unconscious appears as a white privilege, not readily available to the racially subjugated of the world, those who are wounded and made to dwell in the zone of nonbeing ("since the racial drama is played out in the open, the black man has no time to 'unconsciousnessize' it," writes Fanon[26]), the anti-colonial Fanon still insists on the hermeneutic and transformative value of psychoanalysis. His writings on Algeria, in particular, draw attention to the sociopolitical contexts of suffering and trauma.

In *Psychoanalysis Under Occupation*, Lara Sheehi and Stephen Sheehi embrace a similar stance. While they acknowledge a tradition of psychoanalysis that "depoliticizes and diminishes, if not dismisses, the conditions under which Palestinians are subjects of Israeli colonial rule,"[27] they focus their energy on the ways psychoanalysis can and does speak to the "psycho-affective effects of colonialism."[28] Psychoanalysis on this view is in fact indispensable for decolonization, supplying Palestinians (both as clinicians and patients) with the tools and spaces needed for resistance and liberation—working through society's distortions—and not merely adjustment or adaptation to the inhuman world of the Occupation. Psychoanalysis is particularly well-situated to account for the ways the Occupation normalizes a "sadistic regime of *asphyxiation*."[29] In a telling anecdote, Sheehi and Sheehi recall the comments of Samah Jabr, director of the Mental Health Unit at the Palestinian Ministry of Health: "When an Israeli woman psychoanalyst complained that Israelis just need space and time to breathe among the tensions created by the 'Palestine-Israel conflict,' Jabr replied: 'We live in a reality where the more Israelis breathe, the more Palestinians choke.'"[30] For Zionists to breathe, Palestinians must not. This is a disturbing conclusion. Psychoanalysis pushes us to reckon with the reality of coloniality.

Fanon's stretching of psychoanalysis recenters race and the colonial situation. He is not distorting but dislocating the collective unconscious, where "dislocation" entails, as Žižek puts it, "that elements are thoroughly re-contextualized, integrated into a new symbolic and social space which confers on them a new meaning unrelated to the original meaning—one can in no way 'deduce' this new meaning from the original one."[31] Fanon's dislocation or stretching remains both inventive and critical precisely because his anti-colonial critique does not mechanically reproduce psychoanalytic truisms (about the Oedipal family,[32] for instance) nor does it open to identity politics or "race reductionism" (of the sort: "all mental disorders as 'nothing but' the consequence of imperialism and colonialism"[33]). Samah Jabr and Elisabeth Berger put it succinctly: "Fanon saw the need to integrate the understanding of individual psychology and pathology with an analysis of the social forces that act upon, with, and through the individual psyche."[34] It is ill-advised to decouple Palestinian mental health from the colonial situation or the "context of dispossession."[35] Fanon has no interest in reifying the pathology of the colonized. Quite the contrary, the overwhelming thrust in

Fanon's oeuvre is to jam the impulse to ontologize the wretched (via essence or context), to seal, in this instance, the Palestinian in the deadening Occupation, or "the black man in his blackness"—while simultaneously foregrounding the devastating impact of the white gaze in an anti-Black or colonial world.[36]

In his tart rebuttal to Mignolo's reading, Žižek points out that, far from authorizing a decolonial retreat from universality into non-Western particularity, Fanon did not simply cut his ties with European thinkers ("Fanon himself . . . dealt extensively and intensively with Hegel, psychoanalysis, Sartre, and even Lacan"[37]), but actively adopted and adapted Western thought to productively fit the colonial situation.[38] Žižek's psychoanalytic-Marxist interventions ought to be read in light of Fanon's own worlding of psychoanalysis. In this light, conscripting Fanon to a decolonial project represents an ironically un-Fanonian move, distorting Fanon's commitment to a global solidarity that did not exclude Europeans or the labor of psychoanalysis. Consider:

> I am a man, and I have to rework the world's past from the very beginning. I am not just responsible for the slave revolt in Saint Domingue. Every time a man has brought victory to the dignity of the spirit, every time a man has said no to an attempt to enslave his fellow man, I have felt a sense of solidarity with his act.[39]

Exceptionalism, and the separation of distinct zones of difference that it relies on, is anathema to Fanon's politics (I will return to this matter in more detail in Chapter 5). Fanon's work suggests instead that overinvestment in the non-European's difference or cultural diversity, in "subaltern perspectives,"[40] can point to a form of narcissism itself in need of decolonization.

Fanon's anti-identitarian ethos resonates with Žižek's own understanding of the subject of psychoanalysis, which clashes with the reduction of psychoanalysis to particularized, purely Western concerns: *curing* private bourgeois individuals of their neurosis. Provincializing psychoanalysis need not mean abandoning psychoanalysis. Rather, provincialization is the first step in worlding psychoanalysis, which begins precisely by troubling claims both to certainty and to the "individual" as the unit of classic psychoanalysis. At the same time, psychoanalysis has always been concerned with the political and thus relevant to politics. The unconscious always exceeds the contours of the individual. "The clinical is political," Nadia Bou Ali writes, "because the unconscious is always already social."[41] Symptoms have social causes. As Françoise Vergès insightfully discerns, this sense of the unconscious aligns with Fanon's outlook; it resonated with the ways he understood "individual alienation and political alienation" to be "related" insofar as "both are the product of social, political, and cultural conditions that must be transformed."[42] This commitment to transformation also tapped into psychoanalysis' skeptical propensities. Commenting on psychoanalysis as practiced by Lacan, Žižek notes, "the most outstanding feature of [Lacan's] teaching is permanent self-questioning," or "permanent hystericization"[43] of the Master's knowledge. This quote brings to mind Fanon's concluding sentence of *Black Skin, White Masks*: "My final prayer: O my body, always make me a man who questions!"[44] O my body, make me a man who refuses racial interpellation! Skepticism emerges as a technique of the self, in the Foucauldian sense, a technology of revolutionary self-care or "voluntary inservitude."[45] Hysterical questioning of the colonizer is Fanon's categorical imperative.

Fanon's sociogeny—as he argues, "we shall see that the alienation of the black man is not an individual question. Alongside phylogeny and ontogeny, there is also sociogeny"[46]—troubles received (Western) knowledge *and* stretches psychoanalysis, translating it into a language that speaks to the *historical* condition of the wretched of the earth. It leaves behind a normative legacy of psychoanalysis that seeks to define the normal/abnormal. Fanon troubles the question of normativity when it comes to Black subjects dwelling in an anti-Black world: "A normal black child, having grown up with a normal family, will become abnormal at the slightest contact with the white world."[47] The white world, in its "normal" operation, cannot but generate enduring complexes in racialized bodies. Fanon's decolonization of the mind speaks to this situation, but his response clashes with any appeal to cultural rootedness as a form of withdrawal from coloniality or delinking/relinking to one's precolonial culture.

Ross Posnock is fully justified in adapting Julia Kristeva's words "against origins and starting from" to describe Fanon's anti-identitarian politics.[48] To elevate or mystify precolonial reality means to remove or cover over any structural tensions at the heart of Indigenous culture. "Non-European particularity," explains Ilan Kapoor, is imbued "with a certain authenticity" and is in principle untainted and thus retrievable by the decolonial critic.[49] It is this dimension of the influential *Négritude* movement that spurs Fanon's critique. If Fanon praises *Négritude*'s anti-colonial stance and its crucial work to raise Black political consciousness, he still finds its phantasmatic claims of a "golden past" disconcertingly vague and counterproductive; indeed, "to be locked in the substantialized 'tower of the past'" is detrimental to decolonization and genuine liberation.[50] Fetishization of cultural difference always risks playing into the hands of the colonizers, who prefer to fix non-Europeans in their otherness, who are the first to champion "the rescue of indigenous traditions" and to style themselves as "defenders of indigenous style."[51] Fanon does not follow the *Négritude* movement in singularizing Blackness, in nurturing and protecting its authenticity, but stresses instead that "there is not *one* Negro—there are *many* black men."[52]

Whereas *Négritude* then and decoloniality now promise an end to alienation by way of return to a harmonious Whole, Fanon's concept of disalienation proposes a more nuanced assessment. Disalienation is the fruit of anti-colonial, Marxist, and psychoanalytic labor. Disalienation embodies the labor of negativity;

it reorients our gaze to the brutality of "social and economic realities," which affect both Natives and settlers, colonized and colonizers, Black folks and white oppressors, without, of course, obfuscating the differential allocation of power that colonial/white privilege presupposes.[53] To put psychoanalysis to the service of decolonizing the mind is to put it in relation with the non-European and colonialism. It means thinking disalienation in all its facets and complexities. As Sheehi and Sheehi observe, "the psychotherapeutic process [involving Palestinian patients and Palestinian therapists] produces disalienation, a consciousness in the colonial patient, an awareness that they are sociogenic subjects forged by the violence pressed upon them and the material of their individual and collective subjectivity that resides in their body and psyche."[54] The health of the colonized, her disalienation, the possibility of "forgiveness and repair," are all predicated on the radical transformation of the colonial surroundings. Sheehi and Sheehi quote Fanon approvingly: "there will be an authentic disalienation only to the degree to which things, in the most materialistic meaning of the word, will have been restored to their proper places."[55] Within the settler-colonial order of things, disalienation will be wanting. The psychic and the political are intertwined. Fanon once told Beauvoir that "all political leaders should be psychiatrists as well."[56] For disalienation to take hold, the colonial state of affairs must be overturned.

Antagonism Within and Without

Like Fanon, Žižek unmasks the false universalism of Western discourse without retreating to a pristine mode of precolonial existence or becoming mired in "a non-reflective anti-Eurocentrism."[57] Demystification of abstract universalism does not necessarily open to difference, to a view of difference extracted and liberated from Western grasp. Žižek often turns to the example of the Dalits or "untouchables," members of the lowest caste in India, in order to imagine antagonisms otherwise. The first antagonism is obvious enough: the colonized Indians vs. the British colonizers. For Žižek, however, this framing of the antagonistic relation doesn't exhaust the colonial situation. For the Dalits, the antagonism from without was supplemented by an antagonism from within. "True victory over colonization" did not mean a return to any "'authentic' precolonial existence, even less any 'synthesis' between modern civilization and pre-modern origins." No, the Dalits wanted "the *fully accomplished loss of these pre-modern origins*." What British colonialism and its dissemination of the English language paradoxically opened up was an opportunity to dispel the fantasy of wholeness, to denaturalize the positionality of the Dalits in society and to move the underground of their culturally ontologized inferiority: "A large proportion of Dalits welcomed English and in fact even the colonial encounter as a whole. For Ambedkar (the foremost political figure of the Dalit caste) and his legatees, British colonialism—unwittingly and incidentally—gives scope for the so-called rule of law and formal equality for all Indians."[58] The Dalits took advantage of the ontological upheaval brought about by British colonialism by turning to the "antagonism inherent"[59] in India's society. *The colonial wound enabled as it disabled*.

For Fanon and Žižek, both class and race reductionisms are to be avoided. A classic Marxist intervention foregrounds political economy. It aims at correcting the distortions of the libidinal economy: *don't misrecognize your true enemy (capitalism) for your racialized neighbor (the timeless object of scorn and phobia)*. Fanon and Žižek proceed by heuristically separating alienation generated by phantasmatic aspirations (the desire to become white, to replace the colonizer, etc.) from alienation rooted in one's material existence. The alienation stemming from collective fantasies involves an overcoming or traversal of the subject's fantasies of plenitude, and the correlative avowal that a degree of alienation is a permanent feature of all human existence—though, in this morbid universe, alienation is also lived differently by differently racialized subjects.[60] This alienation finds its origins in the workings of ideology, which projects the fantasy of personal and social wholeness, and thus covers up the symbolic order's inherent instability. The colonized's desire to return to Indigenous ways of living and thinking untouched by colonization feeds a dubious logic of completeness, fostering nostalgic beliefs in a phantasmatic return to the full plenitude of unsullied enjoyment, to "*a time before the settler*"; my alienation would disappear if the white colonizers leave our land.[61] Against this model of withdrawal, Žižek insists on social reality's incompleteness and dividedness, exposing the social antagonisms and "structural inconsistency" of the symbolic order—a psychoanalytic understanding of reality that is distorted in attempts to resolve constitutive alienation as a purely historical wound.[62] Decoloniality generates the illusion of a healed wholeness by locating the cause of the colonized's alienation *exclusively* in the colonial encounter (which can, in principle, be overcome): decoloniality mistakes alienation as primarily a disruption of social reality, rather than seeing it as one of its main features. By contrast, a worlding psychoanalysis, following Fanon and Žižek, refuses to fill the *gap* between all of reality and the colonized's experience of it by explaining the inconsistencies in reality away, attributing them solely to an external force like CMP that can be removed. As discussed in Chapter 1, the psychoanalytic subject is precisely *not* sustained by a nostalgic yearning for a lost/absent ideal, the embodiment of the non-European's true nature/ontology.

Fanonian critique does not stop at the colonial world, or to put it more accurately, does not isolate the colonial situation from the economic situation. The alienation stemming from historico-material conditions also demands a direct confrontation with the crushing realities of racial capitalism. But to fully engage capitalism's voracious presence in the lives of the wretched, Fanon turns to a psychoanalytic register. Libidinal economy meets political economy.

A sociogenesis harnesses the psychoanalytic gaze to what Fanon calls the "collective unconsciousness," which he describes as "the repository of prejudices, myths, and collective attitudes of a particular group . . . it is cultural, i.e., it is acquired."[63] The collective unconsciousness refers to a colonial/anti-Black libidinal economy: the implicit rules and principles regulating personal and collective desires and fears, the production, circulation, and consumption of the *Blackened* wretched of the earth. Simply put, a given society's libidinal economy governs our deep sense of who affectively matters, belongs, counts—and who effectively does not. Mignolo might retort that this is Fanon's rebuff of Eurocentrism, evidenced in psychoanalysis' allegedly intrinsic abstract universalism, which is accused of ignoring the colonial situation. But Mignolo's binarization (European vs. Non-European) is quite foreign to the anti-colonial brand of psychoanalysis espoused by Fanon, who, on the contrary, as I have been arguing, insists on the need to move beyond easy Manicheanism, beyond the notion that "it was once all so simple with the bad on one side and the good on the other."[64] Fanon, however, does make a further distinction between differing forms of historical (vs constitutive) alienation:

> The motivations for disalienating a physician from Guadeloupe are essentially different from those for the African construction worker in the port at Abidjan. For the former, alienation is almost intellectual in nature. It develops because he takes European culture as a means of detaching. For the latter, it develops because he is victim to a system based on the exploitation of one race by another and the contempt for one branch of humanity by a civilization that considers itself superior.[65]

Fanon's interpretive sensitivity to the multiple causes of historical alienation reminds the reader of his Marxist framework and the importance of class struggle. Fanonian decolonization does not ignore political economy; moreover, it is inhospitable to identitarian attachments and identity politics. Decolonizing the mind surely must reckon with society's political economy and scrutinize, as Fanon does in *The Wretched of the Earth*, the emergence of the Black elite who push out the white colonizers only to replace them. Again, "some blacks can be whiter than the whites."[66]

The antagonism within can fully emerge retroactively after the encounter with the colonizer (as in the case of the Dalits in India) or it can emerge as a by-product of the encounter, when there is complicity with the occupying power. The Palestinian Authority (PA) is a case in point of an internal antagonism erupting in *a time after the settler*. While the antagonism from without is clearly discernible in the Zionist settler/occupier, Ali Abunimah reminds us that the PA is an enemy within the West Bank. We can witness the PA's shameless complicity with Israel on two interrelated levels. First, the PA complies with the settler state's orders, doing its dirty work on a regular basis. As Tamara Nassar documents, PA forces quell "Palestinian opposition and resistance to help Israel maintain its occupation in the West Bank while promoting the illusion of Palestinian autonomy and representation."[67] Second, President Mahmoud Abbas and the PA benefit economically from the Occupation. While purporting to advance the national interests of the Palestinian people, the PA is enriching the pockets of a small Palestinian elite class "by deepening its political, economic, and military ties with Israel and the United States, often explicitly undermining efforts by Palestinian civil society to resist."[68] The neoliberal capture of Occupied Palestine is undeniable, as evidenced by the widening economic gap between the haves (the leaders of the PA, their associates, the Palestinian bourgeoisie, etc.) and the have-nots (the permanently unemployed, the low-wage laborers, the living-dead of Gaza, etc.). Let's not forget that the call for a two-state solution coming from Western powers and Arab allies is a yearning to return to the Oslo days, which gives us what Toufic Haddad names "Palestine Ltd."[69] Palestinian liberation gave way to the "neoliberal conflict resolution" model, where the Western donor class's involvement in aiding the PA was predicated on the belief that "the market's invisible hand would guide Israelis and Palestinians to peace, provided the international community financially and politically backed this arrangement and facilitated the creation of an adequate incentives arrangement."[70] The PA ushered in a post-political reality, foreclosing the political from the Symbolic:

> It is almost as though the generations of sacrifice of the national liberation movement which struggled to realize "Palestine"—"from the river to the sea" as a homeland saying goes—has now been realized but in a transmogrified form. Palestine Ltd. becomes neoliberalism's Janus-faced version of the former Palestine, emptied of any emancipatory content, and replaced with the economic and political structures which enforce and deepen the state of oppression and fragmentation which Palestinians sought to overcome in the first place through their national liberation movement.[71]

Under PA leadership, freedom and social justice lose their purchase on the world. Post-political Palestine is an Occupied Palestine ready for business and/as corruption. As Michel Warschawski also notes, "the Oslo period was the period of the most classically colonial relationship with the natives: favors, a class of go-betweens to manage the occupied population's daily life, and a native police to keep order."[72] Oslo did nothing to stall Zionist futurology: Israel is slowly inching its way to a Greater Israel.

As a general principle, Israel sadistically punishes its Palestinian collaborators: though the PA typically acquiesce to Western pressure and does the bidding of the occupier, Israel's "subcontractor"[73] is always accused of not doing enough for Israeli security, failing to adequately crack down on Palestinian resistance.

The PA's limited hegemony creates the conditions for what some have described as a "double colonization."⁷⁴ Persecuted by the IOF/settlers and agents of the PA, Palestinians are faced with innumerable challenges. Palestinian civil society yearns for more; Palestinians desire a new order. Their discontent with the neoliberal status quo festers. Soberly, Abunimah paints a grim picture of the struggles ahead, alerting us to the "antagonism inherent" in Occupied Palestine: "If these are indeed the [neoliberal] foundations of a future Palestinian state, then a people who have struggled for so long for liberation from Zionism's colonial assault can only look forward to new, more insidious forms of economic and political bondage."⁷⁵ Is decoloniality able to meet these demands, these internal and external problems facing Palestinians? An ability to think anti-coloniality *with* class struggle appears lacking in the decolonial arsenal.

Decolonization as Materialist Project

In 1972, Huey P. Newton, cofounder and theorist of the Black Panther Party, in a conversation with the renowned Freudian psychoanalyst Erik Erikson, expressed even greater skepticism about the political viability of nationalist forms of decolonization in light of America's ever-expanding hegemonic global reach. Since no colony or neocolony, no matter who runs it, is protected from the claws of US imperialism, Newton stresses the historical rupture that complicates the old paradigm of Third World politics:

> We in the Black Panther Party saw that the United States was no longer a nation. It was something else; it was more than a nation. It had not only expanded its territorial boundaries, but it had expanded all of its controls as well. We called it an empire. Now at one time the world had an empire in which the conditions of rule were different—the Roman Empire. The difference between the Roman and the American empires is that other nations were able to exist external to and independent of the Roman Empire because their means of exploration, conquest, and control were all relatively limited.
>
> But when we say "empire" today, we mean precisely what we say. An empire is a nation-state that has transformed itself into a power controlling *all* the world's lands and people.
>
> We believe that there are no more colonies or neocolonies. If a people is colonized, it must be possible for them to decolonize and become what they formerly were. But what happens when the raw materials are extracted and labor is exploited within a territory dispersed over the entire globe? When the riches of the whole earth are depleted and used to feed a gigantic industrial machine in the imperialist's home? Then the people and the economy are so

integrated into the imperialist empire that it's impossible to "decolonize," to return to the former conditions of existence.

If colonies cannot "decolonize" and return to their original existence as nations, then nations no longer exist. Nor, we believe, will they ever exist again.[76]

Instead of rallying behind the familiar project of decolonization, Newton powerfully argues for a critique of global capitalism in a kind of worlding of solidarity.

Žižek, who favorably quotes the passage above, follows Newton closely, underscoring "the limitation of local (national) resistance to the global reign of capital," rhetorically asking, "Is this not our predicament today, much more than in Newton's time?"[77] But I wonder if the will to decolonize here is not given short shrift. Fanon would surely agree with the need to put political economy front and center (a "decolonized capitalism"[78] is still a capitalism, which means no liberation from exploitation: "the people discover that the iniquitous phenomenon of exploitation can assume a black or Arab face"[79]), but he would also put into relief the need for decolonizing the mind as a psychoanalytic intervention, a way to dislodge the lure of colonized identity (politics) and block the pull to retreat into particularity. A critique of global capitalism cannot sideline the need to scrutinize this seemingly intractable passion for identity. If Newton expands Fanon's concerns beyond the pitfalls of national consciousness, factoring in the monstrous expansion of the US Empire, Žižek dismisses the project of decolonization in, I would say, its current decolonial mode. A truly liberatory decolonizing project, as I have been arguing, requires a different framing, one that takes seriously the full psychic and material force of decolonizing the mind—to decolonize in the Fanonian sense is precisely *not* to become what the colonized formerly were; it is to struggle against the human propensity of wanting to return to one's "original existence." It is a critical engagement of/with the colonized in her compromised and divided form.

Fanon situates decolonizing of the mind as a process that inescapably requires reckoning with global capitalism. As Žižek points out, "What Fanon clearly saw is that today's global world is capitalist, and as such cannot be effectively problematized from the standpoint of local pre-capitalist cultures."[80] While Mignolo often treats capitalism as a Western obsession rather than a global problem, I find the compartmentalization of capitalism along with its Marxist critique both unhelpful and problematic. Not unlike Afropessimism, decoloniality is underpinned by a separatist logic that undermines the possibility of universal politics and cross-racial solidarities. In his polemic against Žižek, Mignolo avers: "In the non-European World, communism is part of the problem rather than the solution. Which doesn't mean that if you are not communist, in the non-European world, you are capitalist."[81] Decolonial activists and scholars fight against "the necessity of war," the logic of "success and competition which engender corruption and selfishness" and fight for the goals of "harmony" and "the plenitude of life."[82] But Mignolo's decolonial ideals of "harmony" and "plenitude of life" are so abstract, devoid of substance, as to make them ripe for ideological manipulation. Arjun Appadurai is right in detecting in decoloniality's proponents a penchant for the precolonial "pristine" and a tendency toward the "cultification of the Indigenous." What happens to antagonisms (from within and without) when harmony and plenitude (the possibility of a frictionless world free from the evils of capitalism) are posited as ideals?[83] As with Occupied Palestine, it is wrong to conceive of neoliberalism as exclusively a Western problem. Relinking to a local pre-capitalist culture, even if such a thing is possible, will not shield you from the reach of global capitalism.

Decoloniality's merit lies in exposing the reality of *epistemicide*, the silencing of Indigenous peoples, the denial of their agency, and barring of their involvement in official knowledge production. But it remains unclear how delinking from the West (including its agitation for class struggle) would immunize the Global South from the relentless and voracious march of globalized capitalism. As Ilan Kapoor points out, "Mignolo looks to 'delinking from capitalism' epistemologically as though decolonized knowledge production will undo not just neoliberal ideology but the structures of global capitalism."[84] Decoloniality depicts the subaltern/Global South somewhat naively as though they were free from contradiction, failure, or disagreement. Delinking from Western narratives of resistance will not halt nor redirect the march of capital. Decolonization and the critique of capitalism must go hand in hand. For Fanon, decolonization was never about auto-enclosure, a retreat into one's borders, nor was it about identitarian politics or nationalism: it is "an agenda for total disorder."[85] With the event of decolonization, nothing remains the same, "everything has to be rethought. . . . Perhaps everything needs to be started over again."[86]

Mignolo approvingly cites Jean-Paul Sartre's prologue to Fanon's *The Wretched of the Earth,* in which Sartre indicates a shift in Fanon's audience: "Listen, pay attention, Fanon is no longer talking to us."[87] Sartre's commentary is however not without its shortcomings, and to imagine that Fanon is now exclusively addressing a non-European readership distorts the revolutionary's ethos and desired reach. How else can we explain Fanon's prolonged engagement with Sartre himself, and how he disseminated the ideas of Sartre's *Critique of Dialectical Reason*, which came out in 1960, to the Armée de Libération Nationale (ALN), the military wing of the National Liberation Front (FLN)? For Fanon, the anti-colonial struggle needed to harness European thought, to dislocate it, in order to unleash its critical and universalist force. As Adam Shatz points out, Sartre's Marxist work resonated with Fanon, "Sartre's formulations—about the dehumanization of the colonized, counterviolence, the battle against scarcity and dispossession, and decolonization as the creation of a new world—struck a powerful chord with Fanon."⁸⁸ While we don't know specifically what Fanon lectured about at ALN training camps, Robert Bernasconi interestingly speculates that Fanon introduced the Algerian militants to Sartre because "it was not enough . . . that these fighters were committed to their particular struggle. He wanted them in addition to think about the struggle in more global terms."⁸⁹ It is safe to say that Sartre and Mignolo overstate Fanon's turn to a new audience of colonial subjects, especially in light of the fact that Fanon ends *The Wretched of the Earth* with an inclusive address, a radical call for solidarity over sectarianism: "For Europe, for ourselves, and for humanity, comrades, we must turn over a new leaf, we must work out new concepts, and try to set afoot a new man."⁹⁰

The invention of this "new man" today continues to face many obstacles from within and without. From without, global capitalism has reshaped the struggle for national sovereignty, making the return to a precolonial reality a ruse and a cruel fantasy (as Newton and Žižek argue). From within, Fanon witnessed the psychic investment in the colonizers' ways of being among the colonized intellectuals and the elite:

> The [colonized] intellectual who . . . has adopted the abstract, universal values of the colonizer is prepared to fight so that colonist and colonized can live in peace in a new world. But what he does not see, because precisely colonialism and all its modes of thought have seeped into him, is that the colonist is no longer interested in staying on and coexisting once the colonial context has disappeared.⁹¹

Rather than fostering anti-colonial consciousness, colonized intellectuals and the native bourgeoisie reproduced the colonial order and its naturalized state-violence. "Decolonization is always a violent event," writes Fanon, and this violence must also be guided toward internal colonialism, the colonized's own psyche.⁹² Decolonization demands self-violence, a traumatic undoing of the self—a "tabula rasa," that is, the active clearing, or rather scraping, of the colonized's slate.⁹³ This type of violence, as Erik Vogt puts it, is "directed primarily against those fantasies that keep subjects bound to their own subjection and oppression by promising, for instance, some particular cultural or even national identity supposedly providing alternative avenues of escape from the capitalist (neo)-colonialist system."⁹⁴ Fanonian self-violence is first and foremost a counter-violence, a violence aimed at weakening the hold of hegemonic fantasies, a painful experience of revolutionary undoing, an attempt to throw off the yoke of colonization (what is responsible for the subjugated's inferiority complex) in the name of a political vision. Žižek puts into relief the pedagogical value of Fanonianism insofar as it foregrounds the "'work of the negative,' of the Hegelian process of *Bildung*, of educational self-formation," casting a shattering self-violence "as a violent reformation of the very substance of subject's being."⁹⁵

We can further describe this self-violence as a kind of symbolic suicide, linking it to the Lacanian act. Decolonization functions as both an individual and collective act, radically transforming the social coordinates of the wretched: "An act does not occur *within* the given horizon of what appears to be 'possible'—it redefines the very contours of what is possible (an act accomplishes what, within the given symbolic universe, appears to be 'impossible,' yet it changes its conditions so that it creates retroactively the conditions of its own possibility)."[96] Alenka Zupančič underscores the ontologically transformative impact on the subject of the act: "Every real act is a 'suicide of the subject.' The subject may be born again in this act, but only as a new subject. The act is an act only if afterwards the subject is no longer the same as before. It is always structured as a symbolic suicide."[97] This "new subject" reborn through this suicidal act recalls Fanon's framing of decolonization as "truly the creation of new men."[98] Decolonization is a project of liberation: "The 'thing' colonized becomes a man through the very process of liberation."[99]

The identity of the (formerly) colonized is thus at stake; there is no partial decolonization, where *only* the Indigenous or colonized's difference is recognized and affirmed (the ideological illusion of a wholeness restored), overcoming their *epistemicide* by delinking from the West and relinking to their precolonial culture (satisfying the demands of decoloniality), feeding, in turn, a pacified, depoliticized "harmonious" global multiculturalism fully compatible with the viciousness of global capitalism. This is why decolonizing the mind must be given its full psychoanalytic force. As an act, it seeks nothing less than to traverse the fundamental fantasy of the (formerly) colonized, the Indigenous as framed and contained in its rooted identity by decoloniality. The act comes with no guarantee of success—whence the drama of decolonization. A would-be act can always miss its target: "This lack of guarantee is what the critics cannot tolerate; they want an Act without risk—not without empirical risks, but without the much more radical 'transcendental risk' that the Act will not only simply fail, but radically misfire."[100] Without the possibility of radical failure, then, no act could ever take place. When an act does happen, when the impossible is rendered possible, when, for example, the sway of colonialism loses its psychic and material hold on the subjugated, the subject of the act undergoes an ontological transformation; "you" are no longer the same as before, as you were prior to the act, to the event of decolonization.[101]

Revolutionary vs. Reactionary Suicide

By aligning "decolonizing the mind" with symbolic suicide, are we pulling the rug out from under the feet of Indigenous scholars and activists committed to securing land sovereignty? Isn't a successful decolonization ultimately a return to sovereignty? This is, after all, the Afropessimist critique of sovereignty: if, for the Native, an atavistic *"time before the settler"*[102] exists, for the Black person there is no return to plenitude possible. The Afropessimists decry political sovereignty, seeing it as underpinned by a specious metaphysics, one that generates and relegates the unsovereign to the zone of nonbeing.[103] The slave/Black stands as the constitutive other of the master/sovereign human, unworthy and incapable of (enjoying the fruits of) sovereignty. Cognizant and generally supportive of the work of the Afropessimists, Indigenous scholars retort, however, that Afropessimism's blistering critique of sovereignty must be tempered by an account of the settler-colonial situation. Jettisoning sovereignty, ruling out any possibility for agency or self-determination, would be tantamount to what Indigenous scholars Glen Coulthard and Leanne Simpson describe as a "form of auto-genocide."[104] To give up claims to Indigenous land and jurisdiction is to embrace nothing short of a collective suicide. Sovereignty is something Indigenous communities *cannot not want*.[105]

Moreover, however, we can add that Indigenous sovereignty need not be tethered to a murderous vision of humanity dictated by the logic *I am sovereign because you're not*. Anishinaabe curator Wanda Nanibush ties this other sovereignty to her deployment of "Indigenous with a 'capital I,'" which, she affirms, "is about sovereignty movements, land rights, the rights of the earth, return to Indigenous women's role in our societies and much more dreaming that cannot be contained in a policy document."[106] Indigenous sovereignty dislocates Western sovereignty. It departs from it in insisting on collective survival; affirming the goal of Indigenous sovereignty may not be an Afropessimist embrace of abolition (the unsovereign), but it disrupts various settler techniques of pacification and the settler's ideological agenda for redressing grievances. It points to an alternative way of being-in-the-world.

I want to meditate further on the relation between national sovereignty and symbolic suicide. Are the two mutually exclusive? If a Fanonian decolonization must involve a degree of self-violence, and if a Lacanian act's emancipatory force lies in its disruptive potential, in its potential for ontological upheaval, sovereignty (of the wretched) might be better understood as the fruit of a process that affirms symbolic suicide rather than avoiding it. How we get to national sovereignty has, of course, everything to do with the ways we conceive of symbolic suicide. In a 2019 *New York Times* op-ed, Danny Danon, then Israel's ambassador to the United Nations, made a request that Palestinians accept national surrender, something akin to "national suicide."[107] Danon positions himself as a truth-teller, delivering to Palestinians the "uncomfortable truth" about "Palestinian national identity": it is motivated not by building a better life for its people but by destroying Israel.[108] A familiar Orientalization of Palestinians sets in. Danon aligns Israel with the West, while Palestinian desire for unity and political liberation fosters a "culture of hate and incitement" toward

Israel and its Jewish people. There is no Palestinian liberation without its anti-Semitic supplement. Danon argues that it is in the interest of both Palestinians and Israelis that Mahmood Abbas accept that they have been defeated, so that the Arabs should give up on their aspirations for statehood and stop engaging in fruitless acts of terrorism. "Knowing when to give up is often the first step to making peace," writes Danon.[109] Basically, Palestinians need to act like adults and concede Israeli victory. Currently, they are acting like immature children in going on about national sovereignty. Once they accept the reality of defeat—and thus embrace national suicide—both parties could live in peace. Danon's call for national suicide here shares nothing with the symbolic violence connected to either Fanon or Žižek. Danon is really calling for the completion of colonization, for more colonizing of the Palestinian mind: accept your inferior place and adjust to your new (even more submissive) role in Greater Israel, that is, in the actualized Zionist order of things. As Sheehi and Sheehi sum it up, "The cognitive slippage, logical fallacies, and structural solipsism within Danon's argumentation represent the *reality-bending* of settler colonialism that has otherwise established itself as hegemonic normalcy."[110] Danon's perverse solution, dripping with paternalism, Orientalism, and the ideology of "might makes right," can only imagine coexistence with Palestinians as complete submission.

Another symbolic suicide is possible. Žižek is keen to frame his discussions of symbolic suicide in relation to the wretched, the part of no-part. This makes sense insofar as the liberal Left has turned these sites for potential ontological upheaval into a symbolic factory for identity politics tethered to a post-political futurology (Danon's fantasized decaffeinated Palestinians fit this identitarian logic). And yet, as Žižek observes, you cannot simply transform one piece of the dyad and revolutionize the system. In addressing Black symbolic suicide more specifically, Žižek begins his discussion with the controversy surrounding Terblanche Delport. At a Johannesburg conference in South Africa, Delport, a white, male scholar from South Africa, provoked consternation in his audience when he called on his country's white people "to commit suicide as an ethical act." Delport elaborates on what he meant:

> The reality [in South Africa] is that most white people spend their whole lives only engaging black people in subservient positions—cleaners, gardeners, etc. My question is then how can a person not be racist if that's the way they live their lives? The only way then for white people to become part of Africa is to not exist as white people anymore. If the goal is to dismantle white supremacy, and white supremacy is white culture and vice versa, then the goal has to be to dismantle white culture and ultimately white people themselves. The total integration into Africa by white people will also automatically then mean the death of white people as white as a concept would not exist anymore.[111]

Derek Hook casts Delport's reasoning in psychoanalytic terms: "Delport's rhetorical and deliberately provocative suggestion is perhaps not as counter-intuitive or crazy as it at first sounds. Arguably, it is the gesture of giving up what one is—the shedding of narcissistic investments, and symbolic and fantasmatic identities—that proves a necessary first step to becoming what one is not, but might become."[112] Symbolic suicide here takes aim at the ruling class, those who have economic and ontological priority within their society. If Danon's call to the subjugated Palestinians is "to commit suicide as a colonial act," Delport's call targets the powerful, urging them to commit to a psychic and material divestment in the existing anti-Black structures of privilege.

Žižek considers this form of collective symbolic suicide, favored by Delport, from the standpoint of Blacks rather than whites. Malcolm X is Žižek's paradigmatic example. *He gives up what he is as a necessary first step to becoming what he is not, but might become.* Žižek interprets Malcolm X's radical renaming as first and foremost an emancipatory gesture—a symbolic suicide that opens to a universalist vision. Adopting X in place of the patronymic Little figures a universalizing move that does not restrict Black radicalism to a thingified vision of the past (the temptation of *Négritude* and liberal identity politics) and instead forms the basis for an anti-racist, anti-colonial critique. To the champions of sectarianism, calling for a return to Africa, Malcolm can be heard saying, "I would prefer not to." Indeed, as Žižek notes,

> The point of choosing X as his family name and thereby signaling that the slave traders who brought the enslaved Africans from their homeland brutally deprived them of their family and ethnic roots, of their entire cultural life-world, was not to mobilize the Blacks to fight for the return to some primordial African roots, but precisely to seize the opening provided by X, an unknown new (lack of) identity engendered by the very process of slavery which made the African roots forever lost. The idea is that this X which deprives Blacks of their particular tradition offers a unique chance to redefine (reinvent) themselves, to freely form a new identity much more universal than white people's professed universality.[113]

On the one hand, slavery in all its metaphysical devastation disabled the being of Blacks, producing Black ~~being~~, resulting in an unbridgeable gap between Blacks and the past. On the other hand, because there was no organic Whole to return to, Malcolm had to invent a new identity and contribute to the creation of a new human. X names what does not coincide with itself. X is a *becoming* X.

Malcolm X's suggestive symbolic suicide can be read productively in relation to Huey P. Newton's explicit distinction between revolutionary suicide and reactionary suicide. For Newton, reactionary suicide comes about when people are "deprived of human dignity, crushed by oppressive forces, and denied their right to live as proud and free human beings." Stripped of economic prospects and dignity, Black people are plagued by "a feeling of not existing," as Fanon puts it.[114] To be Black is to be thrown into "a permanent struggle against an omnipresent death."[115] What is biological death for a subject always already dead, blackened by America's necropolitical regime? Suicide is the tragic *reaction* to this state of ~~being~~. Biological death catches up with social death, "a death of the spirit rather than of the flesh."[116] Newton argues that "it is better to oppose the forces that would drive me to self-murder than to endure them."[117] The state will kill you (biological death); the state has already killed you (social death). As David Marriott avers, "black life is already decapitated, so to speak, and only by killing itself (rather than being endlessly killed) can it more abundantly live as resistant."[118] Newton understands this decapitation materially and economically. Black people are becoming more and more unemployable under the racial capitalist regime, deprived further and further of their substance, joining "the ranks of the lumpens, who are the present unemployables"[119] (if the worker has nothing but his labor-power to sell, the unemployables are *less-than-nothing*[120]). In this *becoming lumpen of the world*, Newton speculates on what the permanently unemployable mean for the struggle for economic justice: "Every worker is in jeopardy because of the ruling circle, which is why we say that the lumpenproletarians have the potential for revolution, will probably carry out the revolution, and in the near future will be the popular majority."[121] Likewise, Fanon finds in the lumpenproletariat a fruitful figure for emancipation insofar as their attachment to any faction of society is not a priori secured: "The lumpenproletariat, this cohort of starving men, divorced from tribe and clan, constitutes one of the most spontaneously and radically revolutionary forces of a colonized people."[122]

Caught up indefinitely in the zone of nonbeing (the stagnate state of living in an anti-Black world), the Black lumpenproletariat can and must pass through this hellish zone and embrace the exposure to/of self-destitution in revolutionary suicide. This form of resistance recalls Cash's revolutionary suicide/violence in *Sorry to Bother You*, where the *equi-sapiens révolté* resists the racial capitalist world that banishes blackened life from the human. Revolutionary suicide is not a "death wish" (understood as a pathological desire for self-destruction); it is resistance at its zero-level. Newton writes, "We have such a strong desire to live with hope and human dignity that existence without them is impossible."[123] Risking death is the price of liberation. In *Revolutionary Suicide* and *To Die for the People*, Newton compares Black political activism to the Warsaw uprising of the oppressed in 1944:

> If we do nothing, we are accepting the situation and allowing ourselves to die. We will not accept that. If the alternatives are very narrow we still will not sit around, we will not die the death of the Jews in Germany. We would rather die the death of the Jews in Warsaw![124]

When scholars call our actions suicidal, they should be logically consistent and describe all historical revolutionary movements in the same way. Thus the American colonists, the French of the late eighteenth century, the Russians of 1917, the Jews of Warsaw, the Cubans, the NLF, the North Vietnamese—any people who struggle against a brutal and powerful force—are suicidal.[125]

One can hear an echo of Fanon's voice: *Every time a man has brought victory to the dignity of the spirit, every time a man has said no to an attempt to enslave his fellow man, I have felt a sense of solidarity with his revolutionary suicide.* And as Žižek would say, this is why we are not dealing here with the usual fetishist disavowal but with revolutionary suicide as a courageous act of taking a risk and ignoring one's limitations: *I know I am socially dead, but I'll do it nonetheless.*[126] Courage, self-respect, and dignity create the conditions for social upheaval, the impetus for upending society's "intolerable conditions."[127] Hannah Zeavin, with good reason, reads Aaron Bushnell's act of self-immolation as an instance of revolutionary suicide. A 25-year-old member of the US Air Force, Bushnell set himself on fire outside the Israeli embassy in Washington, DC, in February 2024 in protest of Israel/America's genocidal war. Hours before his self-immolation, Bushnell posted on social media, "Many of us like to ask ourselves, 'What would I do if I was alive during slavery? Or the Jim Crow south? Or apartheid? What would I do if my country was committing genocide?' The answer is, you're doing it. Right now."[128] But as Zeavin avers, "protest gets pathologized when justice movements produce impermissible disruptions: to traffic, business as usual, or—most vehemently—to thought. We must protect Aaron Bushnell from this playbook so that the meaning of his death is not taken from him—or from us."[129] Indeed, any support for Palestinians is automatically pathologized by the political class and biased media coverage. Being pro-Palestinian, taking up the cause of Palestinian liberation, is a mental and moral disorder. Against its immediate depoliticization, we must insist on Bushnell's self-sacrifice as a revolutionary act. Bushnell *dared to jolt* the American status quo. He refused a world that passivizes us to the world's "crime of crimes," the ugliest of cruelties visited on Palestinians.[130]

Revolutionary suicide is a reaction against oppression (of any life), but unlike its reactionary counterpart, it takes on a quasi-actional or counter-reactional quality; it is always a reaction, but a reaction that is generative and, more importantly, does not cloister Black revolutionaries in their own being. At its core, revolutionary suicide is fueled by a public use of *ressentiment*; it registers a refusal to normalize state violence, to accept denigration as a constitutive part of your daily life, and a willingness to put one's body in harm's way in order to overturn the status quo.[131] Newton casts revolutionary suicide in global terms: "If the Black Panthers symbolize the suicidal trend among Blacks, then the whole Third World is suicidal, because the Third World fully intends to resist and overcome the ruling class of the United States."[132] Revolutionary suicide universalizes Black grievances, cutting across societies and worlds, and turning personal oppression into a common cause.

Malcolm X's symbolic suicide was also a revolutionary suicide, an act of self-violence and a confrontational exposure to state violence. X is a *No!* to white America and its global imperialist regime. In this respect, if Palestinians are indeed suicidal, it is not in the ways Danny Danon cynically imagines they should be. Thinking decolonizing the mind along with Malcolm X's symbolic suicide and Newton's revolutionary suicide sets the stage for a reckoning with Zionism. What do these suicides look like for the settler and the Native? Let's begin with the settler. Wouldn't a symbolic suicide take the form of anti-Zionism, enacting the injunction to de-Zionize? Edward Said was implicitly asked this question in his final interview, and answered in the negative: "I don't like to use words like that [de-Zionization, de-Zionize]. Because that's obviously a signal that I'm asking the Zionists to commit hara-kiri. They can be Zionists, and they can assert their Jewish identity and their connection to the land, so long as it doesn't keep the others out so manifestly."[133] Said observed that asking Israelis to de-Zionize would effectively be akin to asking them to commit symbolic suicide (hara-kiri). Instead, he preferred a process of gradual transformation of Israel.

> *Following this logic [no people can make an exclusionary claim to the land], it would then be necessary to replace the present Israel with a New Israel, just as the New South Africa replaced the old. Unjust state mechanisms would have to be dismantled.*
>
> Yes. Correct. Let's say reformed. I am ill at ease with talk of dismantling. It is apocalyptic language. And I would like to use words that are as little as possible taken from the context of apocalypse and miraculous rebirth. This is why I don't say de-Zionize. It's like waving a red flag in front of an angry bull. I don't see what purpose it serves. So I prefer to talk about transformation. The gradual transformation of Israel.[134]

Said oscillates between "dismantled" and "reformed" in relation to oppressive state mechanisms, displaying his preference for a less aggressive mode of engagement with his Jewish neighbor. Said resists the lure of apocalyptic language in describing what he hopes to see on the Israeli side. But does the word "reformed" adequately describe a reckoning with settler identity and settler desire—which would necessitate dismantling its supremacist core? Given the current state of Israel, I wonder if it is possible for Israeli Jews to transform themselves, to give up their subjective attachment to Jewish supremacy, without a process of de-Zionization. Isn't there a limit to suspending a more agonistic approach to changing your enemy's identity and worldview? Any external pressure can be said to harden the heart of Zionists. Wouldn't BDS also be guilty of arresting the process of transformation? The same can be said about the ICJ rulings on Israel's genocidal war and illegal occupation of Palestinian land, turning Israel into a state pariah and likely to harden the hearts of Jewish Israelis. Even the language of "giving up" Jewish sovereignty troubles Said:

Are you saying to Israelis that they should give up the idea of Jewish sovereignty?

I am not asking people to give up anything. But Jewish sovereignty as an end in itself seems to me not worth the pain and the waste and the suffering it produced. If, on the other hand, one can think of Jewish sovereignty as a step toward a more generous idea of coexistence, of being-in-the-world, then yes, it's worth giving up.[135]

But can you experience the move from Jewish sovereignty (in its expansive and exclusionary form) to a mode of coexistence and a being-in-the-world that opens to a being-with-Palestinians as something other than an ontological upheaval?

It might be necessary here to make a distinction between an apocalyptic language and a language that talks of ontological upheavals. The apocalyptic discourse that worries Said (and should worry the rest of us) is one that evokes a metaphysical register that transcends the worldly, the historically contingent. For example, Netanyahu should be prosecuted as a war criminal because of his undeniable violation of international law, not because he is the incarnation of pure evil. Metaphysics comes to justify the cruelest of violence and destruction. Witness Netanyahu's repertoire. Early in Operation Iron Swords, Netanyahu resorted to catastrophic imagery, comparing Hamas to Israel's ancient nemesis Amalek: "Blot out the memory of Amalek from under heaven," reads the passage from the Book of Deuteronomy. Netanyahu's message to contemporary Israel is that of absolute decimation of Palestinians and their world: "The biblical commandment is to completely destroy all of Amalek. And when I'm talking about completely destroy, we're talking about killing each and every one of them—including babies, including their property, including the animals—everything."[136] As Netanyahu tells us, the IOF "are determined to eradicate this evil from the world, for our existence and, I add, for all of humanity."[137] Palestinian punishment, Said would again say, is conceived in unacceptable terms. The language of "bombing the enemy into the Stone Age" (used in the context of Vietnam, Iraq, Afghanistan, and now in Gaza) imposes an apocalyptic horizon, in the sense of a divinely sanctioned catastrophe.[138] Anti-colonial critique must avoid duplicating the language of fundamentalism while insisting on the project of radical change, on the need for ontological upheaval, a change in being that is not ordained by a higher power, is not the result of a deeper metaphysical necessity, and does not come with guarantees. Zionism is a racist ideology, but it is not pure evil. Apocalyptic language seals Palestinians and Jewish Israelis in their being, leading to the complete destruction of your foe's being. Still, decolonizing the mind is a self-violent practice. For Ziofascists and others, Said's axioms of equality and freedom for all will be read as threatening, anti-Semitic, a violent linguistic assault on their being—you are depriving me of my biblical claim to the land of Judea and Samaria.

Before entertaining a horizon where Palestinians and Israeli Jews can aspire to a nonviolence to come, isn't there a need to reckon with settler identity? Can you decolonize the mind without de-Zionizing the mind? Against the interpretation/accusation that anti-Zionism entails the destruction of the Jewish people, Judith Butler counters that anti-Zionism is an ethical and political call for "dismantling" Israel as a racist state, and replacing it with a state that upholds the equality and freedom of both peoples.[139] As with Audre Lorde's agitation to dismantle the master's house, dismantling the settler's house is a violent act.[140] Let's be honest: to dismantle is a violent verb, though not necessarily "apocalyptic" as Said warns.[141] Dismantling, in this instance, is at once destructive and generative. You don't dismantle for the sake of dismantling; you dismantle in order to inaugurate a new, worldly socioeconomic order, a new human, and a new mode of relationality.

So if dismantling as such is not the problem, maybe we can meet Said halfway and argue for a mode of dismantling that originates from within Israel, where Israelis will do this reckoning in different ways and at different levels of intensity—perhaps not all reckonings would involve ontological upheaval. Žižek has in the past evoked the figure of the *refuseniks*, Israeli soldiers who refuse to complete their compulsory military service in the Occupied Territories, as a promising political possibility.[142] The *refuseniks*, like any Israeli citizen, inherit a racist playbook, an ideology that instructs them to treat Palestinians as less than human. But they choose not to love Israel unconditionally or mechanically, and instead keep their distance from the phantasmic pull of "Israelism,"[143] of Zionist hegemony, and to act in ways that are contrary to their dominant formation, which foregrounds the inculcation of Jewish privilege and priority and inscription in the sanctioned order of things. Similarly, a number of Israeli activists are standing with Palestinians, willingly putting themselves in harm's way; they are risking their lives, their jobs, and standing within their society for protecting the Israeli government's "approved enemy." Against settler activity preventing much-needed aid convoys heading to Gaza at the Tarqumiya checkpoint, members of "Standing Together" provide a humanitarian guard, disrupting the plans of disrupters who operate more or less with impunity (the Israeli police force tends to look away; arrests and prosecutions are rare). Standing Together defines itself as "a progressive grassroots movement mobilizing Jewish and Palestinian citizens of Israel against the occupation and for peace, equality, and social justice," and its motto is "refuse hatred and choose empathy."[144] Alon-Lee Green, the national codirector of Standing Together, says that movement is engaged in "a fight over the lives of innocent people in Gaza."[145] Green, on the one hand, stresses the abject condition of Gazans ("these are people who have lost their homes [and] their land, people facing starvation") and, on the other, he casts their intervention as a reckoning with the "soul" of Israeli society: "it's also a battle . . . over the question of whether we can remain human in the face of fear, in the face of trauma; whether we can make sure that we choose life over death, or we choose solidarity over hatred and starvation."[146] Solidarity here intimates a beyond the pleasure principle. Narrow self-interest encourages one to go along with the government's genocidal war, choosing death, hatred, and starvation of Palestinians. The settlers lash out at the peace activists and accuse them of aiding Hamas. The settlers' sentiment constitutes the status quo: "Across Israel, people are being detained, fired from their jobs, and even attacked for expressing sentiments interpreted by some as showing sympathy for Hamas."[147] Standing with Palestinians in Israel and in much of the world means aiding Hamas. Emanuel Yitzhak Levi, another activist, recognizes the colossal challenge they are confronted with: "[they] are a minority within a minority in Israel."[148]

As with the group Standing Together, the investment in Israel's "soul," in the idea of Israel, is also evidenced in other Israeli activists aiding Palestinians in the West Bank, where after October 7 settler terrorism boomed. The IOF and police do not really interfere—or rather, they contribute to the humiliation, intimidation, and the "rampages" (the prosecutor assigned to the case described settler attacks as a "dispute between neighbors").[149] Peace activist Netta Ben Porat says of this, "I truly feel terrible guilt. In the name of my security, we are inflicting terrible wrongs on innocent people, simple people. We are destroying communities."[150] Ben Porat feels interpellated by the Palestinian crisis, stating, "I can't do otherwise." She was "paralyzed" after October 7, but she returned to help. Elaborating on her motivations, Ben Porat states: "I don't do it out of pity or because I love Palestinians"; rather "I do it because it's hard for me to accept what we [Israelis] are doing—it's hard for me *to accept what has become of us*."[151] Here the emphasis is on reclaiming Israeli identity. A running thread among the activists is that Palestinian suffering and precarity are unacceptable. They feel guilty. In the name of Jewish security, the Israeli military has decimated innocent Palestinians.

In "The Uses of Anger," Lorde meditates on the limits of guilt, on what it can and cannot do. She voices her doubts about the liberal elevation of guilt as an end in itself, as an end to racism, and as an end to her Black anger:

> I cannot hide my anger to spare you guilt, nor hurt feelings, nor answering anger; for to do so insults and trivializes all our efforts. Guilt is not a response to anger; it is a response to one's own actions or lack of action. If it leads

to change then it can be useful, since it becomes no longer guilt but the beginning of knowledge. Yet all too often, guilt is just another name for impotence, for defensiveness destructive of communication; it becomes a device to protect ignorance and the continuation of things the way they are, the ultimate protection for changelessness.[152]

With the Israeli activists, guilt does not translate as impotence, inaction, and frustration, but rather acts as a steppingstone to something more. They are habitually putting their bodies in harm's way. It is the "beginning of knowledge"—of relating to Palestinians differently, ethically, and politically as beings under constant threat of settler and state terrorism. Is it the beginning of decolonizing the mind? Possibly, if activists are capable of imagining Palestinians other than helpless/innocent victims. Itay Mashiach describes most of the Israeli activists as falling into two age groups: "Either they themselves are in their early 20s, or their children are in their early 20s. Both groups are pessimistic, but also espouse a worldview that centers around the here-and-now, in doing good—without thinking about a long-term political solution, without visions of either a binational state or two different states. They are not caught up in the booby-trapped discourse of 'what should be done.'"[153] Pessimistic and pragmatic, they want to do "what they feel needs to be done."[154]

This critico-pragmatic orientation has its merits; it leads to clear, actionable tactics for helping Palestinians. But this refusal to get bogged down into larger, abstract questions runs the risk of becoming a dead end. For Palestinians, *what should be done?* is not an abstract question at all. The hooligan settlers are a synecdoche of the settler-colonial regime. The message of Standing Together also sounds good. It is preferable to having unhinged settlers terrorizing and murdering Palestinians in the West Bank and blocking desperately needed food delivery into Gaza. But does it have to be a choice between helping Palestinians in their everyday existence and considering the ramifications of seeing Israel as an apartheid settler state (which means tying your tactics for helping Palestinians to a reckoning with the racist character of Israel)? If helping Palestinians is meant to make you feel less guilty about being an Israeli citizen, then the effect of your activism will be of limited political value for Palestinians. It would be infinitely closer to a "settler move to innocence" than to symbolic/revolutionary suicide. We must subject this grassroots peace movement to a materialist critique, to "the ruthless critique of all that exists," as Marx puts it.[155] Empathy is not a politics. Worse, the image of an empathetic Israel minus a reckoning with the material colonial situation *normalizes* the Occupation. It fails to isolate Israel as an apartheid state. It helps to sustain a Zionist Israel with a human face. And this is why the Palestinian Campaign for the Academic and Cultural Boycott of Israel, an important organization in the BDS movement, justly accused Standing Together of "whitewashing Israel's genocide."[156]

On the Palestinian side, symbolic suicide returns us to the question of Indigeneity, which has become constitutive of the Palestinian question. Palestinian Indigeneity sits at the forefront of any critique of settler colonialism, challenging Zionist narratives of autochthony, which render Palestinians mere trespassers on the land of Palestine. In Fanonian fashion, to speak of Indigeneity is to insist on the original/objective violence of the colonizer, and Palestinian violence is a counter-violence against an all-powerful Zionist invader. At the same time, Indigeneity is ripe for ideological capture by the champions of liberal identity politics, foreclosing, in turn, a genuine *politics* of decolonization.

For this reason, drawing an analogy with Žižek's interpretation of Malcolm X's radical renaming, I want to consider Edward Said's plea for the exilic mode as equally constitutive of Palestinian identity. For Said, exile has become "the fundamental condition of Palestinian life," a condition that brings together all Palestinians.[157] Rather than fetishizing his own Palestinian difference, elevating it over that of his Jewish counterpart, Said playfully identifies with the signifier Jew, embracing an exilic cosmopolitan mode, designating himself as a "Jewish-Palestinian": "Of course. I'm the last Jewish intellectual. You don't know anyone else. All your other Jewish intellectuals are now suburban squires. From Amos Oz to all these people here in America. So I'm the last one. The only true follower of Adorno. Let me put it this way: I'm a Jewish-Palestinian."[158] Said gives up what he is (based on a rooted Palestinian identity, sealed in his Palestinianness, as Fanon might say) as a necessary first step to becoming what he is not, but might become, a Jewish intellectual, a Jewish-Palestinian. Said, the iconic thinker of the Palestinian question, embraces a Jewish legacy of critical deracination, countering a dogma of national rootedness, where "saying, we need a home" translates into "making others homeless."[159] This is the tradition of what Žižek names the "uncanny Jew":

> A Jew resisting identification with the State of Israel, refusing to accept the State of Israel as his true home, a Jew who "subtracts" himself from this State, and who includes the State of Israel among the states towards which he insists on maintaining a distance, to live in their interstices. And it is this uncanny Jew who is the object of what one cannot but designate as "Zionist anti-Semitism," the foreign excess disturbing the community of the nation-state. These Jews, the "Jews of the Jews themselves," worthy successors of Spinoza, are today the only Jews who continue to insist on the "public use of reason," refusing to submit their reasoning to the "private" domain of the nation-state.[160]

What Žižek and Said are attracted to here is a Jewish tradition fundamentally at odds with Zionism. It maintains and nurtures a critical distance from the organic given, from community as such. For Said, exile is marked by a melancholic disposition, "the unhealable rift forced between a human being and a native place, between the self and its true home: its essential sadness can never be surmounted."[161] In living with this insurmountable sadness, however, the exile must also resist the impulse to fetishize what has been *historically* lost, to alchemically transform the lost "true home" into a *mythical* object (what decoloniality succumbs to). Palestinian Indigeneity meets the exilic Palestinian. Palestinians are emphatically Indigenous to historic Palestine—Said fought all his life for Palestinians to be granted "the permission to narrate,"[162] the permission to decolonize the minds of an indifferent Western audience—but so are other cultures:

> Palestine is and has always been a land of many histories; it is a radical simplification to think of it as principally or exclusively Jewish or Arab. While the Jewish presence is longstanding, it is by no means the main one. . . . Palestine is multicultural, multiethnic, multireligious. There is as little historical justification for homogeneity as there is for notions of national or ethnic and religious purity today.[163]

From his reflections on exile, Said elaborates the worldly hermeneutic of the contrapuntal, which he characterizes as the "core quality of the exilic intellectual practice"[164]; it centers internal dividedness and multiplicity, a subject out-of-joint: "Most people are principally aware of one culture, one setting, one home; exiles are aware of at least two, and this plurality of vision gives rise to an awareness of simultaneous dimensions, an awareness that—to borrow a phrase from music—is *contrapuntal*."[165] A contrapuntal reading of identity resists and rails against the figure of sovereignty aligned with the ideals of self-possession and self-mastery, self-sameness and indivisibility, with *ipseity*, or selfhood, as the individual manifestation of unassailable power. It opens to something like a "soft" or unheroic symbolic/revolutionary suicide:

> This does not mean a diminishing of Jewish life as Jewish life or a surrendering of Palestinian Arab aspirations and political existence. On the contrary, it means self-determination for both peoples. But it does mean being willing to soften, lessen and finally give up special status for one people at the expense of the other.[166]

Here Said makes the demand *to give up* exclusivity, a status that is premised on the negation of the other's status/being. It will require shattering illusions and "false idols"[167] (with Zionism, as Naomi Klein argues, being at the top of the list of murderous idols), letting go of one's sense of superiority and priority; it will involve a defection of sorts, a decision to go against a Zionist-sanctioned form of self-interest. This process of giving up is the sine qua non for liberation and justice, the key psychic, social, and often ontological upheaval required to decolonize the mind and live in exilic relation with one another.

Chapter 4
Radical Others and Real Neighbors
The Politics of the Faceless

Facelessness marks the racialized other in all its exposure and vulnerability; to be faceless already gestures to an ontological and symbolic violation, evoking a naked alterity thrust into the Fanonian zone of nonbeing. Facelessness is arguably synonymous with a state of abjection. Your very humanity becomes a contested matter. This chapter takes up the challenges in thinking facelessness ethically and politically, attending to the frictions between the two registers. My reflections are structured in three parts. First, I turn to Saidiya Hartman's formulation of the "position of the unthought,"[1] or, in Christina Sharpe's terms, "a call for, and recognition of, black studies' continued imagining of the unimaginable"[2]: Black abjection as the life of the slave then and the life of the Black individual now. For Hartman, it is Blackness, *the* figure of pure abjection, that the humanist paradigm forecloses from thought and concern. Next, I relate Hartman's notion of Black abjection to the position of the Palestinians, exploring the ethics and politics of the faceless through a critical (re)reading of Emmanuel Levinas's notorious interview after the 1982 massacres of hundreds in the Sabra and Shatila refugee camps. Levinas's dismissal of his interlocutor's question—*Isn't the Palestinian the other of the Israeli?*—functions unwittingly as a meta-commentary on the precarity of the naked human face and the limits of a Levinasian ethics: What can an ethics infatuated "with the inassimilable other, the irreducible other"[3] tell us about the Palestinian other, the other other? If the face is that which resists and exceeds ontology, what is its role in politics when it is ethics that is deemed "first philosophy"? In *Totality and Infinity*, Levinas writes, "The relation with the Other, or Conversation, is a non-allergic relation, an ethical relation."[4] This ethical relation, however, never materializes for Levinas when it comes to the Palestinian. Here, Fanon helps radically rewrite the Levinasian account: *The colonial relation with the Native, or Subjugation, is an allergic relation, an unethical relation*. The ethical scene in a Palestinian-Israeli encounter cannot be evacuated of politics and power dynamics.

Asymmetry, a defining feature of Levinas's ethical relation, must be seen as rooted in history and ideology, lest it be reduced to a phantasmatic abstraction, making it, in turn, complicit with a murderous and expansionist Zionism, with the settler-colonial project of expulsion and extraction.

If Levinas obfuscates in his interview (not wanting to be pigeonholed into a social script that reproduces the violence of ontology) and brackets the face of the Palestinian (refusing to engage it as "unique" or "absolutely other"), and if Fanon helps us resituate and centralize the colonial situation missing from the dyadic Levinasian relation, so that the singular other is historically marked by its positionality (though not necessarily determined by it), Žižek pursues what we might call a "politics of the faceless" by adopting and adapting the biblical figure of the neighbor—the "neighbor" of the injunction to "love your neighbor as you love yourself" (Leviticus 19:18)—opening, in turn, alternative routes for rethinking the face and facelessness of the Palestinian. This neighbor, to which I turn in the third movement of the chapter, is a concretization or embodiment of the Lacanian Real, a reminder and remainder of this Real, an intolerable or traumatic stain which persists untranslated, irreducible to my interpretive mastery, unconceptualizable in humanist terms. From this vision of the neighbor emerges an ethico-political injunction: "to love and respect your neighbor . . . does not refer to your imaginary *semblable*/double, but to the neighbor qua traumatic Thing."[5] The "Real" of the other is impossible, but it is an impossibility that paradoxically needs to be sustained:

> The Real is impossible but it is not simply impossible in the sense of a failed encounter. It is also impossible in the sense that it is a traumatic encounter that *does* happen but which we are unable to confront. And one of the strategies used to avoid confronting it is precisely that of positing it as this indefinite ideal which is eternally postponed. One aspect of the real is that it's impossible, but the other aspect is that it happens but is impossible to sustain, impossible to integrate. And this second aspect, I think, is more and more crucial.[6]

The real neighbor is neither assimilable to that which we already know, nor a radical alterity à la Levinas mysteriously exempt from the workings of symbolic mediation. As Cornel West notes, there is a sense of the biblical neighbor in Fanon's notion of the wretched, though in this case it is the vulnerability of the neighbor ("the widows, the elderly, the disabled, those who have been victimized by white supremacy or homophobia or patriarchy or imperial subjugation and so forth"), not its uncanny otherness, that is foregrounded.[7] In *Black Skin, White*

Masks, Fanon expresses his commitment to the neighbor as a resistance to the enslavement of others: "If the question once arose for me about showing solidarity with a given past, it was because I was committed to myself and my neighbor [*prochain*], to fight with all my life and all my strength so that never again would people be enslaved on this earth."[8] Fidelity to a "given past" arouses solidarity and action yet also risks freezing this movement. Fanon's neighbor is *irreducible* to a *semblable* (the other with whom I share a colonial past). This neighbor belongs to a different order. The biblical exhortation to love and commit is not grounded in a shared humanity with the other (my imaginary/symbolic counterpart, which always threatens congealing around an identity or the available Western humanism), but in the acknowledgment of the unknown, of a humanity/humanism to come, that will have first to be unwritten and de-gentrified.

Lastly, this chapter considers the ontological and political ramifications of thinking about Palestinians and Blacks, and indeed the human itself, without a face. My wager is that we must pursue a *politics* of the faceless, where facelessness is not so much a condition to be overcome (through appeal to ontological upgrades), but a relation to reorient away from the mystifying lure of dyadic ethics toward an emancipatory universal politics, of humans and beyond, a path/void opened up by the paradoxical figure of the "real" neighbor—the extimate stranger, the outsider, the suspicious, currently exemplified or given a face, a barred face, by the figures of the Black and the Palestinian, the slave and the savage, the nonhuman and the "human animal."[9] Such a wager involves entertaining hopelessness as a politically generative orientation. What might emerge from, or be introduced by, this encounter with the faceless is potentially a questioning of my being as such, and the ends to which my affective dispositions and hopes have been turned. How does the affect of and from the faceless other impact my being? Can my social coordinates be altered in any way (the ontological question)? If so, what forms can/should this transformation take (the political question)?

Black Abjection and the Position of the Unthought

In the cruel afterlife of slavery, Blacks are formally afforded the same rights as whites, but in practice, they still occupy the position of the unthought, of absolute abjection. Blackness in its otherness remains a challenge to humanist thought, which struggles to "imagine the unimageable." Black abjection is the outside that remains inaccessible to white liberals and non-Black people of color. The existing humanist grid, the humanist grammar of suffering, fails to account for and engage with Black abjection. Saidiya Hartman takes up the impulse to identify as that which, within this humanist grid, characterizes white liberal indignation over racial violence. She denounces white liberalism's penchant for recognition as a form of appropriation. Indeed, there is no white liberal outrage without the mechanism of narcissistic identification with "Blackness." For Hartman, "It's as though in order to come to any recognition of common humanity, the other must be assimilated, . . . utterly displaced and effaced: 'Only if I can see myself in that position can I understand the crisis of that position.' That is the logic of the moral and political discourses we see everyday—the need for the *innocent* black subject to be victimized by a racist state in order to see the racism of the racist state."[10] For white liberals to relate to Black bodies, the latter must be humanized, that is, assimilated, libidinally rewritten as white bodies; once freed of their "Blackness," they can be recognized as "innocent," worthy of identification.

Black rage objects to this "softer" version of anti-Blackness. If you're Black in white liberal civil society, you must either be an abject victim or a thug. The abject victim affords empathy or sympathy, the thug indifference or contempt. But in terms of the politics of the human, a reified idealization of Black bodies is no less problematic than a reified degradation; *negrophilia* and *negrophobia* are two sides of the same coin insofar as they both traffic in abstractions, in calcified differences.[11] Ontologically, *negrophilia* is not the remedy to *negrophobia*, but its accomplice in thingifying individuals. More importantly, Fanon generalizes this insight and positions the unleashing of the human—its breaking free from the straitjacket of essentialism—at the center of collective resistance. Fanon's *parti pris* is that *we*—the wretched of the world along with their allies—can collectively alter and critically reimagine the ontology underpinning the social world. Our calling is to introduce the impossible into the colonial/racial possible.

In *Scenes of Subjection*, Hartman warns against the seductions of empathy, turning to white abolitionist John Rankin's empathic musings. She attends to his language, quoting him: "My flighty imagination added much to the tumult of passion by persuading me, for the moment, that I myself was a slave, and with my wife and children placed under the reign of terror. I began in reality to feel for myself, my wife, and my children—the thought of being whipped at the pleasure of a morose and capricious master, aroused the strongest feelings of resentment, but when I fancied the cruel lash was approaching my wife and children . . . every indignant principle of my bloody nature was excited to the highest degree."[12] The intent of Rankin is clearly discernible: he wants "to rouse the sensibility of those indifferent to slavery by exhibiting the suffering of the enslaved and facilitating an identification between those free and those enslaved."[13]

But as Hartman observes, Rankin's outrage, the pathos of the imagined scene, is not unproblematic. Rankin assimilates the slave into a phantasy of himself. The "common humanity" secured by Rankin is built on a lie offered as compassion or benevolence. By imaginatively projecting himself and his family into the assumed position of the slave, Rankin feels moral indignation and repulsion at the system of slavery. And yet, we repeat Hartman's question: Is there an actual recognition of the slave's humanity and subjectivity? Rankin's "idiopathic identification"[14] leads to the *humanization* of the slave, but at what cost? It is a rehumanization that, in practice, further dehumanizes. By symbolically cannibalizing the captive Black body, so that the image of the slave fits into and is controlled by his imaginary schema, Rankin effectively evacuates the other's alterity, the specificity of the situation, erasing the suffering of the enslaved ("the terror of the mundane and quotidian"[15]), and relegates Black abjection (slavery's terror as inflicted on Black folks) to the position of the unthought. For Rankin, the enslaved affords no resistance; its malleability as a commodity authorizes the white liberal's narcissism and "makes the captive body an abstract and empty vessel vulnerable to the projection of others' feelings, ideas, desires, and values."[16] Instrumentalization crowds out rehumanization, treating "the captive body as a vessel for the uses, thoughts, and feelings of others."[17] What we get with Rankin is anti-Blackness with an empathic face: *I care about you only insofar as I possess you and use you for my psychic and symbolic benefit*.

To be sure, there are concrete and pragmatic benefits to being "humanized," even to have others (allies) humanize your plight. White liberals can be moved to alleviate Black suffering, take up the cause of abolition, and fight for an expansion of civil rights. Liberals can lift up the voices of the racially marginalized and echo the cries of Black protesters. We can all recall the iconic image at Black Lives Matter protests expressing, "We are human too." And yet the humanist discourse, despite its investment in anti-oppressive rhetoric, overlooks "the dangers of a too-easy intimacy."[18] Humanist discourse promises to heal Black suffering, but, in doing so, it also displaces and consigns Black bodies to the zone of nonbeing. Hartman meditates on the paradoxical condition of Black folks after the abolition of slavery, where a Black individual is both formally granted full equality under the law and kept in an ontologically compromised position. Critical Black Studies' "obsession" with slavery, as Hartman puts it, stems from the crushing fact of anti-Blackness, "because black lives are still imperiled and devalued by a racial calculus and a political arithmetic that were entrenched centuries ago. This is the afterlife of slavery."[19] Black people dwell in "the time of slavery," in a "future created by" slavery.[20] They live with "the tragic entanglement" of the contemporary with the Middle Passage, marked by "the weight of dead generations upon the present."[21] The life of the enslaved is no human life at all; death is ontologically baked into sociality insofar as "no humans are involved" and the enslaved are "seen as already dead."[22]

In the same vein, Hortense Spillers comments on this treacherous slavery beyond slavery:

> Even though the captive flesh/body has been "liberated," and no one need pretend that even the quotation marks do not *matter*, dominant symbolic

activity, the ruling episteme that releases the dynamics of naming and valuation, remains grounded in the originating metaphors of captivity and mutilation so that it is as if neither time nor history, nor historiography and its topics, shows movement, as the human subject is "murdered" over and over again by the passions of a bloodless and anonymous archaism, showing itself in endless disguise.[23]

Ontical liberation coupled with ontological enslavement constitutes the Black condition. Black abjection produced under slavery persists in contemporary life, in the United States and beyond, in the global circulation and consumption of anti-Blackness. Given this situation, I want to ask, What kind of problem do Black abjection and Black suffering pose for philosophical thinking? Is it an impasse, an irredeemable problem of thought, a limit-case for the humanist grammar of suffering? Is Black abjection without analog? Or does its force lie in the challenge to the paradigm of the human[24]—in the redefinition of *the very universality of what it means to be human*? And if so, is it then a preoccupation that implicates all of us? In the next section, I want to draw on the predicament laid out by Hartman, lingering on abjection as a crisis and displacement of the face—the touchstone of Levinasian ethics.

The Human and the Faceless

As Judith Butler notes, the Levinasian face does not designate "the literal face"; instead, we should understand it as "a demand that is exercised by the other not to kill."[25] George Yancy extrapolates and translates the experience of *negrophobia* into a Levinasian register: "As I move along urban streets, the white imaginary projects upon my Black body all of its fears, rendering my Black body the instantiation of evil. . . . In Levinasian terms, my 'face' does not appear in the form of the imperative 'Thou shall not murder.'"[26] Blackness, or a blackened face, indexes criminality rather than vulnerability. In white civil society, the face of the Black subject does not operate the same way as a human face ought to, as the face of the Levinasian other, of the radical other. An anti-Black libidinal economy underpins my world, regulates my desires and fears; it "positions the Black imago as a phobogenic object"—a faceless image of Black people haunts the white lifeworld, "saturates the collective unconscious."[27] Who is afforded the privileges of the face is an effect of power or political ontology; it is intrinsically linked to a racial matrix that divides and hierarchizes faces, elevating white faces (read as human faces) while denigrating blackened (blackened *because* denigrated) faces.

Racialization, as the ontological mutation of others into subhuman inferiors, objects among other objects, constitutes a powerful social and political mechanism by which some beings are excluded from "the category of the human as it is performed in the modern west."[28] Those who are deemed not-quite-human and nonhuman are surveilled, terrorized, abandoned, denied love, or simply rendered superfluous. As with Yancy's comment, however, the Levinasian register is evoked only to underscore its inadequacy in addressing the nonface of the racialized other because that face never conveys the prohibition against murder, does not trigger a sense of infinite responsibility, an ethics suspended for those bodies "born" faceless. The blackened other, the other of the radical other, appears always already defaced, a face minus its ethical command, which is not a face at all. The face-to-face is aborted *ab initio*. Can one evoke a Levinasian framework without inferring the limits of its discourse in racial matters? Can it intervene and return the face to the racialized other? Is Levinasian ethics an adequate response to the abjection of the racialized other, an apt and generative resource for thinking otherwise? I propose to answer these questions by returning to the controversial radio interview that Levinas, along with Alain Finkielkraut, gave to Shlomo Malka shortly after the massacre of hundreds of Palestinians between September 16 and 18, 1982, at the Sabra and Shatila refugee camps in West Beirut, Lebanon, at the hands of Lebanese Christian Phalangist militia in Israeli-occupied Lebanon.

I want to take up an anti-colonial politics of the faceless and pursue the avenues that Levinas himself willfully and carelessly foreclosed. As I see it, the interview is more than an embarrassment for Levinas and Levinasian ethics. It was a missed opportunity for philosophy to take up the Palestinian question. I juxtapose the Levinas interview with the 2023 open letter "Philosophy for Palestine" signed by philosophy professors in North America, Latin America, and Europe who express their solidarity with the Palestinian people in the face of the genocidal campaign launched by Israel after the October 7th Hamas attack in southern Israel. The statement indexes philosophy's ongoing efforts to reckon with its racial past, with its "historically exclusionary practices and in engaging directly with pressing and urgent injustices."[29] The interview, read in its historical context, or retroactively in light of philosophy's self-critique, tells us something about the limits of the face when confronted with the faceless non-European enemy (enemy *because* faceless, or faceless *because* enemy, or faceless *because* non-European, etc.). And a bit more theoretically, identification and misidentification of the face stage the incommensurability and cross-contamination of ethics and politics, with notions of justice, sovereignty, and neighborly love straddling the two.

It is almost impossible not to reread the interview in light of the carnage taking place in Gaza right now (and the West Bank and Lebanon) as I write this chapter. Palestinian abjection and Israel's unconscionable role in its production was an ethico-political concern then as it is one now. Malka starts the interview with the observation that "the events at Sabra and Chatila have shaken Jewish communities throughout the world, beginning with Israeli society itself."[30] And given Levinas's standing as a philosopher who has harnessed Judaism's ethical force (Malka describes Levinas as "without doubt the philosopher who has given Judaism its most exacting expression"[31]), Levinas seems the ideal philosopher to comment on the grave situation. Levinas's highly meditative answer about Israel's innocence and responsibility vis-à-vis the massacres compels Malka to formulate the question in more concrete if not naïve terms: "Emmanuel Levinas, you are the philosopher of the 'other.' Isn't history, isn't politics the very site of the encounter with the 'other,' and for the Israeli isn't the 'other' above all Palestinian?"[32] Levinas's sharp response takes the form of an authoritative correction, a philosophical lesson in phenomenology:

> My definition of the other is completely different. The other is the neighbor [*prochain*], who is not necessarily my kin [*proche*] but who may be. But if your neighbor attacks another neighbor, or treats him unjustly, what can you do? Then alterity takes on another character, in alterity we can find an enemy, or at least we are faced with the problem of knowing who is right and who is wrong, who is just and who is unjust. There are people who are wrong.[33]

Levinas rejects Malka's elevation of the Palestinian as Israel's radical other, the outside of the Zionist order of things. Levinas's unequivocal "no" to his interlocutor's question reflects the philosopher's phenomenological ethics. At one level, Levinas's response is consistent with his *philosophical* orientation. The other's face is irreducible to ontical elements; it transcends cultural markers and physical features. Still, there is something deeply unsatisfying about the Levinasian model. It displays a philosophical failure to think and engage (with) the Palestinian other. To Enrique Dussel's objection that Levinas "has never thought that the other could be an Indian, an African, an Asian," we can add "a Palestinian."[34] Levinas has no desire to transcend Europe and conceive of the other *otherwise* (here I'm intentionally evoking Levinas's second major work, *Autrement qu'être*. Levinas's *otherwise than being* does not open to those who inhabit the zone of nonbeing in a quasi-permanent fashion).

The other as infinitely foreign cannot simply mean either abstract human (European) or neighbor-kin (the Jewish other)—Levinas fails to confront the Palestinian as infinitely foreign (to the Israeli). Indeed, as he writes elsewhere, "the best way of encountering the Other is not even to notice the color of his eyes!"[35] Philosophy is not sociology nor critical race theory. Alterity is not an effect of cultural discourse, whose meaning is relationally determined. Likewise, processes of racialization do not, or cannot, factor into his reading of Palestinians. Philosophically speaking, Palestinians do not hold any special status for Israelis. They are no different from Jordanians, Koreans, or Swedes. A neighbor could be kin but not necessarily. When neighbors are at war, decisions must be made.

Here we pass from ethics to politics: whenever you find yourself in front of more than one neighbor, you have to decide. Levinas acknowledges the complication that the third—the other of the other—introduces in the face-to-face relation: "The responsibility for the other is an immediacy antecedent to questions, it is proximity. It is troubled and becomes a problem when a third party enters."[36] There is an incommensurability that exists between ethics and politics/justice. As the title of one of Levinas's essays makes clear, "Politics After!,"[37] ethics takes priority over politics. *Ethics first!* indexes the subordination of politics to ethics, to what "transcends the political order," as Derrida puts it in *Adieu*.[38]

In the neighbor's alterity, one can find an enemy or a friend, Levinas tells us. Does your kin (fellow Jew) take precedence over the Arab neighbor? In principle, it shouldn't, but, in practice, it did and does. For Levinas, the abject Palestinian never troubles the Zionist politics of justice; the Palestinian other is not an *autrui*, an ethical other, or rather he is not treated as such. It is also not inconsequential that Levinas is less than convinced about Palestinian identity/Indigeneity, as he puts it in that very essay "Politics After!":

> The origins of the conflict between Jews and Arabs go back to Zionism. This conflict has been acute since the creation of the State of Israel on a small piece of arid land which had belonged to the children of Israel more than thirty centuries before and which . . . has never been abandoned by the Jewish communities. During the Diaspora they continued to lay claim to it and since the beginning of this century their labours have made it flower again. But it also happens to be on a small piece of land which has been inhabited by people who are surrounded on all sides and by vast stretches of land containing the great Arab people of which they form a part. *They call themselves Palestinians*.[39]

Levinas repeats ideological Zionist tropes: metaphysical Indigeneity and how the state of Israel made the desert bloom. When Levinas is faced with "the problem of knowing who is right and who is wrong, who is just and who is unjust," it matters a great deal that he imagines "Palestinians" (as they call themselves) as part of the great Arab hordes encircling the precarious state of Israel and its biblically sanctioned inhabitants.[40] Framed in such a way, all Jewish Israelis occupy the position of the timeless Victim; Israel's occupation of Lebanon was motivated by a righteous impulse. *Israeli Jews must be protected.* "There are people who are wrong" means there are Palestinians, namely the PLO fighters hiding in the Sabra and Shatila refugee camps, who are wrong in threatening the lives of Jews in Israel. Self-defense, the defense of the Jewish people, is not to be hastily condemned. Michael L. Morgan doesn't see a conflict between the demands of infinite responsibility and those of self-defense: "to acknowledge the primacy of infinite responsibility is not to rule out practical and prudential considerations, especially, say, self-defense."[41] Zionism itself is in the business of shielding Jews from harm: "For Levinas, then, there is a sense in which Zionism is about self-defense, protection, and security."[42] Self-defense is self-defense and Israel, like any other nation, has a right to it. What Morgan and others forget, however, is that the occupier's right to self-defense is not enshrined in international law. Self-defense is not self-defense when you are protecting people residing on stolen land. Self-defense is not a right to subjugate with impunity. In any case, self-defense serves as a significant qualifier to the infinite responsibility that the face of the Palestinian ought to have elicited.

Levinas with Finkielkraut highlight the positive Israeli reaction to the Palestinian massacres. Over 300,000 Israelis marched in Tel Aviv protesting their government's inaction, objecting to their leaders' failure to prevent the massacres from taking place.[43] For Levinas and Finkielkraut, the mass protests prove "this image of Zionism, this truth of Israel,"[44] that Israel's messianic demands are irreducible to political efficacy, and that the government's violence will be kept in check by the righteous Jewish people of Israel. Ironically, Palestinian abjection creates the condition for celebrating Zionist virtue.[45] Attention shifts from the horrors of the massacre to its notable reception. Levinas and Finkielkraut give comfort to Israeli Jews, telling them that they have a stronger conscience than the Begin government and its war criminal, defense minister Ariel Sharon (who was to become a cruel prime minister himself).

Levinas ends the interview on a seemingly pertinent note, expressing the primacy of the other over the land, claiming that "a person is more holy than a land, even a holy land."[46] Really? Isn't this too little, too late? Is the Palestinian more holy than the idea/l of Israel? What is the rhetorical effect of stating that a "person is more holy than a land" when the Palestinian neighbor has already been defaced, her alterity determined as an enemy of the Jewish people? Isn't Levinas exempting Israelis from confronting their historical and ongoing mistreatment of Palestinians? The faceless Palestinian never prompts Levinas to reckon with Israel's colonial regime, with *the fact of Zionism*. Judith Butler takes Levinas to task for neglecting to extend the primacy of the face to Palestinians. In the domain of politics, Butler imagines a more rigorous Levinasian rethinking of the enemy's face that could open onto an ethics of the Palestinian, especially when that face is politically demonized and thus rendered void:

> For Levinas, the prohibition against violence is restricted to those whose faces make a demand upon me, and yet these "faces" are differentiated by virtue of their religious and cultural background. This then opens up the question of whether there is any obligation to preserve the life of those who appear 'faceless' within his view or, perhaps, to extend his logic, by virtue of not having a face, do not appear at all. We have not yet seen a study of the "faceless" in Levinas.[47]

While I can sympathize with Butler's project to read Levinas otherwise, a Levinas against Levinas, as it were, a position that I myself have taken up in the past, I have become more skeptical of Levinasian ethics, of the desire or project to formulate what a genuine encounter between Levinas and the Palestinian other might look like.[48] So I am not proposing a study of the "faceless" in Levinas here. Rather, I want to consider the faceless in relation to Black and Palestinian abjection and ask if the effort to invest in the face, in an ever more expanding and inclusive idea of the face, is not part and parcel of the problem. Leaving the climate of Levinas's thinking is a precondition for thinking the relation between ethics and politics differently.

Confronted with the Palestinian question, Levinas's evasive strategies enrage. What happens when seeing the face of one's kin is premised on defacing the neighbor's face, when privileging the state of Israel is premised on disprivileging the Palestinian people? Levinas sees the vulnerability of his fellow Israeli Jews but not that of his Palestinian foes. He is responsive to the demands of his kin but cruelly indifferent to the call of Palestinians. The face of the Palestinian never registers as a supplication of the weak to the mighty. The Palestinian stands for the *reducible* other. Levinas's kin-neighbor is *substantialized* as his fellow Jew, "the neighbor as like or as resembling, as looking like," as Derrida might put it.[49] The face of his *semblable*, which trumps the faceless Palestinian, is secured and given a greater sense of urgency insofar as the politics of Zionism is being matched if not surpassed by the ethics of Zionism, as it was put on full display by the large protests in Tel Aviv. Levinas's ethical Zionism, no less than political Zionism, obfuscates the colonial reality of Palestine/Israel. At no time does Levinas ponder the responsibility of Israel, Jews, and the Zionist movement for ethnic cleansing, for pushing the Indigenous inhabitants of the land into Lebanon and neighboring Arab nations. "Why do the Sabra and Shatila refugee camps exist in the first place?" is a question that Levinas never entertains. This is not a mere oversight but speaks to a "reckless indifference"[50] (to the histories of the Native, the non-European, the enslaved, etc.) that Levinas's Zionism only amplifies. *Palestinians are all living in a future created by the Nakba*. All Palestinian existence is informed if not structured by the Nakba. The "tragic entanglement," to evoke Hartman's language, of the Palestinian past with the present—the idea of an ongoing Nakba—never preoccupies Levinas, never alters his thinking.

Nakba does not register for Levinas, namely because Zionism is unimaginable as a colonial project, as the ideological and phantasmatic narrative that legitimatizes, and continues to legitimize, the systematic murder, dispossession, and displacement of the Palestinian people. The state of Israel is only understood as the Zionist solution to anti-Semitism. At this level, Israel is unimpeachable. To be against (the idea of) Israel is to be for anti-Semitism, which Levinas treats as a paradigm of human suffering: "Anti-Semitism is the archetype of all internment. Social aggression, itself, merely imitates this model. It shuts people away in a class, deprives them of expression and condemns them to being 'signifiers without a signified' and from there to violence and fighting."[51] Levinas evokes the same sentiment in his dedicatory epigraph to *Otherwise than Being*: "To the memory of those who were closest among the six million assassinated by the National Socialists, and of the millions on millions of all confessions and all nations, victims of the same hatred of the other man, the same anti-Semitism."

If the Jew is the paradigmatic suffering subject, what happens to the dispossessed Palestinian? If Israel can only be seen through the Shoah, what happens to the native inhabitants of historic Palestine? Levinas's elevation of the Shoah cannot be separated from his/Europe's devaluation of colonialism. In *Discourse on Colonialism*, Aimé Césaire offers an anti-colonial rebuke to the Western outrage over the Holocaust, exposing the subject of the outrage as "the very distinguished, the very humanistic, the very Christian bourgeois":

> What he cannot forgive Hitler for is not the *crime* in itself, *the crime against man*, it is not *the humiliation of man as such*, it is the crime against the white man, the humiliation of the white man, and the fact that he applied to Europe colonialist procedures which until then had been reserved exclusively for the Arabs of Algeria, the coolies of India, and the blacks of Africa.[52]

The West only cares about its own. Hitler betrayed his own. Not holding back, Césaire's anti-colonial intervention indicts Europeans and their inner Hitlers: the moral bourgeois subject "has a Hitler inside him, that Hitler *inhabits* him, that Hitler is his *demon*."[53] Europeans were beneficiaries of Hitlerism abroad (colonialism), but Hitlerism at home was an aberration, was deemed unacceptable. Césaire's mode of address—*Hey Europe, you have a problem*—finds a receptive ear in Fanon who is stupefied by Europe's murderous track record: "When I look for man in European lifestyles and technology I see a constant denial of man, an avalanche of murders."[54] This passage from Fanon echoes Benjamin's famous observation that "Every document of civilization is also a document of barbarism."[55] Every iteration of the human face is also an iteration of its defacement. Recalling hearing a political speech by Césaire, Fanon quotes him from memory:

> When I switch on my radio and hear that black men are being lynched in America, I say that they have lied to us: Hitler isn't dead. When I switch on my radio and hear that Jews are being insulted, persecuted, and massacred, I say that they have lied to us: Hitler isn't dead. And finally when I switch on my radio and hear that in Africa forced labor has been introduced and legalized, I say that truly they have lied to us: Hitler isn't dead.[56]

When I flip the channel and hear that undocumented children are being targeted in their schools by Trump immigration raids, I say they have lied to us: Hitler isn't dead. When I flip the channel and see that Blacks are being humiliated, harassed, and murdered by the US police, I say that they have lied to us: Hitler isn't dead. And finally when I flip the channel and see that Gazans are being bombed in hospitals, I say that truly they have lied to us: Hitler isn't dead. We're living in the afterlife of Hitler. A Hitler as the embodiment of colonialism is irreducible to the horrors of biological racism. Hitler stands for a racial matrix that generates beings who matter and nonbeings who are genocidable. Following Césaire and Fanon, colonialism and anti-Blackness need a hearing in the West. But this is not meant as a zero-sum game. Understanding the Shoah as a form of colonialism "should be welcomed as it allows us to at least rethink—if not think anew—the problem of European modernity and its devastating misanthropic foundations."[57] De-Nazification must pass through decolonization.[58] This approach to an expansive colonialism returns us to Europe's earlier crimes in order to better appreciate their lingering and crushing presence on our global lives today.

Indirectly disclosing the limits of a phenomenological framework, like Levinas's, that ignores the workings of Blackness, Fanon stresses the ways in which his "race" appears as overdetermined from the outside, epidermalized,[59] captured by a surface ontology, a colonial ontology that violently reifies or *blackens* him. The image of his body is deemed, and consequently rendered, inferior. Fanon contrasts the social perception of Blacks to Jews. Jews can pass as white, can remain undetected by the anti-Semitic gaze. They become a problem once they're perceived as Jews. In contrast, Blacks are always already perceived as Black, always already a problem: "The Jew is not liked as soon as he has been detected. But with me things take on a *new* face."[60] This new face is also a no face. The blackening of the face is unavoidable. And a blackened face is a faceless face. A face reduced to the biological register, a "face" that is a thing, not a fellow subject, is no face at all. Black ~~being~~ "represents the biological danger," "is nothing but biological."[61] The ~~face~~ of the Black is "below-Otherness,"[62] dwelling in a realm of pure corporeality; the face-to-face is suspended, or better yet, aborted as a failed ethical encounter. The colonized in Occupied Palestine suffers the same fate. The settler-colonial context skews the unfolding of the ethical scene (which in principle can take place anywhere). Levinas can imagine "the relation with the Other, or Conversation, [as] a non-allergic relation, an ethical relation"[63] whereas Fanon implores us to see *the colonial relation with the Native, or Subjugation, as an allergic relation, an unethical relation*. Settler colonialism breeds allergic relations. Born translated, deemed a "problem" *ab initio*, Indigenous alterity is met with settler hostility. An Orientalized image of the Palestinian sets in. There is no ethics with the Native in the colonizers' Manichean world. If, "*in Europe, evil is symbolized by the black man*,"[64] in Israel, evil is symbolized by the Palestinian.[65] Those deemed "absolute evil" and the "enemy of values"[66] are then cast aside, shoved into the zone of nonbeing; colonial structures are applied and enforced; an ontological division is erected and preserved, separating the humans from the barbarians. As Patrick D. Anderson notes, "Taking the colonizer/colonized dualism as the fundamental structure of colonial social ontology, Fanon and other anticolonial theorists recognize that this dividing line separates the zone of being, in which the colonizers reside, from . . . the 'zone of nonbeing,' in which the colonized reside."[67]

While the settler enjoys their "zone of being," Césaire reminds us that settler colonialism decivilizes the settler. Here, the referential range of "settler" is not limited to the Occupied Territories or to those in illegal settlements or outposts. There is an inner settler in all Israelis, for under a Zionist horizon, settlers are interpellated in the disfiguration of Palestinians, in the making of Palestinians as faceless human animals. Levinasian ethics seems ill-equipped to counter Zionism's zoological reason. To be sure, we can say that zoological reason reduces the Palestinian to an economy of the Same that fails to bear witness to the radical alterity of the Indigenous other. Animalizing the other is often the first step in defacing the other/enemy. At best, Levinasian ethics can offer a sentimentalist orientation toward the other; the other becomes subjected to the vicissitudes of empathy: the face is retrievable in the good Palestinian, the innocent Palestinian, and so on. At worst, Palestinian facelessness gets stuck in a depoliticized ethical loop—Are Palestinians human, not-quite-human, or nonhuman? Are we talking about Gazans, West Bankers, Jerusalemites, refugees in the diaspora, or Palestinian citizens of Israel?—divorced from the asphyxiating settler-colonial context. Levinas may speak of the "imperialism of the same"[68]—the totalitarian and authoritarian logic underpinning ontology, while vaguely hinting at European tyranny—but it is the imperialism of a philosophical approach that disavows the colonial situation, and its own colonial and carceral logic, that proves to be more damning and violent for Palestinians.

From Ethics to Politics

In sharp contrast to Levinas, who does nothing to unsettle the relation to the Palestinian as a relation of comprehension, Fanon helps us understand the *lived experience* of Zionism, that the Palestinian-Israeli dyad as fundamentally a racial relation, a relation involving two different species, two types of neighbors, where no ethical relation is in fact possible insofar as the settler wants *ontocide*, the elimination of the Native's being. Žižek cuts through Levinas's disavowals and double talk about an ethics of alterity and infinite responsibility: "What Levinas is basically saying is that, as a principle, respect for alterity is unconditional (the highest sort of respect), but, when faced with a concrete other, one should nonetheless see if he is a friend or an enemy. In short, in practical politics, the respect for alterity strictly means nothing."[69] Žižek expresses his distrust of Levinas's singularization of the face, the radical alterity of the face—described as "a being beyond all attributes."[70] Infinite ethical responsibility proves politically disastrous.

Žižek questions the ethical and political status of the face. Unlike Dussel and others "more Levinasian than Levinas," Žižek has no interest in democratizing the face. Rather, Žižek undertakes to unpack the ideological dimension of the face. The singular face still relies on mediation. To perceive the neighbor's face is already to have domesticated the neighbor. Levinas's "ethical petrification"[71] of otherness, his slight gentrification of the face (it is made at once legible as *face,* and bearable as other, by the big Other), gives us the imaginary-symbolic neighbor. The face, here, ironically functions to stabilize rather than disrupt the image of/relation to the other: intersubjective relationality can be forged and sustained.[72] For the real neighbor, Žižek turns to Primo Levi's account of the *Muselmann,* the desubjectified, living-dead of Auschwitz. With the *Muselmann,* we are confronted with the "zero-level neighbor."[73] In the encounter with the real neighbor, "one cannot discern in his face the trace of the abyss of the Other in his/her vulnerability, addressing us with the infinite call of our responsibility. What one gets instead is a kind of blind wall, lack of depth."[74] This "'faceless' face," as Žižek puts it, is a "neighbor with whom no empathetic relationship is possible."[75] The real neighbor reminds and alerts us that the inhuman is constitutive of the human: "What Levinas fails to include in the scope of 'human' is, rather, the *inhuman* itself, a dimension which eludes the face-to-face relationship between humans."[76] This monstrous dimension of the neighbor resonates here with Derrida's account of the radical other—the "other as absolute unlike, recognized as nonrecognizable, indeed as unrecognizable, beyond all knowledge, all cognition and all recognition."[77] This inhuman and faceless neighbor stages the political scene.

For Levinas, the face falters at the political level; we are no longer dealing with the dyadic relation of self/other, but with the other of the other, the other of or beyond the face-to-face relation. But whereas Levinas tips the political scales in favor of his Jewish neighbor, falling back on a rather traditional autonomous and sovereign subject, blocking the demands of the Palestinian other, and neutralizing its interruptive force, Žižek insists that "the true ethical step is the one *beyond* the face of the other, the one of suspending the hold of the face, the one of choosing *against* the face, for the *third.*"[78] In his ethno-national landscape, Levinas's kin-neighbor possesses a face, the other's face is secured, while Žižek's faceless neighbor*s* do not, and that's the point. Justice must be blind and not favor a particular face over another (faceless) face:

> This coldness *is* justice at its most elementary. Every preempting of the Other in the guise of his or her face relegates the Third to the faceless background. And the elementary gesture of justice is not to show respect for the face in front of me, to be open to its depth, but to abstract from it and refocus onto the faceless Thirds in the background.[79]

As with Black ~~subjects~~—racialized bodies living in a necropolitical space, relegated to the zone of nonbeing, "stand[ing]-in for humanity, a 'universal singular,'"[80] embodying the de-gentrification of the human—Palestinians subtract themselves from Israeli apartheid; they negate their negation. In Israel proper, the Israeli state considers, categorizes, and interpellates the Palestinian citizens of Israel as *Arab* citizens, thus indexing the linguistic subtraction/erasure of their Palestinianness. In affirming their Palestinianness (not as a thingified identity or fetish but as an instance of refusal), these citizens disidentify with the fakeness of Israeli democracy; their Palestinianness is "the element which sticks out of the existing Order, which, while internal to it, has no proper place within it"[81]; indeed, Israel does not cover up its anti-Palestinianness; it displays its racism in plain sight. In 2018, the Knesset passed the "Basic Law," which states, in unambiguous terms, that Israel is the Nation State of the Jewish People. If the Palestinians within the Zionist polity are a constant object of scrutiny, the Palestinians without, those in Occupied Palestine, are Israel's surplus humanity—their presence is a demographic threat (to be countered with security by "transfer"), a justification for both a Greater Israel (security by settlements) and the Israeli military-industrial complex (security by genocide). It is clear that Palestinians within and beyond the Green Line have no proper place within the Zionist state. They are and continue to be Israel's symptoms. Why? To fully accommodate Palestinians—to treat them as free and equal subjects, to uphold the democratic ideals of reciprocity or mutual recognition—would necessarily scramble the Zionist order of things, rendering inoperative Israeli social coordinates. Israeli lives' mattering would no longer be predicated on the un-mattering of Palestinian lives. There is no (non-genocidal) political solution to the Palestinian problem without abolishing the entire Zionist system.[82]

If Palestinians are the faceless thirds of the Israelis—and our global neighbors insofar as we are today saturated by mediatic images of Palestinians and violence—what follows from the Levitical injunction "to love the neighbor as yourself"? Jolting the humanist West out of its comfort with that injunction, Žižek reactivates a more radical Jewish biblical view of the neighbor as "inert, impenetrable, enigmatic."[83] In this instance, the neighbor is not unquestionably good, nor your *semblable*, to be valued without reservation. On the contrary, this neighbor is the embodiment of the Lacanian Real, bearer of an impenetrable monstrousness. The real neighbor (the dispossessed) hystericizes me, dispossesses me. "Love your neighbor" propels me to imagine the unimaginable. In its political form, the biblical injunction takes up the difficult task—even traumatizing task insofar as loving/thinking the dispossessed unsettles my social coordinates—the task of identifying with/loving society's undesired, the desubjectivized others, those faceless others, whose ~~faces~~ fail to convey humanity and grievability.[84] Indeed, you're commanded to love the unlovable, the menacing, the one marked by an "opaque monstrosity,"[85] who is simply not like you. This love of the neighbor favors an anti-tribalist politics. As Alenka Zupančič argues, "love for your neighbor actually always involves a relation with an 'inhuman partner.'"[86] Loving here is radically depersonalized, "stripped of ordinary feelings,"[87] never mechanical and implies an overcoming or suspension of my "pathological" inclinations, to put it in Kantian terms. Narcissistically speaking, *the neighbor is not one of us*. She is a stranger and does not accommodate herself to my whims. And yet, we also share with the real neighbor this strangeness, a subject without its symbolic veneer, a common monstrosity, if you will, an inhuman core, an "abyss of impenetrability."[88] Žižek is fond of repeating Hegel's insight that "the secrets of the ancient Egyptians were secret also for the Egyptians themselves."[89]

To love the neighbor is thus to decline a sanctioned embrace of the other based on sentimentalist humanism, empathy, or basic familiarity. A politics of the faceless suspends "the hold of the face."[90] It first "smashes" the imaginary neighbor's face, shakes the Zionist libidinal economy at its source (its capacity to generate images of Israeli coherence at the expense of a demonized Arab other), cutting the "umbilical link" that tethers justice to a given situation.[91] Blocking the lure of the neighbor's face, in turn, disrupts a social logic that would manipulate us into acting/judging according to the pleasure principle and social standards of one's organic community—ironically what generates and sustains the Palestinian as a phobogenic object. Second, a politics of the faceless reorients us to the *becoming* faceless of the Palestinians, to the material conditions and colonial processes that have de-gentrified them and labeled them non- or less than human. This is done, however, not in order to re-gentrify (re-humanize) Palestinians so that they fit within the humanist grammar of suffering—at the expense of Black people, who are further consigned to the "faceless background" anytime a new or improved humanism is affirmed—but to hasten ontological upheavals, to occasion a reckoning with the matrix of the human, with the very ways in which we have up till now imagined the grievable, the human, against the faceless—the Black, the Savage, the colonized. Against a reflexive liberal politics of recognition (I shall humanize you by assimilating you), I want to suggest a politics of the faceless that confronts the abjection of the faceless by precisely declining the humanist gentrification of the dispossessed.

Beyond Humanity and Hope

Attentiveness to Palestinian abjection can only be achieved via grappling with the topics of anti-Blackness and the position of the unthought for a politics of the wretched.[92] With a nod to Hartman, the politics of the faceless opens unto the position of the colonial unthought. How do we attend to the Palestinian condition, to their living hell, to the specificity of their facelessness? We can start by declining the lure of empathy. *No!* to a Rankin-style idiopathic identification that *humanizes* the Palestinians while simultaneously effacing their difference. Rankin lives on in today's humanitarian reason, in its "mobilization of empathy rather than the recognition of rights,"[93] in its struggle for and investment in Palestinian victimhood. To be sure, arguing for your humanity, your status as a victim, as a subject who has been wronged, is something Palestinians "cannot not need," to adapt Spivak's formulation.[94] The Palestinian question must pass through the fraught discourse of victimhood. Needing the label of victim reflects a pharmacotic need. It is a remedy that risks doing further harm by compounding the original wound. Or to put it differently, attending to Palestinian testimonials imposes a double bind. On one level, any Palestinian or pro-Palestinian activist is summoned by the cries coming out of Gaza and the West Bank; they feel an ineluctable need to share, talk about, or center these voices.[95] We Are Not Numbers, a youth-led Palestinian nonprofit project in the Gaza Strip, powerfully echoes BLM activists' insistence that "We are human too."[96] Neither numbers nor nonhumans trigger empathy. Palestinian voices narrativize the ways in which the Israeli military's indiscriminate bombardment of Gaza is destroying Palestinian lives and the civilian infrastructures that support such lives. These testimonies are acts of cultural self-formation. To bear witness to their testimonies is to carry forward a vision of Palestinians as defiant and resisting—not helpless—slowing down or even pushing back against their symbolic and biological elimination. Israel's spaces of death are *not-all*. Again, *existence is resistance*. Their "presence" is an affront to Zionist sensibilities. To foreground Palestinian "presence" is, in the words of Lara Sheehi and Stephen Sheehi, "to amplify the internal worlds of the Palestinian people, to represent them as they are—as full selves and not exclusively as objects of erasure or victims of racist, settler colonialism and, simultaneously, benefactors of our pity."[97] The voices of the Palestinian faceless serve an invaluable purpose. They humanize Palestinians and, or rather because, they speak truth to power, tell the "truth of Israel"—a truth that is fundamentally at odds with Finkielkraut's and Levinas's version.

At the same time, as Jamil Khader observes, "articulating the Palestinian struggle for freedom in terms of Palestinian humanity is a slippery strategy."[98] Empathic identification, the sine qua non of humanization, always runs the risk of depoliticizing, distorting, or nullifying the structural suffering of Palestinians. The West pays attention to Palestinians and feels for their plight only during unusual times, as in the relentless bombings of Gaza since October 7. In these moments, many do empathize with Palestinians, especially when their innocence and abjection are assured; liberals are far more receptive to the testimonies of women and children (in the West's cultural imaginary, adult male Palestinians are invariably associated with terror). If seeing Palestinians as victims necessitates a shift in the framing of the Palestinian body, the mediatic circulation of Palestinians suffering ironically cements their image as abject objects. For the capricious liberal observer, Palestinians move from the status of nonbeing to a being sealed in their victimhood.

But, in the mundane days of the life-stifling Occupation, when objective violence goes along humming, care for or interest in the condition of Palestinians wanes. When the Occupation is on cruise control, the unbearable quotidian—and Palestinian resistance to their social death—does not make mainstream news. Levinas, though in many ways the anti-Rankin, is no help either, but for the opposite reason. Messianic tribalism locks Levinas in his Zionism. The vulnerable Palestinian never moves Levinas, never interrupts the latter's modality of being, because the former's face is never properly *seen*. The challenge, as Hartman notes, is "to bring that position [of the unthought] into view without making it a locus of positive value, or without trying to fill in the void."[99] Again, Palestinians do not want Western pity; they demand universal justice, or simply a fair hearing. In making this happen, our task is, I believe, to focus and linger on the "faceless Thirds," on the Palestinians who have been relegated by Zionist settler colonialism and its Western defenders to the "faceless background,"[100] to the zone of nonbeing—a space of violence and resistance.

Wretchedness abounds in the Gaza Strip. Palestinians are undergoing a violent process of disfigurement, being reduced to the "zero-degree of social existence."[101] Orphaned children are growing up in what Fanon describes as "an apocalyptic atmosphere."[102] Living in a state of hyper-alertness—there are no safe places in Gaza—the "disinherited" Palestinians perceive their material existence as "a permanent struggle against an omnipresent death."[103] If they are still *in* this ugly world, defiantly struggling for their life, they are surely not *of* it.[104] Their abandonment by Western powers is stultifying. The Israeli population's overall support for the genocide of Palestinians shocks the conscience. If, for Levinas, Israel's fate lies in living up to the ethical demands of Zionism, for its victims, Zionism—in its dominant muscular form—treats occupation as a prelude to annexation, and assumes a murderous *comprehension* of Palestinians. Reducing Palestinians to anti-Semitic Arabs—an existential and eternal threat to the Zionist polity—can only lead to Indigenous erasure. Palestinian rage is not to be understood; Orientalism supplies an interpretive framework that effectively defaces Palestinian identity/otherness. Arab alterity never exceeds the idea of the Palestinian in Levinas or the Israeli government.[105] It is contained only to be better eliminated. This is the situation that we're confronting today in Palestine/Israel. Not much has changed since the massacres of Sabra and Shatila. Palestinians remain faceless in the eyes of Western leaders and corporate media—the latter are, let's make it clear, not passive observers but active participants in the invisibilization of Palestinians—except there is nowhere near the same level of Israeli moral repulsion at their government's subjugation and elimination of Palestinians. Ethical Zionism is overwhelmed by political Zionism. And this has been the case for some time now. When the idea of ethical Zionism is advanced, it is more often than not a way to distract and cover over political Zionism's carnage. Look over here, not there. The "Peace Camp" in Israel is practically nonexistent. The liberal-Zionist position has collapsed on its internal contradictions. The criminal Zionist dictum of "maximum land, minimum Arabs" has the tacit buy-in of the majority of Israel Jews.[106]

At one time, talk of annexation was confined to the obscene underbelly of Israeli society, to the fringe of Israeli politics. Now, Netanyahu has normalized annexation; it is out in the open, fully naturalized and accepted as a "security" concern. Even the Netanyahus, Ben-Gvirs, and Smotrichs of Israel cannot say in public that they sadistically crave "annihilation for annihilation's sake." But they can couch their ferocious hatred in the ideological language of security and the global war on terror (a language quite familiar to Western powers). At an event called the "Victory of Israel Conference: Settlement Brings Security," a number of Israeli ministers pushed for illegal Gaza settlements after the war.[107] The end justifies the means. The Gaza War is just another chapter in the "War on Terror." It is not simply that Palestinian injury is unacknowledged—Palestinian *being* is itself the object of that denial.[108] It is Jewish supremacy unleashed. It is clear that Israel's assaults on the Gaza Strip and the West Bank are not about managing or disciplining Palestinians but about punishing or killing them for being Native, for not disappearing.[109] A Greater Israel is not just aspirational, it is a concrete genocidal political project.

Liberals in the Global North hesitate, fed by their leaders' promises to return to the two-state solution. What we can call the "manufacturing of hope" jumpstarts the liberal fetishist disavowal: *I know very well that Palestinians are trapped in a living hell, but all the same I believe my government will resolve the problem with the "two-state solution."* Adding "credibility" to your liberal stance, you flex your "inner Thomas Friedman" and call for the ousting of Netanyahu and his band of crazies. The belief that things will get better prevents a critical engagement with the Occupation and Israeli settler reality. This is the "cruel optimism" of the liberal audience who is witnessing the Palestinian genocide streamed live.[110] It is "cruel optimism" with a twist: Western liberals get optimism, and Palestinians receive the cruelty of that optimism.

To put it plainly, the liberal belief in hope blunts a confrontation with the genocidal Occupation. By imagining and believing in the possibility of an autonomous and sovereign Palestinian state, knowledge of Palestinian suffering is contained or neutralized, and the social coordinates of American liberals are left unaltered. Hopelessness here is paradoxically far more helpful and politically generative. We must see the situation as utterly hopeless. The options under today's Zionist horizon are dead ends. Hope gives life to the current order of things, ensuring its brutal existence and prolonging America's aggressive geopolitical ways. This is not a capitulation to the seduction of nihilism, collective despair, or apathy. Indeed, it takes courage to be hopeless. Žižek frequently defends a "courage of hopelessness," a formulation he borrows from Giorgio Agamben.[111] Without hopelessness, we would imagine reform as the only option for change. Affirming hopelessness, harnessing its negative powers, disrupts the business-as-usual mentality. It paints a stark image of the state of affairs: Western powers will lament Israeli military excess but shamelessly continue to shield it from the International Court of Justice, placing Israel above international law[112]; the Palestinian people will be kept in a perpetual limbo awaiting Israeli largesse. Today's "nostalgia for Oslo," for the defunct two-state solution, is frankly insulting.[113] Over thirty years of lies and theft since the 1993 Oslo Accords should disabuse anyone of the viability and desirability of the two-state solution, but here we are.

The effort to renormalize the two-state solution is symptomatic of our cynical world—it doesn't matter if we are actually doing anything about the Palestinians (or about the internally colonized Black folks in the United States); what counts is that we are *talking* about doing something. The two-state solution—under the asymmetrical conditions concocted in Oslo—is a subterfuge, a distraction from the very real annexation drive of Israeli politics. But how do we derail the two-state solution without ending up in the ultimate catastrophe, Netanyahu's miserable and fascist one-state solution (the Zionist solution to the Palestinian problem)?

Žižek has more recently advocated the importance of giving the Palestinian people hope, drawing on comments from Ami Ayalon, a former leader of Shin Bet. Ayalon underscored the idea that there is no security and peace unless Palestinians have hope for a state of their own: "We Israelis will have security only when they, Palestinians, will have hope. This is the equation."[114] Žižek agrees as well with Ayalon that releasing Marwan Barghouti, the jailed leader of the Second Intifada, to negotiate on behalf of the Palestinian people will be a positive step toward realizing a two-state solution. This return to the two-state solution should give us pause, however. Achieving Palestinian self-determination, as Edward Said argued before the ink of the Oslo Accords had dried, must be predicated on "freedom, sovereignty and equality, rather than perpetual subservience to Israel."[115] This is what the international community needs to insist on in any future negotiations between Palestinians and Israelis. Hope, absent a reckoning with Israeli settler colonialism, is most likely to yield an archipelago of Bantustans rather than anything resembling Indigenous sovereignty. The recognition of a Palestinian state by Spain, Ireland, and Norway is by no means an insignificant development; it indicates to Israel and its US enabler that they are not calling all the shots, that you need to reconsider your plans for a Greater Israel. At the same time, recognition of a Palestinian state can come to function as a fetish preventing us from confronting the realities on the ground.[116] What kind of Palestinian state are we talking about? Is the language of a Palestinian state seeking to infuse new life into the dead two-state solutions? If you are for a two-state solution, tell Palestinians what will happen to the Palestinian right of return or to the 700,000 settlers or so living in illegal settlements and outposts. Liberal Zionists fear a civil war. But can matters change in Palestine/Israel without some degree of social upheaval (consider the Civil Rights Movement in the United States and the movement to end Apartheid in South Africa—both nonviolent movements created violent changes)? Can this upheaval be willed in the name of an emancipatory, imagined future *for both peoples*?

The BDS movement itself does not take a position on a one-state or a two-state solutions. Rather, it aims to compel Israel to respect international law and basic rights by

1. Ending its occupation and colonization of all Arab lands and dismantling the Wall. International law recognizes the West Bank, including East Jerusalem, Gaza, and the Syrian Golan Heights as occupied by Israel.

2. Recognizing the fundamental rights of the Arab-Palestinian citizens of Israel to full equality.

3. Respecting, protecting, and promoting the rights of Palestinian refugees to return to their homes and properties as stipulated in UN Resolution 194.

These are three basic rights without which the Palestinian people cannot exercise their inalienable right to self-determination.[117]

A partition that does not prioritize international law and Palestinian basic rights will yield what Rashid Khalidi accurately describes as a "one-state plus multiple-Bantustans solution,"[118] and will thus be detrimental to a just peace. The official endorsers of the two-state solution must explain to Palestinians and the global community writ large why/how Israel's lack of conformity to international law and human rights is conducive to genuine peace. The United States' response to the ICJ opinion on Israeli Occupation is symptomatic of Western disavowal: *yes, we know very well that the settlements are illegal and hamper the peace process, but all the same we believe that the "breadth" of the court's ruling* [which also calls for the evacuation of settlers and reparations for Palestinians] *"will complicate efforts to resolve the conflict."*[119] Biden-Harris administration, can you tell the skeptics of the two-state solution why Israel's security needs transcend international law?[120] When is the right to self-defense the right to subjugate, arrest, and torture?[121]

A "ruthless analysis," what Žižek preaches, is precisely what is lacking in the current nostalgic return to the two-state solution.[122] Isn't the two-state solution being used primarily to appease global anxiety/rectify America's own global standing in the guise of giving Palestinians hope? And its value (the idea of a Palestinian state) increases even more when the belligerent Israeli government openly resists it, dismissing a framework for Palestinian statehood as rewarding terrorism. The two-state solution is a metonym for an Israel after Netanyahu/

Smotrich/Ben-Gvir. "This troika," according to Žižek, "functions as a fetish which allows the Western liberal to contain what is wrong with Israel to a minority of fundamentalist fanatics who spoil the innocent Zionist project, i.e., to avoid confronting the much more unsettling fact that the notion of Israel from the river to the sea is inscribed into the basic Zionist problem (today, over 80 percent of Jews in Israel support it)."[123] Liberals must check their righteous anger at Netanyahu's coalition; their orchestrated outrage only helps to obfuscate the colonial situation, impeding a confrontation with Zionism's asphyxiating violence and voracious hunger for a Greater Israel.

The charade of a post-expansionist Israel (the Jewish state after Netanyahu) is unlikely to fool Palestinians (again). It is the courage of hopelessness rather than hope under Western eyes that is more likely to sustain the Palestinian desire for self-determination. In the current Palestine/Israel context, hope means compromising on that desire — with the right of return of the refugees, which is enshrined in international law, being the first right likely to be sacrificed at the altar of the two-state solution. Like Said and Butler, Žižek, in an earlier piece from 2014, turned to the idea of a binational state as a political response to the stalled negotiations:

> To those who dismiss the bi-national state as a utopian dream disqualified by the long history of hatred and violence, one should reply that, far from being utopian, *the bi-national state already is a fact*. The reality of today's Israel and West Bank is that it is one state (i.e. the entire territory is *de facto* controlled by one sovereign power, the State of Israel), divided by internal borders, so that the task should rather be to abolish the apartheid and transform it into a secular democratic state.[124]

Against the "'pragmatic' solution" of the two-state solution, the "utopian invention" of a binational state constitutes "the only 'realistic' choice."[125] Binationalism, a just one-state solution, is also a *lost cause* (what can only appear "from within the space of skeptical wisdom" as "crazy") and thus ripe for the courage of hopelessness.[126]

Hopelessness opens to skeptical *pessimism*. Here we might take our cue from Žižek's book *Too Late to Awaken* and assume that the Netanyahu catastrophe has already happened, that "we're already five minutes past zero hour,"[127] that Western powers have dropped all their bad faith efforts to defer the looming annexation — you can have all of Palestine (basically repeating the Balfour Declaration of 1917; Palestinians were not consulted then and they have not been consulted now). Palestinians, of course, have been aware of the death of the two-state solution for some time now.[128] They (activists and academics, not the PA) resist and refuse to compromise on their unity and accept either a settler Israeli apartheid regime or their symbolic and ontological disappearance as a fait accompli. Their slogan "From the river to the sea, Palestine will be free" refuses to assuage or conform to liberal sensibilities (which mirror the baseless accusations that Palestinian freedom and equality are metonyms for Jewish genocide[129]); the chant expresses their resistance, their will to live in a world that is both unimaginable and intolerable for Zionists and their Western sponsors. The Global South is already with the Palestinians; it is up to the West to awaken from this nightmare (namely their political leaders, since we're witnessing a generational shift on the Palestinian question). If we perceive a total annexation of Palestinian land as our fate, as unavoidable, "and then project ourselves into that future, adopting its standpoint, we will retroactively insert into its past (the past of the future) counterfactual possibilities ('If we were to do that and that, this colonial catastrophe wouldn't have occurred!')."[130] Thus, assuming that a genocidal Palestinian erasure has already occurred enables us to meditate on what the international community (mainly the United States) might have done otherwise. If we had reckoned with Israeli settler colonialism, stood with Palestinians in their struggle for justice ("a courageous act of taking a risk and ignoring my limitations"[131] — who am I to go against Israeli propaganda and open myself to the ire of Zionists and their weaponized charges of anti-Semitism?), and finally admitted, as Edward Said pointed out long ago, that the Oslo Accords were nothing more than "an instrument of Palestinian surrender, a Palestinian Versailles," the failed peace process/fascist one-state solution wouldn't have occurred.[132] Without critical hopelessness, politics takes the face of comfort or unjust armistice — the "peace" that those in power always yearn for. Without the courage of hopelessness, there can only be more necropolitics, more Indigenous destruction and dispossession — only a Zionist futurology.[133]

Hopelessness can be generative, not just debilitative. The genocidal assault on Gaza has stunned the world community, but we are witnessing the extent to which the Palestinian question touches us all. "We all have a stake in Palestine," as Niko Block notes.[134] The becoming faceless of the world is happening; we're seeing it; we're funding it. Something must change. Neighborly love takes on its full political force when it halts the march of indifference to the plight of the faceless thirds. The world in its current configuration — the world under Western eyes — is inhospitable to the faceless Palestinian, unresponsive to the Palestinian cause. This impasse must be broken. The Palestinian question stands as a symptom that can only be addressed by a radical overhaul of the global system itself. Just peace and Palestinian liberation require a new hearing, a new world.

Chapter 5
Against Exceptionalism

The rhetoric of exceptionalism pervades our cultural imaginary. Exceptionalism is at work whenever an entity (an individual, an idea) is marked as unusually different. This marking itself is in some sense value neutral. But the exceptional has come in some fields to occupy a privileged epistemic and moral position. The field of trauma studies is a case in point. Exceptionalism here is linked to questions of suffering and our ability to respond ethically and politically to it. Exceptionalism, as it is wielded, can be said to be paradigm-shaping. For many anti-racist scholars and activists, the Holocaust, or Shoah, the Hebrew word for "catastrophe," has functioned this way. As we saw with Levinas in the previous chapter, the Shoah comes to serve as "the" model for understanding trauma and human suffering, even as it stands outside and above the other examples that it helps explicate. And yet the paradigm's universal appeal has been contested or, better yet, provincialized in recent years. David Scott questions the status of the Holocaust as "the primal scene of the original crime, and the extermination camp the fundamental paradigm, of modern Western power."[1] Bare life in front of a relentless and cruel sovereign power is not unique to the Shoah but characterizes the Middle Passage and colonialism as well. Afropessimist Wilderson directly challenges the perceived authority of the Shoah, turning instead to the Maafa, a Swahili term meaning "great disaster," "calamity," or "terrible occurrence." Reacting against the paradigm of the Shoah, Wilderson proceeds to prioritize anti-Blackness in his genealogy of traumas. In doing so, Wilderson leans for support on Fanon, who, in a passage of *Black Skin, White Masks*, relativizes the Holocaust through a passing comparison with the Middle Passage: "[Jews] have been hunted, exterminated, and cremated, but these are *just minor episodes in the family history*. The Jew is not liked as soon as he has been detected. But with me things take on a *new* face. I'm not given a second chance. I am overdetermined from the outside. I am a slave not to the 'idea' others have of me, but to my appearance."[2] Unlike the Shoah, which is presented as a "family drama" among humans, the Maafa involves a metaphysical cut in the human—

the "new face" is a faceless face. For the Afropessimist, the term *Muselmann*, which stands for bare life or the unrecognizable as human only tells part of the story. Drawing on Primo Levi's writings, Giorgio Agamben had described this figure as "der *Muselmann*—a being from whom humiliation, horror, and fear had so taken away all consciousness and all personality as to make him absolutely apathetic."[3] Wilderson updates Agamben's (and Levi's) account of the living-dead: "Agamben is not wrong so much as he is late. Auschwitz is not 'so unprecedented' to one whose frame of reference is the Middle Passage, followed by Native American genocide."[4] Chattel slavery surpasses all other catastrophes insofar as its devastation of Africans is irreducible to a historical event.

Africans lose their historical attributes as they are de-worlded and de-gentrified by their capture, and so the Maafa's ramifications are ontological through and through: Africans' very being has undergone mutation and disfiguration.

In this chapter, I question the logic informing paradigms of trauma that ontologize and essentialize events such as the Shoah and the Maafa, making them unique, incomparable exceptions that encapsulate or inaugurate the violence of Western modernity while standing outside and above the order they founded. Such paradigms are prone not only to the impasses of identity politics, but they also tend to block multidirectional, comparative approaches to history and invalidate the solidarity movements required to dismantle the racial colonialist and capitalist structures that continue to destroy lives today. Exceptionalism is arguably weaponized to break up cross-racial solidarity movements for Palestine. It is also used to discredit other modes of unrecognized suffering, as in repeated implications that one cannot be for Jewish security and Palestinian liberation at the same time.[5] Putting an end to the Nakba is deemed tantamount to putting an end to the Jewish people. Toni Morrison's dedication of her novel *Beloved* to "Sixty Million and more" has ungenerously been read through a similar lens as the author's bid to one-up the Shoah in a game of Oppression Olympics (on the grounds that framing the Middle Passage and slavery as having claimed six million lives times ten minimizes the horrors of the Holocaust).[6] Models of the Shoah and Maafa that ontologize anti-Semitism and anti-Blackness work against one another by de-historicizing these differing forms of violence, transforming them into quasi-eternal foundations that shape political possibilities. Thus ontologized, the Shoah becomes an ever-present danger whose potential reoccurrence must be given priority over other political concerns and claims. Reading politics through this lens drives organizations like the Anti-Defamation League, for example, to equate all criticism of Zionism or the state of Israel with dangerous anti-Semitism. Likewise, Afropessimist critics who take enslavement to be a singular ontological holocaust like no other often condemn the impulse to compare anti-Blackness to other forms of violence, ruling out, in turn, the possibility of cross-racial solidarities based on a shared condition of exclusion. In an effort to avoid the urge to rank that follows almost effortlessly from such ontologization, with competing charges of "relativizing" when critics dare to compare and contextualize, I mobilize the appeal to the universal undergirding the labor of Žižek and of Fanon. Unlike partisans invested in the exceptionality of the Shoah or the Maafa, Fanon and Žižek have no truck with the substantialization-reification of suffering, which locks injured bodies in their victimhood. In their anti-racist politics, they fiercely write against "the taboo of comparison,"[7] opting to de-ontologize the "pure" victim: there are no timeless Victims, no victims to fetishize or shield from comparison.[8] We might say that their hermeneutico-political motto is to de-exceptionalize and to multiply examples of substanceless universals.

Both Fanon and Žižek read racial trauma and racist violence in light of the eviscerating ontological effects of an imperialist capitalism that divides the world and segregates its peoples. The colonized and internally colonized, or those racialized as disposable, worthless, or unemployable—in other words, the world's surplus humanity—cannot and should not, for Fanon and Žižek, be made exceptional, for to do so is to reduce them to their static being, rather than attending instead to the necropolitical processes geared toward these beings' ontological undoing. I argue that we should examine this difference between an abject body and the processes invested in the body's destruction through Fanon's notion of the "zone of nonbeing."[9] Anybody in principle can be relegated to this zone of ontological deprivation, but some are more vulnerable to this violence than others. For those who are rendered wretched, the zone of nonbeing takes on a quasi-ontological permanence, denying the subject the ability to redefine itself (opened up by the destitution of the social ego), to emerge as a new kind of subject. Rather than fixing or essentializing the being of the victimized or enslaved (as a precondition for their elevation or exceptionalization), however, attending carefully to the zone of nonbeing invites comparison, and compels us to ask: What are the collective and historical necropolitical conditions that pushed, and continue to push, targeted bodies into the zone of nonbeing (the realm of nonhumanity/not-quite-humanity)? How do these conditions systematically strip them of their symbolic veneer and imaginary familiarity? How does the entry of one group into the zone of nonbeing converge and diverge with that of another? And what possibilities for shared action emerge when we adopt this framework?

The Shoah and Israel

Zionists committed to the establishment and maintenance of a Jewish nation-state in the land of Palestine, whether for religious or political reasons, have been deeply invested in tying Israel's future to the Shoah, particularly in recent decades. For many partisans of the state, if Israel is eclipsed, so too will be the hard-fought lessons of the Holocaust. If Palestinian suffering displaces Jewish suffering (in its capacity to mobilize global attention and support), what happens to the status of the Shoah as unprecedented and precedent-setting? If the Israeli state loses credibility, won't it energize Holocaust deniers and facilitate the circulation of their appalling and perverse narratives? Israel's loss of support among younger American Jews and among the broader public in the Global North (as witnessed in growing protests against Israel's military actions in Gaza following the October 7, 2023, attacks) produces anxiety among Zionists. As a response to intensified critiques of Israeli state violence among the anti-racist, pro-Palestinian Left, partisans of the state have doubled down on the ideological link between Israel and the Shoah, arguing that such critiques are tantamount to anti-Semitism or even genocidal intent. As Judith Butler pointedly observes, staunch defenders of Israel "cheapen, inflate, and instrumentalize"[10] the charge of anti-Semitism for expedient political benefits. Calling a person, a group, or a university anti-Semitic is often devastating, expelling the accused from the realm of the credible while exposing them to potential economic and physical harm. Such charges often harness the force of "cancel culture," bypassing the labor of critique and dialogue in favor of asserting Zionism as an identity in need of protection from harm, rather than a political position open to scrutiny and debate.

Evocations of the Shoah frequently function to shield Israel from legitimate scrutiny. Because it is so historically loaded, the charge of anti-Semitism casts critique as murderous, and distracts from the Israeli state's dispossession and displacement of Indigenous Palestinians and its well-documented apartheid practices.[11] In times of crisis, the cry of "Never Again"—mediated by an ultra-nationalist Zionist governing coalition in Israel, by European governments cautious about repeating the fascist crimes of the past, and also by Christian Zionists in the United States spanning the ideological spectrum, from President Biden's Democratic liberalism to Evangelical messianism to far-right, white Christian nationalist xenophobia—resonates with a range of Western publics who hear in this call a dire warning of threat to the differing world orders in which they are invested. Contributing to this horizon is the fact that anti-Semitism in the West, spurred by the political gains and normalization of white supremacy and xenophobia, is very real, very dangerous, and rising, from verbal abuse to vandalism to physical attacks. Yet responses to such current events that read them through the lens of the Shoah frequently conflate Jewishness with Zionism. This can be seen most visibly in Germany where the debates over Holocaust historiography have been particularly contentious. Historian Dirk Moses observes how "we are witnessing . . . nothing less than a public exorcism performed by the self-appointed high priests of the *Katechismus der Deutschen*." He adds that this "catechism" is constituted by five elements:

1. The Holocaust is unique because it was the unlimited *Vernichtung der Juden um der Vernichtung willen* (exterminating the Jews for the sake of

extermination itself), distinguished from the limited and pragmatic aims of other genocides. It is the first time in history that a state had set out to destroy a people solely on ideological grounds.

2. It was thus a *Zivilisationsbruch* (civilizational rupture) and the moral foundation of the nation.

3. Germany has a special responsibility to Jews in Germany and a special loyalty to Israel: "*Die Sicherheit Israels ist Teil der Staatsräson unseres Landes*" (Israel's security is part of Germany's reason of state).

4. Antisemitism is a distinct prejudice—and was a distinctly German one. It should not be confused with racism.

5. Antizionism is antisemitism.[12]

This catechism promotes a redemptive story for Germany: the sacrifice of Jews in the Holocaust by Nazis plays an intrinsic role in securing Germany's "geopolitical legitimacy."[13] The Shoah is more than an "important historical event"; it functions as a "sacred trauma," a founding trauma of sorts, making the suffering of Jews constitutive of German identity and thus incredibly difficult to question, shake, or overcome.[14]

All of the elements of this German catechism are at work in a statement released by Nicole Deitelhoff, Rainer Forst, Klaus Günther, and Jürgen Habermas—representing the German intelligentsia with stated ties to the Frankfurt tradition of critical theory—who purport to correct the hermeneutico-political scene through an appeal to philosophical reason. In response to charges that Israel is committing "genocide"[15] in its campaign in the Gaza Strip, the authors begin by authoritatively outlining "some principles that should not be disputed," principles that form "the basis of a rightly understood solidarity with Israel and Jews in Germany."[16] The letter expresses concern for the Gazan population, noting that "principles of proportionality, the prevention of civilian casualties and the waging of a war with the prospect of future peace must be the guiding principles" informing Israeli actions.[17] But the authors then go on to uphold a curious contradiction, in which Jewish life is deemed both separate yet indistinguishable from Israeli statehood. "Israel's actions," they write, "in no way justify anti-Semitic reactions, especially not in Germany. It is intolerable that Jews in Germany are once again exposed to threats to life and limb and have to fear physical violence on the streets."[18] At the same time, they assert, "the democratic ethos of the Federal Republic of Germany, which is orientated towards the obligation to respect human dignity, is linked to a political culture for which Jewish life and Israel's right to exist are central elements worthy of special protection in light of the mass crimes of the Nazi era."[19] Israel's right to exist flows from the crime of the Shoah, by this logic, and is worthy of the same protections as Jewish life more generally; indeed, the state itself is endowed with rights akin to those of an individual. Once established as indisputable, this principle blocks any analysis that questions Israel's right to exist in the form of an exclusionary ethno-state.

Objections to the catechism unleash ire. Achille Mbembe is accused of "relativizing" the Shoah and of being anti-Israel because he, like anti-colonial thinkers Fanon and Césaire before him, turns to European colonialism and racial slavery for a recalibration of human suffering from a non-European perspective. To recall from the previous chapter, Césaire linked colonialism and chattel slavery to the Shoah in order to trouble the Holocaust's place in the European imaginary; in doing so, Césaire's bold intervention inaugurated what Michael Rothberg calls a "multidirectional" approach to trauma studies. Mbembe, for his part, highlights how a necropolitical project defines settler colonialism. Necropolitics in the colony is after *"the generalized instrumentalization of human existence and the material destruction of human bodies and populations."*[20] And Mbembe considers the Israeli occupation of Palestine "the most accomplished form of necropower."[21] The settler state does not manage death for the sake of life; rather, settler sovereignty is constitutively necropolitical, subjecting Palestinian life to "the power of death."[22] Mbembe's commitment to Palestine, to bringing attention to the Palestinian people, outraged the high priests of the catechism.[23] As an anonymous author (who sought to hide their identity from fear of backlash) put it, "those who are critical of Israel's treatment of Palestinians [like Mbembe] are portrayed as antisemitic and unfit for public debate. Their 'civil death' is thereby declared, allowing for 'character assassination,' with the deliberate and sustained effort to damage the reputation or credibility of an individual and with the aim to erase the debate about structural, colonial violence."[24]

German memory politics cannot accommodate Palestinian concerns. It casts any political resistance to Israeli occupation as, by definition, illegitimate violence akin to the harm or murder of an individual. The Israeli state's right to exist is taken as the starting point or precondition for analysis; the state's actions, including its mass bombardment of Gaza, are viewed as purely defensive reactions to an anti-colonial resistance that can only be read as genocidal. According to this hermeneutic, either you stand with Israel and Jewish life, or you stand with Hamas and the extermination of the Jewish people. The global outbursts of Palestinian support in light of the blatantly unjust and illegal actions of the Israeli state in the wake of October 7 can only be read through this lens as hate marches, as indeed then British home secretary Suella Braverman described them.[25] Israel's foreign minister Eli Cohen went so far as to align United Nations leadership itself with Hamas, stating that his government "will stop working with those who cooperate with the propaganda of the terrorist organization Hamas."[26]

The protection of Jewish life, of a life that has been subjected to historical and ongoing racism, must be unquestionably affirmed, but the protection of a racist settle state should not. No state should be granted such a right, particularly a racist state. On the contrary, Germany and all other Western nations must reckon with their historical and ongoing complicity with both anti-Semitism and Israel's racist campaign against Palestinians.[27] When Deitelhoff, Forst, Günther, and Habermas argue that "the elementary rights to freedom and physical integrity as well as to protection from racist defamation are indivisible and apply equally to all,"[28] we should, I argue, understand "equally to all" to include Palestinians and their supporters as well.

Critiques of the eliminatory logic of Israeli settler colonialism have time and time again been rebuffed by allegations that they are "relativizing" the Holocaust, as if attention to the genocide of Palestinians (speaking, writing, and marching against Israel's genocidal war on Gaza) can only come at the expense of Jews, as if recognition that Palestinian lives matter (that civilian lives are legally protected by international law and that collective punishment is legally and ethically prohibited by any system bound by universalist principles) must invalidate the lives of Jews.[29] What Zionists fearful of the global examples of solidarity movements with Palestine see in them is tragically and ironically a projection of their own logic onto Palestinians and those who actively stand with them. For this muscular Zionism, the mattering of Jewish life—the public and psychological "wage" of Jewishness, as we might call it, to adopt and adapt Du Bois's formulation[30]—is predicated on the un-mattering of Palestinian lives. For Jewish lives to count, Palestinian lives must not. For Jewish lives to be mourned, Palestinian lives must not be. The "derealization" of their killing, as Butler puts it, contributes to the systematic undoing of a framework that would enable us to read or label Palestinian civilian deaths as Palestinian human deaths.[31] Zionist ideology Orientalizes and rewrites the being of Palestinians, turning them into bloodthirsty terrorists.

A liberal counter to Zionist discourse might be to humanize Palestinians, to reverse the settler's logic of dehumanization, and to see Palestinians as victims and Israelis as victimizers. To be sure, there are concrete and pragmatic benefits to this approach: people who are moved by Palestinian suffering can take up the cause of Palestinian liberation or, at least, march for ceasefire. Empathy can play a generative role in the Palestinian struggle in that it helps proponents of a cause meet people where they are. It can paint the Palestinians in this case as oppressed and cast the IOF as their oppressors. As outsiders have been confronted with images of civilian death in Gaza, particularly deaths of women and children, Palestinians have begun to be perceived by some as "the victims of the victims," as Said puts it in *The Question of Palestine*.[32] And to be clear, this has been a positive change in that it has become possible for a growing number of Westerners to view Palestinians as capable of being wronged, as suffering an injustice at the hands of Israel (as contrasted with blaming Palestinians for their own misery). But here too, we run into an impasse. Victimhood is a pharmakon that should give us pause. It helps Palestinians by giving them recognition, but it harms them by reifying them, reducing them to a state of abjection. Western liberal support is more often than not conditional on perceiving Palestinians as abject creatures. Humanitarian reason imposes an interpretive framework, an identificatory field, guiding liberal outrage at Israel's massacre of Palestinians in particular ways. Palestinians literally live or die based on the success or failure of empathic identification. But as Saidiya Hartman has shown in *Scenes of Subjection*, empathic identification brings humanization at a cost, namely the evacuation of the other's alterity.[33] Why is it that most people can stand with Palestinians only when they are dead or dying? The pathos of suffering is powerful. And yet, that same pathos can also foreclose other possibilities. An anti-racist Left cannot rely on the powers or whims of empathy. It must break with the prevailing ideological coordinates secured by liberalism's humanitarian reason. Such a reason is interested in the management of global politics, not in its radical transformation.

By means of a contrast with another ongoing war, the war in Ukraine, we can observe that Westerners readily empathize with the suffering of Ukrainian civilians while simultaneously, without tension or contradiction, embracing their armed struggle for liberation. In the West, we seem to have no trouble viewing Ukrainians as victims *and* freedom fighters struggling against an imperialist Russia. What prevents an analogous approach to the Palestinian struggle? Many factors undoubtedly play a role, but the one that I would like to emphasize here is the settler-colonial context and its occlusion in public debates. This framing of the antagonism is still foreign to Western liberal discourse, which tends to interpret what is happening in Palestine/Israel as a fundamentally deracialized, unbalanced "conflict" between two parties over territory—with Israel perhaps using more force than needed to protect itself and secure its borders. As I've argued in this book, liberals in the United States in particular, where elected officials and Cabinet secretaries routinely reference a two-state solution, still believe in a moderate Israel, an Israel minus its ethno-nationalist fascists, that is, an Israel without its Netanyahus, Ben-Gvirs, and Smotrichs. A return to the Israeli status quo, however, is *not* a return to a democratic Israel. From its creation, Israeli leaders, regardless of party, have never wanted to make "just peace" with the Palestinians.[34]

On the failure of the peace process and the two-state solution, Edward Said lamented that Israel "conceded nothing" other than recognizing the PLO as the representative of the Palestinian people. Liberal Zionists—that is, Zionists who believe the state of Israel can be both Jewish and democratic, and can exist peacefully alongside its Palestinian neighbors—welcomed the skewed terms of the Oslo Accords. Said singles out Amos Oz, "the Israeli 'dove' [who] reportedly put it in the course of a BBC interview, 'this is the second biggest victory in the history of Zionism.'"[35] It is not a matter of quarreling over who secured a better deal for their people, but rather that there is something unsettling in seeing the Oslo Accords as the biggest victory for Zionism second only, presumably, to the creation of Israel itself. Zionism from the standpoint of its victim, as Said reminds us, aligns victory with land expropriation and ethnic cleansing. Said in many ways was prescient. Thirty years after the Oslo Accords, illegal settlements have multiplied, Gaza is in ruins, and settler violence against Palestinians in the West Bank is at an all-time high. This critical assessment of the peace process is the bitter pill that liberal Zionists and liberals more generally have a hard time swallowing. The problem with Israel does not simply lie with its prime ministers but with the settler colonialism that is constitutive of its national identity. Identifying the Palestinian cause with the struggle against settler-colonial logic signals a shift by putting front and center the struggle for liberation, which itself is tied to sovereignty over land.

While liberals psychically resist and postpone reckoning with their libidinal economy, in which Brown or Arab bodies plus violence unconsciously equals terrorism and produces anxiety in any context, recasting Palestinians as freedom fighters helps re-center the settler-colonial situation. It troubles the Orientalist answer (imported by Zionists fleeing yet shaped by European norms and still prevalent throughout Israel and the West today), which lays the blame on the being of Palestinians, on their inherent savagery and hate. The liberal attachment to humanitarian reason enables *some* distance from this tenacious and deeply ingrained Zionist framework—what contributes to the unpopularity of the War on Gaza—but it can go only so far in its adjustment of the Palestinian image and thus falls short in confronting the colonial situation. Anti-colonial reason returns us to the Palestinian cause and a Zionist libidinal economy that does its best to invisibilize the cause or castigate it as anti-Semitic in the echo chamber of the West's political imaginary.

An Anti-Zionist Hermeneutic and the Settler-Colonial Situation

An anti-racist critique must emerge through an "anti-Zionist hermeneutic,"[36] where an anti-colonial reason is operative. Rather than casting Palestinians exclusively as victims, such a hermeneutic foregrounds the settler-colonial context in its interpretation of Israel's racist war. When we see Israeli cabinet members talk about their right to self-defense and how their war campaign conforms to international law, we must adopt a skeptical attitude and recognize these leaders as settlers who are doing what all modern-day imperialist settler states do: deny their (ongoing) crimes, namely the elimination of the Indigenous population and the dispossession of their land, under cover of democratic and humanitarian norms. There is a crushing continuity between the Palestinian dispossession in 1948 and Israel's 2023–4 genocidal war in Gaza and the ongoing ethnic cleansing taking place in the Occupied West Bank. Yet Israeli defense minister Yoav Gallant, standing next to his American counterpart Lloyd Austin at a news conference, can express that "unlike our enemies, we are defending our values and we operate according to international law."[37] Really? Hasn't Israel accumulated a long list of documented war crimes and crimes against humanity, including:

- the indiscriminate and disproportionate bombing of the Gaza Strip
- the targeting of schools, hospitals, and places of worship
- the targeting of journalists
- the starvation of Gazans
- the weaponization of water
- the prevention of medical care
- the forced displacement of nearly two million Palestinians
- the destruction of civilian housing and infrastructure
- the use of white phosphorus bombs on civilians
- the making of Gaza uninhabitable
- the complete siege of Gaza, which constitutes an instance of collective punishment clearly forbidden under international law.

Mainstream print and television media in the United States, having already given a pass to Israel's state terror and manufactured consent for the genocide, tend to rehearse Israeli government talking points, often citing evidence produced by the IOF without sufficiently questioning its provenance or reliability.[38] Time and time again, Western journalists betray their mission to hold those in power accountable. There is certainly no *J'accuse* emerging from this camp, though independent outlets have taken up this charge. When journalists fail to dispute the veracity of Gallant's claims, they end up amplifying misleading claims, and sometimes outright lies, coming from Israeli and US state authorities. Here we might revisit Gallant's words and ask what exactly is meant by "our" values. An anti-Zionist hermeneutic exposes that these values are indeed our Western values: the racist values of Western imperialism, of the sovereign settler, of the brutal and sadistic colonizer who regards and treats the Native as a "human animal," an irritant, a subhuman requiring containment by whatever means necessary: ethnic cleansing and genocide, either in their slow (West Bank) or accelerated (Gaza) mode.

The United States is complicit in more than the historical, discursive underpinnings of Israeli state violence; the Gaza War is, as Jeremy Scahill argues, a "joint U.S.–Israeli operation."[39] Or as former Israeli peace negotiator Daniel Levy puts it, "America is playing the role as a member of the axis of Zionist extremism" (joining Germany in its indefensible defense of Israel).⁴⁰ The United States is clearly on the side of Palestinian elimination. Any American president is almost overdetermined to support (a Greater) Israel.⁴¹ Yet both powers must give the *appearance* that Israel is a liberal state waging a war for its survival. Gallant must perform Israel's democratic *pose* and claim that it is abiding by international law, that it will do its best to minimize Palestinian fatalities, but "we [Austin and Gallant] both know the complexities of war. We both fought brutal terror organizations, we know that it takes time" ⁴² (meaning: we'll play along and say that we're not going after civilian targets, shooting journalists, and bombing hospitals, but, of course, we will continue to do so). This is an orchestrated dance: the United States publicly reminds Israel to look out for the welfare of Palestinian civilians, to limit the collateral damage, while greenlighting and feeding Israel's operation. On one hand, the Biden-Harris administration expresses its "disappointment" in the number of Palestinian deaths, but it doesn't take any action to stop Israel's scorched-earth mission. Rather than immediately halting any military support, let alone sanctioning the occupying force for its criminal acts, the United States has actually sped up its provision of arms to Israel, circumventing normal congressional approval.⁴³ Genocidaire solidarity prevails.

So when Palestinian deaths happen, Israel and the United States return to a well-trodden playbook, which lays the blame firmly on Hamas either for infecting or radicalizing all Gazans with their hateful ideology (the "there are no innocent civilians in Gaza" justification) or for its irresponsible treatment of its own people as human shields, immunizing, in turn, the IOF—the self-proclaimed exception that sets the standard, as the "most moral army in the world"—protecting the state, as much as it can, from any moral or legal responsibility.⁴⁴ Accusations of Israeli war crimes and crimes against humanity are aggressively countered on two distinct but interrelated levels. First, Israeli officials would have us believe that the state is acting as any Western liberal state would; it is merely defending its borders from the non-European barbarians in Gaza. Israel flexes its sovereignty through its overwhelming use of military force. It acknowledges that it is disproportionate, but it rhetorically asks, what else do you expect when your Indigenous foe is a "human animal"? Pronounced at the height of global sympathies for Israel after the October 7th attack, the label of "human animal," wielded to demonize the Palestinian enemy, is losing its rhetorical force in the face of extreme Palestinian carnage. This is where the turn to abstraction appears, announcing the second line of argumentation. If you're uncomfortable with or critical of Israel's official position (that "human animals" can only be met with annihilation), then you're complicit with terrorist actions that harm Jewish lives, or worse, you condone such violence. You must answer/confess (your failure to protect Jewish lives): Do you condemn Hamas?⁴⁵ Do you condemn the genocidal chants "Free, Free Palestine" and "Global Intifada"? Any hesitation—any attempt to question the terms of the question, *Are you asking me to condemn the killing of civilians, armed resistance, or resistance as such? Are you asking me to give up on Palestinian unity and equality and accept indefinite Palestinian subjugation?*—invites scrutiny and further speech surveillance, opening yourself (or your group) to the world-canceling charge of anti-Semitism.

Israeli state propaganda (or hasbara) appeals to Western desires and worries. On one hand, Israel asserts its phantasmatic sovereignty, typically experienced as state violence when nothing is really happening, the default mode of the Occupation. Under conditions of war, Israeli sovereignty is enacted in the Dahiya Doctrine, a disproportionate use of force, making collective punishment a feature, not a bug of the military campaign.[46] Western leaders are envious of such unrestrained exercise of sovereign power, reminiscent of older colonial days where *might made right*. On the other hand, Zionists exceptionalize the Shoah to foreground Jewish vulnerability, upholding the figure of the Jew as the timeless Victim, the object of eternal hate (of which Hamas and the pro-Palestinian Left are only the more recent examples) in the Western cultural imaginary. Hamas fighters are transformed into Nazis (their hatred is naturalized, removed from the historical and contingent situation of the Occupation). Nonviolent actions such as the BDS movement or the 2018 Great March of Return do not shield Israel's critics from retaliation. Even Jews and Jewish organizations (such as Jewish Voice for Peace and IfNotNow) protesting the Occupation and the military campaign in Gaza have been labeled anti-Semitic and accused of being traitors.[47] Any opposition to Israel's colonial violence can in principle transform you into a "new Nazi."

Omer Bartov offers some explanation for this impulse to overread the Holocaust in everything pertaining to Israeli security. Describing the ways in which his generation, those who were born after the Shoah, lived with the imminent threat of another catastrophe, Bartov writes:

> for many of my generation there was something embarrassing, even detestable about the entire thing: those terrifying figures with the numbers tattooed on their forearms, those vacant gazes of broken men and women on the bus, those endless, solemn commemorations in the sun-drenched school yard, those vacuous speeches by politicians and the never-ending bluster about never again going like sheep to the slaughter, and our own mute and inarticulate terror that any moment a horde of Nazis could suddenly show up on our street and kill everyone as they did then.[48]

Hamas's attack was brutal, and no doubt has been viscerally experienced as akin to an attack by hordes of Nazis. But transforming this description of experience into an ahistorical claim of identity—that Hamas *are* Nazis—mystifies the situation. It transforms all who stand between Israel and the elimination of Palestinians into anti-Semites. Bartov warns against such a misuse of Holocaust memory to legitimize a horrific campaign.[49] "Never again, now" as a categorical imperative is infinitely more expansive; it makes a universalist plea for the Global North to reckon with its colonial history and support of Israel's revolting domination of the Indigenous Palestinian population. It is an injunction against the reduction of *any* living beings to bare life, to horizonless futures. One can acknowledge that Hamas's attack understandably triggered for a number of Israeli Jews and Jews in the diaspora unbearable memories of the Shoah *and* at the same time denounce the Israeli government's exploitation of this suffering to realize their expansionist plans.

An anti-Zionist hermeneutic historicizes and contextualizes Palestinian rage, intimating that the problem is not October 7 but the relentless dispossession and murder of Palestinians, which began seventy-five years ago in 1948. It sheds light on Israel's imperialist desires and ultimate colonial plan: the eradication of the Indigenous Palestinians. An anti-Zionist hermeneutic pays serious attention to Gallant's "human animals" charge, questioning the impulse to see in it a mere rhetorical flourish, or simply an expression of Israel's desire for vengeance after Hamas's attack. This phrase goes beyond that and speaks to a certain ontologization of Palestinians, authorized by a Zionist settler-colonial reality, where a human matrix racializes and expels the Indigenous Palestinian from the privileges of the human: the type of being who enjoys her human rights, who is (and is expected to be) afforded care and grievability. Or to put it more pointedly, Palestinians are not simply dehumanized and expelled from the human(ist) paradigm; in the Zionist settler's Eurocentric "overrepresentation"[50] of the Human, the Palestinian functions as the Israeli Jew's constitutive outside, the "human animal," the Orientalized savage, the pure abject, the immobile exterior against which it defines itself. Settler Orientalism here is both an *epistemicide* and *ontocide*; it is an ontological machine that discursively defines the Palestinian to dominate her being. With this ontological crime, which underpins the physical violence endlessly visited on the Indigenous population, the Palestinian becomes utterly emptied of agency and subjectivity. Israel's terrifying answer to the Palestinian question is elimination from the river to the sea, by whatever means necessary. An anti-Zionist hermeneutic rejects wholesale the Western/Zionist framework and proceeds to translate otherwise; it constantly and stubbornly returns us to the Occupation and the settler-colonial context.

Sovereignty and/as Anti-Blackness

What exactly follows from such an anti-racist orientation? How does anti-Zionist critique invite or compel us to imagine Palestinian futures? Is the ultimate end of the anti-racist Indigenous struggle (the recognition of) Palestinian sovereignty in a future state? Does Palestinian sovereignty guarantee Palestinian humanity? If so, what are the implications? In seeking their self-determination, are Palestinians unwittingly subscribing to a murderous ontology whose history is constitutively marked by anti-Blackness? Answering these last questions necessitates an encounter with Afropessimism and its challenges.

As I've discussed in this book, Afropessimism has cast a critical light on global anti-racist discourses that ground themselves in or plead for the recognition of the excluded, of their humanity and sovereignty. Why? Because the appeal to humanity and sovereignty feeds an anti-Black world. To be sovereign is an aspiration of all *human* beings. To be fully human is to be sovereign, to be in possession of oneself. To be human is *not* to be a slave—the paradigmatic example of the nonhuman, the unsovereign. Wilderson enters the scene by challenging the paradigmatic status of the Shoah, which conditions Western reason, as is clearly demonstrated, for instance, in the statements of Habermas and others. As we have seen, the shadow of the Shoah overdetermines the defense of the state of Israel, absolving its leaders of genocidal intent, as if the suffering of European Jewry, culminating in the redemptive state of Israel, guarantees their moral integrity. Wilderson insists that the Shoah and the Maafa are two incomparable traumas, stating starkly: "Jews went into Auschwitz and came out as Jews, Africans went into the ships and came out as Blacks. The former is a Human holocaust; the latter is a Human *and* a metaphysical holocaust. That is why it makes little sense to attempt analogy: the Jews have the Dead (the *Muselmann*) among them; the Dead have the Blacks among them."[51] The parallel drawn here is striking. If the *Muselmann* (who stands for the faceless, for bare life, the real or unfathomable neighbor, life under conditions of systemic destruction as in Auschwitz) exceeds the category of the Jews in its utter abjection and persecution, Blacks exceed the category of the dead in their zero-level of being. They are not only symbolically dead, their nonhumanity is paradoxically beyond death's purview and register.

"Chattel slavery, as a condition of ontology and not just as an event of experience, stuck to the African like Velcro," adds Wilderson.[52] He does not stop here. In one of his paradigmatic scenes of the ontological difference between anti-Blackness and Indigenous suffering, which completely neglects the wage of Jewishness, in the Zionist settler-colonial context, Wilderson recalls his Palestinian friend's story about his encounter with an Ethiopian IOF soldier. His friend had just lost his cousin during the First Intifada. Standing in solidarity with the Palestinian cause, Wilderson listens to his friend's process of working through his grief:

> At one point Sameer spoke of being stopped and searched at Israeli checkpoints. He spoke in a manner that seemed not to require my presence. I hadn't seen this level of concentration and detachment in him before. That was fine. He was grieving. "The shameful and humiliating way the soldiers run

their hands up and down your body," he said. Then he added, "But the shame and humiliation runs even deeper if the Israeli soldier is an Ethiopian Jew." The earth gave way. The thought that my place in the unconscious of Palestinians fighting for their freedom was the same *dishonorable* place I occupied in the minds of Whites in America and Israel chilled me. I gathered enough wits about me to tell him that his feelings were odd, seeing how Palestinians were at war with Israelis, and White Israelis at that. How was it that the people who stole his land and slaughtered his relatives were somehow *less* of a threat in his imagination than Black Jews, often implements of Israeli madness, who sometimes do their dirty work? What, I wondered silently, was it about Black people (about *me*) that made us so fungible we could be tossed like a salad in the minds of oppressors and the oppressed?[53]

Wilderson draws attention to the unacknowledged exploitation of Black Jews, how they are manipulated or enticed by white Jews to come to Israel in order to do their "dirty work." His Palestinian friend collaborates with Israeli anti-Blackness. Though he rightly exposes a latent anti-Blackness in the Palestinian collective unconsciousness—confirming the Afropessimist's insistence on the global status of anti-Blackness—Wilderson responds to his Palestinian friend's anti-Blackness in a strikingly narrow fashion, failing to register the full impact of the settler-colonial context: how the wage of Jewishness breeds contempt for Palestinians, how anti-Palestinianness is baked in the Zionist social order.

The least we can say is that he recklessly underreads the situation, conveniently registering a straight line from the Arab Slave Trade in Eastern Africa, which began in 600 CE, to the present. There is only Arab/Palestinian *negrophobia*.[54] There is never a consideration of the wage of Jewishness and the ontological protections that it affords those who can claim it. Wilderson does not ask nor ponder what might be provoking his friend's outrage. Might it be the Ethiopian Jew's status as a newcomer, an outsider, who "share[s] the historical situatedness of being part of the process of Palestinian dispossession,"[55] and is in a position of absolute control vis-à-vis the Native, denigrating, humiliating, and policing with impunity the land's Indigenous population? One might retort that the Ethiopian Jew doesn't quite fit the settler/Native binary. His "sovereign capacity"[56] is significantly qualified, and that he is better understood as a migrant, an *arrivant* or a colonized migrant, for whom the "processes of migration" rather than "those of colonialism" captures his predicament.[57] There is merit to this argument. A rigid binarism settler/Native could, in this instance, yield an impoverished analysis. In a similar vein, Lorenzo Veracini proposes that we see settler colonialism as "a system of power relations that simultaneously *but separately* engulfs both indigenous and exogenous subalterns."[58] At one level, the Ethiopian IOF exemplifies an "exogenous subaltern"; at the other, the Palestine/Israel situation complicates his status as such. The Ethiopian IOF may be a migrant, but he is a migrant with a gun, sanctioned by a Zionist polity to deny Indigenous sovereignties and kill Palestinians with impunity; so in this respect, he shares much with the paradigmatic settler. But none of these considerations really matter for Wilderson.

By bracketing the settler-colonial situation, along with Israel's anti-Palestinian libidinal economy, Wilderson neglects the ways in which the wage of Jewishness helps to cement the settler/Native antagonism; the wage both elevates Ethiopian Jews over Palestinians and is premised on both the devaluation of the Native and the fulfillment of the eliminative project of settler colonialism: the eliminationist dream of a land without Palestinians. Whereas Wilderson divides the scene neatly with the Palestinian friend representing "degraded humanity" (with the possibility of redemption) and the Ethiopian soldier exemplifying "abject inhumanity" (with no hope of redemption), an eye for the operation of the wage of Jewishness, and the ways it enables the actualization of sovereign capacities, troubles the grounds and political usefulness of this abstract or ontological distinction.[59] Again, it is little consolation to his Palestinian friend that in theory he holds some abstract ontological priority (degraded humanity is better than nonhumanity) over the Black IOF soldier. What Afropessimist reason evacuates is history, the dynamic but asymmetrical power relation between Palestinians and Jews, which is, implicitly, dismissed as merely ontical, not touching "anti-Black formation," the unifying ontological scene of anti-Blackness.[60]

Is this a fatal limitation of Afropessimism? Is it always an instance of "exceptionalist Americanism"?[61] Or is the issue more peculiar to Wilderson's Afropessimist musings? Christina Sharpe is an author who is often described as being shaped by Afropessimist thought while also making nuanced contributions to it. In her impactful 2016 work, *In the Wake: On Blackness and Being*, Sharpe revisits the dualling racisms of anti-Blackness and anti-Semitism, though the topic is staged for the reader, at least initially, in far less antagonistic terms than we find in Wilderson's text. In a subsection of chapter one titled, "On Existence in the Wake/Teaching in the Wake," Sharpe shares her experience of teaching a year-long course on chattel slavery and the Shoah named "Memory for Forgetting," which tackles the histories and aesthetic interventions surrounding the two traumas. Meditating on the challenges of teaching this course, Sharpe discusses her puzzlement at the ways her undergraduate students were far more responsive to the material dealing with the Holocaust. Students demonstrated far more empathy for works dealing with the Shoah than the North American holocaust of enslavement.

In light of this experience, she flipped the sequence of the materials when she retaught the course. There was no noticeable difference. Slavery and its afterlives still did not resonate with her students in ways analogous to the Shoah. Sharpe ponders why and how to break up the received knowledge of North America slavery. In their attitudes toward the formerly enslaved, students tended not only to downplay the horror of slavery, but they imagined Africans as always already lost to the world without their European enslavers: "students would say things about the formerly enslaved like, 'Well, they were given food and clothing; there was a kind of care there. And what would the enslaved have done otherwise?'"[62] Sharpe unpacks the cruel indifference of "otherwise": "The 'otherwise' here means: What lives would Black people have had outside of slavery? How would they have survived independent of those who enslaved them?"[63] Sharpe's response to her students' identificatory deficiencies is brilliant. She returns to a scene from Claude Lanzmann's *Shoah* that introduces the viewer to Chelmno massacre survivor Simon Srebnik as he returns to Poland after living in Israel: "In this scene," Sharpe writes,

> Srebnik is surrounded by the townspeople who remember him as the young boy with the beautiful voice who was forced by the Germans to sing on the river every morning. At first the townspeople are glad to see him, glad to know that he is alive. Soon, though, and with ease, their relief and astonishment turn into something else, and they begin to speak about how they helped the Jewish residents of Chelmno, and then they begin to blame the Jews of Chelmno for their own murder. The camera stays on Srebnik's face, as it becomes more and more frozen into a kind of smile as these people surround him. Some of these people who are brought out of their homes by his singing on the river—as if he is a revenant—are the very people who by apathy or more directly abetted the murder of thousands of the town's Jewish residents.[64]

The scene produces a predictable response—"the students are appalled by all of this. They feel for him"[65]—and this empathy for Srebnik can then be used as a springboard for envisioning the position of the formerly enslaved who not only re-encounter but are forced to live among people who remain indifferent to their lives or even desirous of their death: "I ask them if they can imagine if, after the war's end, Simon Srebnik had no place to go other than to return to this country and this town; to these people who would have also seen him dead; who had, in fact, tried to kill him and every other Jewish person in Chelmno."[66] This figure who cannot return home describes "the condition in the post–Civil War United States of the formerly enslaved and their descendants; still on the plantation, still surrounded by those who claimed ownership over them and who fought, and fight still, to extend that state of capture and subjection in as many legal and extralegal ways as possible, into the present. The means and modes of Black subjection may have changed, but the fact and structure of that subjection remain."[67]

Sharpe allows us to formulate the relation between anti-Semitism and anti-Blackness as a question: How does a certain understanding of trauma, which conforms to the paradigmatic role of the Shoah, perpetuate or cover over an anti-Black perspective? There is no prohibition against comparison, but still, there is a prioritization of a Black experience of suffering that is entangled with the reality of gratuitous violence. Her approach seems to resonate with Michael Rothberg's idea of "multidirectional memory": "Against the framework that understands collective memory as competitive memory—as a zero-sum struggle over scarce resources—I suggest that we consider memory as multidirectional: as subject to ongoing negotiation, cross-referencing, and borrowing; as productive and not privative."[68] The importance of my trauma is not premised on trivializing yours. On one hand, Sharpe's course welcomes a "multidirectional" approach to trauma.[69] In Sharpe's text, there is a clear pedagogical value in teaching both traumas together. A necessary provincializing of the Shoah is done for the purposes of learning about the enslaved and "Black life in the aftermath of slavery."[70] On the other, in pressing the relevance of thinking the Middle Passage with the Shoah, Sharpe makes an Afropessimist move by exceptionalizing the condition of the formerly enslaved. The condition in the post–Civil War United States exceeds the condition of Holocaust survivors in the post–Second World War era. After the Shoah, the comparison implies, survivors can make a home elsewhere, only returning to the site of historical violence if they choose to, while the descendants of the enslaved have no other choice than to remain in the place of their capture. The afterlife of slavery insists on the perverse reality of slavery that remains after it has been rendered illegal. Ontical changes in the law do not automatically change the law of anti-Blackness that circulates freely in white civil society's collective unconscious. Anti-Blackness persists today. "Blackness cannot be separated from slavery," Wilderson insists.[71] Today, a Black individual remains ontologically a slave. Gratuitous violence follows Black folks wherever they go. Unlike contingent violence, which occurs when there is a trespass or transgression, gratuitous violence does not need any reason for its devastating eruption: "the Slave's relationship to violence is open-ended, gratuitous, without reason or constraint," whereas "the human's relationship to violence is always contingent."[72] "Living in the wake," as Sharpe calls it, "means living the history and present of terror, from slavery to the present, as the ground of our everyday Black existence; living the historically and geographically dis/continuous but always present and endlessly reinvigorated brutality in, and on, our bodies while even as that terror is visited on our bodies the realities of that terror are erased."[73] For the Afropessimist, the fact of gratuitous violence pertains exclusively to Black bodies. The fault of Blacks lies in their Blackness.

Is a multidirectional approach still salvageable from Sharpe's account? I think so, but it requires pursuing a couple of moments of absence. What is only implied at this point in the narrative is where Srebnik is able to go after the war: it is Israel, where he currently resides. Israel is the land of the Jews, which any Jewish person can claim as their home. Srebnik can flee anti-Semitism (which he is painfully reminded of upon his return to Chelmno) in Israel, but there is no place where Black people can escape the ubiquitous anti-Blackness of the world. What is missed here is the structure of dispossession on which such an escape from anti-Semitism is premised, namely, the dispossession of Palestinians—beginning with the Nakba—through which the modern state of Israel is constituted as a nation-state for Jewish citizens above all (the only citizens who count as full subjects). The point of Sharpe's example is not of course to devalue Palestine, but rather to demonstrate how empathy does and does not circulate and what attachments are, or can be, made in an anti-Black world. Yet Palestine plays an unsettling role in this example, for Sharpe hints at the question of the Nakba at the very beginning of her story, when she gives a brief account of the origins of her title for the trauma course: "I teach a course called Memory for Forgetting. The title came from my misremembering the title of a book that Judith Butler mentioned in an MLA talk on activism and the academy in San Diego in 2004. The book was Mahmoud Darwish's *Memory for Forgetfulness*."[74] A Palestinian poet indirectly inspires the idea for the course, and the displacement of Palestinians renders possible an Israel that can create (or at least pretend that it does) a space free of violence for Jews like Srebnik—a space which is unavailable for Blacks, and which, I would add, is also unavailable for Palestinians insofar as they "live" under the interminable Zionist gaze in both the Occupied Territories and Israel proper. Black lives, like Palestinian lives, are precisely lived under occupation: "I'm interested in ways of seeing and imagining responses to terror in the varied and various ways that our Black lives are lived under occupation"[75] Under the occupier's gaze, Blacks have to "*turn white or disappear [se blanchir ou disparaître]*"[76] while Palestinians have to "*de-Palestinize or get out.*"[77] Respite from the asphyxiating gaze of the occupier is a privilege of the few.

In Sharpe's text, then, there are three traumas at play: the Shoah, the Maafa, and the Nakba. The exceptionalization of any trauma invariably serves an ideological aim: monopolizing and policing the claims of victimhood. Refusing the taboo of comparison (Thou Shalt Not Compare the Shoah, the Maafa, etc.) does not mean relativizing the force of world-ending traumas, or at least it does not have to. Thinking trauma comparatively counters the urge to exceptionalize and reify the image of the wretched, the subject of ontological upheaval. Put differently, a global anti-racism worthy of its name should not be in the business of anointing the next exemplary Victim—as per the assimilative formulas "the new Jew is . . . " or "the new slave is . . . " Such a global anti-racism would decline both the liberal position (elevating only those whose suffering we can empathize with) and the separatist invitation to the Oppression Olympics (elevating a single form of suffering as distinct and unique).

De-exceptionalizing the victim characterizes Fanon's critical approach to the suffering of others and the perils of pathos. Edward Said praised Fanon's generative predilection to de-exceptionalize. Understanding and pleading for a cause never translated into fetishizing any given wretched, elevated above others and for others to follow. Fanon's commitment to the Algerian cause was unimpeachable, but it never came at the expense of hermeneutic expansiveness. A generous multidirectional sensibility underpins Fanon's anti-colonial critique. As Said testifies:

> It is inadequate only to affirm that a people was dispossessed, oppressed or slaughtered, denied its rights and its political existence, without at the same time doing what Fanon did during the Algerian war, affiliating those horrors with the similar afflictions of other people. This does not at all mean a loss in historical specificity, but rather it guards against the possibility that a lesson learnt about oppression in one place will be forgotten or violated in another place or time.[78]

The contrast between Fanon and the Afropessimists is startling. Whereas Afropessimist reasoning dictates that the Maafa is "without analog,"[79] a Fanonian gesture refuses to interpret "things in isolation"[80] and creates connections between horrific realities. The same applies to the gatekeepers of the Shoah. The specificity of the Holocaust is not diluted by comparison, by evocations of the suffering of Palestinians (whether the Nakba of '48 or the one unfolding in plain sight today, in front of our eyes).

A Plea for De-Exceptionalizing the Wretched

In this final part of the chapter, I want to look more closely at a different way of framing the questions of trauma, suffering, and victimhood beyond exceptionalism. As we have seen in the previous chapters, Fanon conceptualizes racial violence in ontological terms, positing the zone of nonbeing as the unbearable condition of wretched existence, with which Black bodies are particularly familiar. Fanon introduces his concept almost immediately in the introduction to *Black Skin, White Masks*:

> There is a zone of nonbeing, an extraordinarily sterile and arid region, an incline stripped bare of every essential, from which a genuine new departure can emerge. In most cases, the black man cannot take advantage of this descent into a veritable hell.[81]

The wretched dwell in the paradoxical site of the zone of nonbeing. Here, Fanon conceptualizes the wretched as Black bodies who experience only the zone's worst features. If the zone of nonbeing is potentially emancipatory insofar as it gestures toward a state where the individual's attachment to her social ego has been compromised (an existential crisis—*who am I?*), this life-affirming existentialist potential underpinning the idea of the zone of nonbeing is itself quickly compromised since, as Fanon intimates, Black folks typically fail to grasp this freedom; the zone gains a quasi-irreversible reality in an anti-Black world. Born in the zone of nonbeing, most Blacks remain caught in this mire of nothingness, arrested in their descent with no way out in sight.

Commenting on the zone of nonbeing, Žižek surprisingly quotes a mistranslation of Fanon's passage:

> Recall Fanon's claim that "the Negro is a zone of non-being, an extraordinarily sterile and arid region, an utterly declining declivity": is the experience that grounds today's "afro-pessimism" not a similar one? Is the insistence of afro-pessimists that Black subordination is much more radical than that of other underprivileged groups (Asians, LGBT+, women . . .), i.e., that Blacks should not be put into the series with other forms of "colonization," not grounded in the act of assuming that one belongs to such a "zone of non-being"?[82]

Now (creative) mistranslations of Fanon are not new. Perhaps the most famous instance is Charles Lam Markmann's translation of chapter 5 of *Black Skin, White Masks*, "L'expérience vécue du noir" ("The Lived Experience of the Black Man") as "The Fact of Blackness." In Markmann's rendering, Fanon's phenomenological subject drops out in favor of a structural optic that highlights the crushing reality of anti-Blackness (Markmann's translation is understandably favored by the Afropessimists who are less interested in Fanon's phenomenological adventures). Žižek's quoted translation, "the Negro is a zone of non-being, an extraordinarily sterile and arid region, an utterly declining declivity," deviates considerably from the French. We can compare the French to Žižek's quotation and to the two standard English translations of Fanon's text, those of Richard Philcox and Charles Lam Markmann:

> Il y a une zone de non-être, une région extraordinairement stérile et aride, une rampe essentiellement dépouillée, d'où un authentique surgissement peut prendre naissance.[83]

> the Negro is a zone of non-being, an extraordinarily sterile and arid region, an utterly declining declivity [. . .] [Žižek]

> There is a zone of nonbeing, an extraordinarily sterile and arid region, an incline stripped bare of every essential[,] from which a genuine new departure can emerge. [Philcox]

> There is a zone of nonbeing, an extraordinarily sterile and arid region, an utterly naked declivity[,] where an authentic upheaval can be born.[84] [Markmann]

The first thing to notice is the problematic ontologization of the zone of nonbeing by assigning it to the "Negro," the Black man, where it is clear from Fanon's text that he wants to avoid starting with an identitarian dilemma. The "Il y a une zone de non-être" characterizes the condition of the destitute, the wretched, for whom their being is a wasteland, for whom social identity is eviscerated. Now, Žižek seems to have retroactively filled this empty space from the following sentence where Fanon concretizes the zone of nonbeing by naming Blacks as the "victim" of this hellish condition. He says that "In most cases, the black man cannot take advantage of this descent into a veritable hell [*Dans la majorité des cas, le Noir n'a pas le bénéfice de réaliser cette descente aux véritables Enfers*]." This is the pessimism embodied in the Afropessimists' Fanon, which Žižek appears to endorse. While there are strong points of resonance between the Afropessimists and Žižek—their general orientations are anti-reformist in nature and both embrace a certain "courage of hopelessness"—I think that Žižek, like the Afropessimists, narrows the meaning and range of Fanon's zone of nonbeing. And this is connected to the second element of significance in Žižek's quotation of the first sentence. It is a partial translation that cuts off "from which a genuine new departure can emerge." *The way down is also the way up*. Fanon's zone of nonbeing accounts for, but is not reducible to, the detrimental effects of *negrophobia*.

Fanon is adopting and adapting here a Sartrean existentialist insight. Transcendence for Sartre is synonymous with radical human freedom; it introduces a gap between consciousness and my social ego. Ironically, this is a part of Fanon's sentence that holds a revolutionary potential that echoes Žižek's own reflections on what he calls the "proletarian position."[85] The proletarian position *stretches* the classic Marxist identification of the proletariat with the working class. Žižek turns to different sites of potential resistance, pursuing "*different proletarian positions*."[86] The candidates for this proletarian position are those wretched beings "who are deprived of their substance, like ecological victims, psychological victims, and, especially, excluded victims of racism, and so on."[87] What binds these proletarian positions together is a common investment in class struggle, in the political belief that the symbolic order is *not-all*, that society does *not* exist as "a positive order of being."[88]

Perhaps we can reduce the gap between Fanon and Žižek by reinterpreting the figure of the Black subject in the United States as a concrete universality: this Black subject incarnates the reality of social violence and the constitutively excluded. "In today's concrete constellation," Žižek writes, "the violence to which blacks are exposed is not just a neutral case of social violence but its privileged, exemplary case—to reduce it to a particular case of violence means to ignore the true nature of violence in our society."[89] The abused Black body stands for those ostracized bodies caught up in the ontological inferno of the zone of nonbeing.

As the BLM movement underscores, to be Black in America is to be marked for early termination. "The immanence of death"[90] haunts Black bodies. "The Black [is] the constitutive outside for those who would construct themselves as *the* Human."[91] Access to this imaginary-symbolic ideal, "*the* human" is predicated on the exclusion of the Black. "*The* human" stands for a false universalism. Žižek gives the constitutive outsideness of the Black body a universalist twist. The Black person, we might say, "sticks out of the existing Order, which, while internal to it, has no proper place within it,"[92] The surplus humanity of Blacks conveys paradoxically their universal humanity. In a crucial gesture, Žižek links this sense of universality to his conceptualization of the proletariat: "To take Marx's classic example, 'proletariat' stands for universal humanity not because it is the lowest, most exploited class, but because its very existence is a 'living contradiction'— that is, it gives body to the fundamental imbalance and inconsistency of the capitalist social Whole."[93] Žižek also notes that Marx never simply collapsed the proletariat into the working class. The latter denotes an "'objective' social category, a topic of sociological study," while the former points to "a certain subjective position," "the class 'for itself,'" "social negativity."[94] Žižek reactivates the proletariat as a "category of truth, the revolutionary subject proper."[95] Having said that, Žižek also cautions against a nostalgia for "a 'predestined' revolutionary subject"[96] (hence the shift to proletarian positions) as in the days of Marx, or in its replacement by nomadic subjects (the refugees as the face of the Global South). If Marx's revolutionary subject is "indisposed,"[97] we should not exceptionalize a new one. Rather, Žižek opts to multiply the sites of resistance, dislocating the field of class struggle and recasting it to include "different *proletarian positions*," different positions of universality embodied in the wretched of the earth, substanceless subjects, the worst off in the world.

So is Žižek contradicting himself by exceptionalizing the Black subject of Fanon and the Afropessimists, by contrasting it to other marginalized identities? Not necessarily. What Žižek seems to appreciate in Fanon and the Afropessimists is the way they articulate exclusion outside the rhetoric of identity and identity politics. "Is the insistence of afro-pessimists that Black subordination is much more radical than that of other underprivileged groups (Asians, LGBT+, women…), i.e., that Blacks should not be put into the series with other forms of 'colonization,' not grounded in the act of assuming that one belongs to such a 'zone of non-being'?"[98] Asians, LGBT+, and women may not be the privileged subjects of society, but they are still *of* this world. Their identity is legible by society, and they have an investment in the world and the world is, to some measure, invested in them. In stark contrast, the zone of nonbeing indexes ontological destitution, marking a break with identity politics and its reformist social remedies. The Black ~~subject~~—the subject under erasure, emptied of its ontological reserves—embodies the proletarian position, provided she does not get co-opted by the liberal managers of anger, the champions of identity politics.

If the notions of the zone of nonbeing and the proletarian position name a certain modality of ontological fraughtness, the Afropessimists ontologize this condition as an inescapable anti-Blackness. But, whereas the Afropessimists exceptionalize the Black subject, Žižek's proletarian position multiplies the sites of resistance, including, in principle, the position of non-Blacks. Yes, the Black is in a zone of nonbeing, but so are the Jew and the Palestinian. No one has a monopoly over the zone of nonbeing. One's thrownness into the zone of nonbeing is not a divine punishment; it is not God but a symbolic order that unjustly condemns you. The source of disenfranchisement is worldly, historical, taking place under varying necropolitical conditions that rip at the individual's being. The hooligan Jewish settlers terrorizing Palestinians in the West Bank frontier, often with the full backing of the IOF, are clearly not in the same position as the *Muselmann* in Auschwitz. Or to look back at Wilderson's example of his Palestinian friend and IOF Ethiopian soldier, Ethiopian Jews are systematically racially discriminated against in Israel. So, as in the United States, Blacks in Israel are in the zone of nonbeing. At the same time, to be a Palestinian living in the Occupied Territories or in Israel proper also positions you *structurally* below any Jewish person—including Ethiopian Jews. The psychic wage of Jewishness does not factor into Wilderson's account. For Wilderson, what is of significance is the shared anti-Blackness of Palestinians and non-Black Jews alike. There is no room for a multidirectional intervention. The fact that Israel's libidinal economy nourishes both anti-Palestinianness and anti-Blackness (though the latter is attenuated if you're Black and Jewish) in its citizens is set aside. Anti-Blackness must take precedence over anti-Palestinianness. That the violence of anti-Palestinianness in Palestine/Israel is as gratuitous for Israeli society as the violence of anti-Blackness is for white American society never gets a hearing. My retort to Wilderson is that acknowledgment of the full weight of anti-Palestinianness is not anti-Black (by minimizing the structural role of anti-Blackness), but rather the means to better understand the constitutive role of anti-Palestinianness and anti-Blackness in Israel's colonial matrix of the human, in its overrepresentation of the Human.

The zone of nonbeing and the gratuitous violence that engulfs it must always be historicized *and* "desedimentized." The zone of nonbeing is a social reality mediated by external forces (the white gaze in Fanon's key example); understanding who or how one comes to occupy it necessitates a reckoning with the differential power relations at work in the caging of being, in the unmaking of life or the making of "daily death."[99] The labor of racial desedimentation, as Nahum Chandler develops it, lies in the will "to make tremble" identificatory categories "by dislodging the layers of sedimentated premises that hold it in place."[100] Desedimentation is a check on ontology's grammar, on its propensity to fix, confuse, or explain away the scene of *ontocide*. As with the zone of nonbeing, the proletarian positions name societies' symptoms, pointing to the lived, dynamic, and historical space that produced them, a space which, by definition, cannot be sedimented, ontologized, or abstracted from the worldly flux of human existence. When Zionists and Israel's staunch defenders exceptionalize the Holocaust, they ironically repeat what Žižek dubs "the rightist slogan 'to each his or her own place'"[101]: Israeli Jews are always the victims and the Palestinians always the aggressors. In the Zionist order of things, differences are calcified— Jewishness is fetishized, Palestinianness demonized, pushed further and further into the zone of nonbeing.

To exceptionalize is thus both a protective and an accusatory gesture; it is both to defend and to attack. This is why there is some daylight between BLM activists and the Afropessimists. After the Hamas attack on October 7, BLM Grassroots, for example, affirmed that they stand in solidarity with their "Palestinian family":

> As Black people continue the fight to end militarism and mass incarceration in our own communities, let us understand the resistance in Palestine as an attempt to tear down the gates of the world's largest open air prison. As a radical Black organization grounded in abolitionist ideals, we see clear parallels between Black and Palestinian people. We, too, understand what it means to be surveilled, dehumanized, property seized, families separated, our people criminalized and slaughtered with impunity, locked up in droves, and when we resist they call us terrorists. We, too, dream of a world where our people may live freely on decolonized land. May the borders, checkpoints, prisons, police and watchlists that terrorize our communities crumble and may the world we build from their ashes honor those who have fallen in struggle.[102]

Indeed, many BLM activists do not exceptionalize their Black agenda but see common cause with Palestinians and other Indigenous groups. What they share in common is not some identity but the cruel and banal experience/structure of exclusion, the fact of being *in but not of* the world; the wretched are habitually policed, humiliated, subjugated, tortured, or exploited by a symbolic order but have "no 'proper place' within it."[103] The colonized and the internally colonized occupy a proletarian position, banished, as it were, to dwell endlessly in the zone of nonbeing. The Left cannot forfeit these proletarian positions to liberals who would immediately manage (meaning co-opt) the rage of the excluded and channel it into identitarian outlets (meaning defang it). The true opposite of exceptionalism here is solidarity. And, as for Fanon and Žižek, revolutionary solidarity or solidarity of/with the wretched must pass through class struggle, taking form through an unwavering reckoning with racial capitalism.

It is telling that many critics who are invested in exceptionalizing anti-Semitism or anti-Blackness often define what is specific about their account of suffering and victimization in stark contrast to the proletarianization of workers, along with class struggle as the main driving force for political change and a new social order. In *Is Theory Good For Jews?*, Bruno Chaouat, for example, laments the expansion of the Shoah to speak about the commodification of workers, arguing that the example of Jewish suffering and trauma gets diluted and loses its specificity once it is generalized to apply to the condition of workers.[104] The "class-struggle framework" is blamed for evacuating "all nuances of oppression."[105] The Left reduces the Holocaust to "social oppression and economic domination," absent any recognition of its "racial and metaphysical determinations."[106] With no distinctions between the camp and the factory, you "drift into downright Holocaust denial."[107] For Chaouat and others, this is the same Left that cares for workers and the Palestinians at the expense of Jews and Israel, maligning/provincializing the latter in order to defend/elevate the former. In *Afropessimism*, Wilderson interrogates the "assumptive logic of Marxism," its belief in "working-class redemption,"[108] in a class struggle that, opening to communism, would entail a restoration of the worker's equilibrium, of his status as *homo faber*, a creative being, which under capitalism generated a state of disequilibrium (alienation from self, labor, and fellow human beings). Anti-Blackness is better understood when one displaces the political economy in favor of an examination of white civil society's libidinal economy.

But when class struggle is expanded or "stretched" to account for proletarian positions, such objections to the Marxist framework must be revisited. When read alongside the proletarian position, the zone of nonbeing gives us a more elastic vision of what a global anti-racist critique can look like. It further clarifies the differences between liberal and leftist interventions. Liberals are at home when defending the interests of marginalized and often racialized groups. What is excluded from their perspective is precisely the proletarian position. As Žižek avers,

> Liberals who acknowledge the problems of those excluded from the socio-political process see their goal as the inclusion of those whose voices are not heard: all points of view should be listened to, all interests taken into account, the human rights of everyone guaranteed, all ways of life, cultures and practices respected. The obsession of this form of democracy is the protection of all kinds of minorities: cultural, religious, sexual, etc. The formula of democracy here is patient negotiation and compromise. What gets lost is the proletarian position, that of universality embodied in the excluded.[109]

And when the question of poverty or class comes up, liberals are quick to convert the working class into an identity, displacing "class struggle" in favor of "classism."[110]

The idea of the proletarian position enables us to reconceptualize the fields of struggle. The worker, the permanently unemployed and unemployable, the

Jew, the Black, and the Palestinian (among a multitude of candidates) are not to be hierarchized, crudely pitted against one another for the benefit of a liberal Oppression Olympics, which would determine which identity vying for attention deserves more recognition and accommodation within the existing world order. The wretched are societies' symptoms, the order's exploited, undesired, abject, or phobic beings, and they urge/hail us to identify with them as *"the only point of true universality."*[111] What makes any marginalized figure a potential concrete universality is their ability to stage for the world the stakes of their existence and struggle. What do they mean for justice and democracy? Étienne Balibar captures this sentiment when he describes "the Palestinian cause [as] a *test* for the recognition of right, and the implementation of international law."[112] If the Israeli state behaves like the imperial and colonial powers of old in plain daylight, *how do we as people of conscience respond to their blatant injustice?* The scandal of Gaza lies in the devastation of Palestinian lives while being told by Western powers and corporate media that Israel has a right to defend itself, meaning that it has the right to butcher women and children, has the *right to deny rights*, to deny the human rights of Palestinians, the right of health, the right to clean water, and so on. If the occupier has a right to defend itself, doesn't the occupied? Activists, academics, and everyday people are moved by the massacres that they are witnessing. But this is where we should recall Said's admiration of Fanon's multidirectional impulse to multiply his examples of affliction. The horrors visited on Palestinians are not self-enclosed. The world is on fire. What is happening in Palestine—the indiscriminate killing of civilians, the humiliation and torture of suspects, the caging of people, state violence masquerading as law, abandonment and neglect—is also happening in Sudan, Syria, Burkina Faso, and DR Congo, to name only a few examples.

The viciousness of Israel's US-funded campaign against Palestinians should concern us all. Disaster opens to "disaster occupation,"[113] which, in turn, opens to genocide. Gaza is taking on a "potent symbol of the plight of surplus humanity around the world," write William I. Robinson and Hoai-An Nguyen.[114] It is occurring in parallel with what Mbembe describes as *"the Becoming Black of the world,"* where, under late capitalism, a generalized commodification of human life is taking place, noticeably visible in the Global South, but inching itself onto the shores of the Global North, already hitting hard the poor, the racialized, and the internally colonized. The gap separating the slave and the worker is evaporating. This is yet another iteration of the afterlife of slavery—a multidirectional supplement to Afropessimism, if you will. Or to put it slightly differently, the mayhem happening in Palestine must be seen as a direct feature of this *becoming Black/wretched of the world*, deeply imbricated with "the global status quo," where, as Michael Marder puts it, we witness "the neoliberal policies of divesting public funding and condemning . . . the most vulnerable to perishing."[115] Class struggle—against imperialisms of all shades, the tyranny of market value, the gentrification and displacement of poor communities and communities of color, the risk-inducing neoliberal cannibalization of the commons, and the blotted military-industrial complexes—*and* the Palestinian fight for justice (must) imply one another.

Said is here again extremely pertinent: "And just because you represent the sufferings that your people lived through which you yourself might have lived through also, you are not relieved of the duty of revealing that your own people now may be visiting related crimes on *their* victims."[116] Unlike the Israeli state and its apologists, who weaponize Jewish suffering in order to shield Israel from censure and critique, Said refuses to exceptionalize Palestinian suffering. Whereas the "Israeli manifesto," as Gilles Deleuze describes this national project in an exchange with Elias Sanbar, rests on the notion that "we are not a people like any other people"—on the demand that the world honor their "exceptional status," acknowledging the singularity of their suffering—the "Palestinian manifesto" declares that Palestinians are "a people like any other people."[117] Waziyatawin draws attention to similar narratives of exceptionalism underlining Israel's and the United States' accounts of their origins: "the Zionist ideology that underpins Israeli colonial occupation is the same as the Manifest Destiny ideology that underpinned US colonial expansion, in that both are based on a belief in a divinely-sanctioned right to occupy someone else's land."[118] The claim "a people like any other people" makes no appeal to a theological framework to justify the Palestinian cause. The Palestinian claim to universality is grounded in a sharedness with other peoples. If Palestinians cynically played the pathos card to cover over Jewish suffering, they would undermine the cause for justice. It is a duty for Palestinians to scrutinize the actions of their own people. "Never solidarity before criticism"[119] applies internally to the various Palestinian factions. The suffering of civilians should not become an occasion for celebration. If it does, Palestinians risk compromising their own cause. There is no justice in wielding the "rhetoric and politics of blame"[120] to elevate your identity at the expense of others. The Palestinian fight for freedom and equality can never truly materialize unless you extend these same values to Israeli Jews. The universality of the Palestinian cause is premised on freedom and equality for all.

Freedom and equality are thus axiomatic. Freedom without equality can lead to cruel and unbearable situations such as the condition of Black folks following the abolition of slavery when their "freedom from bondage" came with a "freedom to starve."[121] There is no shared world—no democratic politics as such—unless freedom and equality are defended and made available to all. A neoliberal Palestine is not a free Palestine. An anti-Semitic Palestine is not a free Palestine. An anti-Black Palestine is not a free Palestine. Palestine hails us. Angela Davis describes Palestine as "a moral litmus test for the world."[122] Palestine is a test for what a settler-colonial state and its Western sponsors can get away with without paying a heavy price: *Will there be a reckoning with this miserable "era of impunity"?*[123]

Exceptionalizing Palestine, synonymous with sedimentizing Palestinian identity, ironically forecloses this reckoning *à venir*, transforming the abject Palestinian into the next empathic object for liberals to cathect or fetishize, and does more harm than good in the long run, since humanitarian reason operates by crowding out anti-colonial reason. Almost by necessity, by its pragmatic demands, humanitarian reason brackets anti-colonial futures, invisibilizes the Indigenous struggle for liberation, and, in turn, seals the Palestinians in their victimhood.[124] Though immensely needed, humanitarian aid cannot be the end goal. We cannot settle for a pre-October 7 Gaza and let humanitarian reason exhaust what must be done in Palestine/Israel. We cannot forget that the Occupation is a monster that creates monsters in abundance, a destroyer of lives *and* worlds.

Refusing the Occupation must also mean refusing the global status quo and/as the racist and neocolonial carving of the world. Solidarity with Palestine compels us all to "universalize the crisis" as Said envisaged the task of the intellectual.[125] Such solidarity agitates for universal emancipation and decries all forms of exceptionalism that unjustly serve the merciless needs of capital, shrink our access to the commons, monopolize social power, legitimize a permanent state of war, demonize the enemy, close us off to the sufferings of others, nurture narcissistic predilections, and, in the end, breed apartheid thinking and murderous ontologies. Palestine—from the river to the sea—remains an antagonistic site of defiance and invention only if the global affective response to the pain and anger of the Palestinian people is matched and surpassed by an insurgent anti-imperialist call for justice in Palestine and beyond. Palestine is our past, present, and future.

Conclusion

Unleashing the Human, or Anti-colonial Reason

Anti-colonial reason does not follow decoloniality's agitations to delink from the West, from Western modernity and its vicissitudes. It declines the lures of authenticity and precolonial times. Fanonian anti-colonial reason adopts a critical or dialectic attitude toward the West, hungering to stretch and dislocate its paradigms so that they are better able to speak to the colonial situation. It returns us to fundamental questions, none bigger than that of the "human," a status granted to some and denied to many others, a line separating zones of life from the zones of death into which too many are cast. For Žižek and the Pro-Human Camp Network to which he lends his voice, dehumanization—epitomized today in "the dehumanization of Gazans, Palestinians, and Muslims, and the dehumanization of Israelis and Jews in general"[1]—constitutes a major political problem, ethical wrong, and intellectual error that must be called out and combatted wherever it occurs. Dehumanization, which serves to "rationalize indiscriminate killing," conflates civilians and combatants, and denies human rights, proceeds by flattening depth and evacuating particularity.[2] The human is a person, irreducible to the social given, "not merely a representation of a collective identity, history, events, or political orientation."[3] Dehumanizing a person is tantamount to locking them in their race, religion, nation, or ideology.

In the face of such violence, Fanon's anti-racist, anti-colonial practices insist on *unleashing the human* from these material and symbolic shackles. Fanon repeatedly refuses the impulse to essentialize and fetishize, on the part of those who dehumanize and those resisting their own dehumanization alike:

> We shall show no pity for the former colonial governors or missionaries. In our view, an individual who loves Blacks is as "sick" as someone who abhors them. Conversely, the black man who strives to whiten his race is as wretched as the one who preaches hatred of the white man. The black man is no more

inherently amiable than the Czech; the truth is that we must unleash the man [*lâcher l'homme*].[4]

As Ato Sekyi-Otu argues, the idea, and ideal, of unleashing the human is crucial to Fanon's project: "From the beginning, the central question for Fanon was always that of releasing possibilities of human existence and history imprisoned by the colonization of experience and the racialization of consciousness."[5] The human is dear to the anti-colonial Fanon.

The act of unleashing the human, of breaking the cages of colonialism and its neocolonial successors, is, however, violent; it upends the status quo. It is a counter-violence, leveled against a racist regime that delights in sealing individuals in their being and nonbeing. (Neo)colonialism, wherever it holds sway, wreaks havoc on the human. Fanon's psychiatric work in Algeria provided myriad examples of the violence these regimes did to the colonizer and the colonized, the torturer and the tortured. While treating a French police officer who was beating his wife and three children, it became clear to Fanon that the officer's sadistic behavior and interpersonal problems at home were directly related to his torturing of Algerians and not simply the general stress of wartime. Yet this realization did not trigger an existential reckoning for the French torturer or plant the seeds for a future resistance. What he wanted from Fanon was to live the contradictions of the regime without friction, to go on dehumanizing and torturing Arabs at work while returning to a "normal" (human) life at home—to his *zone of interest*.[6] Such a demand represents a fundamental betrayal of the sole right Fanon claims for himself: "I acknowledge one right for myself: the right to demand human behavior from the other [*exiger de l'autre un comportement humain*]."[7] Anti-colonial reason insistently recalls that the West's decivilizing mission projects an image of the human that necessarily comes at the expense of the non-European. In the face of this violation, anti-colonial reason demands human behavior from the West. It demands a new grammar of the human—illegible and impossible from the standpoint of white reason.

The dual challenge, as I see it, is to condemn dehumanization *and* to "unleash the human" at the same time—to unsettle, that is, the very category of the human on which the term "dehumanization" relies. How do we do this? It cannot be by recycling the liberal language of humanism with modest updates. Judith Butler is right when they say that Fanon is invested in "a way of thinking about the human beyond humanism."[8] Humanism ironically functions here as a zone of nonbeing for those who do not meet humanity's standards, who are in but not of the human world. Exiting the zone of nonbeing means exiting humanism without simultaneously abandoning the human. Fanon's project of a new humanism—where the greatest leap consists in inventing a "new human"—dislocates extant paradigms. Fanon subjects humanism to dialectical transformation; he takes the human out of its European context and resituates it within the Manichean universe of the colonizer, which is structured by a different, anti-colonial logic.[9] Fanon's dislocation unwrites and rewrites Western humanism.

What does this dislocation look like today, however, against the daunting background of Gaza, where Western reason is flexing its genocidal muscles, eradicating the humanity and being of the Palestinian neighbor? A fight against dehumanization must pass through the liberal West, which insidiously masks its racism in the language of reason and human rights. Franco Berardi puts it well when he says, "I used to believe that reason and human rights were to be intended as universal values, but now [after Gaza] I understand that, for European intellectuals, universal means: *white*."[10] When reason and human rights are (re)claimed as the exclusive property of the white West, atrocities to non-whites follow and are effortlessly legitimized by the political class and mainstream media discourse. Here the wretched do not merely occupy a position of degraded humanity, patiently awaiting their ontological upgrade from the liberal elite; their very position of inferiority is *needed* to enable whites to establish themselves, to ground their humanity. Slightly stretching an Afropessimist analysis, I argue that there is no whiteness/humanity without the wretched (of which the Black/slave is certainly a crushing, though not exhaustive, image), the constitutive outsider — the real neighbor, the faceless face, the other other. This antagonism between the human and the wretched preoccupies anti-colonial reason. When Israeli civil society, under the sway of a supremacist Zionism, depends on anti-Palestinian violence (on its efficiency and the libidinal kick that it produces) for its coherence, when Israeli humanity establishes and reaffirms itself against the being of the Palestinian (interpellated as human animal), decrying dehumanization can only take you so far before it starts obfuscating the racial matrix of the human. The universality of humanity in its current form is a sham. The discourse of human rights has been exposed as myopic and toothless; it matters only if it receives the backing of Western powers (without which the UN Security Council is impotent) and aligns with those the West deems protectable (Israelis, not Palestinians). Human rights discourse is part of the master/settler's tools and thus will not dismantle the master/settler's house.[11]

But universality is not a privilege of white folks. Both Fanon and Žižek ask us to persist and resist the temptation to jettison universality altogether as corrupt and murderous. It is surely that, but it is also much more. Universality can, must, be de-Westernized, de-whitened, and unleashed. Human rights can be reclaimed outside the stifling parameters of humanitarian reason if they are politicized anew. Tools dislocated and re-invented can prove to be more trenchant and emancipatory. Pro-Palestinian solidarity movements are not only asking for a ceasefire and aid; they are animated by a counter-desire, the political demand for Palestinian liberation. They refuse Israel's manufactured "new normal," and embrace the Palestinian cause as a universalist calling, in line with Ghassan Kanafani's revolutionary vision: "The Palestinian cause is not a cause for

Palestinians only, but a cause for every revolutionary, wherever he is, as a cause for the exploited and oppressed masses in our era."[12] The signifier "Palestine" discloses "the colonial nature of the rest of the world," as Noura Erakat puts it.[13] The force of Palestine lies in its capacity to make you care about others, not as an image of yourself, but in all their wretchedness. Palestine illuminates the faceless neighbors of the world.

In the asphyxiating reality that surrounds us, the liberal Left is of little help. Ontological upheavals, radical ruptures, are frowned upon. If you are dwelling in the zone of nonbeing (the world's surplus humanity, the wretched, the nothing and less-than-nothing), this liberalism offers limited options: formulate your grievances in tribalist or identitarian terms (you'll receive a friendly audience unless you're too violent and/or your identity happens to be Palestinian); accept your position on the grounds you might make things worse (beware the election of the likes of Trump or Le Pen—be quiet and make sure to vote for the reproduction of what is[14]). The power of the status quo is bewitching. The beneficiaries don't want to let it go, even when they are exposed to the horrors unfolding within it. Fetishist disavowal, as Žižek stresses, points to "the material force of ideology which makes us refuse what we see and know."[15] When the liberal Left looks at the misery all around the world, it wants to intervene and lessen human suffering but understands global problems only through the depoliticized lenses of humanitarian reason.[16] The liberal Left's default mode is effectively counterrevolutionary. *Yes, liberal powers can be convinced that Palestinians are victims (collateral damage), but don't cast them as freedom fighters, as agents demanding justice—that's anti-Semitic*. Under settler/liberal eyes, Indigenous "active resistance" itself is automatically demonized and pathologized.[17] Humanitarian reason delegitimizes counter-violence in all its manifestations. Structural inequities and injustices, at home and abroad, are not to be reckoned with. Consequently, Palestinians get revengeful genocide from Israel, but "compassionate genocide" from the United States (genocide plus humanitarian aid, sometimes in the form, moreover, of airdropped pallets that literally kill Gazans).[18]

Anti-colonial reason demands more. It summons you to resist, to see your resistance as a form of undoing. To the many liberals who delight in targeting who or what they perceive as a challenge to the moral status quo, preferring global violence in its objective mode, invisible—basically, someone else's problem—we may say in the spirit of Max Horkheimer,[19] *Whoever is not willing to talk about systemic anti-Blackness should also keep quiet about Trump's threat and the populist Right. Whoever is not willing to talk about Israeli state terrorism should also keep quiet about Hamas. Whoever is not willing to talk about the anti-Arab racism of the French Republic should also keep quiet about Marine Le Pen and the National Rally.*

Dispossession and displacement are features, not bugs, of the new global order. The misery and death, political and biological, of the faceless thirds that mark today's global horizon herald dystopian futures. The normalization of man-made evil threatens to take hold. At the same time, a politics of the faceless is mobilizing, working toward "collectivizing our catastrophic condition."[20] *Ressentiment* trembles in anticipation of its public use. Resistance keeps intensifying. A counter-violence dreams of ontological mutations and social change. Solidarities are multiplying. What world will this be? What world do we want? Are we witnessing a genocidal glimpse into "what is yet to come,"[21] a "dress rehearsal"[22] for future catastrophes, a terrifying Gazafication of the world? Perhaps it is not hyperbole to say that the future of humanity and the world will depend on our critical response to the resurgence of colonial cruelty in Palestine and beyond.

Afterword
A Small Note on a Great Book
Slavoj Žižek

I owe Zahi Zalloua two sleepless nights—that's how long it took me to swallow the manuscript of his *Fanon, Žižek, and the Violence of Resistance*. The book is much more than "interesting": it shattered me profoundly not only because it applied some of my thoughts to a specific domain of violence in relations between races. Zalloua also articulated my thoughts in a much more consequent and consistent way than I did in my often-messy writings. Since I am unable to add anything meaningful to the specific topic of the book, I will limit myself to how Zalloua compelled me to reformulate my own premises on violence.

The standard liberal motto apropos violence—it is sometimes necessary to resort to it, but it is never legitimate—is not sufficient: from the radical emancipatory perspective, one should turn this motto around. For the oppressed, violence is always legitimate (since their very status is the result of the violence they are exposed to), but never necessary—it is always a matter of strategic consideration whether to use violence against the enemy or not. What does this amount to?

Patrick Stewart (a left-wing Socialist actor who superbly played Lenin in the 1974 TV series *Fall of Eagles*) says as Lenin (and the imagined words fit the real Lenin perfectly): "Objectively, the enemy can be your best friend, your lover, your party colleague, the chairman of your local branch, the editor of your party journal. The battle that's coming now is not with the tsar, it is with ourselves."[1] I first misread these lines, reading them not the way they are obviously meant, as a globalized suspicion ("your enemy can be even your best friend, one among your closest circle"), but in the opposite sense: your greatest friend is the one whom you perceive as your enemy. However, my misreading also delivers its own truth: since the goal of the revolutionary activity is to bring about an actual revolution (taking power), the enemy's gestures which unwittingly create conditions for the revolution are very helpful.

That's why Lenin was horrified by Stolypin's reforms which, if successful, would postpone revolution for decades. (Pyotr Arkadyevich Stolypin served as the third prime minister and the interior minister of the Russian Empire from 1906 until his assassination in 1911. Known as the greatest reformer of Russian society and economy, Prime Minister Stolypin initiated major agrarian reforms, known as the Stolypin reforms, that granted the right of private land ownership to the peasantry. His reforms caused unprecedented growth of the Russian state, which was halted by his assassination. Lenin was relieved by Stolypin's death: he immediately grasped that the final result of his reforms would have been a satisfied peasant class with no will to engage in revolutionary activity. Stolypin was thus the true enemy, and the hardliners who cancelled his reforms after his death were objectively our friends . . .).

The point is thus not to engage in unconstrained physical violence but to tell the truth, to *unleash the violence of words which shatter and mobilize people*. The actual political violence that may follow should be practiced in a Gandhian way, taking into account all the usual humanitarian considerations—no such constraints hold for the Word at its beginning, and for the violence that sustains it. This is why the structure of state power that best fits our predicament should be triple, not just democracy plus a stupid monarch elected by a lot, but added to it, a collective body standing for social wisdom (not just experts). Take ecology: the necessary tough measures needed to cope with ecological threats cannot be left to a democratic vote. Today, in an age when the fateful limitation of the Western model of multiparty liberal democracy is becoming more and more obvious, the need to supplement liberal democracy with another mechanism of power is also growing.

There is no reason to despise democratic elections; the point is only to insist that they are not per se an indication of Truth—as a rule, they tend to reflect the predominant doxa determined by the hegemonic ideology. There can be democratic elections which enact an event of Truth—the election in which, against the skeptic-cynical inertia—the majority momentarily "awakens" and votes against the hegemonic ideological opinion; however, the very exceptional status of such a surprising electoral result proves that elections as such are not a medium of Truth. This position of a minority which stands for All is more than ever actual today, in our post-political epoch in which the plurality of opinions reigns: under such conditions, the universal Truth is by definition a minority position. As Sophie Wahnich points out, in a democracy corrupted by media, this is what "the freedom of the press without the duty to resist" amounts to: "The right to say anything in a political relativism instead of a demanding and sometimes even lethal ethics of truth."[2] In such a situation, the uncompromisingly-insisting voice of truth (about ecology, about biogenetics, about AI, about the excluded . . .) cannot but appear as "irrational" in its lack of consideration for the opinions of others, in its refusal of the spirit of pragmatic compromises, in its apocalyptic finality.

What grounds a truth is the experience of suffering and courage, sometimes in solitude, not the number and force of the majority. This, of course, does not mean that there are infallible criteria for the truth: the assertion of Truth involves a kind of wager, a risky decision; one should cut out its path, sometimes even enforce it. Those who tell the truth are, as a rule, first not understood; they struggle (also with themselves) and seek for the proper language to tell it. It is the full recognition of this dimension of risk and wager, of the absence of any external guarantee, which distinguishes the authentic truth-engagement from any form of "totalitarianism" or "fundamentalism." But, again: how are we to distinguish clearly this "demanding and sometimes even lethal ethics of truth" from the sectarian attempts to impose one's own position upon all others? How can we be sure that the voice of the minoritarian "part of no-part" is effectively the voice of universal truth and not merely a particular grievance?

The first thing to bear in mind here is that the truth we are dealing with is not "objective" truth, but the self-relating truth about one's own subjective position; as such, this truth is an engaged truth, measured not by its factual accuracy but by the way it affects the subjective position of enunciation. In his Seminar 18 on "a discourse which would not be of a semblance," Lacan provided a succinct definition of the truth of interpretation in psychoanalysis: "Interpretation is not tested by a truth that would decide by yes or no, it unleashes truth as such. It is only true inasmuch as it is truly followed." There is nothing "theological" in this precise formulation, only the insight into the properly dialectical unity of theory and practice in (not only) psychoanalytic interpretation: the "test" of the analyst's interpretation is in the violent truth-effect it unleashes in the patient. And Zalloua's book certainly did this to me.

Notes

Introduction

1. James Baldwin, "Not everything that is faced can be changed; but nothing can be changed until it is faced" (James Baldwin, "As Much of the Truth as One Can Bear," *The New York Times*, January 14, 1962, https://timesmachine.nytimes.com/timesmachine/1962/01/14/118438007.pdf?pdf_redirect=true&ip=0).
2. Frantz Fanon, *Black Skin, White Masks*, trans. Richard Philcox (New York: Grove Press, 2008), 90.
3. Gautam Basu Thakur, "Fanon's 'Zone of Nonbeing': Blackness and the Politics of the Real," in *Lacan and Race: Racism, Identity, and Psychoanalytic Theory*, ed. Sheldon George and Derek Hook (New York: Routledge, 2022), 284.
4. Fanon, *Black Skin*, 6.
5. Fanon, *Black Skin*, 94.
6. Fanon, *Black Skin*, 18.
7. Slavoj Žižek and Glyn Daly, *Conversations with Žižek* (Cambridge: Polity Press, 2004), 120.
8. Žižek, "The Jacobin Spirit," *Jacobin*, May 26, 2011. https://jacobin.com/2011/05/the-jacobin-spirit.
9. Žižek, "The Jacobin Spirit." In a similar vein, Marc Lamont Hill questions a simple opposition between violence and nonviolence: "We must prioritize peace, but we must not romanticize or fetishize it. We must advocate and promote nonviolence at every opportunity, but we cannot endorse a narrow politics of respectability that shames Palestinians for resisting, for refusing to do nothing in the face of state violence and ethnic cleansing" (Eli Day, "Marc Lamont Hill Has Secured His Place in the Proud Black Anti-Colonial Tradition," *In These Times*, December 11, 2018. https://inthesetimes.com/article/marc-lamont-hill-cnn-palestine-israel-apartheid-jim-crow-black-radical). Josh Ruebner puts the matter even more forcefully: "No example exists in the historical record of a colonized, brutalized people accepting their fate without meting out in small measure a taste of the overwhelming violence inflicted upon them by the colonizer. To demand that Palestinians eschew violence while Israel continues to trample over them is to exceptionalize Palestinians, to illegitimately concede on their behalf their right to freedom, to acquiesce in and buttress Israel's drive to permanently control all of historic Palestine and do everything conceivable to erase the Palestinians' irrefutable existence and resiliency" (Josh Ruebner, "'Die, Son of a Whore!' 'Give Him One in the Head.' This

Is What It Sounds Like When Israeli Security Kills Palestinian Kids," *Salon*, October 19, 2015. https://www.salon.com/2015/10/19/die_son_of_a_whore_give_him_one_in_the_head_this_is_what_it_sounds_like_when_israeli_security_kills_palestinian_kids/.

10 Žižek, "Some Concluding Notes on Violence, Ideology and Communist Culture," *Subjectivity* 3, no. 1 (2010): 101.

11 Somdeep Sen, "There Is Nothing Surprising About Hamas's Operation," *Al Jazeera*, October 8, 2023. https://www.aljazeera.com/opinions/2023/10/8/there-is-nothing-surprising-about-hamass-operation.

12 Žižek and Daly, *Conversations with Žižek*, 121.

13 Fanon, *Black Skin*, 204.

14 Žižek, "Some Concluding Notes," 105.

15 Jacques Lacan, *On Feminine Sexuality, The Limits of Love and Knowledge, 1972–1973: Encore, The Seminar of Jacques Lacan, Book XX*, trans. Bruce Fink (New York: Norton, 1998).

16 As Lacan argues, the "relation between the subject and the phallus . . . forms without regard to the anatomical distinction between the sexes" (Lacan, "The Signification of the Phallus," in *Écrits: The First Complete Edition in English*, trans. Bruce Fink [New York: Norton, 2006], 576).

17 Žižek, *For They Know Not What They Do* (New York: Verso, 2008), 123.

18 Žižek, *For They Know*, xxii.

19 Žižek, *For They Know*, xxii.

20 Žižek, *The Puppet and the Dwarf: The Perverse Core of Christianity* (Cambridge, MA: MIT Press, 2003), 69.

21 Žižek, *Less Than Nothing: Hegel and the Shadow of Dialectical Materialism* (New York: Verso, 2012), 958.

22 Jacques Rancière, *Disagreement: Politics and Philosophy*, trans. Julie Rose (Minneapolis: University of Minnesota Press, 1999), 11.

23 Žižek, *Demanding the Impossible*, ed. Yong-June Park (Cambridge: Polity Press, 2013), 60.

24 Žižek, *The Universal Exception*, ed. Rex Butler and Scott Stephens (New York: Continuum, 2006), 179.

25 Achille Mbembe, *Critique of Black Reason*, trans. Laurent Dubois (Durham: Duke University Press, 2017), 1.

26 Fanon, *The Wretched of the Earth*, trans. Richard Philcox (New York: Grove Press, 2004), 1.

27 Žižek, "Human Rights and Its Discontents," Lecture at Bard College, November 15, 1999. http://www.lacan.com/zizek-human.htm.

28 Žižek, *In Defense of Lost Causes* (New York: Verso, 2008), 6.

29 Žižek, *The Parallax View* (Cambridge, MA: MIT Press, 2006), 9.

30 Immanuel Kant, "An Answer to the Question: What Is Enlightenment?" in *What Is Enlightenment? Eighteenth-Century Answers and Twentieth-Century Questions*, ed. James Schmidt (Berkeley: University of California Press, 1996), 60.

31 Žižek, *Violence: Six Sideways Reflections* (New York: Picador, 2008), 143.
32 Žižek, "Anti-Semitism and Its Transformations," in *Deconstructing Zionism: A Critique of Political* Metaphysics, ed. Gianni Vattimo and Michael Marder (New York: Bloomsbury, 2014), 6.
33 Žižek, "A Leftist Plea for 'Eurocentrism,'" *Critical Inquiry* 24, no. 4 (1998): 988.
34 Ato Sekyi-Out, "Dialectics in Dispute, with Aristotle as Witness," in *Violence, Slavery and Freedom between Hegel and Fanon*, ed. Ulrike Kistner and Philippe Van Hauteix (Johannesburg: Wits University Press, 2020), 2.
35 Fanon, *Black Skin*, 195n.10.
36 Fanon, *Black Skin*, 89.
37 Fanon, *Black Skin*, 95.
38 Fanon, *Black Skin*, 204.
39 Charles Taylor, "The Politics of Recognition," in *Multiculturalism: Examining the Politics of Recognition*, ed. Amy Gutmann (Princeton: Princeton University Press, 1994), 25.
40 Christopher Chen, "Race and the Politics of Recognition," in *The Sage Handbook of Frankfurt Critical Theory*, ed. Beverly Best, Werner Bonefeld, and Chris O'Kane (London: SAGE Publications Ltd., 2018), 932–51.
41 Fanon, *Black Skin*, xii.
42 Lewis R. Gordon, "Through the Hellish Zone of Nonbeing: Thinking through Fanon, Disaster, and the Damned of the Earth," *Human Architecture: Journal of the Sociology of Self-Knowledge* 5, no. 3 (2007): 11.
43 Žižek, "Hegel: The Spirit of Distrust," in *Reading Hegel*, ed. Slavoj Žižek, Frank Ruda, and Agon Hamza (Cambridge: Polity Press, 2022), 23; see Judith Butler, "Hegel for Our Times," *IAI News*, November 22, 2019. https://iai.tv/articles/hegel-for-our-times-judith-butler-auid-1273?fbclid=IwAR1-A3knyBu7-LlbYwnSl5i2Frf6GAMK_JUBDEfWj0Xvm2RGqFlufXRBB7A.
44 Žižek, "Hegel: The Spirit of Distrust," 23.
45 Žižek, "Hegel: The Spirit of Distrust," 23.
46 Fanon, *Black Skin*, xii; see also David Marriott, "Blackness: N'est Pas?" *Propter Nos* 4 (2020): 27–51.
47 Geo Maher, *Decolonizing Dialectics* (Durham: Duke University Press, 2017), 57.
48 Fanon, *Black Skin*, xiii.
49 Fanon, *Black Skin*, 193.
50 Ulrike Kistner and Philippe Van Hauteix, "Hegel/Fanon: Transpositions in Translations," in *Violence, Slavery and Freedom between Hegel and Fanon*, ed. Ulrike Kistner and Philippe Van Hauteix (Johannesburg: Wits University Press, 2020), vii.
51 Fanon, *Black Skin*, 192, translation modified.
52 Fanon, *Black Skin*, 192.
53 Fanon, *Black Skin*, 191.
54 Fanon, *Black Skin*, 194–5.

55 Fanon, *The Wretched of the Earth*, 44.
56 Fanon, *Black Skin*, 191.
57 Fanon, *Black Skin*, 193.
58 Fanon, *The Wretched of the Earth*, 4.
59 Fanon, *The Wretched of the Earth*, 5.
60 Žižek, *Freedom: A Disease Without Cure* (New York: Bloomsbury, 2023), 82.
61 Žižek, *Freedom*, 81.
62 Fanon, *Black Skin*, 194.
63 Fanon, *Black Skin*, 194.
64 Fanon, *Black Skin*, 195.
65 Fanon, *Black Skin*, 196.
66 Fanon, *Black Skin*, 196.
67 As Adam Shatz observes, "Like most of his fellow islanders, he seems to have been unaware of the Martinican slave revolt of 1848, which immediately preceded emancipation, or of the sporadic slave uprisings that had rocked the island throughout its history" (Adam Shatz, *The Rebel's Clinic: The Revolutionary Lives of Frantz Fanon* [New York: Farrar, Straus and Giroux, 2024], 19). See also Rebecca Hartkopf Schloss, *Sweet Liberty: The Final Days of Slavery in Martinique* (Philadelphia: University of Pennsylvania Press, 2009); Chris Bongie, *Islands and Exiles: The Creole Identities of Post/Colonial Literature* (Stanford: Stanford University Press, 1997).
68 Like many thinkers and activists, Fanon decries the route of departmentalization—rather than radically breaking from France—chosen for Martinique by Aimé Césaire, the politician.
69 Fanon, *Black Skin*, 197.
70 Fanon, *Black Skin*, 197.
71 Jean Améry, *At the Mind's Limits: Contemplations by a Survivor on Auschwitz and Its Realities*, trans. Sidney Rosenfeld and Stella P. Rosenfeld (Bloomington: Indiana University Press 1980), 71. Améry's bold defense of *ressentiment* finds its political undoing when it comes to Zionism and the state of Israel. Améry regresses to the private use of *ressentiment*, failing to find common cause with the oppressed of Israel: namely, the Palestinians in their political struggle against colonial erasure, against the machinery of settler colonialism. Améry's position on Israel is effectively counterrevolutionary, legitimizing state violence against the native Palestinians. Not unlike Améry's *ressentimental* resistance to Germany's post-Nazism rhetoric, Palestinian *ressentiment* expresses a refusal to allow the crime of Indigenous genocide to become a moral reality for the Zionist settler. It is as if Améry brackets the negativity of *ressentiment*, or it simply allows it to take a back seat to his tribalistic attachment to Israel: "For me, Israel is not an auspicious promise, not a biblically legitimized territorial claim, no Holy Land. It is simply the place where survivors have gathered, a state in which every inhabitant still, and for a long time to come, must fear for his life. My solidarity with Israel is a means of staying loyal to those of my comrades who perished" (Améry, "My Jewishness," in *Essays on Antisemitism, Anti-Zionism, and the Left*, ed. Marlene Gallner [Bloomington: Indiana University Press, 2022], 85).

72 Žižek, *Violence*, 189–90.
73 Žižek, *Violence*, 190.
74 Zahi Zalloua, *The Politics of the Wretched: Race, Reason, and Ressentiment* (New York: Bloomsbury, 2024).
75 Originally published as "Beantwortung der Frage: Was is Aufklärung?" in the journal *Berlinische Monatsschrift*.
76 Fanon, *The Wretched of the Earth*, 5.
77 James Penney, "Passing into the Universal: Fanon, Sartre, and the Colonial Dialectic," *Paragraph* 27, no. 3 (2004): 62.
78 Nancy Fraser, *Justice Interruptus: Critical Reflections on the "Postsocialist" Condition* (New York: Routledge, 1997), 24.
79 Fanon, *The Wretched of the Earth*, 89, translation modified.
80 Jacques Rancière, "Who Is the Subject of the Rights of Man?" *The South Atlantic Quarterly* 103, no. 2 (2004): 304.
81 Susan Neiman, "Fanon the Universalist," *The New York Review*, June 6, 2024. https://www.nybooks.com/articles/2024/06/06/fanon-the-universalist-the-rebels-clinic-shatz/.
82 Glen Sean Coulthard, *Red Skin, White Masks: Rejecting the Colonial Politics of Recognition* (Minneapolis: University of Minnesota Press, 2014), 6.
83 "Colonial relations of power are no longer reproduced primarily through overtly coercive means, but rather through the asymmetrical exchange of mediated forms of state recognition and accommodation" (Coulthard, *Red Skin*, 15).
84 Jodi A. Byrd, *The Transit of Empire: Indigenous Critiques of Colonialism* (Minneapolis: University of Minnesota Press, 2011), xxiii.
85 W. G. Sebald, "Against the Irreversible. On Jean Améry," in *On the Natural History of Destruction* (Toronto: Alfred A. Knopf, 2003), 156, translation modified.
86 Byrd, "The Past Is Never Dead," *The Cornell Daily Sun*, May 14, 2024. https://cornellsun.com/2024/05/14/byrd-the-past-is-never-dead/.
87 Fraser, *Justice Interruptus*, 23.
88 Flavio Zenun Almada, "The Particular Lived Experience of the Black in Portugal," in *Fanon Today: Reason and Revolt of The Wretched of the Earth*, ed. Nigel Gibson (Québec: Daraja Press, 2021), 37.
89 Ato Sekyi-Otu, *Homestead, Homeland, Home: Critical Reflections* (Ottawa: Dajara Press, 2023), ii.
90 Sekyi-Otu, *Homestead, Homeland, Home*, ii.
91 Fanon, "Why We Use Violence," in *Political Writings* from *Alienation and Freedom*, ed. Jean Khalfa and Robert J. C. Young (New York: Bloomsbury, 2021), 655.
92 Fanon, "Why We Use Violence," 655.
93 Fanon, "Why We Use Violence," 654.
94 Adam Shatz catalogs some of the charges leveled at the protesters: "The protesters were. . . accused of making Jews feel unsafe with their ritualised denunciations of Zionism, of grandstanding, of engaging in a fantasy of 1968-style rebellion, of ignoring Hamas's cruelties or even justifying them, of romanticising

armed struggle in their calls to 'globalise the intifada,' of being possessed by a Manichean fervour that blinded them to the complexities of a war that involved multiple parties, not just Israel and Gaza" (Adam Shatz, "Israel's Descent," *London Review of Books*, June 20, 2024. https://www.lrb.co.uk/the-paper/v46/n12/adam-shatz/israel-s-descent).

95 Nigel Gibson, *Fanon: The Postcolonial Imagination* (Cambridge: Polity Press, 2003), 13.

96 Žižek, *Like a Thief in Broad Daylight: Power in the Era of Post-Humanity* (New York: Allen Lane, 2018), 128.

97 Fanon, *The Wretched of the Earth*, 51.

98 Fanon, *The Wretched of the Earth*, 96.

99 Shatz, *The Rebel's Clinic*, 155.

100 Aimé Césaire, "La révolte de Frantz Fanon," *Jeune Afrique*, December 13–19, 1961, my translation. https://www.jeuneafrique.com/178228/politique/la-r-volte-de-frantz-fanon-par-aim-c-saire/.

101 Fanon, *A Dying Colonialism*, trans. Haakon Chevalier (New York: Grove Press, 1965), 25.

102 Fanon, *Black Skin*, 206.

103 For Sartre, the violence of the colonized toward the colonizer is a necessity and a good: "A single duty, a single objective: drive out colonialism by *every* means. . . . [T]his irrepressible violence is neither a storm in a teacup nor the reemergence of savage instincts nor even a consequence of resentment: it is man reconstructing himself. . . . [N]o indulgence can erase the marks of violence: violence alone can eliminate them. . . . [K]illing a European is killing two birds with one stone, eliminating in one go oppressor and oppressed: leaving one man dead and the other man free" (Jean-Paul Sartre, "Preface," in *The Wretched of the Earth*, trans. Richard Philcox [New York: Grove Press, 2004], lv).

104 Fanon, *The Wretched of the Earth*, 23.

105 Mark LeVine, "Fanon's Conception of Violence Does Not Work in Palestine," *Al Jazeera*, October 10, 2023. https://www.aljazeera.com/opinions/2023/10/10/fanons-conception-of-violence-does-not-work-in-palestine.

106 LeVine, "Fanon's Conception of Violence."

107 LeVine, "Fanon's Conception of Violence."

108 Rashid Khalidi, "The Neck and the Sword: Interviewed by Tariq Ali," *New Left Review* 147 (2024): 7.

109 Khalidi, "The Neck and the Sword," 7.

110 Robert J. C. Young rightly takes issue with Hannah Arendt's dismissive early critique of Fanon's alleged glorification of violence. Young exposes Arendt's misleading quotation from Fanon's *The Wretched of the Earth*: "In citing Fanon on violence, Arendt deliberately excises this emphasis on the reciprocal, reactive dimension to the originary violence of colonization. So she criticizes Fanon for endorsing violence by means of the following quotation: 'the practice of violence which binds men together as a whole, since each individual forms a violent link in the great chain, a part of the great organism of violence which has surged upward'" (Hannah Arendt, *On Violence* [New York: Harcourt Books, 1970], 67).

Arendt dishonestly leaves out the words "in reaction to the settler's violence in the beginning" following "has surged upward." Young concludes: "So it wasn't that Arendt just neglected to take the Algerian situation of reciprocal violence into account when discussing Fanon's essay on violence—she deliberately removed it from his own sentence in order to allow her characterize Fanon's validation of anti-colonial violence as a decontextualized, dehistoricized irrational rage and deep hatred which she could then associate with the Black student and Black Power movements in the US in her own time" (Robert J. C. Young, "Frantz Fanon and Hannah Arendt: Anger and Racism," *The Comparatist* 48 [2024]: 173). In our own time, Arendt's legacy lives on in today's liberal gatekeepers who virulently object to anti-colonial protests, involving many students of color, at the Gaza encampments at US universities and beyond. See also Kathryn T. Gines (Kathryn Sophia Belle), *Hannah Arendt and the Negro Question* (Bloomington: Indiana University Press, 2014).

111 Nicki Kattoura and Geo Maher, "Israel-Palestine War: Why Must Palestinians Condemn Themselves for Daring to Fight Back?" *Middle East Eye*, November 9, 2023. https://www.middleeasteye.net/opinion/israel-palestine-war-why-condemnation-trap.

112 Cofounder of the Black Panther Party Huey P. Newton comments on the boomerang effect of anti-colonial violence: "Fanon made a statement during the Algerian war that impressed me; he said it was the 'Year of the Boomerang' which is the third phase of violence. At that point, the violence of the aggressor turns on him and strikes a killing blow. Yet the oppressor does not understand the process; he knows no more than he did in the first phase when he launched the violence. The oppressed are always defensive; the oppressor is always aggressive and surprised when the people turn back on him the force he has used against them" (Huey P. Newton, *Revolutionary Suicide* [New York: Penguin Books, 1973], 117).

113 A. Dirk Moses, "More than Genocide," *Boston Review*, November 14, 2023. https://www.bostonreview.net/articles/more-than-genocide/.

114 Vladimir Ze'ev Jabotinsky, "The Iron Wall," November 4, 1923. https://www.jewishvirtuallibrary.org/quot-the-iron-wall-quot. Though Zionists claim a metaphysical Indigeneity to the land of Israel, they also saw themselves ideologically as European settlers colonizing native land. Tom Segev captures well this ambivalence at the core of Zionist identity: "Zionist leaders in Palestine were furious at British administrators who classified them as *natives*, an insulting colonialist term. The Zionists maintained that the natives were the Arabs; they, the Zionists, represented European culture" (Tom Segev, *Elvis in Jerusalem: Post Zionism and the Americanization of Israel* [New York: Metropolitan Books, 2002], 33).

115 Jabotinsky, "The Iron Wall." To be sure, Jabotinsky's honesty about the Zionist project—how it understood itself as an agonistic movement in relation to the native population—was not shared by all Zionists. Whereas Jabotinsky readily admitted that "the use of massive force against the Arab majority would be necessary to implement the Zionist program," Theodor Herzl and his followers "protested the innocent purity of their aims and deceived their Western listeners, and perhaps themselves, with fairy tales about their benign intentions toward the Arab inhabitants of Palestine" (Rashid Khalidi, *The Hundred Years' War on Palestine: A History of Settler Colonialism and Resistance, 1917–2017* [New York: Metropolitan Books, 2020], 16–17).

116 Perhaps we need to make an additional distinction here between Israel's expectation that Palestinians (as any occupied people) would fight back against an occupier and Israel's colonial belief that the Palestinians are simply *inferior*, incapable of breaking through its high-tech border defenses and boldly striking the enemy on their own soil. The surprise thus lies not in the fact that Hamas attacked, that the brutal raid was "unprovoked," but that Hamas was not contained and succeeded in its attack. Israel never expected this level of sophistication from the savage Natives next door. The genocidal onslaught must be read, then, at least in part, as Israel's response to its narcissistic wound, its attempt to recapture its former phantasmatic self—its sense of superiority and invulnerability—by turning the Gaza Strip into rubble. See Joseph Massad, "Just Another Battle or the Palestinian War of Liberation?" *The Electronic Intifada*, October 8, 2023. https://electronicintifada.net/content/just-another-battle-or-palestinian-war-liberation/38661; Jodi Dean, "Palestine Speaks for Everyone," *Verso Books*, April 9, 2024. https://www.versobooks.com/blogs/news/palestine-speaks-for-everyone; Haidar Eid, "Gaza 2023: Our Warsaw Uprising Moment," *Al Jazeera*, October 10, 2023. https://www.aljazeera.com/opinions/2023/10/10/gaza-2023-our-warsaw-uprising-moment.

117 Moses, "More than Genocide."

118 See A. Dirk Moses, *The Problems of Genocide: Permanent Security and the Language of Transgression* (New York: Cambridge University Press, 2021).

119 Black for Palestine, "2015 Black Solidarity Statement with Palestine." https://www.blackforpalestine.com/2015-statement.html; and Black for Palestine, "Black Solidarity with Gaza - #CeasefireNow." https://www.blackforpalestine.com/2023statement.html.

120 Žižek, *Less than Nothing*, 996.

121 Franco "Bifo" Berardi, "Sabotage and Self-Organization," *Ill Will*, May 6, 2024. https://illwill.com/sabotage-and-self-organization.

122 Michael Smerconish, *CNN Transcripts*, May 11, 2024. https://transcripts.cnn.com/show/smer/date/2024-05-11/segment/01.

123 Shatz gives some credence to these accusations: "There is, of course, a grain of truth to these criticisms. Like 'defund the police,' 'from the river to the sea' is appealing in its absolutism, but also dangerously ambiguous, fuel for right-wing adversaries looking for evidence of calls for 'genocide' against Jews. And there was, as there always is, a theatrical dimension to the protests, with some students imagining themselves to be part of the same drama unfolding in Gaza, confusing the rough clearing of an encampment ('liberated zones') with the violent destruction of a refugee camp" (Shatz, "Israel's Descent").

124 Žižek, *Less Than Nothing*, 996.

125 Fanon, *The Wretched of the Earth*, 3.

126 Fanon, *The Wretched of the Earth*, 7.

127 As Samuel P. Catlin rightly observed, the students at the encampment are throwing a wrench in what Lee Edelman refers to as "reproductive futurism," a politics thoroughly invested in the Child, which incarnates innocence and universal hope, the "citizen as an ideal, entitled to claim full rights to its future share in the nation's good, though always at the cost of limiting the rights 'real'

citizens are allowed" (Lee Edelman, *No Future: Queer Theory and the Death Drive* [Durham: Duke University Press, 2004], 11). The university—despite its rhetoric of wanting to produce critical graduates who can meet the challenges of an ever-changing world—is meant to serve an ideological function, nurture the Child/Student, so that the reproduction of the status quo appears effortless. "What is most libidinally threatening to the social order about protest 'on campus,'" writes Catlin, "is that the students themselves incite and participate in it" (Samuel P. Catlin, "The Campus Does Not Exist," *Parapraxis* 4 [Summer 2024]. https://www.parapraxismagazine.com/articles/the-campus-does-not-exist). Protecting the Child/Student becomes problematic. The threat is coming from within the sacrosanct space of the university. Students in solidarity with Palestine are unruly and must be disciplined. Consequently, they are set apart from the innocent Child— embodied now by Jewish students who *feel* threatened by pro-Palestinian verbal assaults—so they become disaffiliated by presidential fiat, punished and rendered outsiders to campus life. See also Daniel Spaulding, "On Hating Students," *e-flux*, May 28, 2024. https://www.e-flux.com/education/features/610182/on-hating-students.

128   Bruno Maçães, "Gaza and Ukraine Have Divided the World into Geopolitical Tribes," *The New Statesman*, November 15, 2023. https://www.newstatesman.com/world/middle-east/2023/11/gaza-ukraine-world-geopolitical-tribes?utm_source=substack&utm_medium=email.

129   Amnesty International's Annual Report 2023/24 notes: "In a conflict that defined 2023 and shows no sign of abating, evidence of war crimes continues to mount as the Israeli government makes a mockery of international law in Gaza" (Amnesty International, "The State of the World's Human Rights," *Amnesty International's Annual Report 2023/24*, April 24, 2024. https://www.amnesty.org/en/latest/news/2024/04/amnesty-international-sounds-alarm-international-law-flagrant-rule-breaking-governments-corporate-actors/.

130   "Ukrainian Letter of Solidarity with Palestinian People," *Commons*, November 2, 2023. https://commons.com.ua/en/ukrayinskij-list-solidarnosti/.

131   Fanon, *Black Skin*, 201.

132   Nigel Gibson, "Fanon, Movement, Self-Movement," in *Fanon Today: Reason and Revolt of The Wretched of the Earth*, ed. Nigel Gibson (Québec: Daraja Press, 2021), 274.

133   Žižek, *Violence*, 1–2.

134   Žižek, *Violence*, 2.

135   Žižek, *Violence*, 2.

136   Fawas Turki, *The Disinherited: Journal of a Palestinian Exile, With an Epilogue 1974* (New York: Monthly Review Press, 1974), 160.

137   Žižek, "Anti-Semitism and Its Transformations," 8; see also Saree Makdisi, *Palestine Inside Out: An Everyday Occupation* (New York: Norton, 2008).

138   Sara Roy, "Econocide in Gaza," in *Deluge: Gaza and Israel From Crisis to Cataclysm* (New York: OR Books, 2024), 38.

139   Roy, "Econocide in Gaza," 39.

140 David E. Sanger and Peter Baker, "Biden Is 'Outraged.' But Is He Willing to Use America's Leverage With Israel?" *The New York Times*, April 3, 2024. https://www.nytimes.com/2024/04/03/us/politics/biden-israel-gaza.html.

141 But even that care has limited ethical and political value. Western bodies standing with Palestinian bodies are devalued; their worth tainted, their judgment condemned, their humanity degraded. This is happening, though at different levels of intensity, both in Gaza and on college campuses. To stand against genocide is a threat to Zionist reason. To stand with Palestinians is a dangerous proposition. Palestine provokes anxiety.

142 "This is why shooting someone point-blank is for most of us much more repulsive than pressing a button that will kill a thousand people we cannot see" (Žižek, *Violence*, 43).

143 Žižek, "Assange Is Free, But Are We?" *Project Syndicate*, June 27, 2024. https://www.project-syndicate.org/commentary/julian-assange-freed-but-media-still-carrying-water-for-the-powerful-by-slavoj-zizek-2024-06.

144 Achille Mbembe, "Nicolas Sarkozy's Africa," trans. Melissa Thackway, *Africultures*, August 7, 2007. http://africultures.com/nicolas-sarkozys-africa-6816/.

145 Joe Sacco, "The War on Gaza—1-26-24," *The Comics Journal*, January 26, 2024. https://www.tcj.com/the-war-on-gaza-1-26-24/.

146 Joseph Krauss, "In Israel's Call For Mass Evacuation, Palestinians Hear Echoes of Their Original Catastrophic Exodus," *AP News*, October 13, 2023. https://apnews.com/article/israel-palestinians-gaza-evacuation-history-nakba-a1bec1ee3477573e80b39b4044a48111.

147 Joshua Leifer, "A 'Moral, Strategic, and Diplomatic Abyss,'" *The New York Review*, July 2, 2024. https://www.nybooks.com/online/2024/07/02/a-moral-strategic-and-diplomatic-abyss-israel/.

148 Amy Goodman and Juan González, "Holocaust Scholar Raz Segal Loses Univ. of Minnesota Job Offer for Saying Israel Is Committing Genocide," *Democracy Now!* June 18, 2024. https://www.democracynow.org/2024/6/18/raz_segal_university_of_minnesota.

149 Joseph Massad, "Why Academic Scholarship on Israel and Palestine Threatens Western Elites," *Middle East Eye*, June 18, 2024. https://www.middleeasteye.net/opinion/why-academic-scholarship-israel-palestine-threatens-western-elites.

150 Seyla Benhabib, "Ethics without Normativity and Politics without Historicity," *Constellations* 20, no. 1 (2013): 151.

151 "Philosophy for Palestine," November 1, 2023. https://sites.google.com/view/philosophyforpalestine/home.

152 Benhabib, "An Open Letter to My Friends Who Signed 'Philosophy for Palestine,'" *Medium*, November 4, 2023. https://medium.com/amor-mundi/an-open-letter-to-my-friends-who-signed-philosophy-for-palestine-0440ebd665d8.

153 Patrick Wolfe, "Settler Colonialism and the Elimination of the Native," *Journal of Genocide Research* 8, no. 4 (2006): 388.

154 "Settler moves to innocence are those strategies or positionings that attempt to relieve the settler of feelings of guilt or responsibility without giving up land or

power or privilege, without having to change much at all . . . . [S]ettler moves to innocence are hollow, they only serve the settler" (Eve Tuck and K. Wayne Yang, "Decolonization Is Not a Metaphor," *Decolonization: Indigeneity, Education, and Society* 1, no. 1 [2012]: 10).

155 Benhabib, "Ethics without Normativity," 158.

156 Zalloua, *Continental Philosophy and the Palestinian Question: Beyond the Jew and the Greek* (New York: Bloomsbury, 2017), 107.

157 Khalidi, *The Hundred Years*, 9.

158 Žižek, *Violence*, 117.

159 Žižek, *Violence*, 117.

160 I am drawing here on Žižek's often misunderstood quote, "Gandhi was more violent than Hitler" (Žižek, "Disputations: Who Are You Calling Anti-Semitic?" *The New Republic*, January 6, 2009. https://newrepublic.com/article/62376/disputations-who-are-you-calling-anti-semitic). Violence is not measured by the amount of physical devastation that it generates (how many people you murdered) but by its transformative impact on the social order. Hitler did not alter the capitalistic structure under which he was operating (instead he scapegoated the Jews for Germany's ills), whereas Gandhi created a movement that "effectively endeavored to interrupt the basic functioning of the British colonial state" (Žižek, "Disputations").

161 Ali Abunimah, *The Battle for Justice in Palestine* (Chicago: Haymarket Book, 2014), xi.

162 Oren Ziv, "'I'm Bored, So I Shoot': The Israeli Army's Approval of Free-For-All Violence in Gaza," *+972 Magazine*, July 8, 2024. https://www.972mag.com/israeli-soldiers-gaza-firing-regulations/.

163 Ziv, "'I'm Bored So I Shoot.'"

164 Ziv, "'I'm Bored So I Shoot.'"

165 Denise Ferreira da Silva, "No-Bodies: Law, Raciality and Violence," *Griffith Law Review* 18, no. 2 (2009): 213.

166 Žižek, "Change Things So That Nothing Will Really Change!" *Substack: Žižek Goads and Prods*, July 6, 2024. https://slavoj.substack.com/p/change-things-so-that-nothing-will.

167 Eva Illouz crudely and falsely identifies the elimination of the racist state of Israel (what many of the encampment students are calling for) with the elimination of its Jewish people: "When the young protesters express their wish to eliminate Israel, they also express the wish to annihilate the Jews living in Israel" (Eva Illouz, "The Virtuous Antisemitism of Campus Protests Against Israel," *Haaretz*, May 21, 2024. https://www.haaretz.com/opinion/2024-05-21/ty-article-magazine/.premium/the-virtuous-antisemitism-of-campus-protests-against-israel/0000018f-9aa0-d264-a1bf-deb7652f0000). For a refreshing counter to Illouz's slandering distortions of the students' position, see Joseph Levine, "If You Support Israel in the Middle of a Genocide, You're an Awful Person," *Mondoweiss*, July 6, 2024. https://mondoweiss.net/2024/07/if-you-support-israel-in-the-middle-of-a-genocide-youre-an-awful-person/.

168 Usaid Siddiqui, "Israel's War on Gaza Updates: UN to Add Israeli Army to Child Harm List," *Al Jazeera*, June 7, 2024. https://www.aljazeera.com/news/liveblog/2024/6/7/israels-war-on-gaza-live-hospital-barely-coping-with-dead-and-wounded; Jake Johnson, "Israeli Military Has Killed 500 Gaza Healthcare Workers—Two a Day Since Assault Began," *Common Dream*, June 26, 2024. https://www.commondreams.org/news/healthcare-workers-killed-in-gaza; Léa Peruchon, "'The Livestream Was Critical Evidence': Tracing Attacks on Gaza's Press Buildings," *+972 Magazine*, June 26, 2024. https://www.972mag.com/gaza-press-attacks-israeli-army/; MEE Staff, "War on Gaza: Famine Threat Persists as Half a Million Starving, Monitor Finds," *Middle East Eye*, June 25, 2024. https://www.middleeasteye.net/news/half-million-face-starvation-gaza-report-finds; Peter Beaumont, "'Man-Made Famine' Charge Against Israel is Backed by Mounting Body of Evidence," *The Guardian*, March 20, 2024. https://www.theguardian.com/world/2024/mar/20/man-made-famine-charge-israel-mounting-evidence-un-gaza.

169 Maryam Kashani, "The Wreck Itself: Between Palestine and American Indian Studies' Sovereignty and the Surreal," *Critical Ethnic Studies* 8, no. 1 (2023). https://manifold.umn.edu/read/ces0801-08/section/6ff6ead6-1ee8-4423-b96e-d335990e69f7. The accused enact their own hysterical reaction to the vicious weaponization of the charge of anti-Semitism: "Why Are We What You Are Telling Us That We Are?"

170 Ron Jacobs, "The Israeli Defense Forces Is a Misnomer," *CounterPunch*, June 19, 2020. https://www.counterpunch.org/2020/06/19/the-israeli-defense-forces-is-a-misnomer/.

171 Žižek, *Disparities* (New York: Bloomsbury, 2016), 375.

172 In "A Report from Occupied Territory," James Baldwin describes Northern cities with a large Black population; there, the police "are simply the hired enemies of this population. They are present to keep the Negro in his place and to protect white business interests, and they have no other function" (James Baldwin, "A Report from Occupied Territory," *The Nation*, July 11, 1966. https://www.thenation.com/article/culture/report-occupied-territory/). This observation sadly applies just as well to Palestinians today, who are kept in their "place" by a police force that protects settler interests. In the United States and Israel, state violence characterizes the modus operandi of racist settler states; permanent domination of racialized and dispossessed communities is a feature of social reality. See Timothy Seidel, "'Occupied Territory Is Occupied Territory': James Baldwin, Palestine and the Possibilities of Transnational Solidarity," *Third World Quarterly* 37, no. 9 (2016): 1644–60.

173 Haim Bresheeth-Zabner, *An Army Like No Other* (New York: Verso, 2020), 132.

174 Bresheeth-Zabner, *An Army Like No Other*, 132.

175 Consider the testimonies of police officers about the Georgia International Law Enforcement Exchange (GILEE). Jason P. Armstrong, Chief, Ferguson Police Department, Missouri, says: "What I was most impressed with about the program was learning how the Israeli Police force was trying new ways to bring diversity to their police force and their police leadership. Diversity and representation is one of the main points of contention in American law enforcement. Communities are speaking out about police departments having a balanced representation of the communities they serve. It was eye opening to see those same sentiments

were holding true in Israel. Any law enforcement leader looking to expand their knowledge base and experience once in a lifetime memorable moments, this program is top notch." Rodney Bryant, Acting Chief, Atlanta Police Department, echoes this emphasis on the amount of diversity in the Israeli police force: "One of our greatest challenges in American policing is serving a community that is vastly more diverse than the local police department. Comparatively, the Israeli police are responsible for serving a variety of demographics. I was impressed by the level of community policing efforts employed by the Israeli Police to build relationships and maintain peace among such diverse populations. The mentor shadowing was considerably inimitable and having the opportunity to observe the daily operation of a station and its command staff was enlightening. Although generally ensuring public safety was important, understanding the concerns of the community was equally significant" (https://gilee.gsu.edu/). This sounds persuasive in the abstract, but we must ask, which communities are being served and which ones are being ignored? One wonders if the two Black American officers consulted Palestinian citizens of Israel, who constitute over 20 percent of the Israeli population, about the harassment and violence habitually visited on them, as well as frequent failures to investigate crimes committed in Palestinian neighborhoods in Israel, and police complicity in, if not outright contribution to, anti-Palestinianness. Bringing "diversity to the police force" is a smoke screen, a diversion from the racist status quo that both Black Americans and Palestinians confront daily. Systemic racism is unaffected by an increase in diversity so long as racism is baked into the social order that the police are meant to protect. See Josh Breiner, "Israeli Police Twice as Likely to Solve Murders of Jews Than of Arabs," *Haaretz*, October 10, 2019. https://www.haaretz.com/israel-news/2019-10-10/ty-article/.premium/police-solve-murders-among-jews-at-almost-twice-the-rate-of-those-in-arab-community/0000017f-f90b-d318-afff-fb6b3b800000; Janan Abdu, "How Israel Waged Judicial War Against Palestinian Citizens After the May 2021 Uprising," *Middle East Eye*, August 16, 2022. https://www.middleeasteye.net/opinion/israel-waged-judicial-war-against-palestinian-citizens-after-may-2021-uprising; Amnesty International, "Israeli Police Targeted Palestinians with Discriminatory Arrests, Torture and Unlawful Force," *Amnesty International*, June 24, 2021. https://www.amnesty.org/en/latest/press-release/2021/06/israeli-police-targeted-palestinians-with-discriminatory-arrests-torture-and-unlawful-force/.

176 Žižek, "Hegel: The Spirit of Distrust," 41–2.

177 Haaretz, "Former Israeli MK Quotes Hitler While Discussing Gaza War," *Haaretz*, June 16, 2024. https://www.haaretz.com/israel-news/2024-06-16/ty-article/former-israeli-mk-quotes-hitler-while-discussing-gaza-war/00000190-224f-d231-a1b2-e65f76fe0000.

178 Susan Neiman, "Historical Reckoning Gone Haywire," *The New York Review*, October 19, 2023. https://www.nybooks.com/articles/2023/10/19/historical-reckoning-gone-haywire-germany-susan-neiman/.

179 Žižek, "Anti-Semitism and Its Transformations," 6; see also Joseph Massad, "The Last of the Semites," *Al Jazeera*, May 21, 2013. https://www.aljazeera.com/opinions/2013/5/21/the-last-of-the-semites.

180 Žižek, "Human Rights and Its Discontents," emphasis added.

181 Chandra Talpade Mohanty, *Feminism without Borders: Decolonizing Theory, Practicing Solidarity* (Durham: Duke University Press, 2003), 231. See Ilan Kapoor and Zahi Zalloua, *Universal Politics* (Oxford: Oxford University Press, 2022), 152–5.
182 Žižek, "A Leftist Plea for 'Eurocentrism,'" 988.
183 Mohanty, *Feminism without Borders*, 231.
184 Žižek, *Freedom*, 167.
185 Fanon, *The Wretched of the Earth*, 2.
186 Olúfẹ́mi Táíwò, *Against Decolonisation: Taking African Agency Seriously* (London: C. Hurst & Company, 2022), 23.
187 Sylvia Wynter, "Unsettling the Coloniality of Being/Power/Truth/Freedom: Towards the Human, After Man, Its Overrepresentation—An Argument," *CR: The New Centennial Review* 3, no. 3 (2003): 260.
188 Greg Thomas, "PROUD FLESH Inter/Views: Sylvia Wynter," *ProudFlesh: New Afrikan Journal of Culture, Politics, and Consciousness* 4 (2006): 23.
189 Žižek, *Welcome to the Desert of the Real! Five Essays on September 11 and Related Dates* (New York: Verso, 2002), 2.
190 Edward Said, *Orientalism* (New York: Vintage Books, 2003), xxii.
191 Martin Belam and Lili Bayer, "Middle East Crisis: Famine 'Imminent' in Northern Gaza, UN Report Says, as EU Foreign Policy Chief Calls Area 'Open Air Graveyard'—as It Happened," *The Guardian*, March 18, 2024. https://www.theguardian.com/world/live/2024/mar/18/middle-east-crisis-live-israel-gaza-palestine-al-shifa-live-updates.
192 Saidiya Hartman, *Lose Your Mother: A Journey Along the Atlantic Slave Route* (New York: Farrar, Straus and Giroux, 2007), 6.

Chapter 1

1 François Laruelle, *Intellectuals and Power: The Insurrection of the Victim*, trans. Anthony Paul Smith (Cambridge: Polity Press, 2015), 9.
2 Žižek, "Introduction: Cogito as a Shibboleth," in *Cogito and the Unconscious*, ed. Slavoj Žižek (Durham: Duke University Press, 1998), 7.
3 Žižek, *The Ticklish Subject: The Absent Center of Political Ontology* (New York: Verso, 1999), 266.
4 Žižek, *Less Than Nothing*, 958.
5 Edelman, *No Future*, 132.
6 Edelman, *No Future*, 4.
7 Against Edelman's brand of queer theory, Tiffany Lethabo King, for example, argues that a reckoning with the human must interrogate the "scaffolding that upends and holds [the human] together" (Tiffany Lethabo King, "Humans Involved: Lurking in the Lines of Posthumanist Flight," *Critical Ethnic Studies* 3, no. 1 [2017]: 180). At best, Western self-critique is not sufficient. At worst, it remains oblivious to its anti-Blackness. While radical strands of Western theory are typically

enamored with "self-critique, self-abnegation, and masochism alone," they end up prolonging the subjugation of the racialized other (King, "Humans Involved," 164). Western solutions and pronouncements (about the end or death of the subject, for example) often compound the problem of the other by ignoring the ways in which the category of the human, regardless of its undoing and redoing, is plagued by a genocidal history that persists in the present (coloniality and the afterlife of slavery) and closes off decolonial futures. For King, a true reckoning of the human must pass through "decolonial refusal" and "abolitionist skepticism." Witness the BLM movement: "if Black lives were to be absorbed into the category of the human, the social order and the scaffolding that upends and holds together the human would collapse" (King, "Humans Involved," 180).

8 Žižek questions the subversiveness of Edelman's stance, pointing out that capitalism does not really have a problem with a subject who insists on the void/crack at the heart of its being. While Edelman's anti-politics of prosperity—"radical ethics of *jouissance*"—does promote "the negativity of the death drive," which, in principle, nihilistically aims at "withdrawing from reality into the Real of the 'Night of the World'" (Žižek, *Less Than Nothing*, 141), his queer subject, in practice, still operates from *within* the ideological coordinates of capitalism, subversively dwelling, as it were, in the ideological post-political, where capitalism can and does accommodate Edelman's "radical" but apolitical demands: his drive for an undifferentiated unity of everything. The queer subject is not (*a priori*) a revolutionary subject insofar as "the problem with this [queer] vision of a new fluid subjectivity is not that it is utopian but that it is already predominant—yet another case of the hegemonic ideology presenting itself as subversive and transgressive of the existing order" (Žižek, *The Courage of Hopelessness: Chronicles of a Year of Acting Dangerously* [New York: Allen Lane, 2017], 190–1). See also Kapoor and Zalloua, *Universal Politics*, 84–8.

9 Jared Sexton and Daniel Colucciello Barber, "On Black Negativity, or the Affirmation of Nothing," *Society and Space*, September 18, 2017. https://www.societyandspace.org/articles/on-black-negativity-or-the-affirmation-of-nothing.

10 Frank B. Wilderson III, *Red, White & Black: Cinema and the Structure of U.S. Antagonisms* (Durham: Duke University Press, 2010), 58.

11 Fanon, *Black Skin*, 91. See also "European culture has an imago of the black man that makes him responsible for every possible conflictual situation" (Fanon, *Black Skin*, 146).

12 Calvin L. Warren, *Ontological Terror: Blackness, Nihilism, and Emancipation* (Durham: Duke University Press, 2018), 38.

13 Wilderson, "Biko and the Problematic of Presence," in *Biko Lives! Contesting the Legacies of Steve Biko*, ed. Andile Mngxitama, Amanda Alexander, and Nigel C. Gibson (New York: Palgrave, 2008), 111.

14 Fanon, *Black Skin*, 90.

15 Sexton, "Unbearable Blackness," *Cultural Critique* 90 (2015): 161.

16 Wilderson, *Afropessimism* (New York: Liveright, 2020), 248.

17 Siddhant Issar and James Padilioni, Jr. "'To Address Black Suffering Is to Destroy the World.' An Interview with Frank B. Wilderson, III on *Afropessimism*," *Interfere* 1 (2020): 94.

18 David Marriott, *On Black Men* (New York: Columbia University Press, 2000), 88.
19 Sigmund Freud, *The Interpretation of Dreams*, in *The Standard Edition of the Complete Psychological Works of Sigmund Freud*, vol. 4, ed. James Strachey (London: Hogarth, 1953–74), ix.
20 Žižek, *Less Than Nothing*, 995–6.
21 Todd McGowan, "The Bedlam of the Lynch Mob: Racism and Enjoying Through the Other," in *Lacan and Race: Racism, Identity, and Psychoanalytic Theory*, ed. Sheldon George and Derek Hook (New York: Routledge, 2022), 20.
22 Žižek, "Afterword: With Defenders Like These, Who Needs Attackers?" in *The Truth of Žižek*, ed. Paul Bowman and Richard Stamp (New York: Continuum, 2007), 204.
23 Juan Carlos Canals, "Warrior of the Imaginary: A Conversation with Patrick Chamoiseau," *Sargasso* 1 (2007–8): 9–20.
24 Warren, *Ontological Terror*, 24.
25 Scholars in Black Studies are interpellated "to defend the dead," a formulation Christina Sharpe borrows from NourbeSe Philip's poem "Zong #15." Sharpe carefully unpacks the force of these words: "What does it mean to defend the dead? To tend to the Black dead and dying: to tend to the Black person, to Black people, always living in the push toward our death? It means work. It is work: hard emotional, physical, and intellectual work that demands vigilant attendance to the needs of the dying, to ease their way, and also to the needs of the living" (Sharpe, *In the Wake: On Blackness and Being* [Durham: Duke University Press, 2016], 10). *Zong!* addresses the eighteenth-century massacre on the slave ship Zong, in which the captain ordered more than 130 enslaved captives to be thrown overboard when the ship ran low on drinking water during the Middle Passage. The owners of the boat sought to collect on the insurance due following the loss of their "cargo." When the insurance company refused to pay, the case went to court, which ruled in favor of the owners of the slave ship. The case was appealed, and the verdict was reversed in favor of the insurers; it was determined that it was Zong's captain who erred in failing to maintain a sufficient amount of drinking water.
26 Ernesto Laclau, "Identity and Hegemony: The Role of Universality in the Constitution of Political Logics," in *Contingency, Hegemony, Universality: Contemporary Dialogues on the Left*, ed. Judith Butler, Ernesto Laclau, and Slavoj Žižek (New York: Verso, 2000), 73.
27 René Descartes, *The Passions of the Soul*, trans. Stephen Voss (Indianapolis: Hackett, 1989), 58.
28 René Descartes, *Discourse on Method and Meditations on First Philosophy*, trans. Donald A. Cress (Indianapolis: Hackett, 1998), 35.
29 Freud, "A Difficulty in the Path of Psycho-Analysis," in *The Standard Edition of the Complete Psychological Works of Sigmund Freud*, vol. 17, ed. James Strachey (London: Hogarth, 1953–74), 141.
30 Lacan initially frames psychoanalysis's relation to Cartesianism in strictly antagonistic terms: "It should be noted that this experience [of psychoanalysis] sets us at odds with any philosophy directly stemming from the *cogito*" (Lacan, "The Mirror Stage as Formative of the Function of the I as Revealed in

Psychoanalytic Experience," in *Écrits: The First Complete Edition in English*, trans. Bruce Fink [New York: Norton, 2006], 75).

31 Žižek draws on François Balmès, *Ce que Lacan dit de l'être* (Paris: Presses Universitaires de France, 1999).

32 Ed Pluth, "Psychoanalysis, Science, and Worldviews," *Crisis & Critique* 5, no. 1 (2018): 335, 336.

33 Žižek, *The Ticklish Subject*, 2.

34 Žižek, "Language, Violence and Non-Violence," *International Journal of Žižek Studies* 2, no. 3 (2008): 9.

35 Žižek, *Less Than Nothing*, 36.

36 Žižek, "Language, Violence and Non-Violence," 9.

37 Žižek, *Absolute Recoil: Towards a New Foundation of Dialectical Materialism* (New York: Verso, 2014), 183.

38 Žižek, *Absolute Recoil*, 182.

39 Žižek, *The Ticklish Subject*, 34.

40 Žižek, *Less Than Nothing*, 979.

41 Žižek, "Afterword: Objects, Objects Everywhere," in *Slavoj Žižek and Dialectical Materialism*, ed. Agon Hamza and Frank Ruda (New York: Palgrave Macmillan, 2016), 190–1.

42 Žižek, *Less Than Nothing*, 501.

43 Fanon, *Black Skin*, xii, translation modified. Philcox's translation leaves out a crucial comma after "an incline stripped bare of every essential." See Maher, *Anticolonial Eruptions: Racial Hubris and the Cunning of Resistance* (Berkeley: University of California Press, 2022), 20.

44 As Žižek explains, the public use of reason, "in a kind of short-circuit, by-passing the mediation of the particular, directly participates in the universal," enabling the individual to be modern and cosmopolitan, to break with the "communal-institutional order of one's particular identification" (Žižek, *Violence*, 143).

45 W. E. B. Du Bois, *The Souls of Black Folk* (New Haven: Yale University Press, 2015), 3.

46 See Beata Stawarska, "Struggle and Violence: Entering the Dialectic with Frantz Fanon and Simone de Beauvoir," in *Violence, Slavery and Freedom between Hegel and Fanon*, ed. Ulrike Kistner and Philippe Van Hauteix (Johannesburg: Wits University Press, 2020), 93–115; Matthieu Renault, "Le genre de la race: Fanon, lecteur de Beauvoir," *Actuel Marx*, no. 55 (2014): 36–48; Lewis R. Gordon, *What Fanon Said: A Philosophical Introduction to His Life and Thought* (New York: Fordham University Press, 2015).

47 Simone de Beauvoir, *America Day by Day*, trans. Carol Cosman (Berkeley: University of California Press, 1999), 239.

48 Beauvoir, *America Day*, 239.

49 Beauvoir, *America Day*, 239.

50 Beauvoir, *America Day*, 239.

51 Beauvoir, *The Second Sex*, trans. Constance Borde and Sheila Malovany-Chevallier (New York: Alfred Knopf, 2010), 12.
52 See Žižek, *Violence*, 72.
53 Žižek, *Violence*, 73.
54 Žižek, *Violence*, 72.
55 Žižek, *Violence*, 72.
56 Beauvoir, *The Second Sex*, 12.
57 Beauvoir, *The Second Sex*, 16.
58 "When we declare that the slave in chains is as free as his master, we do not mean to speak of a freedom which would remain undetermined. The slave in chains is free to break them; this means that the very meaning of his chains will appear to him in the light of the end which he will have chosen: to remain a slave or to risk the worst in order to get rid of his slavery" (Jean-Paul Sartre, *Being and Nothingness*, trans. Hazel E. Barnes [New York: Philosophical Library, 1956], 550).
59 Beauvoir, *The Second Sex*, 16–17.
60 Wilderson, *Afropessimism*, 15.
61 Alenka Zupančič, "Desire, Hysteria and the Indirectness of Truth," unpublished manuscript.
62 Wilderson, *Red, White & Black*, 38.
63 Jason Allen-Paisant, *Engagements with Aimé Césaire* (Oxford: Oxford University Press, 2024), 65.
64 Wilderson, *Afropessimism*, 242.
65 Wilderson, *Afropessimism*, 242–3.
66 Žižek, *The Fragile Absolute, or, Why Is the Christian Legacy Worth Fighting For?* (New York: Verso, 2000), 142.
67 Žižek, *The Fragile Absolute*, 144.
68 Žižek, *The Fragile Absolute*, 144.
69 Toni Morrison, *Beloved* (New York: Vintage Books, 2004), 321.
70 Jodi Dean, *Žižek's Politics* (New York: Routledge, 2006), 170.
71 Morrison, *Beloved*, 176. Sethe overhears one of Schoolteacher's zoological lessons to his nephews, "No, no. That's not the way. I told you to put her human characteristics on the left; her animal ones on the right. And don't forget to line them up" (Morrison, *Beloved*, 228). The categorization of Sethe's human and nonhuman characteristics chills her to the bone.
72 Žižek, *The Fragile Absolute*, 146.
73 McGowan, "The Bankruptcy of Historicism: Introducing Disruption into Literary Studies," in *Everything You Always Wanted to Know about Literature but Were Afraid to Ask Žižek*, ed. Russell Sbriglia (Durham: Duke University Press, 2017), 100.
74 Christina Sharpe, "Black Studies: In the Wake," *The Black Scholar* 44, no. 2 (2014): 59.
75 Morrison, *Beloved*, 102.

76 Morrison, *Beloved*, 103.
77 Morrison, *Beloved*, 105.
78 Morrison, *Beloved*, 212.
79 Wilderson, *Red, White & Black*, 28.
80 Wilderson, "Afro-Pessimism and the End of Redemption," *Humanities Futures*. Franklin Humanities Institute: Duke University, October 20, 2015. https://humanitiesfutures.org/papers/afro-pessimism-end-redemption/.
81 Wilderson, *Afropessimism*, 229.
82 Jared Sexton, "African American Studies," in *A Concise Companion to American Studies*, ed. John Carlos Rowe (Malden: Wiley-Blackwell, 2010), 216.
83 Wilderson, *Afropessimism*, 92.
84 Sexton, "The Social Life of Social Death: On Afro-Pessimism and Black Optimism," *InTensions* 5 (2011): 21.
85 Wilderson, "Gramsci's Black Marx: Whither the Slave in Civil Society?" *Social Identities* 9, no. 2 (2003): 233.
86 Fanon, *The Wretched of the Earth*, 93.
87 See H. Samy Alim, "Inventing 'the White Voice': Racial Capitalism, Raciolinguistics & Culturally Sustaining Pedagogies," *Daedalus* 15, no. 3 (2023): 147–66.
88 As Boots Riley notes, "white voice doesn't really exist. White people don't even have it. They use it, and it's a performance. There's a performance of whiteness that is all about saying that everything is OK, you've got your bills paid, and that—and, you know, this kind of smooth and easy thing" (Amy Goodman and Juan González, "Boots Riley's Dystopian Satire 'Sorry to Bother You' Is an Anti-Capitalist Rallying Cry for Workers," *Democracy Now!* July 17, 2018. https://www.democracynow.org/2018/7/17/sorry_to_bother_you_boots_rileys).
89 Žižek, *How to Read Lacan* (New York: Norton, 2006), 80.
90 Sylvia Wynter, "No Humans Involved: An Open Letter to My Colleagues," *Forum N.H.I. Knowledge for the 21st Century* 1, no. 1 (1994): 42.
91 Wynter, "A Black Studies Manifesto," *Forum N.H.I. Knowledge for the 21st Century* 1, no. 1 (1994): 6.
92 Wilderson, *Red, White & Black*, 82.
93 Ashitha Nagesh, "What Exactly Is a 'Karen' and Where Did the Meme Come From?" *BBC News*, July 30, 2020. https://www.bbc.com/news/world-53588201. See also Calvin Warren, "The Karen Call: Emergency, Destiny, and Surveillance," *Critical Philosophy of Race* 10, no. 2 (2022): 141–57.
94 George Yancy, "Afropessimism Forces Us to Rethink Our Most Basic Assumptions About Society," *Truthhout,* September 14, 2022. https://truthout.org/articles/afropessimism-forces-us-to-rethink-our-most-basic-assumptions-about-society/.
95 Wilderson, *Red, White & Black*, 80.
96 Fanon, *Black Skin*, xiii.
97 Mbembe, *Critique of Black Reason*, 4.
98 Zalloua, *Being Posthuman: Ontologies of the Future* (New York: Bloomsbury, 2021), 175.

99 Sexton, "Affirmation in the Dark: Racial Slavery and Philosophical Pessimism," *The Comparatist* 43 (2019): 103.

100 I want to thank Nicole Simek for drawing attention to this scene in the film.

101 Wilderson, "Biko and the Problematic of Presence," 111.

102 Ferreira da Silva, "No-Bodies."

103 Žižek, "Neighbors and Other Monsters: A Plea for Ethical Violence," in *The Neighbor: Three Inquiries in Political Theology*, ed. Slavoj Žižek, Eric L. Santner, and Kenneth Reinhard (Chicago: University of Chicago Press, 2006), 143.

104 Fanon describes his own struggles with the Black imago: "I was responsible not only for my body but also for my race and my ancestors. I cast an objective gaze over myself, discovered my blackness, my ethnic features; deafened by cannibalism, backwardness, fetishism, racial stigmas, slave traders, and above all, yes, above all, the grinning *Y a bon Banania*" (Fanon, *Black Skin*, 92).

105 Robin D. G. Kelley, "Sorry, Not Sorry," *Boston Review*, September 13, 2018. http://bostonreview.net/race-literature-culture/robin-d-g-kelley-sorry-not-sorry#.XMdwpNHrLCE.email.

106 See Chapter 3 of Keeanga-Yamahtta Taylor's *From #BlackLivesMatter to Black Liberation* (Chicago: Haymarket Books, 2016). It is not a surprise that Black faces in high places prefer reform to revolution. Their chances of "success" require the perpetual reproduction of the white status quo at home and abroad. As Cornel West insightfully notes: "We've been talking about reform for the last 50 years. We've had Black faces in high places for the last 50 years. They've become very much beholden to the same police power, the same wall street power, the same Pentagon power, the same presidential power" (Azad Essa, "Cornel West on US Protests: The Chickens Have Come Home to Roost," *Middle East Eye*, June 16, 2020. https://www.middleeasteye.net/news/cornel-west-america-george-floyd-protests-chickens-have-come-home-roost). The Black elite, not unlike other non-white elites, are as allergic to class struggle as any member of the ruling class. Their privileges are contingent on the maintenance of the status quo. See Zalloua, *The Politics of the Wretched*, 92.

107 Lift: "We also need people like you [Cash], people who can be trusted, people that can analyze the challenge and adapt, like a cunning racoon or like a snake or like a tardigrade." See Alim, "Inventing," 152.

108 An Afropessimist might pounce on the trickery of white folks, noting that Blacks are constantly lied to and cheated. Now, Cash's nonhumanity is objectively and materially confirmed. But the film does not stop here. Cash's response is a call for revolutionary violence; it may start with the *equi-sapiens*, but it does not end there. It takes a village to fully sack the master's house.

109 Kelley, "Sorry, Not Sorry."

110 Mbembe, "In Conversation: Achille Mbembe and David Theo Goldberg on *Critique of Black Reason*," *Theory, Culture, and Society*, July 3, 2018. https://www.theoryculturesociety.org/conversation-achille-mbembe-and-david-theo-goldberg-on-critique-of-black-reason/.

111 Mbembe, *Critique of Black Reason*, 6.

112 Grace Blakeley, "No, Capitalism Isn't Democratic," *Tribune*, June 15, 2023. https://tribunemag.co.uk/2023/06/no-capitalism-isnt-democratic.

113 Blakeley, "No, Capitalism."

114 Kelley, "Sorry, Not Sorry."

115 Kelley, "Sorry, Not Sorry."

116 Žižek, *For They Know*, 70.

117 Žižek, *Mad World: War, Movies, Sex* (New York: OR Books, 2023), 71.

118 Catherine Portevin, "Patrick Chamoiseau: 'L'individu doit se fabriquer autour de l'absence," *Philosophie Magazine*, March 22, 2017. https://www.philomag.com/articles/patrick-chamoiseau-lindividu-doit-se-fabriquer-autour-de-labsence.

119 Nicole Simek, *Alchemies of Blood and Afro-Diasporic Fiction: Race, Kinship, and the Passion for Ontology* (New York: Bloomsbury, 2024), 66.

120 Rosa Amelia Plumelle-Uribe, *White Ferocity: The Genocides of Non-Whites and Non-Aryans from 1492 to Date*, trans. Virginia Popper (Dakar: CODESRIA, 2020); Samir Amin, "Ferocity of Whites, Ferocity of Capitalism," *Africa Development / Afrique et Développement* 45, no. 2 (2020): 9–16.

121 Mari Ruti, "Creativity Between Anxiety and Aliveness," *Sublation Magazine*, June 17, 2023. https://www.sublationmag.com/post/creativity-between-anxiety-and-aliveness.

122 Žižek, *Mad World*, 138.

123 Žižek, "The Real of Sexual Difference," in *Reading Seminar XX: Lacan's Major Work on Love, Knowledge, and Feminine Sexuality*, ed. Suzanne Barnard and Bruce Fink (New York: State University of New York Press, 2002), 70.

124 Jacques Derrida, "Force of Law: The 'Mystical Foundation of Authority,'" in *Acts of Religion*, ed. Gil Anidjar (New York: Routledge, 2002), 252.

125 Derrida, *Negotiations: Interventions and Interviews, 1971–2001*, ed. Elizabeth Rottenberg (Stanford: Stanford University Press, 2002), 231.

126 Lacan characterizes the death drive by its capacity "to wipe the slate clean" (Jacques Lacan, *The Seminar of Jacques Lacan, Book VII: The Ethics of Psychoanalysis, 1959–1960*, trans. Dennis Porter, ed. Jacques-Alain Miller [New York: Norton, 1992], 210). It "challenges everything that exists" (Lacan, *The Ethics of Psychoanalysis*, 212), adheres to no external authority, and spurns futurology in all its guises.

Chapter 2

1 Octave Mannoni, "I Know Very Well, but All the Same . . . ," in *Perversion and the Social Relation*, ed. Molly Anne Rothenberg, Dennis A. Foster, and Slavoj Žižek, trans. G. M. Goshgarian (Durham: Duke University Press, 2003), 70.

2 Žižek, *Less Than Nothing*, 859.

3 Žižek, *Violence*, 53.

4   As Amnesty International's Secretary General, Agnès Callamard observes: "Israel's flagrant disregard for international law is compounded by the failures of its allies to stop the indescribable civilian bloodshed meted out in Gaza. Many of those allies were the very architects of that post-World War Two system of law" (Amnesty International, "The State of the World's Human Rights").

5   IfNotNow, October 14, 2021. https://twitter.com/IfNotNowOrg/status/1448709689127030789; see also Branko Marcetic, "A Tidal Wave of State and Private Repression Is Targeting Pro-Palestinian Voices," *Jacobin*, November 3, 2023. https://jacobin.com/2023/11/anti-palestine-mccarthyism-censorship.

6   During the first presidential debate in 2024, Trump labelled Biden "a weak Palestinian, a very bad one," and later, at a campaign stop, doubled down on this line of attack, declaring that Senate Majority Leader Chuck Schumer, who is Jewish, "has become a Palestinian." Calling someone "Palestinian" is now a slur. See Juan Cole, "The Vile Racism of Calling Biden a 'Weak Palestinian,'" *Common Dreams*, June 28, 2024. https://www.commondreams.org/opinion/trump-biden-weak-palestinian; Griffin Eckstein, "'Schumer Has Become a Palestinian': Trump Spews More Rhetoric at Rally," *Salon*, June 28, 2024. https://www.salon.com/2024/06/28/schumer-has-become-a-palestinian-spews-more-rhetoric-at-rally/#:~:text=%E2%80%9CSchumer%20has%20become%20a%20Palestinian,%E2%80%9CPalestinian%E2%80%9D%20as%20a%20slur.

7   See Marc Lamont Hill and Mitchell Plitnick, *Except for Palestine: The Limits of Progressive Politics* (New York: The New Press, 2021).

8   Shannon Sullivan, "White Priority," *Critical Philosophy of Race* 5, no. 2 (2017): 171–82.

9   Black Lives Matter, March 27, 2024. https://twitter.com/Blklivesmatter/status/1765935635490070840.

10 Commenting on Lacan's eye for repetition, Nadia Bou Ali insightfully notes: "Lacan was a subtle analyst of repetition, attentive not only to the phenomenon's more obvious capacity to maintain order but also to its less apparent, transformative potential. He saw in repetition—of traumas, historical events, symptoms and so on—an unconscious plea to change the existing order of things" (Nadia Bou Ali, "Measure Against Measure: Why Lacan Contra Foucault?" in *Lacan Contra Foucault: Subjectivity, Sex and Politics*, ed. Nadia Bou Ali [New York: Bloomsbury, 2019], 1). I read the Gaza protests as performing such a plea, summoning us to change and challenge the racist and exploitive order of things.

11 McGowan, *Universality and Identity Politics* (New York: Columbia University Press, 2020), 183.

12 Sebastian Althoff, "The Condemnation of Hate and the Violence of the Status Quo," *Cultural Politics* 20, no. 1 (2024): 47.

13 Althoff, "The Condemnation of Hate," 49.

14 Randa Abdel-Fattah, "On Zionist Feelings," *Mondoweiss*, December 27, 2023. https://mondoweiss.net/2023/12/on-zionist-feelings/.

15 Sigmund Freud, "Repression," in *The Standard Edition of the Complete Psychological Works of Sigmund Freud*, vol. 14, ed. James Strachey (London: Hogarth, 1957), 147.

16 Bonnie Angelo, "The Pain of Being Black: An Interview with Toni Morrison," in *Conversations with Toni Morrison*, ed. Taylor Danielle-Guthrie (Jackson: University of Mississippi Press, 1994), 257.
17 Hartman, *Lose Your Mother*, 6.
18 Amy Goodman, "Cornel West: Obama's Response to Trayvon Martin Case Belies Failure to Challenge 'New Jim Crow,'" *Democracy Now!* July 22, 2013. https://www.democracynow.org/2013/7/22/cornel_west_obamas_response_to_trayvon.
19 Movement for Black Lives, "A Vision for Black Lives," *Movement for Black Lives*. https://m4bl.org/policy-platforms/.
20 Movement for Black Lives, "A Vision for Black Lives."
21 Žižek, *Heaven in Disorder* (New York: OR Books, 2021), 154–5.
22 BLM Inland Empire, "'To Ally with the Democratic Party Is to Ally Against Ourselves': BLM Inland Empire Breaks with BLM Global Network," *Left Voice*, February 4, 2021. https://www.leftvoice.org/blm-inland-empire-breaks-with-black-lives-matter-global-network/.
23 Žižek, "How to Begin from the Beginning," *New Left Review* 57 (2009): 53.
24 Žižek, *The Parallax View*, 342.
25 Thomas Frank, "Bill Clinton's Crime Bill Destroyed Lives, and There's No Point Denying It," *The Guardian*, April 15, 2016. https://www.theguardian.com/commentisfree/2016/apr/15/bill-clinton-crime-bill-hillary-black-lives-thomas-frank.
26 Too Black, "Unburdened by Palestine: Shedding Black Liberalism for Anti-imperialism," *Mondoweiss*, August 22, 2024. https://mondoweiss.net/2024/08/unburdened-by-palestine-shedding-black-liberalism-for-anti-imperialism/.
27 https://twitter.com/realchrisrufo/status/1712938775834185891.
28 Arlie Russell Hochschild, *Stolen Pride: Loss, Shame, and the Rise of the Right* (New York: The New Press, 2024); Maria T. Zuber, "How to Declare War on Coal's Emissions Without Declaring War on Coal Communities," *The Washington Post*, February 24, 2017. https://www.washingtonpost.com/opinions/how-to-declare-war-on-coals-emissions-without-declaring-war-on-coal-communities/2017/02/24/610c7da2-f864-11e6-bf01-d47f8cf9b643_story.html.
29 JD Vance, Donald Trump's selection for vice-president, is also a great manipulator of (real) pain. In his bestselling memoir *Hillbilly Elegy* (2016), adapted into a Netflix feature film, Vance paints a portrait of the world that nicely coincides with "the new Rightist populism," writes Žižek. In his memoir, Vance recounts "the story of a poor white working-class hero in destitute Appalachia who fights his way to success in a family full of violence and alcohol, with a drug-addicted mother. He succeeds and becomes a millionaire with hard work, against the constant bickering of the big state and corporations which support lazy self-proclaimed 'victims' who lead a more comfortable life than the poor honest white workers" (Žižek, "The Shooting of Trump," *Substack: Žižek Goads and Prods*, July 17, 2024. https://slavoj.substack.com/p/the-shooting-of-trump). Vance, not unlike Trump, identifies a genuine problem—the plight of economically disenfranchised white workers—but mystifies the causes of white precarity. The remedy to poverty (social mobility) is not so much about "money and economics" in this vision as it is about "a lifestyle change" (JD Vance, *Hillbilly Elegy* [New York: HarperCollins Publishers,

2016], 206). Throughout *Hillbilly Elegy*, Vance elevates the importance of family values while systematically degrading the role of the government and its policies in the success or failure in attaining the American dream of social mobility, even though his Yale Law School education was funded in part by the government's G.I. Bill program. See Neema Avashia, "I'm from Appalachia: JD Vance Doesn't Represent Us—He Only Represents Himself," *The Guardian*, July 16, 2024. https://www.theguardian.com/us-news/article/2024/jul/16/jd-vance-hillbilly-elegy-appalachia?utm_term=669b619d92e496a151553926da1b6953&utm_campaign=SaturdayEdition&utm_source=esp&utm_medium=Email&CMP=saturdayedition_email.

30 Josiah Ryan, "'This Was a Whitelash': Van Jones' Take on the Election Results," *CNN*, November 9, 2016. https://www.cnn.com/2016/11/09/politics/van-jones-results-disappointment-cnntv/index.html.

31 Keeanga-Yamahtta Taylor, "The Enduring Power of 'Scenes of Subjection,'" *The New Yorker*, October 17, 2022. https://www.newyorker.com/books/second-read/the-enduring-power-of-scenes-of-subjection-saidiya-hartman.

32 Zalloua, *Žižek on Race: Toward an Anti-Racist Future*, with Preface by Slavoj Žižek (New York: Bloomsbury, 2020), 36.

33 Derrick Bell, *Faces at the Bottom of the Well: The Permanence of Racism* (New York: Basic Books, 2018).

34 Michelle Alexander reminds us how Martin Luther King, Jr. was "cancelled" by mainstream America after his unpopular critique of the Vietnam War. Black liberals of the NAACP condemned MLK's speech as a "serious tactical mistake" ("N.A.A.C.P. Decries Stand Of Dr. King on Vietnam," *The New York Times*, April 11, 1967, 1, 17. https://timesmachine.nytimes.com/timesmachine/1967/04/11/83586963.html?pageNumber=1). MLK's nonviolence was perceived and experienced as a violent threat to American imperialism. Alexander draws a powerful lesson from King's speech: "Of all the incredible speeches that Martin Luther King Jr. gave in his lifetime, I think the one that speaks most directly to our times, and that models what is required of us as we face multiple threats to our democracy and our world, is the speech that King gave when he publicly condemned the Vietnam War—and was immediately canceled" (Michelle Alexander, "Only Revolutionary Love Can Save Us Now," *The Nation*, March 8, 2024. https://www.thenation.com/article/activism/mlk-vietnam-war-speech-gaza-democracy/). Far from being immersed in identitarian preoccupations, MLK today would have been fighting for justice on multiple fronts: "If we are to honor the principles and values for which King sacrificed his life, we must demand a cease-fire in Gaza and an end to the occupation of Palestine. We must speak unpopular truths and organize to save our planet, rebirth our democracy, and embrace human creativity and the natural beauty of our world rather than artificial intelligence and virtual reality. We must also demand a cease-fire in our communities. But I am not talking simply about ending violence in our streets—violence born of trauma, despair, and desperation. Last year was a record-setting year for police killings in the United States, the highest rate of police killings in more than a decade. Even after all the protests and uprisings, even after all the promises of policy reform and change, the killing and violence perpetrated by those who wear badges has continued unabated" (Alexander, "Only Revolutionary Love").

35 Sarah Florini, *Beyond Hashtags: Racial Politics and Black Digital Networks* (New York: New York University Press, 2019), 116.

36 Mitch Smith and Tim Arango, "'We Need Policemen': Even in Liberal Cities, Voters Reject Scaled-Back Policing," *The New York Times*, November 3, 2021. https://www.nytimes.com/2021/11/03/us/police-reform-minneapolis-election.html.

37 Jamelle Bouie, "Biden Says 'Fund the Police.' Well, They Aren't Exactly Hurting for Cash," *The New York Times*, March 4, 2022. https://www.nytimes.com/2022/03/04/opinion/the-police-arent-exactly-running-out-of-cash.html.

38 Akela Lacy, "After Years of Failure on Gun Control, Democrats Push More Police Funding," *The Intercept*, April 19, 2022. https://theintercept.com/2022/04/19/police-funding-democrats-gun-control/.

39 Movement for Black Lives, "The BREATHE Act." https://breatheact.org/.

40 Kelley, "Insecure: Policing Under Racial Capitalism," *Spectre* 1, no. 2 (2020): 14.

41 Kelley, "Insecure: Policing," 12.

42 Steve Inskeep, "The BREATHE Act Is a Counterproposal to Justice in Policing Act," *NPR*, March 23, 2021. https://www.npr.org/2021/03/23/980234498/the-breathe-act-is-a-counterproposal-to-justice-in-policing-act.

43 It is crucial to insist that the police officer need not be white. We can recall the killing of Tyre Nichols on January 7, 2023. After a traffic stop by officers of the Scorpion unit in the City of Memphis, Nichols, a 29-year-old Black man, suffered a severe beating at the hands of five Black officers and died three days later. Black police officers are also formed by anti-Blackness, tormented by the Black imago that unconsciously gnaws at their being (Rick Rojas, Neelam Bohra, and Eliza Fawcett, "What We Know About Tyre Nichols's Lethal Encounter With Memphis Police," *The New York Times*, February 12, 2023. https://www.nytimes.com/article/tyre-nichols-memphis-police-dead.html).

44 Nadia Abu El-Haj, "The Banality of Knowledge," *Critical Ethnic Studies* 7, no. 1 (2021). https://manifold.umn.edu/read/ces0701-banality-of-knowledge/section/8b7e936e-ec4f-4d7d-a436-df82f4df69b8; Abu El-Haj, "'We Know Well, but All the Same . . . ' Factual Truths, Historical Narratives, and the Work of Disavowal," *History of the Present* 13, no. 2 (2023): 245–64.

45 Even when Palestinians are interviewed by mainstream media outlets, it is done in bad faith, in order to manufacture consent for the Gaza War, not to question it or complicate the predominant Zionist narrative. See Mohammed El-Kurd's damning satire of media news, "In Bad Faith with Mohammed El-Kurd." https://www.youtube.com/watch?v=4m1aDlglA-k.

46 Henry A. Giroux, "US Fascism Is Spreading Under the Guise of 'Patriotic Education,'" *Truthout*, April 10, 2023. https://truthout.org/articles/us-fascism-is-spreading-under-the-guise-of-patriotic-education.

47 The Florida Board of Education standards stipulate that students in public schools will be instructed that "slaves developed skills which, in some instances, could be applied for their personal benefit" (Reuters, "Florida Introduces New Guidelines on Teaching Black History, Critics Give Poor Grade," *Reuters*, July 20, 2023. https://www.reuters.com/world/us/florida-introduces-new-guidelines-teaching-black-history-critics-give-poor-grade-2023-07-20/). As with Cotton's comment that slavery was a "necessary evil," the Right dreams of normalizing the trauma of

enslavement by disclosing its benefits not only to whites but also to the enslaved. Statements like those of Senator Cotton and the Florida Board must be ruthlessly criticized, but if the critique is not supplemented by a critique of the liberal fetishist disavowal, it risks exhausting how we critically imagine today's pervasive circulation of anti-Blackness.

48 Right-wing nostalgia is, of course, not limited to white times—there is a nostalgic strain for the heteronormative nuclear family running through the Right's aggressive anti-LGBTQ+ initiatives.

49 Žižek, "Against the Game of Total War," *Substack: Žižek Goads and Prods*, August 10, 2024. https://slavoj.substack.com/p/against-the-game-of-total-war?utm_source=publication-search.

50 The two statutory provisions commonly referred to as the "Leahy Law" (under section 620M of the Foreign Assistance Act of 1961, 22 U.S.C. 2378d) forbid the US government from giving assistance to foreign military units that commit gross violations of human rights. In light of the ICJ rulings and countless reports by human rights groups, this threshold has clearly been met.

51 Jamil Khader, "Ziofascist Violence and the Nakba 2.0: Jouissance and Necrocapitalism in the Consolidation of Extremist Messianic Zionist Far-right Ideology," *Crisis and Critique* 11, no. 1 (2024): 26–54.

52 Eva Illouz, "47 Years a Slave: A New Perspective on the Occupation," *Haaretz*, February 7, 2014. https://www.haaretz.com/2014-02-07/ty-article/.premium/47-years-a-slave/0000017f-decf-df62-a9ff-dedfc4ff0000.

53 Paul Salvatori, "Q&A: 'What Happened in Israel on October 7 Was a Slave Revolt,'" *TRT World*, October 12, 2023. https://headtopics.com/us/q-a-what-happened-in-israel-on-october-7-was-a-slave-revolt-46588280.

54 Hanin Majadli, "Over 30,000 Killed in Gaza, but Even Israel's 'Liberal Left' Says: That's War," *Haaretz*, March 7, 2024. https://www.haaretz.com/opinion/2024-03-07/ty-article-opinion/.premium/over-30-000-killed-in-gaza-but-even-israels-liberal-left-says-thats-war/0000018e-1a3a-d8fb-abff-5f3ad8860000.

55 Illouz, "The Global Left Needs to Renounce Judith Butler," *Haaretz*, March 21. https://www.haaretz.com/opinion/2024-03-21/ty-article/.premium/the-global-left-needs-to-renounce-judith-butler/0000018e-61e7-d507-a1cf-63f7bc380000.

56 To be fair, Illouz has refused to demonize critics of the Israeli state, arguing against anti-BDS legislation, though she herself did not agree with the BDS movement. But the global Left's reaction to the Hamas attacks has soured her position.

57 Zalloua, "The Left and (New) Antisemitism: The Palestinian Question and the Politics of *Ressentiment*," *Crisis and Critique* 9, no. 2 (2022): 390–413.

58 Illouz, "How the Left Became a Politics of Hatred Against Jews," *Haaretz*, February 3, 2024. https://www.haaretz.com/opinion/2024-02-03/ty-article-opinion/.highlight/how-the-left-became-a-politics-of-hatred-against-jews/0000018d-6562-d7f7-adcf-6def4fe50000.

59 Žižek notes Illouz's slippages into interpretive "vulgarity" when describing Judith Butler as an "'intellectual' in quotation marks." Žižek counters: "although I had many disputes with Butler, whatever she is, she is an intellectual in the full sense of the term" (Žižek, "Truth Has the Structure of a Fiction: An Imagined Phone Call," *The Philosophical Salon*, November 20, https://thephilosophicalsalon.com/truth

-has-the-structure-of-a-fiction-an-imagined-phone-call/). Likewise, postcolonial theory—though not without limitations—is not to be summarily dismissed. With an eye for the persistence of colonial bias and reason in the contemporary landscape, postcolonial theorists—like Said, Spivak, and Mbembe—have played a crucial role in provincializing Western philosophy and its preoccupations, creating, in turn, an intellectual space for thinking non-European difference and the Palestinian question (see Zalloua, *Continental Philosophy and the Palestinian Question*).

60 Illouz, "The Global Left."

61 Aviad Kleinberg, "Are All Israelis 'Colonialists' Who Deserve to Die?" *Haaretz*, November 13, 2023. https://www.haaretz.com/israel-news/2023-11-13/ty-article-opinion/.premium/are-all-israeli-babies-colonialist-who-deserve-to-die/0000018b-c87e-d61e-a39b-ddfe0fc10000.

62 Kleinberg, "Are All Israelis."

63 Said, *Representations of the Intellectual: The 1993 Reith Lectures* (New York: Vintage Books, 1996), 32.

64 Gayatri Chakravorty Spivak, *The Post-Colonial Critic: Interviews, Strategies, Dialogues*, ed. Sarah Harasym (New York: Routledge, 1990), 66. Spivak is also quite cognizant of the pitfall of political correctness: "I will have in an undergraduate class, let's say, a young, white male student, politically-correct, who will say: 'I am only a bourgeois white male, I can't speak.' In that situation—It's peculiar, because I am in the position of power and their teacher and, on the other hand, I am not a bourgeois white male—I say to them: 'Why not develop a certain degree of rage against the history that has written such an abject script for you that you are silenced?' Then you begin to investigate what it is that silences you, rather than take this very deterministic position—since my skin colour is this, since my sex is this, I cannot speak. I call these things, as you know, somewhat derisively, chromatism: basing everything on skin color—'I am white, I can't speak'—and genitalism: depending on what kind of genitals you have, you can or cannot speak in certain situations. From this position, then, I say you will of course not speak in the same way about the Third World material, but if you make it your task not only to learn what is going on there through language, through specific programmes of study, but also at the same time through a *historical* critique of your position as the investigating person, then you will see that you have earned the right to criticize, and you be heard. When you take the position of not doing your homework—'I will not criticize because of my accident of birth, the historical accident'—that is a much more pernicious position. In one way you take a risk to criticize, of criticizing something which is *Other*—something which you used to dominate. I say that you have to take a certain risk: to say 'I won't criticize' is salving your conscience, and allowing you not to do any homework. On the other hand, if you criticize having earned the right to do so, then you are indeed taking a risk and you will probably be made welcome, and can hope to be judged with respect" (Spivak, *The Post-Colonial Critic*, 62–3). Needless to say, an actual engagement with postcolonial theory has to engage its theorists and not rely on widespread caricatures.

65 Illouz, "The Global Left."

66 Jacqueline Rose, *The Question of Zion* (Princeton: Princeton University Press, 2005).

67 Fayez Sayegh, *Zionist Colonization in Palestine* (Beirut: Research Center, Palestine Liberation Organization, 1965), 22.

68 Catherine Shoard, "Jonathan Glazer: More than 450 Jewish Creatives Denounce Oscars Speech in Open Letter," *The Guardian*, March 19. https://www.theguardian.com/film/2024/mar/19/jonathan-glazer-more-than-450-jewish-creatives-denounce-oscars-speech-in-open-letter-zone-of-interest. Center-left Zionists typically see the "conflict" between Palestinians and Jewish Israelis as a 1967 problem; they believe that the illegal occupation of Palestinian territories after the Six-Day War must come to an end. The letter's line of reasoning comes straight out of the Israeli far-right playbook, not what you would expect from liberal Hollywood. The anti-colonial Left agrees: 1967 is not the problem. Rather, it locates the source of the Palestine/Israel antagonism in 1948, in the Zionist settler invasion.

69 The specific portion of Glazer's comments that critics have seized upon (and often misquoted) is the following: "We stand here as men who refute their Jewishness and the Holocaust being hijacked by an occupation which has led to conflict for so many innocent people, whether the victims of 7 October in Israel or the ongoing attack on Gaza." What Glazer is denouncing here is not his Jewishness but the instrumentalization of Jewish suffering (symbolized by the Shoah) for the justification of Palestinian genocide. In disidentifying with a genocidal Jewish state, Glazer refuses to have his art contribute to the cynical logic of Zionism that, on one hand, sacralizes Jewish suffering and, on the other, discounts Palestinian suffering. Avowing the latter suffering, and having that knowledge alter one's identity, is precisely what liberal Zionists tend to decline to do, preferring instead to isolate the constitutive role of the former suffering in their day-to-day lives. See Naomi Klein, "The Zone of Interest Is about the Danger of Ignoring Atrocities—Including in Gaza," *The Guardian*, March 14, 2024. https://www.theguardian.com/commentisfree/2024/mar/14/the-zone-of-interest-auschwitz-gaza-genocide. In poignant response to the open letter, over 150 Jewish Hollywood professionals signed a letter in support of Glazer's Oscars comments. The signatories reject the Zionist forced choice, affirming: "We should be able to name Israel's apartheid and occupation—both recognized by leading human rights organizations as such—without being accused of rewriting history" (Ellise Shafer, "Joaquin Phoenix, Elliott Gould, Chloe Fineman and More Jewish Creatives Support Jonathan Glazer's Oscars Speech in Open Letter," *Variety*, April 5, 2024. https://variety.com/2024/film/global/jonathan-glazer-oscars-speech-support-jewish-creatives-open-letter-1235960158/).

70 Illouz neglects to mention that historians immediately refuted Netanyahu's claim that the Mufti of Jerusalem gave Hitler the idea for the Final Solution in 1941. See Jodi Rudoren, "Netanyahu Denounced for Saying Palestinian Inspired Holocaust," *The New York Times*, October 21, 2015. https://www.nytimes.com/2015/10/22/world/middleeast/netanyahu-saying-palestinian-mufti-inspired-holocaust-draws-broad-criticism.html.

71 Rashid Khalidi, *Palestinian Identity: The Construction of Modern National Consciousness* (New York: Columbia University Press, 1997), 5.

72 Odeh Bisharat, "The World Was in Complete Solidarity With Israel. Then the Status Quo Returned," *Haaretz*, November 6, 2023. https://www.haaretz.com/opinion/2023-11-06/ty-article-opinion/.premium/the-world-was-in-complete

-solidarity-with-israel-then-the-status-quo-returned/0000018b-a11c-dc0b-a1cb
-e5de6ced0000.

73 Lara Sheehi and Stephen Sheehi argue that the Palestinians' "perverse" state is explained as either "due to the backwardness of Arab culture or, from a more sympathetic perspective, 'stunted' as a consequence of 'trauma,' 'war,' or occupation" (Lara Sheehi and Stephen Sheehi, *Psychoanalysis Under Occupation: Practicing Resistance in Palestine* [New York: Routledge, 2022], 11). Palestinians are damaged either by the backwardness of their own processes of culturalization or by the debilitating effect of colonial subjugation in the occupied territories. In both instances, the humanity/subjectivity of the Palestinians is politically compromised. The latter explanation may be less Orientalist, but it reifies the victim status of the Palestinians, evacuating any sense of Indigenous agency—*they couldn't do otherwise.*

74 Césaire, *Discourse on Colonialism*, trans. Joan Pinkham (New York: Monthly Review Press, 2000), 35.

75 Sayegh, *Zionist Colonization*, 27.

76 Alice Speri, "Israel Responds to Hamas Crimes by Ordering Mass War Crimes in Gaza," *The Intercept*, October 9, 2023. https://theintercept.com/2023/10/09/israel-hamas-war-crimes-palestinians/.

77 Even Yanis Varoufakis, a strong supporter of Palestinian liberation, overstates the anti-Semitic charge when it comes to the global Left. On the problem of anti-Semitism, Varoufakis answers: "It is always a clear and present danger. And it must be eradicated, especially amongst the ranks of the global left and the Palestinians fighting for Palestinian civil liberties around the world" (Yanis Varoufakis, "The Speech That Got Me Banned From Germany," *Jacobin*, April 13, 2024. https://jacobin.com/2024/04/yanis-varoufakis-germany-banned-palestine-gaza?mc_cid=d49beb4b8d&mc_eid=0317ccf9ee). I completely agree with Varoufakis that anti-Semitism must not be tolerated anywhere, including among the global Left and Palestinian activists. But he seems to repeat the overblown charge that the global Left has a Jewish problem. I don't doubt that some anti-Semites have infiltrated our ranks, but from my experiences, the charge of "new anti-Semitism" (an anti-Semitism coming from the ranks of the anti-colonial, anti-racist Left) leveled at the pro-Palestinian solidarity movement is more often a red herring meant to divert global attention from the Occupation and the genocide of the Palestinian people to Jewish insecurities provoked by valid criticism of Zionism and Israeli state actions.

78 Tamer Nafar, "If Our Eyes Can See the Huge Scope of Atrocity, Can Our Hearts Contain Two Pains at Once?" *Haaretz*, December 5. https://www.haaretz.com/opinion/2023-12-05/ty-article-opinion/.premium/with-no-shortage-of-enemies-only-palestinian-israeli-friendships-can-fix-this-miss/0000018c-3662-de12-a3af-3fefdb2e0000.

79 Seth Ackerman, "Israel's March to a Second Nakba," *Catalyst* 7, no. 4 (2024): 16.

80 Illouz, "The Global Left"; Etan Nechin, "Why Judith Butler Calling Hamas' Slaughter 'Armed Resistance' Is So Depressing," *Haaretz*, March 7, 2024. https://www.haaretz.com/opinion/2024-03-07/ty-article-opinion/.premium/why-judith-butler-calling-hamas-slaughter-armed-resistance-is-so-depressing/0000018e-18a9-d1cc-abfe-dfad4cd90000; Roy Peled, "Judith Butler Is Intentionally Giving Hamas' Terror Legitimacy," *Forward*, March 8, 2024. https://forward.com/opinion

/590612/judith-butler-hamas-terror/; Karl Kraus, "Judith Butler: Powerlessness in Action," *K,* March 15. https://k-larevue.com/en/judith-butler-powerlessness-in-action/; Cary Nelson, "'We Can Have a Debate About Whether Hamas Did the Right Thing': Judith Butler's Moral Relativism," *Fathom*, March, 2024. https://fathomjournal.org/we-can-have-a-debate-about-whether-hamas-did-the-right-thing-judith-butlers-moral-relativism/.

81. Butler, "Contre l'antisémitisme et pour la paix révolutionnaire en Palestine," *Parole D'Honneur*. https://www.youtube.com/watch?v=rIQNBJOq-0E&t=1550s; see also Butler, "After Pantin," *Verso Books*, March 14, 2024. https://www.versobooks.com/blogs/news/after-pantin.
82. Sayegh, *Zionist Colonization*, 46.
83. Butler, "Contre l'antisémitisme."
84. Butler, "Contre l'antisémitisme."
85. Butler, "Contre l'antisémitisme."
86. Butler, "After Pantin."
87. Butler, "After Pantin."
88. Nelson, "'We Can Have a Debate.'" Nelson's accusation of anti-Semitism must be turned back on its vindictive accuser. In policing Butler's speech, deemed beyond the pale, Nelson displays what Žižek names "Zionist anti-Semitism," insofar as Nelson is infuriated by Butler deployment of their Jewishness to denounce Israel's colonial subjugation and state violence (Žižek, "Anti-Semitism and Its Transformations," 6; see also Massad, "The Last of the Semites"). By disidentifying with the Zionist settler-colonial regime, and lending their voice to the Palestinian cause of liberation, Butler refuses to accept the state of Israel as the authority over Jewish matters (unlike Netanyahu's narcissistic reading of the Holocaust imperative "Never Again," Butler reads it as interpellating you—as a Jew—to prevent rather than authorize the genocide of Palestinians). They labor instead to decouple Judaism from Zionism so that another political configuration of Palestine/Israel might emerge.
89. Butler, "There Can Be No Critique," *Boston Review*, December 13, 2023. https://www.bostonreview.net/articles/there-can-be-no-critique/.
90. Butler, "There Can Be No Critique."
91. Žižek, "The Shooting of Trump."
92. Žižek, *Mad World*, 31.
93. See Ella Shohat, "Sephardim in Israel: Zionism from the Standpoint of Its Jewish Victims," *Social Text* 19/20 (Fall 1988): 1–35; Ronit Lentin, *Traces of Racial Exception: Racializing Israeli Settler Colonialism* (New York: Bloomsbury, 2018).
94. Wynter, "Unsettling the Coloniality of Being/Power/Truth/Freedom," 260.
95. Katherine McKittrick, ed. *Sylvia Wynter: On Being Human as Praxis* (Durham: Duke University Press, 2015), 47; see also, Kashani, "The Wreck Itself."
96. Sheehi and Sheehi, *Psychoanalysis Under Occupation*, 206.
97. Illouz urges the global Left to cancel Butler, that is, to not let them "usurp" the Left in their support of Hamas (Illouz, "The Global Left").
98. Sayegh, *Zionist Colonization*, 30.

99 Gilles Deleuze, "The Importance of Being Arafat," in *Two Regimes of Madness: Texts and Interviews 1975–1995*, ed. David Lapoujade (New York: Semiotext(e), 2006), 241.

100 Menachem Begin, *The Revolt* (New York: Dell, 1977), 91. See Žižek, *Violence*, 118–19; Massad, *The Persistence of the Palestinian Question: Essays on Zionism and the Palestinians* (New York: Routledge, 2006), 4.

101 Begin, *The Revolt*, 90–1.

102 Said, "Zionism from the Standpoint of Its Victims," *Social Text* 1 (1979): 7–58.

103 There is also a tendency among Zionists to reclaim the idea of terrorism. Then prime minister Ehud Barak said, "Had I been a Palestinian I would have joined a terrorist organization" (Jonathan Mendilow, *Ideology, Party Change, and Electoral Campaigns in Israel, 1965–2001* [New York: SUNY Press, 2003], 209). Consider also the article by Ben Hecht, the militant Zionist Hollywood scriptwriter, "Letter to the Terrorists of Palestine," in which he praises the terrorist actions of the Zionist paramilitary groups in Mandate Palestine (Žižek, *Violence*, 119).

104 Nechin, "Why Judith."

105 Tuck and Yang, "Decolonization Is Not a Metaphor," 10.

106 Wolfe, "Recuperating Binarism: A Heretical Introduction," *Settler Colonial Studies* 3, no. 3–4 (2013): 257.

107 Wolfe, "Settler Colonialism," 388.

108 Nechin, "Why Judith."

109 Malcolm X condemned and ridiculed the popular Zionist narrative that cast Jewish Indigeneity as a justification for settler colonialism: "Did the Zionists have the legal or moral right to invade Arab Palestine, uproot its Arab citizens from their homes and seize all Arab property for themselves just based on the 'religious' claim that their forefathers lived there thousands of years ago? Only a thousand years ago the Moors lived in Spain. Would this give the Moors the legal and moral right to invade the Iberian Peninsula, drive out its Spanish citizens, and then set up a Moroccan nation where Spain used to be, as the European Zionists have done to our Arab brothers and sisters in Palestine?" (Malcolm X, "Zionist Logic," 1967. www.malcolm-x.org/docs/gen_zion.htm). As Illouz notes, Jews did maintain a presence in the country of Palestine, but let's recall that when the 1917 Balfour Declaration was made, Palestinian Arabs comprised roughly 95 percent of the land's inhabitants. Britain's decision to create a national Jewish homeland in historic Palestine was issued without the consultation of the Indigenous Palestinian people. And contrary to Israeli prime minister Golda Meir, who infamously remarked in 1969 that "There was no such thing as a Palestinian. It was not as though there was a Palestinian people. . . . They did not exist" (Khalidi, *Palestinian Identity*, 147), Rashid Khalidi documents an awareness of Palestinianness or Palestinian identity, at the end of the nineteenth century, that existed prior to the encounter with Zionism, though it was subsequently marked by it. In this sense, Palestinian identity, writes Khalidi, "developed in spite of, and in some cases because of, the obstacles it faced" (Khalidi, *Palestinian Identity*, 6; see also Sayegh, *Zionist Colonization*, 4). Contemporary claims regarding Jewish metaphysical Indigeneity must be heard in the context of Golda Meir's attempts to discredit Palestinianness, painting Palestinians as merely Arabs who

call themselves "Palestinians." See also Teresa Aranguren, Sandra Barrilaro, and Mohammed El-Kurd, *Against Erasure: A Photographic Memory of Palestine Before the Nakba* (Chicago: Haymarket Books, 2024).

110   The Red Nation, "Indigenous Solidarity with Palestine," *The Red Nation*, October 26, 2023. https://therednation.org/statement-of-indigenous-solidarity-with-palestine/.

111   Sheehi and Sheehi, *Psychoanalysis Under Occupation*, 96.

112   "For those who, like me, define themselves as Zionists—believing that, despite its iniquities, the creation of a Jewish national home was legitimate and necessary—writing these words—Jewish fascism—is shocking. But a number of facts leave no choice" (Illouz, "The Third Political Force in Israel Represents What We Must Reluctantly Call 'Jewish Fascism,'" *Le Monde*, November 16, 2022. https://www.lemonde.fr/en/opinion/article/2022/11/16/the-third-political-force-in-israel-represents-what-we-must-reluctantly-call-jewish-fascism_6004446_23.html.

113   Howard Jacobson, "The Founding of Israel Wasn't a Colonial Act—a Refugee Isn't a Colonist," *The New Statesman*, November 29, 2023. https://www.newstatesman.com/ideas/2023/11/founding-israel-palestine-anti-semitism?utm_source=substack&utm_medium=email.

114   Jacobson, "The Founding of Israel."

115   Jabotinsky, "The Iron Wall."

116   David Ben-Gurion, "Ben Gurion: Letter to His Son, October 5, 1937," *Jewish Voice for Peace*. https://www.jewishvoiceforpeace.org/2013/04/06/the-ben-gurion-letter/#:~:text=Dear%20Amos%2C,that%20you%20have%20no%20time.

117   Ben-Gurion, "Ben Gurion."

118   Ben-Gurion, "Ben Gurion."

119   Jabotinsky, "The Iron Wall."

120   Ackerman, "Israel's March," 29.

121   For Israeli finance minister Bezalel Smotrich, a Greater Israel means more than cannibalizing additional Palestinian land. In a 2024 documentary produced by Arte Reportage, *Israel: Extremists in Power*, Smotrich envisions an Israel that extends into neighboring Arab states, including Jordan, Lebanon, Egypt, Syria, Iraq, and Saudi Arabia. As he proclaims, "It is written that the future of Jerusalem is to expand to Damascus" (see MEE Staff, "Bezalel Smotrich Calls for Israel's Borders to Extend to Damascus," *Middle East Eye*, October 11, 2024. https://www.middleeasteye.net/news/smotrich-calls-israels-borders-extend-damascus).

122   Ilan Pappé, *The Ethnic Cleansing of Palestine* (Oxford: Oneworld, 2006), xii–xiii.

123   Pappé, *The Ethnic Cleansing*, xiii.

124   Jacobson, "The Founding of Israel."

125   Jacobson, "The Founding of Israel."

126   In contradistinction to Zionist futurology, revolutionary Palestinian philosophy, in the words of Fawaz Turki, embraces the boundless openness of the future, insisting that the Zionist order of things is not an unbreakable horizon: "If the Palestinian revolution is armed with a philosophy at all, it is armed with the anti-determinist

vision of the open-endedness of the future" (Fawaz Turki, "Meaning in Palestinian History: Text and Context," *Arab Studies Quarterly* 3, no. 4 [1981]: 381).

127 Every Palestinian counter-violence is an opportunity for fewer and fewer Indigenous Palestinians: "The Zionist strategy of branding its brutal policies as an *ad hoc* response to this or that Palestinian action is as old as the Zionist presence in Palestine itself. It was used repeatedly as a justification for implementing the Zionist vision of a future Palestine that has in it very few, if any, native Palestinians" (Pappé, "Israel's Incremental Genocide in the Gaza Ghetto," *The Electronic Intifada*, July 13, 2014. https://electronicintifada.net/content/israels-incremental-genocide-gaza-ghetto/13562).

128 See Sheehi and Sheehi, *Psychoanalysis Under Occupation*, 131.

129 Alon Schwarz, "How to Cover Up a Massacre," *Haaretz*, August 12, 2022. https://www.haaretz.com/israel-news/2022-08-12/ty-article-magazine/how-to-cover-up-a-massacre/00000182-9271-d9bc-affb-f3ff387f0000.

130 Tuck and Yang, "Decolonization Is Not a Metaphor," 35.

131 Schwarz, "How to Cover Up a Massacre."

132 Sheehi and Sheehi, *Psychoanalysis Under Occupation*, 126.

133 Lydia Polgreen, "Restoring the Past Won't Liberate Palestine," *The New York Times*, February 18, 2024. https://www.nytimes.com/2024/02/18/opinion/israel-gaza-palestine-decolonization.html.

134 Polgreen, "Restoring the Past."

135 Fanon, *The Wretched of the Earth*, trans. Constance Farrington (New York: Grover Press, 1963), 315.

136 Fanon, *The Wretched of the Earth*, 1, 239.

137 Fanon, *The Wretched of the Earth*, 2.

138 Fanon, *The Wretched of the Earth*, 2.

139 Said, "The Morning After," *The London Review of Books* 15, no. 20 (October 21, 1993). https://www.lrb.co.uk/the-paper/v15/n20/edward-said/the-morning-after.

140 We should contrast Schwarz's "progressive" account with Israeli historian Benny Morris, who carefully documented Israel's ethnic cleansing, fully acknowledging the existence of the Nakba (Benny Morris, *The Birth of the Palestinian Refugee Problem Revisited* [Cambridge: Cambridge University Press, 2004]). Unlike Schwarz and his fellow historian Pappé, however, Morris does not lament the Nakba; it was necessary for the birth of Israel. The Nakba, we're told, was tragic but justified. If there is regret, it comes in Morris's chilling observation that it would have been preferable, for everyone involved, if Ben-Gurion had completed the ethnic cleansing. Israel would have been "Greater Israel" from the beginning, free of Palestinians from the river to the sea. And Palestinians would have figured out another option. In Morris's reading, there is nothing exceptional about Israel here. Israel is like America: "Even the great American democracy could not have been created without the annihilation of the Indians. There are cases in which the overall, final good justifies harsh and cruel acts that are committed in the course of history" (Ari Shavit, "Survival of the Fittest? An Interview with Benny Morris," *CounterPunch*, January 16–18, 2004. http://www.counterpunch.org/2004/01/16/an-interview-with-benny-morris/). Morris's callousness notwithstanding,

the ignorance of North American history displayed in his comment should give us pause about his understanding of resistance. The American Indian peoples were not "annihilated." Just like the settler's invasion, Indigenous resistance to settler colonialism is *a structure, not an event*; it cannot be divorced from the present nor relegated to the dustbin of history. Indigenous resistance has been co-terminous with settler subjugation. Lakota historian Nick Estes' own account of unyielding native resistance exposes the inadequacies and obfuscations of Morris's recounting: "Like [Israel's] patron, the United States, white historians in the United States have long framed the history of settler colonialism in this nation as a 'conflict' between two equal sides: cowboys and Indians; settlers and savages. Dakota scholar Elizabeth Cook-Lynn reminds us there are no two sides to a story of colonial dispossession and genocide. In a settler nation, there is a clear perpetrator: the settler state. *Like Palestinians, Native people continue to resist systematic colonialism* by the United States. We refuse to be uprooted. Refusal is the basis of all forms of anti-colonial resistance, and we, as the original peoples and nations of these lands, extend unwavering solidarity and support to our Palestinian relatives who struggle for liberation from the same violence that threatens to erase *our* histories and *our* futures" (Nick Estes, "The Liberation of Palestine Represents an Alternative Path for Native Nations," *The Red Nation*, September 7, 2019. https://therednation.org/the-liberation-of-palestine-represents-an-alternative-path-for-native-nations/, emphasis added). Not unlike Tom Cotton's rationalization of chattel slavery as something that was necessary for America's founding, Morris declines a reckoning with the Nakba because it would entail an abandonment or overcoming of the Zionist idea of Israel. Schwarz and Morris show that acknowledging the Nakba does not necessarily existentially transform you nor does it compel you to reimagine a different relationality with the Palestinians. Schwarz wants fellow Zionists to have a healthy relationship with their past, to feel good about feeling bad for Palestinians and the Nakba, whereas Morris wants Zionists to understand the consequences of the Nakba—that it is basically a zero-sum game. It is us or them: "A society that aims to kill you forces you to destroy it. When the choice is between destroying or being destroyed, it's better to destroy" (Shavit, "Survival"). Morris has no remorse in saying that he is operating beyond international law, let alone any universalist ethical framework. Might makes right. If you're supporting Israel's carnage in Gaza, you're supporting world-destroying brutish politics.

141 Abu El-Haj, "'We Know Well,'" 259.
142 Sheehi and Sheehi, *Psychoanalysis Under Occupation*, 116.
143 Jacobson, "The Founding of Israel."
144 Dylan Saba, "A Surge in Suppression: It's Never Been This Bad," *N+1*, October 23, 2023. https://www.nplusonemag.com/online-only/online-only/a-surge-in-suppression/; Whitney Strub, "Palestine Is the Single Most Urgent Free Speech Crisis in the U.S. Today," *Mondoweiss*, November 12, 2023. https://mondoweiss.net/2023/11/palestine-is-the-single-most-urgent-free-speech-crisis-in-the-u-s-today/; Alex Kane, "A 'McCarthyite Backlash' Against Pro-Palestine Speech," *Jewish Currents*, October 20, 2023. https://jewishcurrents.org/a-mccarthyite-backlash-against-pro-palestine-speech; Marcetic, "A Tidal Wave"; Warren Montag, "The New McCarthyism: A Personal Testimony," *Verso Books*, March 6, 2024. https://www.versobooks.com/blogs/news/the-new-mccarthyism-a-personal

-testimony. Illouz, "Genocide in Gaza? Eva Illouz Replies to Didier Fassin," *K*, November 16, 2023. https://k-larevue.com/en/genocide-in-gaza-eva-illouz-replies-to-didier-fassin/.

145 Illouz, "Genocide in Gaza?"

146 Yarden Michaeli, "The Israeli Left's Support for the Gaza War Serves the Interests of Netanyahu, Far-Right," *Haaretz*, January 24, 2024. https://www.haaretz.com/opinion/2024-01-24/ty-article-opinion/.premium/israels-center-left-is-still-serving-netanyahus-reign-by-not-collapsing-the-government/0000018d-3d03-dc44-a5bf-bdb703010000.

147 "The Elephant in the Room," August 4, 2023. https://sites.google.com/view/israel-elephant-in-the-room/petitions/aug-23-elephant-in-the-room?authuser=0.

148 Illouz, "The Global Left."

149 Žižek, "The Shooting of Trump."

150 For Žižek, this invention of the enemy to articulate and affirm self-identity is more typical of a rightist orientation: "What characterizes an authentic emancipatory thought is not a vision of conflict-free harmonious future but the properly dialectical notion of antagonism which is totally incompatible with the Rightist topic of the need of an enemy to assert our self-identity" (Žižek, *Christian Atheism: How to Be a Real Materialist* [New York: Bloomsbury, 2024], 206–7). When liberal Zionists dream of a world free of Hamas, they imagine a conflict-free harmonious future (with decaffeinated Palestinian neighbors) absent a reckoning with its violent settler ontology.

151 Abu El-Haj, "'We Know Well,'" 260.

152 Bisharat, "The World."

153 Žižek, *Violence*, 126.

Chapter 3

1 Jacques Lacan, *The Seminar. Book XI. The Four Fundamental Concepts of Psychoanalysis*, trans. Alan Sheridan (London: Hogarth Press and Institute of Psycho-Analysis, 1977), 233.

2 Lacan, *The Four Fundamental Concepts of Psychoanalysis*, 234.

3 Lacan, *The Four Fundamental Concepts of Psychoanalysis*, 230.

4 Jason Glynos, "Psychoanalysis Operates Upon the Subject of Science: Lacan Between Science and Ethics," in *Lacan and Science*, ed. Jason Glynos and Yannis Stavrakakis (New York: Karnac Books, 2002), 60.

5 Tuck and Yang, "Decolonization Is Not a Metaphor," 19.

6 Césaire, *A Tempest*, trans. Richard Miller (New York: TCG Translations, 2002), 60.

7 Hortense J. Spillers, "Mama's Baby, Papa's Maybe: An American Grammar Book," *Diacritics* 17, no. 2 (1987): 68.

8 Žižek and Daly, *Conversations with Žižek*, 119.

9 Fanon, *The Wretched of the Earth,* 168.

10 Fanon, *The Wretched of the Earth,* 182.
11 Fanon, *The Wretched of the Earth*, 2; Žižek, *Freedom*, 282.
12 Mignolo, *The Politics of Decolonial Investigations* (Durham: Duke University Press, 2021), 33. See also Mignolo, *Local Histories/Global Designs: Coloniality, Subaltern Knowledges, and Border Thinking* (Durham: Duke University Press, 2012), 86–7.
13 José Medina, "Varieties of Hermeneutical Injustice," in *The Routledge Handbook of Epistemic Injustice*, ed. Ian James Kidd, José Medina, and Gaile Pohlhaus (New York: Routledge, 2017), 49. Boaventura de Sousa Santos also observes: "Colonial domination involves the deliberate destruction of other cultures. The destruction of knowledge (besides the genocide of indigenous people) is what I call *epistemicide*: the destruction of the knowledge and cultures of these populations, of their memories and ancestral links and their manner of relating to others and to nature. Their legal and political forms—everything—is destroyed and subordinated to the colonial occupation" (Boaventura de Sousa Santos, "Epistemologies of the South and the Future," *From the European South* 1 [2016]: 18).
14 Mignolo, *The Politics of Decolonial Investigations*, 9.
15 Mignolo, *The Politics of Decolonial Investigations*, 33.
16 "Psychoanalysis came into being precisely to deal with the destabilized members of the Western European middle class, due, as Freud knew well, to the imposition that society enforces 'in the service of cultural ideals'" (Mignolo, *The Politics of Decolonial Investigations*, 31).
17 Mignolo, *The Politics of Decolonial Investigations*, 11.
18 Fanon, *Black Skin*, 199.
19 Mignolo, *The Politics of Decolonial Investigations*, 11.
20 "Neurosis is not of necessity a problem for Indigenous females, at least as far as taking their destiny into their own hands is concerned. Psychoanalysis and psychoanalysts are not needed" (Mignolo, *The Politics of Decolonial Investigations*, 33).
21 Mignolo, *The Politics of Decolonial Investigations*, 32.
22 Mignolo, *The Politics of Decolonial Investigations*, 440.
23 Mignolo, *The Politics of Decolonial Investigations*, 418.
24 Fanon, *Black Skin*, xiv, 80.
25 Fanon, *Black Skin*, 129.
26 Fanon, *Black Skin*, 129.
27 Sheehi and Sheehi, *Psychoanalysis Under Occupation*, 30.
28 Sheehi and Sheehi, *Psychoanalysis Under Occupation*, 58.
29 Sheehi and Sheehi, *Psychoanalysis Under Occupation*, 82.
30 Sheehi and Sheehi, *Psychoanalysis Under Occupation*, 114.
31 Žižek, *Freedom*, 114.
32 "Whether you like it or not the Oedipus complex is far from being a black complex" (Fanon, *Black Skin*, 130).

33 Samah Jabr and Elisabeth Berger, "Fanon and Palestine: The Struggle for Justice as the Core of Mental Health," in *Fanon Today: Reason and Revolt of The Wretched of the Earth*, ed. Nigel Gibson (Québec: Daraja Press, 2021), 133.
34 Jabr and Berger, "Fanon and Palestine," 134.
35 Jabr and Berger, "Fanon and Palestine," 133.
36 Fanon, *Black Skin*, xiv.
37 Žižek, *Trouble in Paradise: From the End of History to the End of Capitalism* (Brooklyn: Melville House, 2014), 184.
38 Safeguarding Fanon from Western contamination is ultimately a fool's errand.
39 Fanon, *Black Skin*, 201.
40 Mignolo, "The Many Faces of Cosmo-polis: Border Thinking and Critical Cosmopolitanism," *Public Culture* 12, no. 3 (2000): 743. The defense of, and right to, cultural diversity can be weaponized. Witness the ways the far Right across the globe has co-opted the grammar of decoloniality. As Miri Davidson disquietly observes, "In France, far-right intellectuals routinely cast Europe as indigenous victim of an 'immigrant colonization' orchestrated by globalist elites. Renaud Camus, theorist of the Great Replacement, has praised the anticolonial canon—'all the major texts in the fight against decolonization apply admirably to France, especially those of Frantz Fanon'—and claimed that indigenous Europe needs its own FLN. A similar style of reasoning is evident among Hindu supremacists, who employ the ideas of Latin American decolonial theorists to present ethnonationalism as a form of radical indigenous critique" (Miri Davidson, "Sea and Earth," *New Left Review*, April 4, 2024. https://newleftreview.org/sidecar/posts/sea-and-earth).
41 Nadia Bou Ali, "Against Zionist Psychoanalysis: Conversation Between the Sword and the Neck," *Psychoanalysis and History* 26, no. 1 (2024): 98.
42 Françoise Vergès, "Chains of Madness, Chains of Colonialism: Fanon and Freedom," in *The Fact of Blackness: Frantz Fanon and Visual Representation*, ed. Alan Read (Seattle: Bay Press, 1996), 49.
43 Žižek, *How to Read Lacan*, 5; Žižek, *Organs without Bodies: On Deleuze and Consequences* (New York: Routledge, 2004), 57. See also Žižek, *The Plague of Fantasies* (New York: Verso, 1997), 125.
44 Fanon, *Black Skin*, 206.
45 Foucault, "What Is Critique?," trans. Kevin Paul Geiman, in *What Is Enlightenment? Eighteenth-Century Answers and Twentieth-Century Questions*, ed. James Schmidt (Berkeley: University of California Press, 1996), 386.
46 Fanon, *Black Skin*, xv. Mignolo overreads Fanon's introduction of "sociogenesis" as purely a disruption of the geopolitics of knowledge, a radical displacement of psychoanalysis.
47 Fanon, *Black Skin*, 122.
48 Ross Posnock, "How It Feels to Be a Problem: Du Bois, Fanon, and the 'Impossible Life' of the Black Intellectual," *Critical Inquiry* 23 (1997): 325.
49 Kapoor, "Žižek, Antagonism and Politics Now: Three Recent Controversies," *International Journal of Žižek Studies* 12, no. 1 (2018): 6.

50 Fanon, *Black Skin*, 201. In its infatuation with Africa, *Négritude* relies on a logic of exemplarity that prevents the Caribbean people from engaging in the necessary work of critical self-fashioning, doing no less damage to them than their prior infatuation with Europe: "Fifteen years before, they [the West Indians] said to the Europeans, 'Don't pay attention to my black skin, it's the sun that has burned me, my soul is as white as yours.' After 1945 they changed their tune. They said to the Africans, 'Don't pay attention to my white skin, my soul is as black as yours, and that is what matters'" (Fanon, "West Indians and Africans," in *Toward the African Revolution*, trans. Haakon Chevalier [New York: Grove Press, 1967], 25).

51 Fanon, *The Wretched of the Earth*, 175.

52 Fanon, *Black Skin*, 115. To be fair, Césaire rejects an exoticized *Négritude*, marked by nostalgia, and entertains this anti-colonial society *à venir* as an invention: "For us, the problem is not to make a utopian and sterile attempt to repeat the past, but to go beyond. It is not a dead society that we want to revive. We leave that to those who go in for exoticism. Nor is it the present colonial society that we wish to prolong, the most putrid carrion that ever rotted under the sun. It is a new society that we must create, with the help of all our brother slaves, a society rich with all the productive power of modern times, warm with all the fraternity of olden days" (Césaire, *Discourse on Colonialism*, 51–2).

53 Fanon, *Black Skin*, xiv.

54 Sheehi and Sheehi, *Psychoanalysis Under Occupation*, 67.

55 Qtd. Sheehi and Sheehi, *Psychoanalysis Under Occupation*, 131.

56 Qtd. in Neiman, Neiman, "Fanon the Universalist."

57 Žižek, *Trouble in Paradise*, 183.

58 Žižek, *Trouble in Paradise*, 192.

59 Žižek, *How to Read Lacan*, 74.

60 As Fanon reminds his white existentialist ally/interlocutor: "Sartre forgets that the black man suffers in his body quite differently from the white man" (Fanon, *Black Skin*, 117).

61 Wilderson, *Afropessimism*, 217.

62 Žižek, "Holding the Place," in *Contingency, Hegemony, Universality: Contemporary Dialogues on the Left*, ed. Judith Butler, Ernesto Laclau, and Slavoj Žižek (New York: Verso, 2000), 310.

63 Fanon, *Black Skin*, 165.

64 Fanon, *The Wretched of the Earth*, 94.

65 Fanon, *Black Skin*, 198–9.

66 Fanon, *The Wretched of the Earth*, 93.

67 Tamara Nassar, "Palestinian Authority Forces Are Israel's Foot Soldiers," *The Electronic Intifada*, June 28, 2021. https://electronicintifada.net/blogs/tamara-nassar/palestinian-authority-forces-are-israels-foot-soldiers; see also Joseph Massad, "Nizar Banat Killing: Why the PA's Days Are Numbered," *Middle East Eye*, June 28, 2021. https://www.middleeasteye.net/opinion/palestine-nizar-banat-killing-why-pa-days-numbered.

68 Abunimah, *The Battle for Justice in Palestine*, 78. See also Andy Clarno, *Neoliberal Apartheid: Palestine/Israel and South Africa after 1994* (Chicago: University of Chicago Press, 2017).

69 Toufic Haddad, *Palestine Ltd.: Neoliberalism and Nationalism in the Occupied Territories* (London: I.B. Tauris, 2016).

70 Haddad, *Palestine Ltd.*, 3.

71 Haddad, *Palestine Ltd.*, 8. But Palestinians never relinquished their desire for freedom and social justice. Their anger then and now at the PA helps to explain Hamas's popularity in Occupied Palestine. When Hamas won the 2006 parliamentary elections, it ran on a platform of anti-colonial resistance and anti-corruption.

72 Michel Warschawski, *Toward an Open Tomb: The Crisis of Israeli Society*, trans. Peter Drucker (New York: Monthly Review Press, 2004), 74.

73 "Abbas' popularity has plummeted in recent years, with polls consistently finding that a large majority of Palestinians want him to resign. The PA's security coordination with Israel is extremely unpopular, causing many Palestinians to view it as a subcontractor of the occupation" (Joseph Krauss, "What Would a New Palestinian Government in the West Bank Mean for the War in Gaza?" *AP News*, February 26, 2024, https://apnews.com/article/israel-palestinian-authority-government-explainer-aefe041e045f2c60918b42f42185f41e).

74 Ahmad Qabaha and Bilal Hamamra, "The Nakba Continues: The Palestinian Crisis from the Past to the Present," *Janus Unbound* 1, no. 1 (2021): 30.

75 Abunimah, *The Battle for Justice in Palestine*, 78–9.

76 Erik H. Erikson and Huey P. Newton, *In Search of Common Ground: Conversations with Erik H. Erikson and Huey P. Newton* (New York: Norton, 1973), 29–30.

77 Žižek, *Surplus-Enjoyment: A Guide for The Non-Perplexed* (New York: Bloomsbury, 2022), 108, 109.

78 Gibson, "Fanon, Movement, Self-Movement," 301.

79 Fanon, *The Wretched of the Earth*, 94.

80 Žižek, *Trouble in Paradise*, 185.

81 Mignolo, "Yes, We Can: Non-European Thinkers and Philosophers," *Al Jazeera*, February 19, 2013. http://www.aljazeera.com/indepth/opinion/2013/02/20132672747320891.html.

82 Mignolo, "Yes, We Can."

83 Žižek, *Trouble in Paradise*, 191.

84 Kapoor, "Intersectionality, Decoloniality, Indigenous Localism: A Critique," *Theory, Culture and Society* (2024): 11.

85 Fanon, *The Wretched of the Earth*, 2.

86 Fanon, *The Wretched of the Earth*, 56.

87 Mignolo, "Yes, We Can"; Sartre, "Preface," lvii.

88 Shatz, *The Rebel's Clinic*, 301.

89. Robert Bernasconi, "Fanon's *The Wretched of the Earth* as the Fulfillment of Sartre's *Critique of Dialectical Reason*," *Sartre Studies International* 16, no. 2 (2010): 36.
90. Fanon, *The Wretched of the Earth*, 239.
91. Fanon, *The Wretched of the Earth*, 9.
92. Fanon, *The Wretched of the Earth*, 1.
93. Fanon, *The Wretched of the Earth*, 1.
94. Erik Vogt, "Žižek and Fanon: On Violence and Related Matters," in *Žižek Now: Cultural Perspectives in Žižek Studies*, ed. Jamil Khader and Molly Anne Rothenberg (Cambridge: Polity Press, 2013), 141.
95. Žižek and Daly, *Conversations with Žižek*, 121.
96. Žižek, "Class Struggle or Postmodernism? Yes, Please!" in *Contingency, Hegemony, Universality: Contemporary Dialogues on the Left*, ed. Judith Butler, Ernesto Laclau, and Slavoj Žižek (New York: Verso, 2000), 121.
97. Alenka Zupančič, "A Perfect Place to Die: Theatre in Hitchcock's Films," in *Everything You Always Wanted to Know About Lacan, But Were Afraid to Ask Hitchcock*, ed. Slavoj Žižek (New York: Verso, 1992), 93.
98. Fanon, *The Wretched of the Earth*, 2.
99. Fanon, *The Wretched of the Earth,* 2.
100. Žižek, *Welcome to the Desert of the Real*, 152–3.
101. Again, any liberation movement can be deprived of its radical substance; the event can be undone and de-eventalized. In *The Wretched of the Earth*, Fanon warned that the rule of the Black bourgeoisie after gaining independence risked betraying the project of decolonization. See also Žižek, *Event: Philosophy in Transit* (London: Penguin Books, 2014), 161–78.
102. Wilderson, *Afropessimism*, 217.
103. Echoing the Afropessimists, Fred Moten defines the "abolition of sovereignty" as "an abolition of a certain horrible and brutal individuated notion of freedom. And it's an abolition of the world that is constructed on that conceptual framework. And if you want to put it in positive rather than negative terms, then it is the project of saving the earth. Or, as the great poet Ed Roberson would say, 'the project of seeing the Earth before the end of the world'" (Nehal El-Hadi, "Ensemble: An Interview with Dr. Fred Moten," *Mice Magazine*, Summer 2018. https://micemagazine.ca/issue-four/ensemble-interview-dr-fred-moten).
104. Glen Coulthard and Leanne Betasamosake Simpson, "Grounded Normativity / Place-Based Solidarity," *American Quarterly* 68, no. 2 (2016): 254.
105. This is akin to Gayatri Chakravorty Spivak's formulation of the double bind as "a persistent critique of what we cannot not want" (Gayatri Chakravorty Spivak, *Critique of Postcolonial Reason: Toward a History of the Vanishing Present* [Cambridge, MA: Harvard University Press, 1999], 110).
106. Walter Mignolo and Wanda Nanibush, "Thinking and Engaging with the Decolonial: A Conversation between Walter D. Mignolo and Wanda Nanibush," *Afterall* (Spring/Summer 2018): 27–8.

107 Danny Danon, "What's Wrong with Palestinian Surrender?" *The New York Times*, June 24, 2019. https://www.nytimes.com/2019/06/24/opinion/palestinian-peace-bahrain-conference.html.

108 Danon, "What's Wrong with Palestinian Surrender?"

109 Danon, "What's Wrong with Palestinian Surrender?"

110 Sheehi and Sheehi, *Psychoanalysis Under Occupation*, 202.

111 Personal communication from Terblanche Delport to Derek Hook, quoted in Derek Hook, "White Anxiety in (Post)apartheid South Africa," *Psychoanalysis, Culture & Society* 25, no. 4 (2020): 613.

112 Hook, "White Anxiety in (Post)apartheid South Africa," 613.

113 Žižek, *Freedom*, 82.

114 Fanon, *Black Skin*, 118.

115 Fanon, *A Dying Colonialism*, 128.

116 Newton, *Revolutionary Suicide*, 2.

117 Newton, *Revolutionary Suicide*, 3.

118 David Marriott, "On Revolutionary Suicide," *Diacritics* 49, no. 4 (2021): 111.

119 Newton, *To Die for the People* (New York: Vintage Books, 1972), 28.

120 I'm drawing here on Žižek's reflections on the refugees who are looking to join the proletariat; they aspire to become "nothing"—beings divested of all substantial content—because they are, strictly speaking, "less-than-nothing" (Žižek, *A Left That Dares to Speak Its Name* [Cambridge: Polity Press, 2020], 31).

121 Newton, *To Die for the People*, 28. Angela Davis also believes that the role of the lumpenproletariat in the struggle for liberation "must be given serious thought" (Angela Davis, "Political Prisoners, Prisons and Black Liberation," in *If They Come in the Morning: Voices of Resistance*, ed. Angela Y. Davis [New York: Verso, 2016], 35).

122 Fanon, *The Wretched of the Earth*, 81.

123 Newton, *Revolutionary Suicide*, 3. In the aftermath of the October 7 attack, Michel Warschawski similarly observed, "the Palestinians are pushed to the limit, but also driven by the thought of a sense of dignity: 'Since we must die, let us die in fighting for our land'" (Michel Warschawski, "We Have Gone Beyond War Crimes in Gaza," *Verso Books*, November 6, 2023. https://www.versobooks.com/blogs/news/michel-warschawski-we-have-gone-beyond-war-crimes-in-gaza). What happens when Palestinians, reduced to naked life, no longer fear biological death? Revolutionary suicide/violence against the occupier crystalizes as the only viable solution (Zalloua, *The Politics of the Wretched*, 127).

124 Newton, *To Die for the People*, 22.

125 Newton, *Revolutionary Suicide*, 5. Haidar Eid and M. Gessen have drawn a parallel between the confinement of Palestinians in Gaza and that of the ghettoized Jews in Nazi-occupied Europe. Gessen sees similarities in their living conditions, while Eid extends the parallel, comparing resistance to the occupation to the Warsaw uprising of the oppressed in 1944. See Eid, "Gaza 2023: Our Warsaw Uprising Moment"; M. Gessen, "In the Shadow of the Holocaust," *The New Yorker*,

December 9, 2023. https://www.newyorker.com/news/the-weekend-essay/in-the-shadow-of-the-holocaust.

126 Žižek, *Surplus-Enjoyment*, 212.

127 Newton, *Revolutionary Suicide*, 3.

128 Tamara Nassar, "Palestinians Mourn 'Heroic' Aaron Bushnell," *The Electronic Intifada*, February 27, 2024. https://electronicintifada.net/blogs/tamara-nassar/palestinians-mourn-heroic-aaron-bushnell.

129 Hannah Zeavin, "Diagnosing Resistance: What Aaron Bushnell's Death Says About Power, Protest, and Pathology," *Bookforum* (Spring 2024). https://www.bookforum.com/print/3004/what-aaron-bushnell-s-death-says-about-power-protest-and-pathology-25343. On social media, Ali Abunimah, the founder of *The Electronic Intifada*, said: "Aaron Bushnell gave his life so that America would hear his message: End the genocide. He kept calling 'Free Palestine' through intense, horrifying pain. He gave his life so people in Gaza might live. There's no greater love than that. I feel sadness and awe for this human being" (https://twitter.com/AliAbunimah/status/1762172816013574315).

130 We can't forget how presidential candidate Barack Obama almost committed career suicide when he displayed, in 2007, sympathy for Palestinians, saying, "no one has suffered more than the Palestinians." Finding himself in a political jam, Obama walked back the statement the only way possible. He cynically blamed the suffering of Palestinians on Palestinians themselves: "Nobody has suffered more than the Palestinian people from the failure of the Palestinian leadership to recognize Israel, to renounce violence, and to get serious about negotiating peace and security for the region" (2008 South Carolina Democratic Debate, http://www.nytimes.com/2007/04/27/us/politics/27debate_transcript.html?pagewanted=all&_r=0). I have strong reservations about Palestinian leadership, but I would still put Israel and the United States ahead of the PA as far as responsibility for Palestinian misery is concerned.

131 We can contrast the public use of *ressentiment* subtending revolutionary suicide with its private use visible among a younger generation of Israeli students and soldiers, who have experienced Operation Iron Swords first-hand. Omer Bartov, who was scheduled to give a talk at Ben-Gurion University of the Negev in Be'er Sheva, Israel, describes his agonistic exchange with students there protesting his lecture. To promote conversation, Bartov invited the ethno-nationalist activists to dialogue. Bartov notes that these students are not necessarily representative of the student body, but they do exemplify "a much more widespread sentiment in the country" (Bartov, "As a Former IDF Soldier and Historian of Genocide, I Was Deeply Disturbed by my Recent Visit to Israel," *The Guardian*, August 13, 2024. https://www.theguardian.com/world/article/2024/aug/13/israel-gaza-historian-omer-bartov?CMP=share_btn_url). These students display their private use of *ressentiment* in doubling down on the righteousness of the Israeli army (despite, or because of, the global outrage over the number of Palestinian civilians' deaths, they repeat that it is the most moral army in the world) and in identifying absolutely with the activities of the IOF, immunizing themselves and fellow soldiers from any critique. Bartov sums up the sentiments he heard repeatedly from these young people and many others: "We have no room in our hearts, we have no room in our thoughts, we do not want to speak about or to be shown what our own soldiers,

our children or grandchildren, our brothers and sisters, are doing right now in Gaza. We must focus on ourselves, on our trauma, fear and anger" ("As a Former IDF Soldier"). No relation is possible with the population of Gaza (a message fully internalized by most of the Israeli society). The faceless Gazan has become Israel's *Muselmann*, the racialized enemy/subhuman of the Zionist apartheid regime, afforded no care nor consideration, only sadistic hostility. According to Bartov, Israeli soldiers are developing a "way of thinking" reminiscent of Nazism: "Having internalised certain views of the enemy—the Bolsheviks as *Untermenschen*; Hamas as human animals—and of the wider population as less than human and undeserving of rights, soldiers observing or perpetrating atrocities tend to ascribe them not to their own military, or to themselves, but to the enemy" (Bartov, "As a Former IDF Soldier"). This way of thinking is not, however, fully new, but finds its roots in Zionism's colonial ambitions. Now the question is how colonialism relates to Nazism. I turn to this topic in Chapter 5.

132   Newton, *Revolutionary Suicide*, 5.
133   Said, "My Right of Return," in *Power, Politics, and Culture: Interviews with Edward W. Said*, ed. Gauri Viswanathan (New York: Vintage, 2001), 451.
134   Said, "My Right of Return," 451–2.
135   Said, "My Right of Return," 452–3.
136   NPR, "Netanyahu's References to Violent Biblical Passages Raise Alarm Among Critics," *Morning Edition*, November 7, 2023. https://www.npr.org/2023/11/07/1211133201/netanyahus-references-to-violent-biblical-passages-raise-alarm-among-critics.
137   Lazar Berman, "Netanyahu: Goal of War Is 'to Defeat the Murderous Enemy, Ensure Our Existence in Our Land,'" *The Times of Israel*, October 28, 2023. https://www.timesofisrael.com/liveblog_entry/netanyahu-goal-of-war-is-to-defeat-the-murderous-enemy-ensure-our-existence-in-our-land/.
138   Edward Said, "Apocalypse Now," *Index on Censorship* 29, no. 5 (2000): 51.
139   Butler, "Contre l'antisémitisme."
140   Audre Lorde, "The Master's Tools Will Never Dismantle the Master's House," in *This Bridge Called My Back: Writings by Radical Women of Color*, ed. Cherríe Moraga and Gloria Anzaldua (New York: Kitchen Table Press, 1983), 94–101.
141   Said, "My Right of Return," 451.
142   Žižek, *Welcome to the Desert of the Real*, 116.
143   *Israelism* (2023). Directed by Erin Axelman and Sam Eilertsen. www.israelismfilm.com.
144   Standing Together, "Where There Is Struggle There Is HOPE." https://www.standing-together.org/en.
145   Lorenzo Tondo and Quique Kierszenbaum, "'Solidarity over Hatred': The Small Band of Israelis Stopping Settlers Obstructing Aid Trucks," *The Guardian*, May 31, 2024. https://www.theguardian.com/world/article/2024/may/31/solidarity-over-hatred-the-small-band-of-israelis-stopping-settlers-obstructing-aid-trucks.
146   Tondo and Kierszenbaum, "'Solidarity over Hatred.'"
147   Tondo and Kierszenbaum, "'Solidarity over Hatred.'"

148 Tondo and Kierszenbaum, "'Solidarity over Hatred.'"
149 Itay Mashiach, "Meet the Israelis Who Are Trying to Physically Block the Ethnic Cleansing Unfolding in the West Bank," *Haaretz*, February 2, 2024. https://www.haaretz.com/israel-news/2024-02-02/ty-article-magazine/.highlight/meet-the-israelis-physically-blocking-the-ethnic-cleansing-unfolding-in-the-west-bank/0000018d-6609-d37c-a9df-ef8b77200000.
150 Mashiach, "Meet the Israelis."
151 Mashiach, "Meet the Israelis," emphasis added.
152 Audre Lorde, "The Uses of Anger," *Women's Studies Quarterly* 25, no. 1/2 (1997): 282.
153 Mashiach, "Meet the Israelis." None of the peace activists interviewed by Itay Mashiach expressed anything remotely close to anti-Zionism. One of the activists, Gil Alexander, drew on his religious Zionism as an explanation for his care of Palestinians: "My religious-Zionist viewpoint is that human rights take precedence over the wholeness of the Land of Israel" (Mashiach, "Meet the Israelis"). Alexander's ethical Zionism elevates any human over the nation-state of Israel.
154 Mashiach, "Meet the Israelis."
155 Karl Marx, "Letters from the *Deutsch-Französische Jahrbucher*," in *Collected Works of Marx and Engels*, vol. 3 (New York: International Publishers, 1975), 142.
156 BDS, "Standing Together: Serving Apartheid Israel's Propaganda," January 25, 2024. https://bdsmovement.net/standing-together-normalization.
157 Said, *The Question of Palestine* (New York: Vintage Books, 1992), xxviii.
158 Said, "My Right of Return," 458.
159 Said, "My Right of Return," 457.
160 Žižek, "Anti-Semitism and Its Transformations," 6.
161 Said, *Reflections on Exile and Other Essays* (Cambridge, MA: Harvard University Press, 2000), 173.
162 Said, "Permission to Narrate," *Journal of Palestine Studies* 13, no. 3 (1984): 27–48.
163 Said, "The One-State Solution," *The New York Times Magazine*, January 10, 1999. https://www.nytimes.com/1999/01/10/magazine/the-one-state-solution.html.
164 Rehnuma Sazzad, *Edward Said's Concept of Exile: Identity and Cultural Migration in the Middle East* (New York: I.B. Tauris & Co. Ltd., 2017), 220.
165 Said, *Reflections on Exile*, 186.
166 Said, "The One-State Solution."
167 Klein, "We Need an Exodus from Zionism," *The Guardian*, April 24, 2024. https://www.theguardian.com/commentisfree/2024/apr/24/zionism-seder-protest-new-york-gaza-israel.

Chapter 4

1 Saidiya V. Hartman and Frank B. Wilderson III, "The Position of the Unthought," *Qui Parle* 13, no. 2 (2003): 183–201.

2   Sharpe, "Black Studies: In the Wake," 59.
3   Emmanuel Levinas, "Peace and Proximity," in *Basic Philosophical Writings*, ed. Adriaan T. Peperzak, Simon Critchley, and Robert Bernasconi (Bloomington: Indiana University Press, 1996), 166.
4   Levinas, *Totality and Infinity: An Essay on Exteriority*, trans. Alphonso Lingis (Pittsburgh: Duquesne University Press, 1969), 51.
5   Žižek, "Neighbors and Other Monsters," in *The Neighbor: Three Inquiries in Political Theology*, with a New Preface, ed. Slavoj Žižek, Eric L. Santner, and Kenneth Reinhard (Chicago: University of Chicago Press, 2013), 140.
6   Žižek and Daly, *Conversations with Žižek*, 71.
7   Cornel West, "Truth," in *Examined Life: Excursions with Contemporary Thinkers*, ed. Astra Taylor (New York: The New Press, 2009), 8–9.
8   Fanon, *Black Skin*, 202, translation modified.
9   Speri, "Israel Responds to Hamas."
10 Hartman and Wilderson, "The Position of the Unthought," 189.
11 Fanon, *Black Skin*, xii–xiii.
12 Hartman, *Scenes of Subjection: Terror, Slavery, and Self-Making in Nineteenth-Century America* (Oxford: Oxford University Press, 1997), 18.
13 Hartman, *Scenes of Subjection,* 18.
14 Zakiyyah Iman Jackson, "Saidiya Hartman by Zakiyyah Iman Jackson," *BOMB*, Winter 2023. https://bombmagazine.org/articles/2022/10/24/saidiya-hartman/.
15 Hartman, *Scenes of Subjection,* 4.
16 Hartman, *Scenes of Subjection*, 21.
17 Hartman, *Scenes of Subjection*, 19.
18 Hartman, *Scenes of Subjection*, 20.
19 Hartman, *Lose Your Mother*, 6.
20 Hartman, *Lose Your Mother*, 133.
21 Saidiya V. Hartman and Tina Campt, "A Future Beyond Empire: An Introduction," *Small Axe*, no. 28 (2009): 20.
22 Hartman, *Lose Your Mother*, 31.
23 Spillers, "Mama's Baby, Papa's Maybe," 208.
24 See Wynter, "Unsettling the Coloniality of Being/Power/Truth/Freedom."
25 Nicolas Weill, "Levinas trahi? La réponse de Judith Butler," *Le Monde*, March 21, 2013. https://www.lemonde.fr/idees/article/2013/03/21/levinas-trahi-la-reponse-de-judith-butler_5994702_3232.html.
26 George Yancy, *Black Bodies, White Gazes: The Continuing Significance of Race in America* (Lanham: Rowman & Littlefield, 2017), xxxv.
27 Wildeson, *Afropessimism*, 13.
28 Alexander G. Weheliye, *Habeas Viscus: Racializing Assemblages, Biopolitics, and Black Feminist Theories of the Human* (Durham: Duke University Press, 2014), 3.
29 "Philosophy for Palestine."

30 Levinas, "Ethics and Politics," in *The Levinas Reader*, ed. Seán Hand (Oxford: Blackwell, 1989), 289.
31 Levinas, "Ethics and Politics," 289.
32 Levinas, "Ethics and Politics," 294.
33 Levinas, "Ethics and Politics," 294.
34 Enrique Dussel, "Anti-Cartesian Meditations: On the Origin of the Philosophical Anti-Discourse of Modernity," trans. Geo Maher, *Journal for Culture and Religious Theory* 13, no. 1 (2014): 21.
35 Levinas, *Ethics and Infinity: Conversations with Philippe Nemo*, trans. Richard A. Cohen (Pittsburgh: Duquesne University Press, 1985), 85.
36 Levinas, *Otherwise than Being, or, Beyond Essence*, trans. Alphonso Lingis (The Hague: Martinus Nijhoff, 1981), 157.
37 Levinas, "Politics After!" in *The Levinas Reader*, ed. Seán Hand (Oxford: Blackwell, 1989), 277–83. "Politics After!" is one of three essays included under the title "Zionisms."
38 Derrida, *Adieu to Emmanuel Levinas*, trans. Pascale-Anne Brault and Michael Naas (Stanford: Stanford University Press, 1999), 83.
39 Levinas, "Politics After!", 277–8, emphasis added.
40 "The assumption of Arab homogeneity enabled fantasies of 'transferring' Palestinians to neighboring countries to make room for Jewish settlers" (Moses, *The Problems of Genocide*, 365).
41 Michael L. Morgan, *Levinas's Ethical Politics* (Bloomington: Indiana University Press, 2016), 274.
42 Morgan, *Levinas's Ethical Politics*, 278.
43 "Israeli television said the protest was the largest in the history of the state, which was created in 1948. Organizers of the rally said the crowd numbered 350,000; the country has a population of about four million" (William E. Farrell, "Israelis, At Huge Rally In Tel Aviv, Demand Begin and Sharon Resign," *The New York Times*, September 26, 1982. https://www.nytimes.com/1982/09/26/world/israelis-at-huge-rally-in-tel-aviv-demand-begin-and-sharon-resign.html).
44 Levinas, "Ethics and Politics," 296.
45 Bartov correctly observes that the type of response caused by the Sabra and Shatila massacre is "inconceivable" now (Bartov, "As a Former IDF Soldier"). The criminality of Operation Iron Swords does not unsettle Israeli society. Palestinian abjection, acknowledged or disavowed, creates the condition for defending, enjoying, and celebrating Zionist identity—Israel vs. the anti-Semitic world. In a personal communication with me, an Israeli activist and historian who prefers to remain anonymous added more context to the different reactions to both catastrophic events: "In 1982 the occupation was only 15 years old and Israeli Jews were hardly aware of the Nakba. They could still hold to a self-image of being Zionist and moral in one and the same time. Since then we had 2 intifadas, a war in Lebanon, many 'rounds' in Gaza etc. The October 7th attack which contained a massacre of some 800 civilians, taking more than 240 hostages among them very young children, fully destroying several Jewish communities, unleashed the darkest forces in the Jewish Israeli society." While "there are very significant pockets of

Jewish-Palestinian solidarity and of resistance to the war and to the atrocities in Gaza, in Israeli universities and in Israeli civil society," they added, Israel's pull to the Right is unmistakable. Under "the rapid Fascitization of the Israeli society and Israel's form of governance," most Israeli Jews "support the war and the genocide and many even want to accelerate it."

46 Levinas, "Ethics and Politics," 297.
47 Judith Butler, *Parting Ways: Jewishness and the Critique of Zionism* (New York: Columbia University Press, 2012), 39.
48 Zalloua, *Continental Philosophy and the Palestinian Question*.
49 Derrida, *Rogues: Two Essays on Reason*, trans. Pascale-Anne Brault and Michael Naas (Stanford: Stanford University Press, 2005), 60.
50 "Philosophy for Palestine."
51 Levinas, "The Name of a Dog, or Natural Rights," in *Difficult Freedom: Essays on Judaism*, trans. Seán Hand (Baltimore: The Johns Hopkins University Press, 1990), 153.
52 Césaire, *Discourse on Colonialism*, 36. In a similar vein, W. E. B. Du Bois relates the horrors of Nazism to Europe's imperialism and racial colonialism: "There was no Nazi atrocity—concentration camps, wholesale maiming and murder, defilement of women or ghastly blasphemy of childhood—which Christian civilization or Europe had not long been practicing against colored folk in all parts of the world in the name of and for the defense of a Superior Race born to rule the world" (W. E. B. Du Bois, *The World and Africa and Color and Democracy*, ed. Henry Louis Gates, Jr. [New York: Oxford University Press, 2007], 15).
53 Césaire, *Discourse on Colonialism*, 36.
54 Fanon, *The Wretched of the Earth*, 236.
55 Walter Benjamin, *Illuminations*, ed. Hannah Arendt, trans. Harry Zohn (New York: Schocken, 1968), 262. Joe Sacco muses on the Janus face of the Enlightenment in relation to its ideals and the devastated reality of Gaza: "One might fairly ask, was the Enlightenment buried in the rubble of Gaza or was the rubble the Enlightenment's logical conclusion?" (Joe Sacco, "The War on Gaza—6-25-24," *The Comics Journal*, June 25, 2024. https://www.tcj.com/the-war-on-gaza-6-25-24/).
56 Fanon, *Black Skin*, 70.
57 Patrick D. Anderson, "Levinas and the Anticolonial," *Journal of French and Francophone Philosophy* 25, no. 1 (2017): 170.
58 To be sure, the Israeli government has not adopted Nazi-style death camps where Palestinians would be killed on an industrial scale. Zionist genocide proceeds differently. Israel has accelerated its de-worlding of Palestinians, transforming the Gaza Strip into a concentration camp where its citizens await death by starvation or attacks. We are dealing with mass starvation at an unprecedented rate and with attacks that could take place anywhere and anytime in Gaza. Evacuation orders mean nothing because there are no safe zones in the Gaza Strip. Safe zones communicated by the Israeli military to Gazans are the cruelest of lies. Despite the documentation of Israeli brutality, most Western leaders continue to maintain the best of relations with their Israeli counterparts as if no genocide, no war crimes, no

crimes against humanity were taking place. See Ghada Ageel, "Gaza's 'Safe Zone' of Horror," *Al Jazeera*, July 8, 2024. https://www.aljazeera.com/opinions/2024/7/8/gazas-safe-zone-of-horror; Mahmoud Mushtaha, "Israel Ordered Thousands To 'Safe' Areas in Gaza City—Then Bombed Them," *+972 Magazine*, July 10, 2024. https://www.972mag.com/gaza-city-israeli-army-attacked-safe-areas/; Human Rights Watch, "Israel: Starvation Used as Weapon of War in Gaza," *Human Rights Watch*, December 18, 2023. https://www.hrw.org/news/2023/12/18/israel-starvation-used-weapon-war-gaza; Neve Gordon and Muna Haddad, "The Road to Famine in Gaza," *The New York Review*, March 30, 2024. https://www.nybooks.com/online/2024/03/30/the-road-to-famine-in-gaza/.

59. Fanon, *Black Skin*, xv.
60. Fanon, *Black Skin*, 95.
61. Fanon, *Black Skin*, 143.
62. Gordon, "Through the Hellish Zone of Nonbeing," 11.
63. Levinas, *Totality and Infinity*, 51.
64. Fanon, *Black Skin*, 165.
65. "The colonial world is a Manichean world. The colonist is not content with physically limiting the space of the colonized, i.e., with the help of his agents of law and order. As if to illustrate the totalitarian nature of colonial exploitation, the colonist turns the colonized into a kind of quintessence of evil" (Fanon, *The Wretched of the Earth*, 6). Israel's apartheid regime is not only interested in disciplining Palestinian bodies (through its Separation Wall and the seemingly endless number of checkpoints); it wants to erode and hollow out their being, and recast it as evil, full of hate and *ressentiment* for the Jewish state. See B'Tselem, "List of Military Checkpoints in the West Bank and Gaza Strip," Updated, June 5, 2024. https://www.btselem.org/freedom_of_movement/checkpoints_and_forbidden_roads.
66. Fanon, *The Wretched of the Earth*, 6.
67. Anderson, "Levinas and the Anticolonial," 154.
68. Levinas, *Totality and Infinity*, 39.
69. Žižek, *Organs Without Bodies*, 106.
70. Levinas, "The *I* and the Totality," in *Entre Nous: Thinking of the Other*, trans. Michael B. Smith and Barbara Harshav (New York: Columbia University Press, 1998), 28.
71. Žižek, *In Defense of Lost Causes*, 165.
72. Donning a white mask both alienates Black people and bestows them with an identity, purporting to transform them into imaginary-symbolic neighbors. Living in an anti-Black world, however, intensifies Black alienation and gives the lie to white civil society's promises. See Basu Thakur, "Blackness and the Politics of the Real," 291–2.
73. Žižek, *The Parallax View*, 113.
74. Žižek, "Neighbors and Other Monsters," 161.
75. Žižek, "Neighbors and Other Monsters," 162.
76. Žižek, *The Parallax View*, 111.

77 Derrida, *Rogues*, 60.
78 Žižek, "Neighbors and Other Monsters," 183.
79 Žižek, "Neighbors and Other Monsters," 183.
80 Žižek, "Neighbors and Other Monsters," 166.
81 Žižek, *In Defense of Lost Causes*, 285.
82 Žižek, *Less Than Nothing*, 763.
83 Žižek, "Neighbors and Other Monsters," 140.
84 Are some of the Jewish Israeli activists discussed in Chapter 3 practicing neighborly love? Maybe. Yifat Mehl, for example, articulates her shifting views and commitments to Israel and Palestinians: "On October 7 I felt very Jewish and very Israeli, and I thought that maybe I wouldn't go back. Let them go to hell. My collective identity was suddenly reinforced. I started to move toward insularity, toward withdrawing within the shared pain, toward what's supposed to be my real identity. Maybe I was afraid that this would happen to me, and that if I forced myself to think about things rationally, it would stop the emotional process I'm undergoing. Maybe that's the reason that at 6 A.M. on October 8 I was on the road. 'I don't know why I went,' she continues. "We didn't even go with the shepherds to their pastures—who even left the house? We simply began to wander among the different communities. These people need to have [access to] water, and the village has a gate, and the army decides when that gate will be opened. That day, the army locked the gate and they ran out of water. We approached them [the soldiers] and they told us, 'You're not ashamed, on a day like this? Why do you even care about them?' I'm not indifferent to that at all. *My reference group is still Israel and Israelis, first and foremost*" (Mashiach, "Meet the Israelis," emphasis added). Mehl's love for the Palestinian neighbor risks undoing her identity; but upon reflecting on her commitment to Palestinians, she forges a measured plan, introduces a calculus of pleasure, tempering her affect for the Palestinian neighbor and reaffirming her alignment with her kin.
85 Žižek, *Christian Atheism*, 182. During Israel's 2008–9 War on Gaza, Operation Cast Lead, then foreign minister Tzpi Livni stated that "Palestinians teach their children to hate us and we teach love thy neighbor" (Nurit Peled-Elhanan, *Palestine in Israeli School Books: Ideology and Propaganda in Education* [New York: I.B. Tauris, 2012], 232). The desire to annihilate Palestinians is so prevalent in Israel, so naturalized and devoid of repulsion, that it generated, in November, after the start of Operation Iron Swords, a video of Israeli children, dubbed "Friendship Song 2023," singing about the virtues of exterminating Palestinians in Gaza. Here is a sample of the song's murderous lyrics: "In another year there will be nothing there. And we will safely return to our homes. Within a year we will annihilate everyone. And then we will return to plow our fields." The video, uploaded by Israel's public broadcaster, Kan News, on its official X page, was taken down due to the global backlash over the song's celebration of genocide. (Rifat Audeh, "It's Not Shocking to See Israeli Children Celebrate the Gaza Genocide," *Al Jazeera*, December 13, 2023. https://www.aljazeera.com/opinions/2023/12/13/its-not-shocking-to-see-israeli-children-celebrate-the-gaza-genocide). Here we have a clear example of Israel's injunction to hate thy neighbor, of its anti-Palestinian libidinal economy; the anticipatory enjoyment of the destruction of Palestinian lives attests to the ways sadism is achieving a normalized state in Israel. Calling for Palestinian elimination

is no longer simply legitimate; there is a sick collective enjoyment in seeing Gaza destroyed and Palestinians liquidated.

86 Alenka Zupančič, "Love Thy Neighbor as Thyself?!" *Problemi International* 3, no. 2 (2019): 100.
87 Zupančič, "Love Thy Neighbor as Thyself?!" 100.
88 Žižek, *Against the Double Blackmail: Refugees, Terror and Other Troubles with the Neighbors* (London: Penguin Random House, 2016), 79.
89 Žižek, *Against the Double Blackmail*, 79.
90 Žižek, "Neighbors and Other Monsters," 183.
91 Žižek, "Neighbors and Other Monsters," 142, 183.
92 Che Gossett, "A Wall Is Just a Wall: Anti-Blackness and the Politics of Black and Prison Abolitionist Solidarity with Palestinian Struggle," *Decolonization* (blog), June 16, 2014. https://decolonization.wordpress.com/2014/06/16/a-wall-is-just-a-wall-anti-blackness-and-the-politics-of-black-and-prison-abolitionist-solidarity-with-palestinian-struggle/.
93 Didier Fassin, *Humanitarian Reason: A Moral History of the Present*, trans. Rachel Gomme (Berkeley: University of California Press, 2012), 6.
94 Gayatri Chakravorty Spivak, *Outside the Teaching* Machine (New York: Routledge, 1993), 284.
95 B'Tselem, "Voices from Gaza." https://www.btselem.org/voices_from_gaza; Sarah Himoud, "Love in a Time of Genocide: A Palestinian Litany for Survival," *Journal of Palestinian Studies* 52, no. 4 (2023): 87–94.
96 Nadine Bloch, "The Art of #BlackLivesMatter," *Waging Nonviolence*, January 8, 2015. https://wagingnonviolence.org/2015/01/art-blacklivesmatter/; Farah Stockman, "What Happens When Palestinians Tell Their Stories Directly to the World?" *The New York Times*, November 12, 2023. https://www.nytimes.com/2023/11/12/opinion/gaza-family-killed-war.html.
97 Sheehi and Sheehi, *Psychoanalysis Under Occupation*, 5.
98 Jamil Khader, "Rehumanizing Palestinians? Radicalize the Struggle!" *The Philosophical Salon*, July 9, 2018. https://thephilosophicalsalon.com/rehumanizing-palestinians-radicalize-the-struggle/.
99 Hartman and Wilderson, "The Position of the Unthought," 185.
100 Žižek, "Neighbors and Other Monsters," 183.
101 Eric L. Santner, "Miracles Happen: Benjamin, Rosenzweig, Freud, and the Matter of the Neighbor," in *The Neighbor: Three Inquiries in Political Theology*, with a New Preface, ed. Slavoj Žižek, Eric L. Santner, and Kenneth Reinhard (Chicago: University of Chicago Press, 2013), 100.
102 Fanon, *A Dying Colonialism*, 26.
103 Fanon, *A Dying Colonialism*, 128.
104 Stuart Hall, "'In But Not of Europe': Europe and its Myths," in *Selected Writings on Race and Difference* (Durham: Duke University Press, 2021), 305–45.
105 "The way in which the other presents himself, exceeding *the idea of the other in me*, we here name the face" (Levinas, *Totality and Infinity*, 59).

106 Nur Masalha, "The Concept of 'Transfer' in Zionist Thinking and Practice: Historical Roots and Contemporary Challenges," *Institute For Palestinian Studies*, no. 7 (2023). https://www.palestine-studies.org/en/node/1654742.

107 Bethan McKernan, "Israeli Ministers Attend Conference Calling for 'Voluntary Migration' of Palestinians," *The Guardian*, January 29, 2024. https://www.theguardian.com/world/2024/jan/29/israeli-ministers-attend-conference-calling-for-voluntary-migration-of-palestinians.

108 Elias Sanbar makes this point in his exchange with Gilles Deleuze: "You will never hear them [Zionists] say: 'the Palestinian people have a right to nothing.' No amount of force can maintain such a position, and they know it. But you will hear them say: 'there is no Palestinian people.' This is why the affirmation of the existence of the Palestinian people is so very powerful, much more so than it might at first appear" (Gilles Deleuze and Elias Sanbar, "The Indians of Palestine," in *Two Regimes of Madness: Texts and Interviews 1975–1995*, ed. David Lapoujade [New York: Semiotext(e), 2006], 200).

109 While an accelerated genocide is visibly and horrifyingly taking place in Gaza, where the Israeli army is the culprit behind Palestinian elimination, in the Occupied West Bank, where forcible removal is also increasing, other, less spectacular forms of violence operate through legal and economic pressure. Palestinians are given a "choice": either tear down your houses or pay crushing economic fines because the construction of your home (on your own land) is deemed illegal within Israel's Kafkaesque legal system governing housing permits. See International Middle East Media Center, "Palestinian Family Forced To Demolish Their Home In Silwan," *IMEMC News*, July 15, 2024. https://imemc.org/article/palestinian-family-forced-to-demolish-their-home-in-silwan/.

110 Lauren Berlant, *Cruel Optimism* (Durham: Duke University Press, 2011).

111 Jordan Skinner, "Thought Is the Courage of Hopelessness: An Interview with Philosopher Giorgio Agamben," *Verso Books*, Interview by Jordan Skinner, June 17, 2014. https://www.versobooks.com/blogs/1612-thought-is-the-courage-of-hopelessness-an-interview-with-philosopher-giorgio-agamben; Žižek, *The Courage of Hopelessness*.

112 The United States is drenched in hypocrisy, which reached a new low when Secretary of State Antony Blinken commemorated the seventy-fifth anniversary of the Geneva Conventions of 1949 with a plea to respect international humanitarian law. In a tweet as convincing as Israel's claim to have "the most moral army," Blinken wrote: "The United States reaffirms our steadfast commitment to respecting international humanitarian law and mitigating suffering in armed conflict. We call on others to do the same" (https://x.com/SecBlinken/status/1823122800095457535; see Olivia Rosane, "'Is This a Joke?': Tlaib Blasts Blinken for Geneva Convention Remarks Amid Gaza Carnage," *Common Dreams*, August 13, 2024. https://www.commondreams.org/news/tlaib-blinken-gaza). With human rights defenders like these . . .

113 Zalloua, *Solidarity and the Palestinian Cause: Indigeneity, Blackness, and the Promise of Universality* (New York: Bloomsbury, 2023), 130.

114 Žižek, "Lenin's Lesson for Israel and Ukraine," *Syndicate*, February 6, 2024. https://www.project-syndicate.org/commentary/lenin-principled-pragmatism fidelity-to-cause-requires-changing-position-by-slavoj-zizek-2024-02#:~:text=If

%20there%20is%20one%20element,blind%20dogmatism%20and%20cynical%20opportunism.

115 Said, "The Morning After."

116 Žižek praises Israeli Jewish intellectuals who have called on all EU member states, the UK, and others to recognize the State of Palestine (Žižek, "Assange Is Free, But Are We?"). The open letter declares that "recognition of a Palestinian state is a matter of principle and historic justice" ("Israeli Public Figures Call On the Remaining EU Member States, the UK, and Other States to Recognize the State of Palestine Without Delay," May 7, 2024. https://estaticos-cdn.prensaiberica.es/epi/public/content/file/original/2024/0510/14/call-by-israeli-public-figures-to-recognize-the-state-of-palestine-7-may-2024-pdf.pdf). The words are promising and might carry some weight within Israel. At the same time, we should be skeptical about its end goal. Eva Illouz is one of the signatories and, as we've seen in Chapter 2, she is a genocide denier, rejects any claims that Israel is a settler-colonial state, and accuses the anti-colonial/global Left of anti-Semitism for not standing unconditionally with Israel.

117 BDS. https://bdsmovement.net/faqs#collapse16233.

118 Khalidi, "The Neck and the Sword," 21.

119 Kanishka Singh, "US Criticizes ICJ Opinion on Israeli Occupation of Palestinian Territories," *Reuters*, July 20, 2024. https://www.reuters.com/world/us-criticizes-icj-opinion-israeli-occupation-palestinian-territories-2024-07-20/; David Kattenburg, "In a Historic Ruling, ICJ Declares Israeli Occupation Unlawful, Calls for Settlements to be Evacuated, and for Palestinian Reparations," *Mondoweiss*, July 19, 2024. https://mondoweiss.net/2024/07/in-a-historic-ruling-icj-declares-israeli-occupation-unlawful-calls-for-settlements-to-be-evacuated-and-for-palestinian-reparations/; Kenneth Roth, "The ICJ Has Demolished Israel's Claims That It Is Not Occupying Palestinian Territories," *The Guardian*, July 22, 2024. https://www.theguardian.com/commentisfree/article/2024/jul/22/the-icj-has-demolished-israels-claims-that-it-is-not-occupying-palestinian-territories.

120 On the question of reparations, Fanon didn't consider them an emancipatory endeavor: "I have neither the right nor the duty to demand reparations for my subjugated ancestors" (Fanon, *Black Skin*, 203). Fanon didn't want to be psychically and materially tethered to the past, immobilizing his identity ("I am not a slave to slavery that dehumanized my ancestors" [Fanon, *Black Skin*, 205]), and, in turn, hindering his projects of liberation and invention. The idea of reparations itself, however, does not condemn you to fix your identity in relation to the past, so that now you are defined by the historical subjugation of your people. Reparations in the context of Palestine mean something different. It is not about making the settlers feel guilty. Žižek is correct in highlighting Fanon's "refusal to capitalize on the guilt of the colonizers" (Žižek, *First as Tragedy, Then as Farce* [New York: Verso, 2009], 117). Settler guilt will not liberate Palestinians. Reparations are irreducible to monetary compensation, which by itself is unlikely to alter the status quo. "According to the UN, reparations also include restituting original property to refugees, aiding their return, ending ongoing violations, holding perpetrators accountable, commemorating the victims, acknowledging wrongs, issuing a public apology, and implementing a variety of measures to prevent the reoccurrence of injustice" (Nadim Khoury, "Transitional Justice in Palestine/Israel: Whose Justice?

Which Transition?" in *Rethinking Statehood in Palestine Self-Determination and Decolonization Beyond Partition*, ed. Leila H. Farsakh [Oakland: University of California Press, 2021], 159). An orientation toward reparations would make it crystal clear for a global audience how the Nakba is not an event but a structure for Palestinians (what Palestinians have been saying for decades). Recognition and reconciliation would be premised on a reckoning with settler colonialism rather than its repression or disavowal by Israel and its Western allies. If the United States wanted to take a stand for justice (and recognize its responsibility since it has basically funded all of the Israeli wars on Gaza), it could earmark the $3.8 billion in military aid that it sends to Israel annually for reparations. And let's not forget for a second the cost of simply clearing the Gaza Strip of its debris once a "permanent" ceasefire is secured. According to the United Nations, the removal of 50 million tons of debris will cost $1.9 billion, and it will take at least $53 billion to rebuild Gaza (United Nations, "Demand for Ceasefire in Gaza Report of the Secretary-General," *United Nations*, January 30, 2025. https://www.un.org/unispal/document/demand-for-ceasefire-in-gaza-needs-assessment-for-gaza-humanitarian-and-socioeconomic-impact-of-gaza-war-un-response-secretary-general-report-a-79-739/.

121 The United Nations Human Rights Office, "Detention in the Context of the Escalation of Hostilities in Gaza," The United Nations Human Rights, July 31, 2024. https://www.ohchr.org/en/documents/reports/detention-context-escalation-hostilities-gaza; Diana Buttu, "Rioting for the Right to Rape Palestinians," *Zeteo*, July 31, 2024. https://zeteo.com/p/rioting-for-the-right-to-rape-palestinians; Buttu, "I Spoke To Palestinians Tortured By Israel. What They Endured Is Unimaginable," *Zeteo*, July 1, 2024. https://zeteo.com/p/israel-sde-teiman-prisoners-palestinians-torture; Oren Ziv, "A Riot for Impunity Shows Israel's Proud Embrace of Its Crimes," *+972 Magazine*, August 1, 2024. https://www.972mag.com/sde-teiman-beit-lid-protests-detainees/.

122 Žižek, "A Soft Focus on War," *In These Times,* April 21, 2010. http://www.inthesetimes.com/article/5864/a_soft_focus_on_war/.

123 Žižek, "The Shooting of Trump."

124 Žižek, "Anti-Semitism and Its Transformations," 9–10.

125 Žižek, *The Parallax View*, 267.

126 Žižek, *In Defense of Lost Causes*, 2; qtd. in Richard Falk, "On 'Lost Causes' and the Future of Palestine," *The Nation*, December 16, 2014. https://www.thenation.com/article/archive/lost-causes-and-future-palestine/.

127 Žižek, *Too Late to Awaken: What Lies Ahead When There Is no Future?* (London: Allen Lane, 2024), 1.

128 Haidar Eid, "The Two-State Solution: The Opium of the Palestinian People," *Al Jazeera*, December 29, 2020. https://www.aljazeera.com/opinions/2020/12/29/the-two-state-solution-the-opium-of-the-palestinian-people; Ali Abunimah, "A Formal Funeral for the Two-State Solution," *Foreign Affairs*, September 19, 2011. https://www.foreignaffairs.com/articles/middle-east/2011-09-19/formal-funeral-two-state-solution?page=show; Leila Farsakh, "Alternatives to Partition in Palestine Rearticulating the State-Nation Nexus," in *Rethinking Statehood in Palestine Self-Determination and Decolonization Beyond Partition*, ed. Leila H. Farsakh (Oakland: University of California Press, 2021), 173–91.

129. Abu El-Haj, "Zionism's Political Unconscious," *Verso Books*, November 17, 2023. https://www.versobooks.com/blogs/news/zionism-s-political-unconscious.
130. Žižek, *Too Late to Awaken*, 2–3.
131. Žižek, *Surplus-Enjoyment*, 212.
132. Said, "The Morning After."
133. Makdisi, *Tolerance Is a Wasteland: Palestine and the Culture of Denial* (Oakland: University of California Press, 2022), 66–7.
134. Niko Block, "Justice Without Exception: Zionist Narrative and the Crisis of Liberalism," *Social Text*, January 10, 2024. https://socialtextjournal.org/periscope_article/justice-without-exception-zionist-narrative-and-the-crisis-of-liberalism/.

Chapter 5

1. David Scott, "Preface: Soul Captives Are Free," *Small Axe* 11, no. 2 (2007): ix.
2. Fanon, *Black Skin*, 95.
3. Giorgio Agamben, *Homo Sacer: Sovereign Power and Bare Life*, trans. Daniel Heller-Roazen (Stanford: Stanford University Press, 1998), 18. Agamben comments in passing on "the ironical name given to the *Muselmann*," which envisions the most abject Jew as a Muslim man (Agamben, *Homo Sacer*, 18). The *Muselmann* is meant to capture bare life, a life beyond race, since racial signifiers attach themselves to humans, and yet the same word is drenched in Orientalism, denoting a racial category born out of Europe's racial matrix. If *Muselmann* symbolizes "Europe's racial antithesis," as Sunera Thobani suggests, then the depiction of suffering Jews as imaginary Muslims compounds their violence by further racializing the inhumanity of their being as less than/worse than Jew (Sunera Thobani, "Empire, Bare Life and the Constitution of Whiteness: Sovereignty in the Age of Terror," *Borderlands* 11, no. 1 [May 2012], 10).
4. Wilderson, *Red, White & Black*, 36.
5. The pro-Palestinian chant "From the River to the Sea, Palestine will be free" is, for example, willfully misread by the pro-Israel camp as an incitement to Jewish genocide rather than an affirmation of Palestinian freedom and equality on the land of historic Palestine. Michigan Democratic Representative Rashida Tlaib's evocation of the "From the River to the Sea" chant led to her censure. She was accused of "promoting false narratives" regarding Hamas's October 7th attack on Israel and of "calling for the destruction of the state of Israel." (Kayla Guo, "House Censures Rashida Tlaib, Citing 'River to the Sea' Slogan," *The New York Times*, November 7, 2024. https://www.nytimes.com/2023/11/07/us/politics/tlaib-censure-house-israel-gaza.html. But, there is both a distortion of the Palestinian version of the slogan and an obfuscation of its actual genocidal Israeli version. The words "between the Sea and the Jordan there will only be Israeli sovereignty" have been part of the Likud Party Platform since 1977. A "call for Palestinian freedom," as Rashid Khalidi points out, is subjected to hermeneutic malpractice by US college administrators and government officials. Whereas they

hear in the pro-Palestinian chant only an "odious and hateful demand," they fail to comment that it is in fact Israel who is ruthlessly dominating Palestinian bodies in "all the land between the Mediterranean and the Jordan River, an area that for all intents and purposes constitutes a single state under a single security regime and a single sovereignty" (Rashid Khalidi, "It's Time to Confront Israel's Version of 'From the River to the Sea,'" *The Nation*, November 22, 2023. https://www.thenation.com/article/world/its-time-to-confront-israels-version-of-from-the-river-to-the-sea/).

6 It is, of course, not outlandish to see Morrison interpellating a Jewish audience with her choice of words. "In the American context," Emily Miller Budick notes, "this dedication cannot, especially to a Jewish readership, but recall the 'six million' of the Holocaust" (Emily Miller Budick, *Blacks and Jews in Literary Conversation* [Cambridge: Cambridge University Press, 1998], 161). Stanley Crouch, however, reads the tentative, even fragile, relation forged in the dedication between the two catastrophes in an antagonistic and unhelpful way. In "Aunt Medea," Crouch describes *Beloved* as "a blackface holocaust novel," written to "enter American slavery into the big-time martyr contest, a contest usually won by references to, and works about, the experience of Jews at the hands of Nazis" (Stanley Crouch, "Aunt Medea," in *Notes of a Hanging Judge: Essays and Reviews, 1979–1989* [New York: Oxford University Press, 1990], 205). Conversely, thinking the Maafa with the Shoah (and vice versa) might enable, as Paul Gilroy intimates, a richer understanding of modernity's operations (Paul Gilroy, *The Black Atlantic: Modernity and Double-Consciousness* [Cambridge, MA: Harvard University Press, 1993], 217).

7 Michael Rothberg and Jürgen Zimmerer, "Enttabuisiert den Vergleich!" *DIE ZEIT*, no. 14, March 31, 2021. https://www.zeit.de/2021/14/erinnerungskultur-gedenken-pluralisieren-holocaust-vergleich-globalisierung-geschichte?utm_referrer=https%3A%2F%2Fwww.google.com%2F.

8 Dirk Moses, "The German Catechism," *Geschichte der Gegenwart*, May 23, 2021. https://geschichtedergegenwart.ch/the-german-catechism/.

9 Fanon, *Black Skin*, xii.

10 Butler, "There Can Be No Critique."

11 On Israeli apartheid, see Amnesty International, "Israel's Apartheid Against Palestinians: Cruel System of Domination and Crime Against Humanity," February 1, 2022. https://www.amnesty.org/en/wp-content/uploads/2022/02/MDE1551412022ENGLISH.pdf; Human Rights Watch, "A Threshold Crossed Israeli Authorities and the Crimes of Apartheid and Persecution," April 27, 2021. https://www.hrw.org/report/2021/04/27/threshold-crossed-israeli-authorities-and-crimes-apartheid-and-persecution#; B'Tselem, "A Regime of Jewish Supremacy From the Jordan River to the Mediterranean Sea: This Is Apartheid," January 12, 2021. https://www.btselem.org/publications/fulltext/202101_this_is_apartheid.

12 Moses, "The German Catechism."

13 Moses, "The German Catechism"; Moses, "Stigma and Sacrifice in the Federal Republic of Germany," *History & Memory* 19, no. 2 (2007): 139–80.

14 Moses, "The German Catechism."

15 Raz Segal, "A Textbook Case of Genocide," *Jewish Currents*, October 13, 2023. https://jewishcurrents.org/a-textbook-case-of-genocide; Omer Bartov, *Genocide, The Holocaust, and Israel-Palestine: First-Person History in Times of Crisis* (New York: Bloomsbury, 2023).

16 Nicole Deitelhoff, Rainer Forst, Klaus Günther, and Jürgen Habermas, "Habermas on Israel: a Principle of Solidarity," *Research Center Normative Orders*, November 15, 2023. https://www.resetdoc.org/story/habermas-israel-principle-solidariety/.

17 Deitelhoff, Forst, Günther, and Habermas, "Habermas on Israel."

18 Deitelhoff, Forst, Günther, and Habermas, "Habermas on Israel."

19 Deitelhoff, Forst, Günther, and Habermas, "Habermas on Israel."

20 Achille Mbembe, *Necropolitics*, trans. Steven Corcoran (Durham: Duke University Press, 2019), 68.

21 Mbembe, *Necropolitics*, 80.

22 Mbembe, *Necropolitics*, 92.

23 Achille Mbembe also claims that Israel's apartheid logic is "far more lethal" than the South African style and "looks like high-tech Jim Crow-cum-apartheid" (Mbembe, "On Palestine," in *Apartheid Israel: The Politics of an Analogy*, ed. Jon Soske and Sean Jacobs [Chicago: Haymarket Books, 2015], viii). Moreover, he insists that "the occupation of Palestine is the greatest moral scandal of our times, one of the most dehumanizing ordeals of the century we have just entered, and the biggest act of cowardice of the last half-century" (Mbembe, "On Palestine," viii). Such remarks put Germany on the defensive, to say the least.

24 Anonymous, "Palestine Between German Memory Politics and (De-)Colonial Thought," *Journal of Genocide Research* 23, no. 3 (2021): 376.

25 Rajeev Syal, Dan Sabbagh, and Kiran Stacey, "Suella Braverman Calls Pro-Palestine Demos 'Hate Marches,'" *The Guardian*, October 30. https://www.theguardian.com/politics/2023/oct/30/uk-ministers-cobra-meeting-terrorism-threat-israel-hamas-conflict-suella-braverman.

26 Dan Primack, "Israel Says It Will Block United Nations Visa Requests," *Axios*, December 26, 2023. https://www.axios.com/2023/12/25/israel-un-visa-requests-block.

27 A new generation of Germans are starting to disidentify with the catechism; they are aware that "Israelis keep electing rightwing governments that entrench the settlement project, thereby ending the illusion of the two-state solution that allows Germans (and Americans) to believe they can reconcile their Zionism with justice for Palestinians" (Moses, "The German Catechism"). A 2021 poll by the Jewish Electoral Institute shows that 25 percent of US Jews consider Israel an "apartheid state," 34 percent draw a parallel between its racism and that of the United States, and 22 percent believe that it is committing genocide against Palestinians (Jewish Electoral Institute, "July 2021 National Survey of Jewish Voters"). https://www.jewishelectorateinstitute.org/july-2021-national-survey-of-jewish-voters/). More generally, as Alexander Sammon notes, "Young voters are far from the president, who publicly remains hawkish and unstinting in a way that has not kept pace with their political attitudes (or even those, to a lesser degree, of the Democratic Party). Biden has continued to pledge unquestioning and total support for Israel, even

as human rights groups sound the alarm about the threat of the Israeli military committing ethnic cleansing against Palestinians, humanitarian groups' inability to deliver anything resembling sufficient aid to Gaza, and comments from Israeli military leaders that indicate a willingness to target civilians" (Alexander Sammon, "Biden Has a Youth-Vote Problem. His Israel Policy Is Making It Worse," *Slate*, October 24, 2023. https://slate.com/news-and-politics/2023/10/biden-polling-israel-palestine-gaza-hamas-war-youth.html).

28 Deitelhoff, Forst, Günther, and Habermas, "Habermas on Israel."
29 Gessen, "In the Shadow of the Holocaust"; Michael Rothberg, "Lived Multidirectionality: '*Historikerstreit 2.0*' and the Politics of Holocaust Memory," *Memory Studies* 15, no. 6 (2022): 1316–29.
30 Du Bois, *Black Reconstruction in America* (New York: The Free Press, 1998), 700–1.
31 Butler, "There Can Be No Critique."
32 Said, *The Question of Palestine*, xxi.
33 "it's as though in order to come to any recognition of common humanity, the other must be assimilated, . . . utterly displaced and effaced" (Wilderson and Hartman, "The Position of the Unthought," 189).
34 Gideon Levy, "Israel Does Not Want Peace," *Haaretz*, July 4, 2014. https://www.haaretz.com/2014-07-04/ty-article/israel-does-not-want-peace/0000017f-db80-df62-a9ff-dfd75c210000; Amy Goodman, "Israeli Writer Gideon Levy: If Netanyahu Wants to Stop the Rockets, He Needs to Accept a Just Peace," *Democracy Now!* July 22, 2014. https://www.democracynow.org/2014/7/22/israeli_writer_gideon_levy_if_netanyahu. Amira Hass, "Palestinian Ghettos Were Always the Plan," *Haaretz*, January 20, 2013. https://www.haaretz.com/2013-01-20/ty-article/.premium/palestinian-ghettos-the-plan-all-along/0000017f-f82b-d044-adff-fbfbb0e80000; Jeff Halper, "The 'Two-state Solution' Only Ever Meant a Big Israel Ruling Over a Palestinian Bantustan. Let It Go," *Haaretz*, June 19, 2018. https://www.haaretz.com/opinion/2018-01-19/ty-article-opinion/.premium/the-two-state-solution-is-dead-let-it-go/0000017f-dbe3-df62-a9ff-dff78aa80000; Butler, "The End of Oslo," *London Review of Books*, September 25, 2011. https://www.lrb.co.uk/blog/2011/september/the-end-of-oslo.
35 Said, "The Morning After."
36 Jasbir Puar, *The Right to Maim: Debility, Capacity, Disability* (Durham: Duke University Press, 2017), 153.
37 U.S. Department of Defense, "Secretary of Defense Lloyd J. Austin III Joint Press Conference With Israeli Defense Minister Yoav Gallant in Tel Aviv, Israel," *Transcript*, December 18, 2023. https://www.defense.gov/News/Transcripts/Transcript/Article/3621107/secretary-of-defense-lloyd-j-austin-iii-joint-press-conference-with-israeli-def/. We can also recall how on the eve of the hearing at The Hague in the Netherlands, initiated by South Africa's lawsuit against Israel for the crime of genocide at the International Court of Justice, an anxious Netanyahu repeats, in a short video, the delusional claim that Israel is operating within the law, and that it is combating "Hamas terrorists, not the Palestinian population, and we are doing so in full compliance with international law" (Michael Hauser Tov, "'Israeli Gov't Is Intent on Destroying Palestinians in Gaza': South Africa Presents Genocide Case

at ICJ," *Haaretz*, January 11, 2024. https://www.haaretz.com/israel-news/2024-01-11/ty-article/israeli-govt-is-intent-on-destroying-palestinians-south-africa-presents-genocide-case/0000018c-f8bc-d517-af9d-fcbe87ae0000.

38 Jamil Khader, "Media's Selective Moral Outrage Manufactures Consent for Palestinian Genocide," *Truthout*, October 18, 2023. https://truthout.org/articles/medias-selective-moral-outrage-manufactures-consent-for-palestinian-genocide/; Ryan Grim, "What Are We Doing??" *The Intercept*, January 29, 2024. https://theintercept.com/2024/01/29/unrwa-funding-genocide-israel/; Jeremy Scahill, "Netanyahu's War on Truth: Israel's Ruthless Propaganda Campaign to Dehumanize Palestinians," *The Intercept*, February 7, 2024. https://theintercept.com/2024/02/07/gaza-israel-netanyahu-propaganda-lies-palestinians/.

39 Scahill, "Netanyahu's War on Truth."

40 The "Axis of Zionist Extremism" echoes the more familiar "Axis of Resistance," which includes primarily Iran, Hezbollah, Hamas, and the Houthis.

41 Even when American presidents are not particularly fond of Netanyahu, as in the case of Bill Clinton and Barack Obama, Israel benefits. In some perverse way, Israel gets more support from the United States when it angers American presidents, who favor Occupation in slow motion, so as to avoid the perception of discord. See Alon Pinkas, "A Short History of 'F**k Him': How Netanyahu Enraged U.S. Presidents, From Clinton to Trump," *Haaretz*, December 13, 2021. https://www.haaretz.com/israel-news/2021-12-13/ty-article/.highlight/a-short-history-of-f-k-him-how-the-trump-netanyahu-affair-unraveled/0000017f-e97b-d62c-a1ff-fd7b5e020000; Sammy Westfall and Joe Snell, "Netanyahu's History of Clashing With U.S. Presidents Spans Decades," *The Washington Post*, July 24, 2024. https://www.washingtonpost.com/world/2024/07/22/netanyahu-united-states-presidents-clinton-obama-israel/?next_url=https://www.washingtonpost.com/world/2024/07/22/netanyahu-united-states-presidents-clinton-obama-israel/.

42 U.S. Department of Defense, "Secretary of Defense Lloyd J. Austin."

43 Julian Borger, "Biden Under Scrutiny After Bypassing Congress to Supply Tank Shells to Israel," *The Guardian*, December 10, 2023. https://www.theguardian.com/world/2023/dec/10/biden-under-scrutiny-bypassing-congress-supply-tank-shells-israel-gaza.

44 While Israel accuses Hamas of embedding itself among Palestinian civilians, using them as human shields, in order to deflect attention from the criminality of its attacks on civilians and civilian infrastructure, the IOF is engaging in this very practice of human shielding, in violation of international and Israeli law. Reports—following *Al Jazeera*'s footage of Palestinians dressed in IOF uniform being used as shields in combat maneuvers, along with collaborating testimonies from Israeli soldiers to the newspaper *Haaretz* and Breaking the Silence, a group of Israeli combat veterans formed after the Second Intifada to document military abuses—outline the pervasiveness of this illegal practice, which is premised on the racist belief that "our lives are more important than their lives," as the soldiers were told by their commanders. Palestinians are not only less than human; they are also less than animal. The lives of our canines are more important than Palestinian lives: "One soldier had been told Palestinian civilians were being used to replace the dog units that search for explosives 'because too many dogs had died,' he added" (Emma Graham-Harrison, "Israeli Forces in Gaza 'Use Civilians as Human

Shields' Against Possible Booby-Traps," *The Guardian*, August 14, 2024. https://www.theguardian.com/world/article/2024/aug/14/israeli-forces-in-gaza-use-civilians-as-human-shields-against-possible-booby-traps); Sharon Zhang, "Israel 'Systematically' Uses Gaza Children as Human Shields, Rights Group Finds," *Truthout*, August 21, 2024. https://truthout.org/articles/israel-systematically-uses-gaza-children-as-human-shields-rights-group-finds/.

45 Žižek urges a shift in our questioning of what he finds unacceptable: "After the October 7 attack, prior to any debate the question automatically posed to anyone who criticized Israel was: 'Do you condemn the Hamas attack?' Now the time has come to turn this question around: 'Do you condemn what IDF [IOF] is doing in Gaza?' The asymmetry is clear: while Palestinians are presumed to *think* about the destruction of Israel, Israel is *actually destroying* Gaza . . . " (Žižek, "Jews Between Assimilation and Zionism," *Substack: Žižek Goads and Prods*, April 27, 2024. https://slavoj.substack.com/p/jews-between-assimilationism-and).

46 Khalidi, "The Dahiya Doctrine, Proportionality, and War Crimes," *Journal of Palestine Studies* 44, no. 1 (2014): 5–13.

47 Amira Jarmakani, "The ADL Is Leading the Attack Against Free Speech on Palestine," *Mondoweiss*, November 20, 2023. https://mondoweiss.net/2023/11/the-adl-is-leading-the-attack-against-free-speech-on-palestine/; Ben Lorber, "The ADL Is Making It Less Safe to Be a Progressive Jew," *In These Times*, November 21, 2023. https://inthesetimes.com/article/adl-defamation-league-jvp-ifnotnow-musk?link_id=5&can_id=839242f129045dcf95563791cad9b53c&source=email-bidens-unflinching-support-for-israels-war-on-gaza-is-derailing-his-reelection-chances-2&email_referrer=email_2121160___subject_2645816&email_subject=the-rise-of-the-far-right-is-a-global-phenomenon-the-adl-is-making-it-less-safe-to-be-a-progressive-jew; Omar Barghouti, "Two Degrees of Separation: Israel, Its Palestinian Victims, and the Fraudulent Use of Antisemitism," in Jewish Voice for Peace, *On Anti-Semitism: Solidarity and the Struggle for Justice* (Chicago: Haymarket Books, 2017), 139–51; Dave Zirin, "The Left Is Not 'Anti-Jewish,'" *The Nation*, November 6, 2023. https://www.thenation.com/article/world/jewish-left-israel-protests/; Antony Lerman, "The Tropes of 'Jewish Antisemitism,'" *The Guardian*, October 5, 2009. https://www.theguardian.com/commentisfree/2009/oct/05/self-hating-jew-antisemitism.

48 Bartov, *Genocide, The Holocaust, and Israel-Palestine*, 164.

49 Omer Bartov, Christopher R. Browning, Jane Caplan, Debórah Dwork, Michael Rothberg, et al. "An Open Letter on the Misuse of Holocaust Memory," *The New York Review*, November 20, 2023. https://www.nybooks.com/online/2023/11/20/an-open-letter-on-the-misuse-of-holocaust-memory/.

50 Wynter, "Unsettling the Coloniality of Being/Power/Truth/Freedom."

51 Wilderson, *Red, White & Black*, 38.

52 Wilderson, *Red, White & Black*, 18.

53 Wilderson, *Afropessimism*, 11.

54 Wilderson, *Red, White & Black*, 182.

55 Wolfe, "Recuperating Binarism: A Heretical Introduction," 264.

56 Lorenzo Veracini, *The Settler Colonial Present* (New York: Palgrave Macmillan, 2015), 37.

57 Nandita Sharma and Cynthia Wright, "Decolonizing Resistance, Challenging Colonial States," *Social Justice* 35, no. 3 (2009): 121. Borrowing the term from Barbadian poet Kamau Brathwaite, Jodi Byrd deploys *arrivants* to refer to people "forced into the Americas through the violence of European and Anglo-American colonialism and imperialism around the globe" (Byrd, *The Transit of Empire*, xix).

58 Veracini, *The Settler Colonial Present*, 47.

59 Wilderson, "Afro-Pessimism and the End of Redemption."

60 See Zalloua, *Solidarity and the Palestinian Cause*, 47–8.

61 Greg Thomas, "Afro-Blue Notes: The Death of Afro-pessimism (2.0)?" *Theory & Event* 21, no. 1 (2018): 291.

62 Sharpe, *In the Wake*, 11.

63 Sharpe, *In the Wake*, 11.

64 Sharpe, *In the Wake*, 12.

65 Sharpe, *In the Wake*, 12.

66 Sharpe, *In the Wake*, 12.

67 Sharpe, *In the Wake*, 12.

68 Rothberg, *Multidirectional Memory: Remembering the Holocaust in the Age of Decolonization* (Stanford: Stanford University Press, 2009), 3.

69 Rothberg's multidirectional approach problematizes the view that "the Holocaust was unique in world history and it cannot be described as a colonial crime" (Rothberg, "We Need to Re-Center the New Historikerstreit," *DIE ZEIT*, July 21, 2021. https://www.zeit.de/kultur/2021-07/dealing-with-the-holocaust-historikerstreit-controversy-genocide-english; see also Rothberg, "Lived Multidirectionality." Putting the Holocaust in dialogue with "memories of colonialism and slavery does not 'relativize' or minimize the Shoah or vice versa" (Rothberg, "We Need to Re-Center").

70 Sharpe, *In the Wake*, 16.

71 Wilderson, *Afropessimism*, 217.

72 Wilderson, *Afropessimism*, 216.

73 Sharpe, *In The Wake*, 15.

74 Sharpe, *In The Wake*, 11.

75 Sharpe, *In the Wake*, 22.

76 Fanon, *Black Skin, White Masks*, trans. Charles Lam Markmann (New York: Grove Press, 1967), 100. "Acceptable being is nonexistence, nonappearance, or submergence. . . . To change things is to appear, but to appear is to be violent since that group's appearance is illegitimate. Violence, in this sense, need not be a physical imposition. It need not be a consequence of guns and other weapons of destruction. It need simply be appearance" (Gordon, "Through the Hellish Zone of Nonbeing," 11). Gordon's gloss applies to the blackened bodies, and I believe to the appearance of Black *and* Palestinian bodies.

77 Zalloua, *Solidarity and the Palestinian Cause*, 59.

78 Said, *Representations of the Intellectual*, 44. A multidirectional sensibility informs Said's discussion of the ways violence is constitutive of the Palestinian experience:

"Violence has been an extraordinarily important aspect of our lives. Whether it has been the violence of our uprooting and the destruction of our society in 1948, the violence visited on us by our enemies, the violence we have visited on others, or, most horribly, the violence we have wreaked on each other—these dimensions of the Palestinian experience have brought us a great deal of attention, and have exacerbated our self-awareness as a community set apart from others" (Said, *After the Last Sky: Palestinian Lives*, with photographs by Jean Mohr [New York: Pantheon, 1986], 5).

79 Wilderson, *Red, White & Black*, 38.
80 Said, *Representations of the Intellectual*, 60.
81 Fanon, *Black Skin*, xii, translation modified. Again, Philcox's translation leaves out a comma after "an incline stripped bare of every essential."
82 Žižek, *Freedom*, 81. Žižek might be relying on Saroj Giri's mistranslation. In *Surplus-Enjoyment*, Žižek quotes the same Fanon passage while discussing Giri's work (Žižek, *Surplus-Enjoyment*, 286). Giri misattributes the lines to Fanon's *The Wretched of the Earth* (Saroj Giri, "From the October Revolution to the Naxalbari Movement: Understanding Political Subjectivity," in *Of Concepts and Methods: "On Postisms" and Other Essays*, ed. K. Murali (Ajith) [Paris: Foreign Languages Press, 2020], 20).
83 Fanon, *Peau noir, masques blancs* (Paris: Seuil, 1952), 6.
84 Fanon, *Black Skin*, 8.
85 Žižek, *In Defense of Lost Causes*, 424.
86 Žižek, *Demanding the Impossible*, 60.
87 Žižek, *Demanding the Impossible*, 102.
88 "'Class struggle' paradoxically precedes classes as determinate social groups . . . every class position and determination is already an effect of the 'class struggle.' This is why 'class struggle' is another name for the fact that 'society does not exist'—it does not exist as a positive order of being" (Žižek, *Living in the End Times* [New York: Verso, 2011], 198).
89 Žižek, "Forward: The Importance of Theory," in *Žižek on Race: Toward an Antiracist Future*, by Zahi Zalloua (New York: Bloomsbury, 2020), xii.
90 Sharpe, *In the Wake*, 15.
91 Sharpe, *In the Wake*, 141n.10.
92 Žižek, *In Defense of Lost Causes*, 285.
93 Žižek, *The Ticklish Subject*, 225.
94 Žižek, "Afterword: Lenin's Choice," in V. I. Lenin, *Revolution at the Gates: Selected Writings of Lenin from 1917*, ed. Slavoj Žižek (New York: Verso, 2002), 336n.208.
95 Žižek, *Like a Thief in Broad Daylight*, 62.
96 Žižek, *In Defense of Lost Causes*, 289.
97 Žižek, *The Relevance of the Communist Manifesto* (Cambridge: Polity Press, 2019), 42.
98 Žižek, *Freedom*, 81.

99 Frantz Fanon, *Toward the African Revolution*, trans. Haakon Chevalier (New York: Grove Press, 1967), 13.
100 Nahum Dimitri Chandler, *X—The Problem of the Negro as a Problem for Thought* (New York: Fordham University Press, 2013), 137.
101 Žižek, *The Ticklish Subject*, 224.
102 Black Lives Matter Grassroots, "Black Lives Matter Grassroots Statement in Solidarity with the Palestinian People," 2023. https://blmgrassroots.org/black-lives-matter-grassroots-statement-in-solidarity-with-the-palestinian-people/.
103 Žižek, *The Ticklish Subject*, 224.
104 Bruno Chaouat is drawing here from Emmanuel Levinas's resistance to the parallels between "the condition of factory workers and the Holocaust," which allegedly minimizes and relativizes the Shoah (Bruno Chaouat, *Is Theory Good for the Jews? French Thought and the Challenge of the New Antisemitism* [Liverpool: Liverpool University Press, 2016], 117).
105 Chaouat, *Is Theory Good for the Jews?*, 119. Chaouat is here reiterating Alain Finkielkraut's argument against "left-wing Holocaust denial" in his *L'avenir d'une négation* (1982).
106 Chaouat, *Is Theory Good for the Jews?*, 119.
107 Chaouat, *Is Theory Good for the Jews?*, 119.
108 Wilderson, *Afropessimism*, 14, 15.
109 Žižek, *Like a Thief in Broad Daylight*, 14–15.
110 Žižek, "Class Struggle Against Classism," *The Philosophical Salon*, May 10, 2023. https://thephilosophicalsalon.com/class-struggle-against-classism/.
111 Žižek, *The Ticklish Subject*, 224.
112 Étienne Balibar, "A Complex Urgent Universal Political Cause," Address Before the Conference of Faculty for Israeli-Palestinian Peace (FFIPP), Université Libre de Bruxelles, July 3–4, 2004. https://users.resist.ca/~elkilombo/documents/%20BalibarBrusseBD480.pdf.
113 Zalloua, *The Politics of the Wretched*, 123–4.
114 William I. Robinson and Hoai-An Nguyen, "Gaza: A Ghastly Window into the Crisis of Global Capitalism," *The Philosophical Salon*, January 15, 2024. https://thephilosophicalsalon.com/gaza-a-ghastly-window-into-the-crisis-of-global-capitalism/.
115 Michael Marder, "The 'Volcano of Occupation' Is Erupting Again: Responding to the Bombings of Gaza," *Basque Museum of Contemporary Art*, December 13, 2023. https://www.amaonline.eus/the-volcano-of-occupation-is-irrupting-again-responding-to-the-bombings-of-gaza/.
116 Said, *Representations of the Intellectual*, 44. Said further adds: "It is always easy and popular for intellectuals to fall into modes of vindication and self-righteousness that blind them to the evil done in the name of their own ethnic or national community" (Said, *Representations of the Intellectual*, 45).
117 Deleuze and Sanbar, "The Indians of Palestine," 199.
118 Waziyatawin, "Malice Enough in Their Hearts and Courage Enough in Ours: Reflections on US Indigenous and Palestinian Experiences under Occupation," *Settler Colonial Studies* 2, no. 1 (2012): 177.

119 Said, *Representations of the Intellectual*, 32.
120 Said, *Culture and Imperialism* (New York: Vintage, 1994), 18.
121 Keeanga-Yamahtta Taylor, "Forward" to Hartman's 2022 edition of *Scenes of Subjection* (New York: W.W. Norton & Co, 2022), xxi.
122 Upfront, "Angela Davis: 'Palestine Is a Moral Litmus Test for the World,'" *Al Jazeera*, October 27, 2023. https://www.aljazeera.com/program/upfront/2023/10/27/angela-davis-palestine-is-a-moral-litmus-test-for-the-world.
123 Noam Chomsky, "An Era of Impunity Is Over," *Catalyst* 5, no. 2 (2021): 141–9.
124 The linking of suffering and victimhood can also take a more aggressive form. Zionist reason weaponizes Jewish shame and injury, so that "when suffering becomes an identity," as Jacqueline Rose puts it, "it has to turn cruel" toward the Palestinian neighbor "in order to be able to bear, or live with, itself" (Jacqueline Rose, *The Question of Zion* [Princeton: Princeton University Press, 2005], 115).
125 Said, *Representations of the Intellectual*, 44.

Conclusion

1 The Pro-Human Camp, "Resist the Dehumanization of Palestinians and Israelis," December 13, 2023. https://www.amnesty.org.il/2023/12/13/%D7%9E%D7%9B%D7%AA%D7%91-%D7%A4%D7%AA%D7%95%D7%97-%D7%94%D7%9E%D7%97%D7%A0%D7%94-%D7%94%D7%A4%D7%A8%D7%95-%D7%90%D7%A0%D7%95%D7%A9%D7%99/.
2 The Pro-Human Camp, "Resist the Dehumanization."
3 The Pro-Human Camp, "Resist the Dehumanization."
4 Fanon, *Black Skin*, xii–xiii.
5 Sekyi-Otu, *Fanon's Dialectic of Experience* (Cambridge, MA: Harvard University Press, 1996), 17.
6 Fanon, *The Wretched of the Earth*, 198–9.
7 Fanon, *Black Skin*, 204.
8 Butler, "Violence, Nonviolence: Sartre on Fanon," in *Senses of the Subject* (New York: Fordham University Press, 2015), 182.
9 Žižek, *Freedom*, 113.
10 Franco Berardi, "Letter to the Hypocrites of Europe," *Institute of Network Cultures*, January 18, 2024. https://networkcultures.org/tactical-media-room/2024/01/18/letter-to-the-hypocrites-of-europe/, emphasis added.
11 Lorde, "The Master's Tools."
12 Qtd in "Introduction," in *Palestine: A Socialist Introduction*, ed. Sumaya Awad and Brian Bean (Chicago: Haymarket Books, 2020), 1.
13 Noura Erakat and Nicki Kattoura, "Palestinians Illuminate the Colonial Nature of the Rest of the World," *Hammer & Hope*, no. 3 (2024). https://hammerandhope.org/article/noura-erakat-palestine-gaza.

14 Gessen captures well the ethical dilemma of the pro-Palestinian protesters. Living with your complicity in helping to reelect an candidate that helped to greenlight a genocide: "They cannot stand to live in a world in which Joe Biden's vice president, who has not voiced any disagreement with the administration's Middle East policies, wins the presidency. It's not that they want Trump to win; it's that the level of political cynicism they are being asked to adopt feels unbearable" (Gessen, "Kamala Harris Is Speaking. Is She Listening?" *The New York Times*, August 10, 2024. https://www.nytimes.com/2024/08/10/opinion/kamala-harris-gaza-detroit.html?unlocked_article_code=1.CE4.-IQS.YV04gsQON5tv&smid=url-share). Too Black formulates this dead-end choice for the Black voter: "Black people in the United States should barter genocide for 'democracy.' . . . Apparently, 'democracy' is when Black people must choose between maintaining our dwindling civil rights or shipping 250-pound bombs to explode Gazan schools full of Palestinians praying in peace" (Black, "Unburdened by Palestine"). Identity politics over solidarity is a losing proposition. Reducing political engagement to the crude logic of self-interest undermines the struggle for economic and racial justice. Political cynicism is a curse and a blackmail. Its logic is unsustainable. The liberal Left must separate itself from the xenophobic Right at a policy level (and thus move closer to an internationalist, anti-colonial Left) lest it waste the younger generation of voters' revolutionary energy for global justice.

15 Žižek, *Less Than Nothing*, 997.

16 See Robert Meister, *After Evil: A Politics of Human Rights* (New York: Columbia University Press, 2010).

17 Sheehi and Sheehi, *Psychoanalysis Under Occupation*, 96.

18 Michael Marder, "Compassionate Genocide," *The Philosophical Salon*, April 22, 2024. https://thephilosophicalsalon.com/compassionate-genocide/.

19 "Whoever is not willing to talk about capitalism should also keep quiet about fascism" (Max Horkheimer, "The Jews and Europe," in *Critical Theory and Society: A Reader*, ed. Stephen Bronner and Douglas Kellner [New York: Routledge, 1989], 78).

20 Agon Hamza and Frank Ruda, "Interview with Alberto Toscano: The Fascism of Our Times," *Crisis and Critique* 11, no. 1 (2024): 259.

21 Mbembe, *Necropolitics*, 97.

22 Žižek, *Pandemic! 2: Chronicles of a Lost Time* (New York: OR Books, 2020), 137.

Afterword

1 See Patrick Stewart as Lenin (All Scenes). https://www.youtube.com/watch?v=dsiU0P-swYE&t=995s.

2 Sophie Wahnich, "Faire entendre la voix de la vérité, un droit révolutionnaire éternel" Manuscript, June 2010.

Bibliography

2008 South Carolina Democratic Debate. http://www.nytimes.com/2007/04/27/us/politics/27debate_transcript.html?pagewanted=all&_r=0.
Abdel-Fattah, Randa. "On Zionist Feelings." *Mondoweiss*, December 27, 2023. https://mondoweiss.net/2023/12/on-zionist-feelings/.
Abdu, Janan. "How Israel Waged Judicial War Against Palestinian Citizens After the May 2021 Uprising." *Middle East Eye*, August 16, 2022. https://www.middleeasteye.net/opinion/israel-waged-judicial-war-against-palestinian-citizens-after-may-2021-uprising.
Abu El-Haj, Nadia. "The Banality of Knowledge." *Critical Ethnic Studies* 7, no. 1 (2021). https://manifold.umn.edu/read/ces0701-banality-of-knowledge/section/8b7e936e-ec4f-4d7d-a436-df82f4df69b8.
Abu El-Haj, Nadia. "'We Know Well, but All the Same . . . ' Factual Truths, Historical Narratives, and the Work of Disavowal." *History of the Present* 13, no. 2 (2023): 245–64.
Abu El-Haj, Nadia. "Zionism's Political Unconscious." *Verso Books*, November 17, 2023. https://www.versobooks.com/blogs/news/zionism-s-political-unconscious.
Abunimah, Ali. *The Battle for Justice in Palestine*. Chicago: Haymarket Book, 2014.
Abunimah, Ali. "A Formal Funeral for the Two-State Solution." *Foreign Affairs*, September 19, 2011. https://www.foreignaffairs.com/articles/middle-east/2011-09-19/formal-funeral-two-state-solution?page=show.
Ackerman, Seth. "Israel's March to a Second Nakba." *Catalyst* 7, no. 4 (2024): 8–55.
Agamben, Giorgio. *Homo Sacer: Sovereign Power and Bare Life*. Translated by Daniel Heller-Roazen. Stanford: Stanford University Press, 1998.
Ageel, Ghada. "Gaza's 'Safe Zone' of Horror." *Al Jazeera*, July 8, 2024. https://www.aljazeera.com/opinions/2024/7/8/gazas-safe-zone-of-horror.
Alexander, Michelle. "Only Revolutionary Love Can Save Us Now." *The Nation*, March 8, 2024. https://www.thenation.com/article/activism/mlk-vietnam-war-speech-gaza-democracy/.
Alim, H. Samy. "Inventing 'the White Voice': Racial Capitalism, Raciolinguistics & Culturally Sustaining Pedagogies." *Daedalus* 15, no. 3 (2023): 147–66.
Allen-Paisant, Jason. *Engagements with Aimé Césaire*. Oxford: Oxford University Press, 2024.
Althoff, Sebastian. "The Condemnation of Hate and the Violence of the Status Quo." *Cultural Politics* 20, no. 1 (2024): 45–59.
Améry, Jean. *At the Mind's Limits: Contemplations by a Survivor on Auschwitz and Its Realities*. Translated by Sidney Rosenfeld and Stella P. Rosenfeld. Bloomington: Indiana University Press, 1980.

Améry, Jean. "My Jewishness." In *Essays on Antisemitism, Anti-Zionism, and the Left*, edited by Marlene Gallner, 78–86. Bloomington: Indiana University Press, 2022.

Amin, Samir. "Ferocity of Whites, Ferocity of Capitalism." *Africa Development / Afrique et Développement* 45, no. 2 (2020): 9–16.

Amnesty International. "Israeli Police Targeted Palestinians with Discriminatory Arrests, Torture and Unlawful Force." *Amnesty International*, June 24, 2021. https://www.amnesty.org/en/latest/press-release/2021/06/israeli-police-targeted-palestinians-with-discriminatory-arrests-torture-and-unlawful-force/.

Amnesty International. "Israel's Apartheid Against Palestinians: Cruel System of Domination and Crime Against Humanity," February 1, 2022. https://www.amnesty.org/en/wp-content/uploads/2022/02/MDE1551412022ENGLISH.pdf.

Amnesty International. "The State of the World's Human Rights." *Amnesty International's Annual Report 2023/24*, April 24, 2024. https://www.amnesty.org/en/latest/news/2024/04/amnesty-international-sounds-alarm-international-law-flagrant-rule-breaking-governments-corporate-actors/.

Anderson, Patrick D. "Levinas and the Anticolonial." *Journal of French and Francophone Philosophy* 25, no. 1 (2017): 150–81.

Angelo, Bonnie. "The Pain of Being Black: An Interview with Toni Morrison." In *Conversations with Toni Morrison*, edited by Taylor Danielle-Guthrie, 255–61. Jackson: University of Mississippi Press, 1994.

Aranguren, Teresa, Sandra Barrilaro, and Mohammed El-Kurd. *Against Erasure: A Photographic Memory of Palestine Before the Nakba*. Chicago: Haymarket Books, 2024.

Audeh, Rifat. "It's Not Shocking to See Israeli Children Celebrate the Gaza Genocide." *Al Jazeera*, December 13, 2023. https://www.aljazeera.com/opinions/2023/12/13/its-not-shocking-to-see-israeli-children-celebrate-the-gaza-genocide.

Avashia, Neema. "I'm from Appalachia: JD Vance Doesn't Represent Us—He Only Represents Himself." *The Guardian*, July 16, 2024. https://www.theguardian.com/us-news/article/2024/jul/16/jd-vance-hillbilly-elegy-appalachia?utm_term=669b619d92e496a151553926da1b6953&utm_campaign=SaturdayEdition&utm_source=esp&utm_medium=Email&CMP=saturdayedition_email.

Awad, Sumaya and Brian Bean, eds. *Palestine: A Socialist Introduction*. Chicago: Haymarket Books, 2020.

Axelman, Erin and Sam Eilertsen, dirs. *Israelism*, 2023. www.israelismfilm.com.

Baldwin, James. "An Open Letter to My Sister, Miss Angela Davis." *The New York Review of Books*, January 7, 1971. www.nybooks.com/articles/archives/1971/jan/07/an-open-letter-to-my-sister-miss-angela-davis/.

Baldwin, James. "As Much of the Truth as One Can Bear." *The New York Times*, January 14, 1962. https://timesmachine.nytimes.com/timesmachine/1962/01/14/118438007.pdf?pdf_redirect=true&ip=0.

Baldwin, James. "A Report from Occupied Territory." *The Nation*, July 11, 1966. https://www.thenation.com/article/culture/report-occupied-territory/.

Balibar, Étienne. "A Complex Urgent Universal Political Cause." Address Before the Conference of Faculty for Israeli-Palestinian Peace (FFIPP). Université Libre de Bruxelles, July 3–4, 2004. https://users.resist.ca/~elkilombo/documents/%20BalibarBrusseBD480.pdf.

Balmès, François. *Ce que Lacan dit de l'être*. Paris: Presses Universitaires de France 1999.

Barghouti, Omar. "Two Degrees of Separation: Israel, its Palestinian Victims, and the Fraudulent Use of Antisemitism." In Jewish Voice for Peace, *On Anti-Semitism: Solidarity and the Struggle for Justice*, 139–51. Chicago: Haymarket Books, 2017.

Bartov, Omer. "As a Former IDF Soldier and Historian of Genocide, I Was Deeply Disturbed by my Recent Visit to Israel." *The Guardian*, August 13, 2024. https://www.theguardian.com/world/article/2024/aug/13/israel-gaza-historian-omer-bartov?CMP=share_btn_url.

Bartov, Omer. *Genocide, The Holocaust, and Israel-Palestine: First-Person History in Times of Crisis*. New York: Bloomsbury, 2023.

Bartov, Omer, Christopher R. Browning, Jane Caplan, Debórah Dwork, Michael Rothberg, et al. "An Open Letter on the Misuse of Holocaust Memory." *The New York Review*, November 20, 2023. https://www.nybooks.com/online/2023/11/20/an-open-letter-on-the-misuse-of-holocaust-memory/.

Basu Thakur, Gautam. "Fanon's 'Zone of Nonbeing': Blackness and the Politics of the Real." In *Lacan and Race: Racism, Identity, and Psychoanalytic Theory*, edited by Sheldon George and Derek Hook, 284–98. New York: Routledge, 2022.

BDS. "Standing Together: Serving Apartheid Israel's Propaganda," January 25, 2024. https://bdsmovement.net/standing-together-normalization.

Beaumont, Peter. "'Man-Made Famine' Charge Against Israel is Backed by Mounting Body of Evidence." *The Guardian*, March 20, 2024. https://www.theguardian.com/world/2024/mar/20/man-made-famine-charge-israel-mounting-evidence-un-gaza.

Beauvoir, Simone de. *America Day by Day*. Translated by Carol Cosman. Berkeley: University of California Press, 1999.

Beauvoir, Simone de. *The Second Sex*. Translated by Constance Borde and Sheila Malovany-Chevallier. New York: Alfred Knopf, 2010.

Begin, Menachem. *The Revolt*. New York: Dell, 1977.

Belam, Martin and Lili Bayer. "Middle East Crisis: Famine 'Imminent' in Northern Gaza, UN Report Says, as EU Foreign Policy Chief Calls Area 'Open Air Graveyard'—as It Happened." *The Guardian*, March 18, 2024. https://www.theguardian.com/world/live/2024/mar/18/middle-east-crisis-live-israel-gaza-palestine-al-shifa-live-updates.

Bell, Derrick. *Faces at the Bottom of the Well: The Permanence of Racism*. New York: Basic Books, 2018.

Ben-Gurion, David. "Ben-Gurion: Letter to his Son, October 5, 1937." *Jewish Voice For Peace*. https://www.jewishvoiceforpeace.org/2013/04/06/the-ben-gurion-letter/#:~:text=Dear%20Amos%2C,that%20you%20have%20no%20time.

Benhabib, Seyla. "An Open Letter To My Friends Who Signed 'Philosophy for Palestine.'" *The Hannah Arendt Center*, November 4, 2023. https://medium.com/amor-mundi/an-open-letter-to-my-friends-who-signed-philosophy-for-palestine-0440ebd665d8.

Benhabib, Seyla. "Ethics without Normativity and Politics without Historicity." *Constellations* 20, no. 1 (2013): 150–63.

Benjamin, Walter. *Illuminations*. Edited by Hannah Arendt. Translated by Harry Zohn. New York: Schocken, 1968.

Berardi, Franco "Bifo." "Letter to the Hypocrites of Europe." *Institute of Network Cultures*, January 18, 2024. https://networkcultures.org/tactical-media-room/2024/01/18/letter-to-the-hypocrites-of-europe/.

Berardi, Franco "Bifo." "Sabotage and Self-Organization." *Ill Will*, May 6, 2024. https://illwill.com/sabotage-and-self-organization.

Berlant, Lauren. *Cruel Optimism*. Durham: Duke University Press, 2011.

Berman, Lazar. "Netanyahu: Goal of War is 'to Defeat the Murderous Enemy, Ensure Our Existence in Our Land.'" *The Times of Israel*, October 28, 2023. https://www

.timesofisrael.com/liveblog_entry/netanyahu-goal-of-war-is-to-defeat-the-murderous-enemy-ensure-our-existence-in-our-land/.

Bernasconi, Robert. "Fanon's *The Wretched of the Earth* as the Fulfillment of Sartre's *Critique of Dialectical Reason*." *Sartre Studies International* 16, no. 2 (2010): 36–46.

Bisharat, Odeh. "The World Was in Complete Solidarity With Israel. Then the Status Quo Returned." *Haaretz*, November 6, 2023. https://www.haaretz.com/opinion/2023-11-06/ty-article-opinion/.premium/the-world-was-in-complete-solidarity-with-israel-then-the-status-quo-returned/0000018b-a11c-dc0b-a1cb-e5de6ced0000.

Black for Palestine. "2015 Black Solidarity Statement with Palestine." https://www.blackforpalestine.com/2015-statement.html.

Black for Palestine. "Black Solidarity with Gaza - #CeasefireNow." https://www.blackforpalestine.com/2023statement.html.

Black Lives Matter Grassroots. "Black Lives Matter Grassroots Statement in Solidarity with the Palestinian People." https://blmgrassroots.org/black-lives-matter-grassroots-statement-in-solidarity-with-the-palestinian-people/.

Blakeley, Grace. "No, Capitalism Isn't Democratic." *Tribune*, June 15, 2023. https://tribunemag.co.uk/2023/06/no-capitalism-isnt-democratic.

BLM Inland Empire. "'To Ally with the Democratic Party is to Ally Against Ourselves': BLM Inland Empire Breaks with BLM Global Network." *Left Voice*, February 4, 2021. https://www.leftvoice.org/blm-inland-empire-breaks-with-black-lives-matter-global-network/.

Bloch, Nadine. "The Art of #BlackLivesMatter." *Waging Nonviolence*, January 8, 2015. https://wagingnonviolence.org/2015/01/art-blacklivesmatter/.

Block, Niko. "Justice Without Exception: Zionist Narrative and the Crisis of Liberalism." *Social Text*, January 10, 2024. https://socialtextjournal.org/periscope_article/justice-without-exception-zionist-narrative-and-the-crisis-of-liberalism/.

Bongie, Chris. *Islands and Exiles: The Creole Identities of Post/Colonial Literature*. Stanford: Stanford University Press, 1997.

Borger, Julian. "Biden Under Scrutiny After Bypassing Congress to Supply Tank Shells to Israel." *The Guardian*, December 10, 2023. https://www.theguardian.com/world/2023/dec/10/biden-under-scrutiny-bypassing-congress-supply-tank-shells-israel-gaza.

Bou Ali, Nadia. "Against Zionist Psychoanalysis: Conversation Between the Sword and the Neck." *Psychoanalysis and History* 26, no. 1 (2024): 93–9.

Bou Ali, Nadia. "Measure Against Measure: Why Lacan Contra Foucault?" In *Lacan Contra Foucault: Subjectivity, Sex and Politics*, edited by Nadia Bou Ali, 1–36. New York: Bloomsbury, 2019.

Bouie, Jamelle. "Biden Says 'Fund the Police.' Well, They Aren't Exactly Hurting for Cash." *The New York Times*, March 4, 2022. https://www.nytimes.com/2022/03/04/opinion/the-police-arent-exactly-running-out-of-cash.html.

Breiner, Josh. "Israeli Police Twice as Likely to Solve Murders of Jews Than of Arabs." *Haaretz*, October 10, 2019. https://www.haaretz.com/israel-news/2019-10-10/ty-article/.premium/police-solve-murders-among-jews-at-almost-twice-the-rate-of-those-in-arab-community/0000017f-f90b-d318-afff-fb6b3b800000.

Bresheeth-Zabner, Haim. *An Army Like No Other*. New York: Verso, 2020.

B'Tselem. "List of Military Checkpoints in the West Bank and Gaza Strip." Updated: June 5, 2024. https://www.btselem.org/freedom_of_movement/checkpoints_and_forbidden_roads.

B'Tselem. "A Regime of Jewish Supremacy From the Jordan River to the Mediterranean Sea: This is Apartheid," January 12, 2021. https://www.btselem.org/publications/fulltext/202101_this_is_apartheid.

B'Tselem. "Voices from Gaza." https://www.btselem.org/voices_from_gaza.

Budick, Emily Miller. *Blacks and Jews in Literary Conversation*. Cambridge: Cambridge University Press, 1998.

Butler, Judith. "After Pantin." *Verso Books*, March 14, 2024. https://www.versobooks.com/blogs/news/after-pantin.

Butler, Judith. "Contre l'antisémitisme et pour la paix révolutionnaire en Palestine." *Parole D'Honneur*. https://www.youtube.com/watch?v=rIQNBJOq-0E&t=1550s.

Butler, Judith. "The End of Oslo." *London Review of Books*, September 25, 2011. https://www.lrb.co.uk/blog/2011/september/the-end-of-oslo.

Butler, Judith. *Parting Ways: Jewishness and the Critique of Zionism*. New York: Columbia University Press, 2012.

Butler, Judith. "There Can Be No Critique." *Boston Review*, December 13, 2023. https://www.bostonreview.net/articles/there-can-be-no-critique/.

Butler, Judith. "Violence, Nonviolence: Sartre on Fanon." In *Senses of the Subject*, 171–97. New York: Fordham University Press, 2015.

Buttu, Diana. "I Spoke To Palestinians Tortured By Israel. What They Endured Is Unimaginable." *Zeteo*, July 1, 2024. https://zeteo.com/p/israel-sde-teiman-prisoners-palestinians-torture.

Buttu, Diana. "Rioting for the Right to Rape Palestinians." *Zeteo*, July 31, 2024. https://zeteo.com/p/rioting-for-the-right-to-rape-palestinians.

Byrd, Jodi A. "The Past is Never Dead." *The Cornell Daily Sun*, May 14, 2024. https://cornellsun.com/2024/05/14/byrd-the-past-is-never-dead/.

Byrd, Jodi A. *The Transit of Empire: Indigenous Critiques of Colonialism*. Minneapolis: University of Minnesota Press, 2011.

Canals, Juan Carlos. "Warrior of the Imaginary: A Conversation with Patrick Chamoiseau." *Sargasso* 1 (2007–8): 9–20.

Catlin, Samuel P. "The Campus Does Not Exist." *Parapraxis* 4 (Summer 2024). https://www.parapraxismagazine.com/articles/the-campus-does-not-exist.

Césaire, Aimé. *Discourse on Colonialism*. Translated by Joan Pinkham. New York. Monthly Review Press, 2000.

Césaire, Aimé. "La révolte de Frantz Fanon." *Jeune Afrique*, December 13–19, 1961. https://www.jeuneafrique.com/178228/politique/la-r-volte-de-frantz-fanon-par-aim-c-saire/.

Césaire, Aimé. *A Tempest*. Translated by Richard Miller. New York: TCG Translations, 2002.

Chandler, Nahum Dimitri. *X—The Problem of the Negro as a Problem for Thought*. New York: Fordham University Press, 2013.

Chaouat, Bruno. *Is Theory Good for the Jews? French Thought and the Challenge of the New Antisemitism*. Liverpool: Liverpool University Press, 2016.

Chen, Christopher. "Race and the Politics of Recognition." In *The Sage Handbook of Frankfurt Critical Theory*, edited by Beverly Best, Werner Bonefeld, and Chris O'Kane, 932–51. London: SAGE Publications Ltd., 2018.

Chomsky, Noam. "An Era of Impunity Is Over." *Catalyst* 5, no. 2 (2021): 141–9.

Clarno, Andy. *Neoliberal Apartheid: Palestine/Israel and South Africa after 1994*. Chicago: University of Chicago Press, 2017.

Cole, Juan. "The Vile Racism of Calling Biden a 'Weak Palestinian.'" *Common Dreams*, June 28, 2024. https://www.commondreams.org/opinion/trump-biden-weak-palestinian.

Coulthard, Glen Sean. *Red Skin, White Masks: Rejecting the Colonial Politics of Recognition*. Minneapolis: University of Minnesota Press, 2014.

Coulthard, Glen Sean and Leanne Betasamosake Simpson. "Grounded Normativity / Place-Based Solidarity." *American Quarterly* 68, no. 2 (2016): 249–55.
Crouch, Stanley. "Aunt Medea." In *Notes of a Hanging Judge: Essays and Reviews, 1979–1989*, 202–9. New York: Oxford University Press, 1990.
Danon, Danny. "What's Wrong With Palestinian Surrender?" *The New York Times*, June 24, 2019. https://www.nytimes.com/2019/06/24/opinion/palestinian-peace-bahrain-conference.html.
Davidson, Miri. "Sea and Earth." *New Left Review*, April 4, 2024. https://newleftreview.org/sidecar/posts/sea-and-earth.
Davis, Angela Y. "Political Prisoners, Prisons and Black Liberation." In *If They Come in the Morning: Voices of Resistance*, edited by Angela Y. Davis, 27–43. New York: Verso, 2016.
Day, Eli. "Marc Lamont Hill Has Secured His Place in the Proud Black Anti-Colonial Tradition." *In These Times*, December 11, 2018. https://inthesetimes.com/article/marc-lamont-hill-cnn-palestine-israel-apartheid-jim-crow-black-radical.
Dean, Jodi. *Žižek's Politics*. New York: Routledge, 2006.
Deitelhoff, Nicole, Rainer Forst, Klaus Günther, and Jürgen Habermas. "Habermas on Israel: A Principle of Solidarity." *Research Center Normative Orders*, November 15, 2023. https://www.resetdoc.org/story/habermas-israel-principle-solidariety/.
Deleuze, Gilles. "The Importance of Being Arafat." In *Two Regimes of Madness: Texts and Interviews 1975–1995*, edited by David Lapoujadem, 241–5. New York: Semiotext(e), 2007.
Deleuze, Gilles and Elias Sanbar. "The Indians of Palestine." In *Two Regimes of Madness: Texts and Interviews 1975–1995*, edited by David Lapoujade, 194–200. New York: Semiotext(e), 2007.
Derrida, Jacques. *Adieu to Emmanuel Levinas*. Translated by Pascale-Anne Brault and Michael Naas. Stanford: Stanford University Press, 1999.
Derrida, Jacques. "Force of Law: The 'Mystical Foundation of Authority.'" In *Acts of Religion*, edited by Gil Anidjar, 228–98. New York: Routledge, 2002.
Derrida, Jacques. *Negotiations: Interventions and Interviews, 1971–2001*. Edited by Elizabeth Rottenberg. Stanford: Stanford University Press, 2002.
Derrida, Jacques. *Rogues: Two Essays on Reason*. Translated by Pascale-Anne Brault and Michael Naas. Stanford: Stanford University Press, 2005.
Descartes, René. *Discourse on Method and Meditations on First Philosophy*. Translated by Donald A. Cress. Indianapolis: Hackett, 1998.
Descartes, René. *The Passions of the Soul*. Translated by Stephen Voss. Indianapolis: Hackett, 1989.
Du Bois, W. E. B. *Black Reconstruction in America*. New York: The Free Press, 1998.
Du Bois, W. E. B. *The Souls of Black Folk: Essays and Sketches*. New Haven: Yale University Press, 2015.
Dussel, Enrique. "Anti-Cartesian Meditations: On the Origin of the Philosophical Anti-Discourse of Modernity." Translated by Geo Maher. *Journal for Culture and Religious Theory* 13, no. 1 (2014): 21–53.
Eckstein, Griffin. "'Schumer Has Become a Palestinian': Trump Spews More Rhetoric at Rally." *Salon*, June 28, 2024. https://www.salon.com/2024/06/28/schumer-has-become-a-palestinian-spews-more-rhetoric-at-rally/#:~:text=%E2%80%9CSchumer%20has%20become%20a%20Palestinian,%E2%80%9CPalestinian%E2%80%9D%20as%20a%20slur.
Edelman, Lee. *No Future: Queer Theory and the Death Drive*. Durham: Duke University Press, 2004.

Edelman, Lee. *The World and Africa and Color and Democracy*. Edited by Henry Louis Gates, Jr. New York: Oxford University Press, 2007.

Eid, Haidar. "Gaza 2023: Our Warsaw Uprising Moment." *Al Jazeera*, October 10, 2023. https://www.aljazeera.com/opinions/2023/10/10/gaza-2023-our-warsaw-uprising-moment.

Eid, Haidar. "The Two-State Solution: The Opium of the Palestinian People." *Al Jazeera*, December 29, 2020. https://www.aljazeera.com/opinions/2020/12/29/the-two-state-solution-the-opium-of-the-palestinian-people.

"The Elephant in the Room," August 4, 2023. https://sites.google.com/view/israel-elephant-in-the-room/petitions/aug-23-elephant-in-the-room?authuser=0.

El-Hadi, Nehal. "Ensemble: An Interview with Dr. Fred Moten." *Mice Magazine*, Summer 2018. https://micemagazine.ca/issue-four/ensemble-interview-dr-fred-moten.

El-Kurd, Mohammed. "In Bad Faith with Mohammed El-Kurd." https://www.youtube.com/watch?v=4m1aDlglA-k.

Erakat, Noura and Nicki Kattoura. "Palestinians Illuminate the Colonial Nature of the Rest of the World." *Hammer & Hope*, no. 3 (2024). https://hammerandhope.org/article/noura-erakat-palestine-gaza.

Erikson, Erik H. and Huey P. Newton. *In Search of Common Ground: Conversations with Erik H. Erikson and Huey P. Newton*. New York: Norton, 1973.

Estes, Nick. "The Liberation of Palestine Represents an Alternative Path for Native Nations." *The Red Nation*, September 7, 2019. https://therednation.org/the-liberation-of-palestine-represents-an-alternative-path-for-native-nations/.

Falk, Richard. "On 'Lost Causes' and the Future of Palestine." *The Nation*, December 16, 2014. https://www.thenation.com/article/archive/lost-causes-and-future-palestine/.

Fanon, Frantz. *Black Skin, White Masks*. Translated by Richard Philcox. New York: Grove Press, 2008.

Fanon, Frantz. *Black Skin, White Masks*. Translated by Charles Lam Markmann. New York: Grove Press, 1967.

Fanon, Frantz. *A Dying Colonialism*. Translated by Haakon Chevalier. New York: Grove Press, 1965.

Fanon, Frantz. "West Indians and Africans." In *Toward the African Revolution*, translated by Haakon Chevalier, 17–27. New York: Grove Press, 1967.

Fanon, Frantz. "Why We Use Violence." In *Political Writings* from *Alienation and Freedom*, edited by Jean Khalfa and Robert J. C. Young, 653–9. New York: Bloomsbury, 2021.

Fanon, Frantz. *The Wretched of the Earth*. Translated by Richard Philcox. New York: Grove Press, 2004.

Farrell, William E. "Israelis, At Huge Rally In Tel Aviv, Demand Begin and Sharon Resign." *The New York Times*, September 26, 1982. https://www.nytimes.com/1982/09/26/world/israelis-at-huge-rally-in-tel-aviv-demand-begin-and-sharon-resign.html.

Farsakh, Leila. "Alternatives to Partition in Palestine Rearticulating the State-Nation Nexus." In *Rethinking Statehood in Palestine Self-Determination and Decolonization Beyond Partition*, edited by Leila H. Farsakh, 173–91. Oakland: University of California Press, 2021.

Fassin, Didier. *Humanitarian Reason: A Moral History of the Present*. Translated by Rachel Gomme. Berkeley: University of California Press, 2012.

Ferreira da Silva, Denise. "No-Bodies: Law, Raciality and Violence." *Griffith Law Review* 18, no. 2 (2009): 212–36.

Florini, Sarah. *Beyond Hashtags: Racial Politics and Black Digital Networks*. New York: New York University Press, 2019.

Foucault, Michel. "What Is Critique?" Translated by Kevin Paul Geiman. In *What Is Enlightenment? Eighteenth-Century Answers and Twentieth-Century Questions*, edited by James Schmidt, 82–98. Berkeley: University of California Press, 1996.

Frank, Thomas. "Bill Clinton's Crime Bill Destroyed Lives, and There's No Point Denying It." *The Guardian*, April 15, 2016. https://www.theguardian.com/commentisfree/2016/apr/15/bill-clinton-crime-bill-hillary-black-lives-thomas-frank.

Fraser, Nancy. *Justice Interruptus: Critical Reflections on the "Postsocialist" Condition*. New York: Routledge, 1997.

Freud, Sigmund. "A Difficulty in the Path of Psycho-Analysis." In *The Standard Edition of the Complete Psychological Works of Sigmund Freud*, Vol. 17, edited by James Strachey, 135–44. London: Hogarth, 1953–74.

Freud, Sigmund. *The Interpretation of Dreams*. In *The Standard Edition of the Complete Psychological Works of Sigmund Freud*, Vol. 4, edited by James Strachey, ix–627. London: Hogarth, 1953–74.

Freud, Sigmund. "Repression." In *The Standard Edition of the Complete Psychological Works of Sigmund Freud*, Vol. 14, edited by James Strachey, 142–58. London: Hogarth, 1957.

Gessen, M. "In the Shadow of the Holocaust." *The New Yorker*, December 9, 2023. https://www.newyorker.com/news/the-weekend-essay/in-the-shadow-of-the-holocaust.

Gessen, M. "Kamala Harris Is Speaking. Is She Listening?" *The New York Times*, August 10, 2024. https://www.nytimes.com/2024/08/10/opinion/kamala-harris-gaza-detroit.html?unlocked_article_code=1.CE4.-IQS.YV04gsQON5tv&smid=url-share.

Gibson, Nigel C. *Fanon: The Postcolonial Imagination*. Cambridge: Polity Press, 2003.

Gibson, Nigel C. "Fanon, Movement, Self-Movement." In *Fanon Today: Reason and Revolt of The Wretched of the Earth*, edited by Nigel Gibson, 270–307. Québec: Daraja Press, 2021.

Gilroy, Paul. *The Black Atlantic: Modernity and Double-Consciousness*. Cambridge, MA: Harvard University Press, 1993.

Gines, Kathryn T. (Kathryn Sophia Belle). *Hannah Arendt and the Negro Question*. Bloomington: Indiana University Press, 2014.

Giri, Saroj. "From the October Revolution to the Naxalbari Movement: Understanding Political Subjectivity." In *Of Concepts and Methods: "On Postisms" and Other Essays*, edited by K. Murali (Ajith), 1–32. Paris: Foreign Languages Press, 2020.

Giroux, Henry A. "US Fascism Is Spreading Under the Guise of 'Patriotic Education.'" *Truthout*, April 10, 2023. https://truthout.org/articles/us-fascism-is-spreading-under-the-guise-of-patriotic-education.

Glynos, Jason. "Psychoanalysis Operates Upon the Subject of Science: Lacan Between Science and Ethics." In *Lacan and Science*, edited by Jason Glynos and Yannis Stavrakakis, 51–88. New York: Karnac Books, 2002.

Goodman, Amy. "Cornel West: Obama's Response to Trayvon Martin Case Belies Failure to Challenge 'New Jim Crow.'" *Democracy Now!* July 22, 2013. https://www.democracynow.org/2013/7/22/cornel_west_obamas_response_to_trayvon.

Goodman, Amy. "Israeli Writer Gideon Levy: If Netanyahu Wants to Stop the Rockets, He Needs to Accept a Just Peace." *Democracy Now!* July 22, 2014. https://www.democracynow.org/2014/7/22/israeli_writer_gideon_levy_if_netanyahu.

Goodman, Amy and Juan González. "Boots Riley's Dystopian Satire 'Sorry to Bother You? Is an Anti-Capitalist Rallying Cry for Workers." *Democracy Now!* July 17, 2018. https://www.democracynow.org/2018/7/17/sorry_to_bother_you_boots_rileys.

Goodman, Amy and Juan González. "Holocaust Scholar Raz Segal Loses Univ. of Minnesota Job Offer for Saying Israel Is Committing Genocide." *Democracy Now!* June 18, 2024. https://www.democracynow.org/2024/6/18/raz_segal_university_of _minnesota.

Gordon, Lewis R. "Through the Hellish Zone of Nonbeing: Thinking through Fanon, Disaster, and the Damned of the Earth." *Human Architecture: Journal of the Sociology of Self-Knowledge* 5, no. 3 (2007): 5–11.

Gordon, Lewis R. *What Fanon Said: A Philosophical Introduction to His Life and Thought*. New York: Fordham University Press, 2015.

Gordon, Neve and Muna Haddad. "The Road to Famine in Gaza." *The New York Review*, March 30, 2024. https://www.nybooks.com/online/2024/03/30/the-road-to-famine -in-gaza/.

Gossett, Che. "A Wall is Just a Wall: Anti-Blackness and the Politics of Black and Prison Abolitionist Solidarity with Palestinian Struggle." *Decolonization* (blog), June 16, 2014. https://decolonization.wordpress.com/2014/06/16/a-wall-is-just-a-wall-anti -blackness-and-the-politics-of-black-and-prison-abolitionist-solidarity-with-palestinian -struggle/.

Graham-Harrison, Emma. "Israeli Forces in Gaza 'Use Civilians as Human Shields' Against Possible Booby-Traps." *The Guardian*, August 14, 2024. https://www .theguardian.com/world/article/2024/aug/14/israeli-forces-in-gaza-use-civilians-as -human-shields-against-possible-booby-traps.

Grim, Ryan. "What Are We Doing?" *The Intercept*, January 29, 2024. https://theintercept .com/2024/01/29/unrwa-funding-genocide-israel/.

Guo, Kayla. "House Censures Rashida Tlaib, Citing 'River to the Sea' Slogan." *The New York Times*, November 7, 2024. https://www.nytimes.com/2023/11/07/us/politics/ tlaib-censure-house-israel-gaza.html.

Haaretz. "Former Israeli MK Quotes Hitler While Discussing Gaza War." *Haaretz*, June 16, 2024. https://www.haaretz.com/israel-news/2024-06-16/ty-article/former -israeli-mk-quotes-hitler-while-discussing-gaza-war/00000190-224f-d231-a1b2 -e65f76fe0000.

Haddad, Toufic. *Palestine Ltd.: Neoliberalism and Nationalism in the Occupied Territories*. London: I.B. Tauris, 2016.

Hall, Stuart. "'In But Not of Europe': Europe and its Myths." In *Selected Writings on Race and Difference*, 305–45. Durham: Duke University Press, 2021.

Halper, Jeff. "The 'Two-state Solution' Only Ever Meant a Big Israel Ruling Over a Palestinian Bantustan. Let It Go." *Haaretz*, June 19, 2018. https://www.haaretz.com/ opinion/2018-01-19/ty-article-opinion/.premium/the-two-state-solution-is-dead-let-it -go/0000017f-dbe3-df62-a9ff-dff78aa80000.

Hamza, Agon and Frank Ruda. "Interview with Alberto Toscano: The Fascism of Our Times." *Crisis and Critique* 11, no. 1 (2024): 252–61.

Hartkopf Schloss, Rebecca. *Sweet Liberty: The Final Days of Slavery in Martinique*. Philadelphia: University of Pennsylvania Press, 2009.

Hartman, Saidiya V. *Lose Your Mother: A Journey Along the Atlantic Slave Route*. New York: Farrar, Straus and Giroux, 2007.

Hartman, Saidiya V. *Scenes of Subjection: Terror, Slavery, and Self-Making in Nineteenth-Century America*. Oxford: Oxford University Press, 1997.

Hartman, Saidiya V. and Tina Campt. "A Future Beyond Empire: An Introduction." *Small Axe*, no. 28 (2009): 19–26.

Hartman, Saidiya V. and Frank B. Wilderson III. "The Position of the Unthought." *Qui Parle* 13, no. 2 (2003): 183–201.

Hass, Amira. "Palestinian Ghettos Were Always the Plan." *Haaretz*, January 20, 2013. https://www.haaretz.com/2013-01-20/ty-article/.premium/palestinian-ghettos-the-plan-all-along/0000017f-f82b-d044-adff-fbfbb0e80000.

Hauser Tov, Michael. "'Israeli Gov't Is Intent on Destroying Palestinians in Gaza': South Africa Presents Genocide Case at ICJ." *Haaretz*, January 11, 2024. https://www.haaretz.com/israel-news/2024-01-11/ty-article/israeli-govt-is-intent-on-destroying-palestinians-south-africa-presents-genocide-case/0000018c-f8bc-d517-af9d-fcbe87ae0000.

Herzl, Theodor. "The Jewish State" (1896). In *The Zionist Idea: A Historical Analysis and Reader*, edited by Arthur Hertzberg, 204–26. Philadelphia: Jewish Publication Society 1997.

Himoud, Sarah. "Love in a Time of Genocide: A Palestinian Litany for Survival." *Journal of Palestinian Studies* 52, no. 4 (2023): 87–94.

Hochschild, Arlie Russell. *Stolen Pride: Loss, Shame, and the Rise of the Right*. New York: The New Press, 2024.

Hook, Derek. "White Anxiety in (Post)Apartheid South Africa." *Psychoanalysis, Culture & Society* 25, no. 4 (2020): 612–31.

Horkheimer, Max. "The Jews and Europe." In *Critical Theory and Society: A Reader*, edited by Stephen Bronner and Douglas Kellner, 77–94. New York: Routledge, 1989.

Human Rights Watch. "Israel: Starvation Used as Weapon of War in Gaza." *Human Rights Watch*, December 18, 2023. https://www.hrw.org/news/2023/12/18/israel-starvation-used-weapon-war-gaza.

Human Rights Watch. "A Threshold Crossed Israeli Authorities and the Crimes of Apartheid and Persecution," April 27, 2021. https://www.hrw.org/report/2021/04/27/threshold-crossed/israeli-authorities-and-crimes-apartheid-and-persecution#.

IfNotNow, October 14, 2021. https://twitter.com/IfNotNowOrg/status/1448709689127030789.

Illouz, Eva. "47 Years a Slave: A New Perspective on the Occupation." *Haaretz*, February 7, 2014. https://www.haaretz.com/2014-02-07/ty-article/.premium/47-years-a-slave/0000017f-decf-df62-a9ff-dedfc4ff0000.

Illouz, Eva. "Genocide in Gaza? Eva Illouz Replies to Didier Fassin." *K*, November 16, 2023. https://k-larevue.com/en/genocide-in-gaza-eva-illouz-replies-to-didier-fassin/.

Illouz, Eva. "The Global Left Needs to Renounce Judith Butler." *Haaretz*, March 21. https://www.haaretz.com/opinion/2024-03-21/ty-article/.premium/the-global-left-needs-to-renounce-judith-butler/0000018e-61e7-d507-a1cf-63f7bc380000.

Illouz, Eva. "How the Left Became a Politics of Hatred Against Jews." *Haaretz*, February 3, 2024. https://www.haaretz.com/opinion/2024-02-03/ty-article-opinion/.highlight/how-the-left-became-a-politics-of-hatred-against-jews/0000018d-6562-d7f7-adcf-6def4fe50000.

Illouz, Eva. "The Third Political force in Israel Represents What We Must Reluctantly Call 'Jewish Fascism.'" *Le Monde*, November 16, 2022. https://www.lemonde.fr/en/opinion/article/2022/11/16/the-third-political-force-in-israel-represents-what-we-must-reluctantly-call-jewish-fascism_6004446_23.html.

Illouz, Eva. "The Virtuous Antisemitism of Campus Protests Against Israel." *Haaretz*, May 21, 2024. https://www.haaretz.com/opinion/2024-05-21/ty-article-magazine/.premium/the-virtuous-antisemitism-of-campus-protests-against-israel/0000018f-9aa0-d264-a1bf-deb7652f0000.

Inskeep, Steve. "THE BREATHE Act Is A Counterproposal To Justice In Policing Act." *NPR*, March 23, 2021. https://www.npr.org/2021/03/23/980234498/the-breathe-act-is-a-counterproposal-to-justice-in-policing-act.

International Middle East Media Center. "Palestinian Family Forced To Demolish Their Home In Silwan." *IMEMC News*, July 15 2024. https://imemc.org/article/palestinian-family-forced-to-demolish-their-home-in-silwan/.

"Israeli Public Figures Call On the Remaining EU Member States, the UK, And Other States To recognize the State of Palestine Without Delay," May 7, 2024. https://estaticos-cdn.prensaiberica.es/epi/public/content/file/original/2024/0510/14/call-by-israeli-public-figures-to-recognize-the-state-of-palestine-7-may-2024-pdf.pdf.

Issar, Siddhant and James Padilioni, Jr. "'To Address Black Suffering is to Destroy the World.' An Interview with Frank B. Wilderson, III on *Afropessimism*." *Interfere* 1 (2020): 92–111.

Jabotinsky, Vladimir Ze'ev. "The Iron Wall," November 4, 1923. https://www.jewishvirtuallibrary.org/quot-the-iron-wall-quot.

Jabr, Samah and Elisabeth Berger. "Fanon and Palestine: The Struggle for Justice as the Core of Mental Health." In *Fanon Today: Reason and Revolt of The Wretched of the Earth*, edited by Nigel Gibson, 127–54. Québec: Daraja Press, 2021.

Jackson, Zakiyyah Iman. "Saidiya Hartman by Zakiyyah Iman Jackson." *BOMB*, Winter 2023. https://bombmagazine.org/articles/2022/10/24/saidiya-hartman/.

Jacobs, Ron. "The Israeli Defense Forces is a Misnomer." *CounterPunch*, June 19, 2020. https://www.counterpunch.org/2020/06/19/the-israeli-defense-forces-is-a-misnomer/.

Jacobson, Howard. "The Founding of Israel Wasn't a Colonial Act—a Refugee Isn't a Colonist." *The New Statesman*, November 29, 2023. https://www.newstatesman.com/ideas/2023/11/founding-israel-palestine-anti-semitism?utm_source=substack&utm_medium=email.

Jarmakani, Amira. "The ADL is Leading the Attack Against Free Speech on Palestine." *Mondoweiss*, November 20, 2023. https://mondoweiss.net/2023/11/the-adl-is-leading-the-attack-against-free-speech-on-palestine/.

Jewish Electoral Institute. "July 2021 National Survey of Jewish Voters." https://www.jewishelectorateinstitute.org/july-2021-national-survey-of-jewish-voters/.

Johnson, Jake. "Israeli Military Has Killed 500 Gaza Healthcare Workers—Two a Day Since Assault Began." *Common Dream*, June 26, 2024. https://www.commondreams.org/news/healthcare-workers-killed-in-gaza.

Kane, Alex. "A 'McCarthyite Backlash' Against Pro-Palestine Speech." *Jewish Currents*, October 20, 2023. https://jewishcurrents.org/a-mccarthyite-backlash-against-pro-palestine-speech.

Kant, Immanuel. "An Answer to the Question: What Is Enlightenment?" Translated by James Schmidt. In *What Is Enlightenment? Eighteenth-Century Answers and Twentieth-Century Questions*, edited by James Schmidt, 58–64. Berkeley: University of California Press, 1996.

Kapoor, Ilan. "Intersectionality, Decoloniality, Indigenous Localism: A Critique." *Theory, Culture and Society* (2024): 1–21.

Kapoor, Ilan. "Žižek, Antagonism and Politics Now: Three Recent Controversies." *International Journal of Žižek Studies* 12, no. 1 (2018): 1–31.

Kapoor, Ilan and Zahi Zalloua. *Universal Politics*. Oxford: Oxford University Press, 2022.

Kashani, Maryam. "The Wreck Itself: Between Palestine and American Indian Studies' Sovereignty and the Surreal." *Critical Ethnic Studies* 8, no. 1 (2023). https://manifold.umn.edu/read/ces0801-08/section/6ff6ead6-1ee8-4423-b96e-d335990e69f7.

Kattenburg, David. "In a Historic Ruling, ICJ Declares Israeli Occupation Unlawful, Calls for Settlements To Be Evacuated, and for Palestinian Reparations." *Mondoweiss*, July

19, 2024. https://mondoweiss.net/2024/07/in-a-historic-ruling-icj-declares-israeli-occupation-unlawful-calls-for-settlements-to-be-evacuated-and-for-palestinian-reparations/.

Kattoura, Nicki and Geo Maher. "Israel-Palestine War: Why Must Palestinians Condemn Themselves for Daring to Fight Back?" https://www.middleeasteye.net/opinion/israel-palestine-war-why-condemnation-trap.

Kelley, Robin D. G. "Insecure: Policing Under Racial Capitalism." *Spectre* 1, no. 2 (2020): 12–37.

Kelley, Robin D. G. "Sorry, Not Sorry." *Boston Review*, September 13, 2018. http://bostonreview.net/race-literature-culture/robin-d-g-kelley-sorry-not-sorry#.XMdwpNHrLCE.email.

Khader, Jamil. "Media's Selective Moral Outrage Manufactures Consent for Palestinian Genocide." *Truthout*, October 18, 2023. https://truthout.org/articles/medias-selective-moral-outrage-manufactures-consent-for-palestinian-genocide/.

Khader, Jamil. "Rehumanizing Palestinians? Radicalize the Struggle!" *The Philosophical Salon*, July 9, 2018. https://thephilosophicalsalon.com/rehumanizing-palestinians-radicalize-the-struggle/.

Khader, Jamil. "Ziofascist Violence and the Nakba 2.0: Jouissance and Necrocapitalism in the Consolidation of extremist Messianic Zionist far-right Ideology." *Crisis and Critique* 11, no. 1 (2024): 26–54.

Khalidi, Rashid. "The Dahiya Doctrine, Proportionality, and War Crimes." *Journal of Palestine Studies* 44, no. 1 (2014): 5–13.

Khalidi, Rashid. *The Hundred Years' War on Palestine: A History of Settler Colonialism and Resistance, 1917–2017*. New York: Metropolitan Books, 2020.

Khalidi, Rashid. "It's Time to Confront Israel's Version of 'From the River to the Sea.'" *The Nation*, November 22, 2023. https://www.thenation.com/article/world/its-time-to-confront-israels-version-of-from-the-river-to-the-sea/.

Khalidi, Rashid. "The Neck and the Sword: Interviewed by Tariq Ali." *New Left Review* 147 (2024): 5–38.

Khalidi, Rashid. *Palestinian Identity: The Construction of Modern National Consciousness*. New York: Columbia University Press, 1997.

Khoury, Nadim. "Transitional Justice in Palestine/Israel: Whose Justice? Which Transition?" In *Rethinking Statehood in Palestine Self-Determination and Decolonization Beyond Partition*, edited by Leila H. Farsakh, 153–72. Oakland: University of California Press, 2021.

King, Tiffany Lethabo. "Humans Involved: Lurking in the Lines of Posthumanist Flight." *Critical Ethnic Studies* 3, no. 1 (2017): 162–85.

Kistner, Ulrike and Philippe Van Hauteix. "Hegel/Fanon: Transpositions in Translations." In *Violence, Slavery and Freedom between Hegel and Fanon*, edited by Ulrike Kistner and Philippe Van Hauteix, vii–xii. Johannesburg: Wits University Press, 2020.

Klein, Naomi. "We Need an Exodus from Zionism." *The Guardian*, April 24, 2024. https://www.theguardian.com/commentisfree/2024/apr/24/zionism-seder-protest-new-york-gaza-israel.

Klein, Naomi. "The Zone of Interest is about the Danger of Ignoring Atrocities—Including in Gaza." *The Guardian*, March 14, 2024. https://www.theguardian.com/commentisfree/2024/mar/14/the-zone-of-interest-auschwitz-gaza-genocide.

Kleinberg, Aviad. "Are All Israelis 'Colonialists' Who Deserve to Die?" *Haaretz*, November 13, 2023. https://www.haaretz.com/israel-news/2023-11-13/ty-article-opinion/

.premium/are-all-israeli-babies-colonialist-who-deserve-to-die/0000018b-c87e-d61e-a39b-ddfe0fc10000.

Kraus, Karl. "Judith Butler: Powerlessness in Action." *K,* March 15. https://k-larevue.com/en/judith-butler-powerlessness-in-action/.

Krauss, Joseph. "In Israel's Call For Mass Evacuation, Palestinians Hear Echoes of Their Original Catastrophic Exodus." *AP News,* October 13, 2023. https://apnews.com/article/israel-palestinians-gaza-evacuation-history-nakba-a1bec1ee3477573e80b39b4044a48111.

Krauss, Joseph. "What Would a New Palestinian Government in the West Bank Mean for the War in Gaza?" *AP News,* February 26, 2024. https://apnews.com/article/israel-palestinian-authority-government-explainer-aefe041e045f2c60918b42f42185f41e.

Lacan, Jacques. "The Mirror Stage as Formative of the Function of the I as Revealed in Psychoanalytic Experience." In *Écrits: The First Complete Edition in English,* translated by Bruce Fink, 753–81. New York: Norton, 2006.

Lacan, Jacques. *On Feminine Sexuality, The Limits of Love and Knowledge, 1972-1973: Encore, The Seminar of Jacques Lacan, Book XX.* Translated by Bruce Fink. New York: Norton, 1998.

Lacan, Jacques. *The Seminar. Book XI. The Four Fundamental Concepts of Psychoanalysis.* Translated by Alan Sheridan. London: Hogarth Press and Institute of Psycho-Analysis, 1977.

Lacan, Jacques. *The Seminar of Jacques Lacan, Book VII: The Ethics of Psychoanalysis, 1959–1960.* Translated by Dennis Porter. Edited by Jacques-Alain Miller. New York: Norton, 1992.

Lacan, Jacques. "The Signification of the Phallus." In *Écrits: The First Complete Edition in English,* translated by Bruce Fink, 575–84. New York: Norton, 2006.

Laclau, Ernesto. "Identity and Hegemony: The Role of Universality in the Constitution of Political Logics." In *Contingency, Hegemony, Universality: Contemporary Dialogues on the Left,* edited by Judith Butler, Ernesto Laclau, and Slavoj Žižek, 44–80. New York: Verso, 2000.

Lacy, Akela. "After Years of Failure on Gun Control, Democrats Push More Police Funding." *The Intercept,* April 19, 2022. https://theintercept.com/2022/04/19/police-funding-democrats-gun-control/.

Lamont Hill, Marc and Mitchell Plitnick. *Except for Palestine: The Limits of Progressive Politics.* New York: The New Press, 2021.

Laruelle, François. *Intellectuals and Power: The Insurrection of the Victim.* Translated by Anthony Paul Smith. Cambridge: Polity Press, 2015.

Leifer, Joshua. "A 'Moral, Strategic, and Diplomatic Abyss.'" *The New York Review,* July 2, 2024. https://www.nybooks.com/online/2024/07/02/a-moral-strategic-and-diplomatic-abyss-israel/.

Lentin, Ronit. *Traces of Racial Exception: Racializing Israeli Settler Colonialism.* New York: Bloomsbury, 2018.

Lerman, Antony. "The Tropes of 'Jewish Antisemitism.'" *The Guardian,* October 5, 2009. https://www.theguardian.com/commentisfree/2009/oct/05/self-hating-jew-antisemitism.

Levinas, Emmanuel. *Ethics and Infinity: Conversations with Philippe Nemo.* Translated by Richard A. Cohen. Pittsburgh: Duquesne University Press, 1985.

Levinas, Emmanuel. "Ethics and Politics." In *The Levinas Reader,* edited by Seán Hand, 289–97. Oxford: Blackwell, 1989.

Levinas, Emmanuel. "The I and the Totality." In *Entre Nous: Thinking of the Other*, translated by Michael B. Smith and Barbara Harshav, 13–38. New York: Columbia University Press, 1998.

Levinas, Emmanuel. "The Name of a Dog, or Natural Rights." In *Difficult Freedom: Essays on Judaism*, translated by Seán Hand, 151–3. Baltimore: The Johns Hopkins University Press, 1990.

Levinas, Emmanuel. *Otherwise than Being, or, Beyond Essence*. Translated by Alphonso Lingis. The Hague: Martinus Nijhoff, 1981.

Levinas, Emmanuel. "Peace and Proximity." In *Basic Philosophical Writings*, edited by Adriaan T. Peperzak, Simon Critchley, and Robert Bernasconi, 161–9. Bloomington: Indiana University Press, 1996.

Levinas, Emmanuel. "Politics After!" In *The Levinas Reader*, edited by Seán Hand, translated by Roland Lack, 277–83. Oxford: Blackwell, 1989.

Levinas, Emmanuel. *Totality and Infinity: An Essay on Exteriority*. Translated by Alphonso Lingis. Pittsburgh: Duquesne University Press, 1969.

Levine, Joseph. "If You Support Israel in the Middle of a Genocide, You're an Awful Person." *Mondoweiss*, July 6, 2024. https://mondoweiss.net/2024/07/if-you-support-israel-in-the-middle-of-a-genocide-youre-an-awful-person/.

LeVine, Mark. "Fanon's Conception of Violence Does Not Work in Palestine." *Al Jazeera*, October 10, 2023. https://www.aljazeera.com/opinions/2023/10/10/fanons-conception-of-violence-does-not-work-in-palestine.

Levy, Gideon. "Israel Does Not Want Peace." *Haaretz*, July 4, 2014. https://www.haaretz.com/2014-07-04/ty-article/israel-does-not-want-peace/0000017f-db80-df62-a9ff-dfd75c210000.

Lorber, Ben. "The ADL Is Making It Less Safe to Be a Progressive Jew." *In These Times*, November 21, 2023. https://inthesetimes.com/article/adl-defamation-league-jvp-ifnotnow-musk?link_id=5&can_id=839242f129045dcf95563791cad9b53c&source=email-bidens-unflinching-support-for-israels-war-on-gaza-is-derailing-his-reelection-chances-2&email_referrer=email_2121160___subject_2645816&email_subject=the-rise-of-the-far-right-is-a-global-phenomenon-the-adl-is-making-it-less-safe-to-be-a-progressive-jew.

Lorde, Audre. "The Master's Tools Will Never Dismantle the Master's House." In *This Bridge Called My Back: Writings by Radical Women of Color*, edited by Cherríe Moraga and Gloria Anzaldua, 94–101. New York: Kitchen Table Press, 1983.

Lorde, Audre. "The Uses of Anger." *Women's Studies Quarterly* 25, no. 1–2 (1997): 278–85.

Maçães, Bruno. "Gaza and Ukraine Have Divided the World into Geopolitical Tribes." *The New Statesman*, November 15, 2023. https://www.newstatesman.com/world/middle-east/2023/11/gaza-ukraine-world-geopolitical-tribes?utm_source=substack&utm_medium=email.

Maher, Geo. *Anticolonial Eruptions: Racial Hubris and the Cunning of Resistance*. Berkeley: University of California Press, 2022.

Maher, Geo. *Decolonizing Dialectics*. Durham: Duke University Press, 2017.

Majadli, Hanin. "Over 30,000 Killed in Gaza, but Even Israel's 'Liberal Left' Says: That's War." *Haaretz*, March 7, 2024. https://www.haaretz.com/opinion/2024-03-07/ty-article-opinion/.premium/over-30-000-killed-in-gaza-but-even-israels-liberal-left-says-thats-war/0000018e-1a3a-d8fb-abff-5f3ad8860000.

Makdisi, Saree. *Palestine Inside Out: An Everyday Occupation*. New York: Norton, 2008.

Makdisi, Saree. *Tolerance Is a Wasteland: Palestine and the Culture of Denial*. Oakland: University of California Press, 2022.

Malcolm X. "Zionist Logic." www.malcolm-x.org/docs/gen_zion.htm.

Mannoni, Octave. "I Know Very Well, but All the Same . . . ." In *Perversion and the Social Relation*, edited by Molly Anne Rothenberg, Dennis A. Foster, and Slavoj Žižek, translated by G. M. Goshgarian, 68–92. Durham: Duke University Press, 2003.

Marcetic, Branko. "A Tidal Wave of State and Private Repression Is Targeting Pro-Palestinian Voices." *Jacobin*, November 3, 2023. https://jacobin.com/2023/11/anti-palestine-mccarthyism-censorship.

Marder, Michael. "Compassionate Genocide." *The Philosophical Salon*, April 22, 2024. https://thephilosophicalsalon.com/compassionate-genocide/.

Marder, Michael. "The 'Volcano of Occupation' Is Erupting Again: Responding to the Bombings of Gaza." *Basque Museum of Contemporary Art*, December 13, 2023. https://www.amaonline.eus/the-volcano-of-occupation-is-irrupting-again-responding-to-the-bombings-of-gaza/.

Marriott, David. "Blackness: N'est Pas?" *Propter Nos* 4 (2020): 27–51.

Marriott, David. *On Black Men*. New York: Columbia University Press, 2000.

Marriott, David. "On Revolutionary Suicide." *Diacritics* 49, no. 4 (2021): 101–33.

Marx, Karl. "Letters from the *Deutsch-Französische Jahrbucher*." In *Collected Works of Marx and Engels*, Vol. 3, 133–45. New York: International Publishers, 1975.

Masalha, Nur. "The Concept of 'Transfer' in Zionist Thinking and Practice: Historical Roots and Contemporary Challenges." *Institute For Palestinian Studies*, no. 7 (2023). https://www.palestine-studies.org/en/node/1654742.

Mashiach, Itay. "Meet the Israelis Who Are Trying to Physically Block the Ethnic Cleansing Unfolding in the West Bank." *Haaretz*, February 2, 2024. https://www.haaretz.com/israel-news/2024-02-02/ty-article-magazine/.highlight/meet-the-israelis-physically-blocking-the-ethnic-cleansing-unfolding-in-the-west-bank/0000018d-6609-d37c-a9df-ef8b77200000.

Massad, Joseph. "Just Another Battle or the Palestinian War of Liberation?" *The Electronic Intifada*, October 8, 2023. https://electronicintifada.net/content/just-another-battle-or-palestinian-war-liberation/38661.

Massad, Joseph. "The Last of the Semites." *Al Jazeera*, May 21, 2013. https://www.aljazeera.com/opinions/2013/5/21/the-last-of-the-semites.

Massad, Joseph. "Nizar Banat Killing: Why the PA's Days Are Numbered." *Middle East Eye*, June 28, 2021. https://www.middleeasteye.net/opinion/palestine-nizar-banat-killing-why-pa-days-numbered.

Massad, Joseph. *The Persistence of the Palestinian Question: Essays on Zionism and the Palestinians*. New York: Routledge, 2006.

Massad, Joseph. "Why Academic Scholarship on Israel and Palestine Threatens Western Elites." *Middle East Eye*, June 18, 2024. https://www.middleeasteye.net/opinion/why-academic-scholarship-israel-palestine-threatens-western-elites.

Mbembe, Achille. *Critique of Black Reason*. Translated by Laurent Dubois. Durham: Duke University Press, 2017.

Mbembe, Achille. "In Conversation: Achille Mbembe and David Theo Goldberg on *Critique of Black Reason*." *Theory, Culture, and Society*, July 3, 2018.

Mbembe, Achille. *Necropolitics*. Translated by Steven Corcoran. Durham: Duke University Press, 2019.

Mbembe, Achille. "Nicolas Sarkozy's Africa." Translated by Melissa Thackway. *Africultures*, August 7, 2007. http://africultures.com/nicolas-sarkozys-africa-6816/.

Mbembe, Achille. "On Palestine." In *Apartheid Israel: The Politics of an Analogy*, edited by Jon Soske and Sean Jacobs. Chicago: Haymarket Books, 2015.

McGowan, Todd. "The Bankruptcy Historicism: Introducing Disruption into Literary Studies." In *Everything You Always Wanted to Know about Literature but Were Afraid to Ask Žižek*, edited by Russell Sbriglia, 89–106. Durham: Duke University Press, 2017.
McGowan, Todd. "The Bedlam of the Lynch Mob: Racism and Enjoying Through the Other." In *Lacan and Race: Racism, Identity, and Psychoanalytic Theory*, edited by Sheldon George and Derek Hook, 19–34. New York: Routledge, 2022.
McGowan, Todd. *Universality and Identity Politics*. New York: Columbia University Press, 2020.
McKernan, Bethan. "Israeli Ministers Attend Conference Calling for 'Voluntary Migration' of Palestinians." *The Guardian*, January 29, 2024. https://www.theguardian.com/world/2024/jan/29/israeli-ministers-attend-conference-calling-for-voluntary-migration-of-palestinians.
McKittrick, Katherine, ed. *Sylvia Wynter: On Being Human as Praxis*. Durham: Duke University Press, 2015.
MEE Staff. "Bezalel Smotrich Calls for Israel's Borders to Extend to Damascus." *Middle East Eye*, October 11, 2024. https://www.middleeasteye.net/news/smotrich-calls-israels-borders-extend-damascus.
MEE Staff. "War On Gaza: Famine Threat Persists as Half a Million starving, Monitor Finds." *Middle East Eye*, June 25, 2024. https://www.middleeasteye.net/news/half-million-face-starvation-gaza-report-finds.
Meister, Robert. *After Evil: A Politics of Human Rights*. New York: Columbia University Press, 2010.
Mendilow, Jonathan. *Ideology, Party Change, and Electoral Campaigns in Israel, 1965–2001*. New York: SUNY Press, 2003.
Michaeli, Yarden. "The Israeli Left's Support for the Gaza War Serves the Interests of Netanyahu, Far-Right." *Haaretz*, January 24, 2024. https://www.haaretz.com/opinion/2024-01-24/ty-article-opinion/.premium/israels-center-left-is-still-serving-netanyahus-reign-by-not-collapsing-the-government/0000018d-3d03-dc44-a5bf-bdb703010000.
Mignolo, Walter D. *Local Histories/Global Designs: Coloniality, Subaltern Knowledges, and Border Thinking*. Durham: Duke University Press, 2012.
Mignolo, Walter D. "The Many Faces of Cosmo-polis: Border Thinking and Critical Cosmopolitanism." *Public Culture* 12, no. 3 (2000): 721–48.
Mignolo, Walter D. *The Politics of Decolonial Investigations*. Durham: Duke University Press, 2021.
Mignolo, Walter D. "Yes, We Can: Non-European Thinkers and Philosophers." *Al Jazeera*, February 19, 2013. http://www.aljazeera.com/indepth/opinion/2013/02/20132672747320891.html.
Mignolo, Walter D. and Wanda Nanibush. "Thinking and Engaging with the Decolonial: A Conversation between Walter D. Mignolo and Wanda Nanibush." *Afterall* (Spring/Summer, 2018): 24–9.
Mohanty, Chandra Talpade. *Feminism without Borders: Decolonizing Theory, Practicing Solidarity*. Durham: Duke University Press, 2003.
Montag, Warren. "The New McCarthyism: a Personal Testimony." *Verso Books*, March 6, 2024. https://www.versobooks.com/blogs/news/the-new-mccarthyism-a-personal-testimony.
Morgan, Michael L. *Levinas's Ethical Politics*. Bloomington: Indiana University Press, 2016.
Morrison, Toni. *Beloved*. New York: Vintage Books, 2004.

Moses, A. Dirk. "The German Catechism." *Geschichte der Gegenwart*, May 23, 2021. https://geschichtedergegenwart.ch/the-german-catechism/.

Moses, A. Dirk. "More than Genocide." *Boston Review*, November 14, 2023. https://www.bostonreview.net/articles/more-than-genocide/.

Moses, A. Dirk. *The Problems of Genocide: Permanent Security and the Language of Transgression*. New York: Cambridge University Press, 2021.

Moses, A. Dirk. "Stigma and Sacrifice in the Federal Republic of Germany." *History & Memory* 19, no. 2 (2007): 139–80.

Movement for Black Lives. "The BREATHE Act." https://breatheact.org/.

Mushtaha, Mahmoud. "Israel Ordered Thousands To 'Safe' Areas in Gaza City—Then Bombed Them." *+972 Magazine*, July 10, 2024. https://www.972mag.com/gaza-city-israeli-army-attacked-safe-areas/.

"N.A.A.C.P. Decries Stand Of Dr. King on Vietnam." *The New York Times*, April 11, 1967, 1, 17. https://timesmachine.nytimes.com/timesmachine/1967/04/11/83586963.html?pageNumber=1.

Nafar, Tamer. "If Our Eyes Can See the Huge Scope of Atrocity, Can Our Hearts Contain Two Pains at Once?" *Haaretz*, December 5. https://www.haaretz.com/opinion/2023-12-05/ty-article-opinion/.premium/with-no-shortage-of-enemies-only-palestinian-israeli-friendships-can-fix-this-miss/0000018c-3662-de12-a3af-3fefdb2e0000.

Nagesh, Ashitha. "What Exactly Is a 'Karen' and Where Did the Meme Come From?" *BBC News*, July 30, 2020. https://www.bbc.com/news/world-53588201.

Nassar, Tamara. "Palestinian Authority Forces Are Israel's Foot Soldiers." *The Electronic Intifada*, June 28, 2021. https://electronicintifada.net/blogs/tamara-nassar/palestinian-authority-forces-are-israels-foot-soldiers.

Nassar, Tamara. "Palestinians Mourn 'Heroic' Aaron Bushnell." *The Electronic Intifada*, February 27, 2024. https://electronicintifada.net/blogs/tamara-nassar/palestinians-mourn-heroic-aaron-bushnell.

Nechin, Etan. "Why Judith Butler Calling Hamas' Slaughter 'Armed Resistance' Is So Depressing." *Haaretz*, March 7, 2024. https://www.haaretz.com/opinion/2024-03-07/ty-article-opinion/.premium/why-judith-butler-calling-hamas-slaughter-armed-resistance-is-so-depressing/0000018e-18a9-d1cc-abfe-dfad4cd90000.

Neiman, Susan. "Fanon the Universalist." *The New York Review*, June 6, 2024. https://www.nybooks.com/articles/2024/06/06/fanon-the-universalist-the-rebels-clinic-shatz/.

Neiman, Susan. "Historical Reckoning Gone Haywire." *The New York Review*, October 19, 2023. https://www.nybooks.com/articles/2023/10/19/historical-reckoning-gone-haywire-germany-susan-neiman/.

Nelson, Cary. "'We Can Have a Debate About Whether Hamas Did the Right Thing': Judith Butler's Moral Relativism." *Fathom*, March, 2024. https://fathomjournal.org/we-can-have-a-debate-about-whether-hamas-did-the-right-thing-judith-butlers-moral-relativism/.

Newton, Huey P. *Revolutionary Suicide*. New York: Penguin Books, 1973.

Newton, Huey P. *To Die For The People*. New York: Vintage Books, 1972.

NPR. "Netanyahu's References to Violent Biblical Passages Raise Alarm Among Critics." *Morning Edition*, November 7, 2023. https://www.npr.org/2023/11/07/1211133201/netanyahus-references-to-violent-biblical-passages-raise-alarm-among-critics.

Pappé, Ilan. *The Ethnic Cleansing of Palestine*. Oxford: Oneworld, 2006.

Pappé, Ilan. "Israel's Incremental Genocide in the Gaza Ghetto." *The Electronic Intifada*, July 13, 2014. https://electronicintifada.net/content/israels-incremental-genocide-gaza-ghetto/13562.

Peled, Roy. "Judith Butler is Intentionally Giving Hamas' Terror Legitimacy." *Forward*, March 8, 2024. https://forward.com/opinion/590612/judith-butler-hamas-terror/.

Peled-Elhanan, Nurit. *Palestine in Israeli School Books: Ideology and Propaganda in Education*. New York: I.B. Tauris, 2012.

Penney, James. "Passing into the Universal: Fanon, Sartre, and the Colonial Dialectic." *Paragraph* 27, no. 3 (2004): 49–67.

Peruchon, Léa. "'The Livestream Was Critical Evidence': Tracing Attacks on Gaza's Press Buildings." *+972 Magazine*, June 26, 2024. https://www.972mag.com/gaza-press-attacks-israeli-army/.

"Philosophy for Palestine," November 1, 2023. https://sites.google.com/view/philosophyforpalestine/home.

Pinkas, Alon. "A Short History of 'F**k Him': How Netanyahu Enraged U.S. Presidents, From Clinton to Trump." *Haaretz*, December 13, 2021. https://www.haaretz.com/israel-news/2021-12-13/ty-article/.highlight/a-short-history-of-f-k-him-how-the-trump-netanyahu-affair-unraveled/0000017f-e97b-d62c-a1ff-fd7b5e020000.

Plumelle-Uribe, Rosa Amelia. *White Ferocity: The Genocides of Non-Whites and Non-Aryans from 1492 to Date*. Translated by Virginia Popper. Dakar: CODESRIA, 2020.

Pluth, Ed. "Psychoanalysis, Science, and Worldviews." *Crisis & Critique* 5, no. 1 (2018): 326–38.

Polgreen, Lydia. "Restoring the Past Won't Liberate Palestine." *The New York Times*, February 18, 2024. https://www.nytimes.com/2024/02/18/opinion/israel-gaza-palestine-decolonization.html.

Portevin, Catherine. "Patrick Chamoiseau: 'L'individu doit se fabriquer autour de l'absence." *Philosophie Magazine*, March 22, 2017. https://www.philomag.com/articles/patrick-chamoiseau-lindividu-doit-se-fabriquer-autour-de-labsence.

Posnock, Ross. "How It Feels to Be a Problem: Du Bois, Fanon, and the 'Impossible Life' of the Black Intellectual." *Critical Inquiry* 23 (1997): 323–49.

Primack, Dan. "Israel Says It Will Block United Nations Visa Requests." *Axios*, December 26, 2023. https://www.axios.com/2023/12/25/israel-un-visa-requests-block.

The Pro-Human Camp. "Resist the Dehumanization of Palestinians and Israelis," December 13, 2023. https://www.amnesty.org.il/2023/12/13/%D7%9E%D7%9B%D7%AA%D7%91-%D7%A4%D7%AA%D7%95%D7%97-%D7%94%D7%9E%D7%97%D7%A0%D7%94-%D7%94%D7%A4%D7%A8%D7%95-%D7%90%D7%A0%D7%95%D7%A9%D7%99/.

Puar, Jasbir. *The Right to Maim: Debility, Capacity, Disability*. Durham: Duke University Press, 2017.

Qabaha, Ahmad and Bilal Hamamra. "The Nakba Continues: The Palestinian Crisis from the Past to the Present." *Janus Unbound* 1, no. 1 (2021): 30–42.

Rancière, Jacques. *Disagreement: Politics and Philosophy*. Translated by Julie Rose. Minneapolis: University of Minnesota Press, 1999.

Rancière, Jacques. "Who is the Subject of the Rights of Man?" *The South Atlantic Quarterly* 103, no. 2 (2004): 297–310.

The Red Nation. "Indigenous Solidarity with Palestine." *The Red Nation*, October 26, 2023. https://therednation.org/statement-of-indigenous-solidarity-with-palestine/.

Renault, Matthieu. "Le genre de la race: Fanon, lecteur de Beauvoir." *Actuel Marx*, no. 55 (2014): 36–48.

Reuters. "Florida Introduces New Guidelines on Teaching Black History, Critics Give Poor Grade." *Reuters*, July 20, 2023. https://www.reuters.com/world/us/florida-introduces-new-guidelines-teaching-black-history-critics-give-poor-grade-2023-07-20/.

Robinson, William I. and Hoai-An Nguyen. "Gaza: A Ghastly Window into the Crisis of Global Capitalism." *The Philosophical Salon*, January 15, 2024. https://thephilosophicalsalon.com/gaza-a-ghastly-window-into-the-crisis-of-global-capitalism/.

Rojas, Rick, Neelam Bohra, and Eliza Fawcett, "What We Know About Tyre Nichols's Lethal Encounter With Memphis Police." *The New York Times*, February 12, 2023. https://www.nytimes.com/article/tyre-nichols-memphis-police-dead.html.

Rosane, Olivia. "'Is This a Joke?': Tlaib Blasts Blinken for Geneva Convention Remarks Amid Gaza Carnage." *Common Dreams*, August 13, 2024. https://www.commondreams.org/news/tlaib-blinken-gaza.

Rose, Jacqueline. *The Question of Zion*. Princeton: Princeton University Press, 2005.

Roth, Kenneth. "The ICJ Has Demolished Israel's Claims That It Is Not Occupying Palestinian Territories." *The Guardian*, July 22, 2024. https://www.theguardian.com/commentisfree/article/2024/jul/22/the-icj-has-demolished-israels-claims-that-it-is-not-occupying-palestinian-territories.

Rothberg, Michael. "Lived Multidirectionality: '*Historikerstreit 2.0*' and the Politics of Holocaust Memory." *Memory Studies* 15, no. 6 (2022): 1316–29.

Rothberg, Michael. *Multidirectional Memory: Remembering the Holocaust in the Age of Decolonization*. Stanford: Stanford University Press, 2009.

Rothberg, Michael. "We Need to Re-Center the New Historikerstreit." *DIE ZEIT*. July 21, 2021. https://www.zeit.de/kultur/2021-07/dealing-with-the-holocaust-historikerstreit-controversy-genocide-english.

Rothberg, Michael and Jürgen Zimmerer. "Enttabuisiert den Vergleich!" *DIE ZEIT*, no. 14, March 31, 2021. https://www.zeit.de/2021/14/erinnerungskultur-gedenken-pluralisieren-holocaust-vergleich-globalisierung-geschichte?utm_referrer=https%3A%2F%2Fwww.google.com%2F.

Roy, Sara. "Econocide in Gaza." In *Deluge: Gaza and Israel From Crisis to Cataclysm*, edited by Jamie Stern-Weiner, 37–55. New York: OR Books, 2024.

Rudoren, Jodi. "Netanyahu Denounced for Saying Palestinian Inspired Holocaust." *The New York Times*, October 21, 2015. https://www.nytimes.com/2015/10/22/world/middleeast/netanyahu-saying-palestinian-mufti-inspired-holocaust-draws-broad-criticism.html.

Ruebner, Josh. "'Die, Son of a Whore!' 'Give Him One in the Head.' This is What It Sounds Like When Israeli Security Kills Palestinian Kids." *Salon*, October 19, 2015. https://www.salon.com/2015/10/19/die_son_of_a_whore_give_him_one_in_the_head_this_is_what_it_sounds_like_when_israeli_security_kills_palestinian_kids/.

Ruti, Mari. "Creativity Between Anxiety and Aliveness." *Sublation Magazine*, June 17, 2023. https://www.sublationmag.com/post/creativity-between-anxiety-and-aliveness.

Ryan, Josiah. "'This Was a Whitelash': Van Jones' Take on the Election Results." *CNN*, November 9, 2016. https://www.cnn.com/2016/11/09/politics/van-jones-results-disappointment-cnntv/index.html.

Saba, Dylan. "A Surge in Suppression: It's Never Been This Bad." *N+1*, October 23, 2023. https://www.nplusonemag.com/online-only/online-only/a-surge-in-suppression/.

Sacco, Joe. "The War on Gaza—1-26-24." *The Comics Journal*, January 26, 2024. https://www.tcj.com/the-war-on-gaza-1-26-24/.

Sacco, Joe. "The War on Gaza—6-25-24." *The Comics Journal*, June 25, 2024. https://www.tcj.com/the-war-on-gaza-6-25-24/.

Said, Edward. *After the Last Sky: Palestinian Lives*, with photographs by Jean Mohr. New York: Pantheon, 1986.

Said, Edward. "Apocalypse Now." *Index on Censorship* 29, no. 5 (2000): 49–53.

Said, Edward. *Culture and Imperialism*. New York: Vintage, 1994.
Said, Edward. "The Gap Grows Wider." *Al-Ahram Weekly* 471 (March 2–8, 2000).
Said, Edward. "The Morning After." *The London Review of Books* 15, no. 20 (October 21, 1993). https://www.lrb.co.uk/the-paper/v15/n20/edward-said/the-morning-after.
Said, Edward. "My Right of Return." In *Power, Politics, and Culture: Interviews with Edward W. Said*, edited by Gauri Viswanathan, 443–58. New York: Vintage, 2001.
Said, Edward. "The One-State Solution." *The New York Times Magazine*, January 10, 1999. https://www.nytimes.com/1999/01/10/magazine/the-one-state-solution.html.
Said, Edward. *Orientalism*, 25th anniversary edition. New York: Vintage, 2003.
Said, Edward. "Permission to Narrate." *Journal of Palestine Studies* 13, no. 3 (1984): 27–48.
Said, Edward. *The Politics of Dispossession: The Struggle for Palestinian Self-Determination 1969–1994*. New York: Vintage, 1994.
Said, Edward. *The Question of Palestine.* New York: Vintage Books, 1992.
Said, Edward. *Reflections on Exile and Other Essays*. Cambridge, MA: Harvard University Press, 2000.
Said, Edward. *Representations of the Intellectual: The 1993 Reith Lectures*. New York: Vintage Books, 1996.
Said, Edward. "Zionism from the Standpoint of Its Victims." *Social Text* 1 (1979): 7–58.
Salvatori, Paul. "Q&A: 'What Happened in Israel on October 7 Was a Slave Revolt.'" *TRT World*, October 12, 2023. https://headtopics.com/us/q-a-what-happened-in-israel-on-october-7-was-a-slave-revolt-46588280.
Sammon, Alexander. "Biden Has a Youth-Vote Problem. His Israel Policy Is Making It Worse." *Slate*, October 24, 2023. https://slate.com/news-and-politics/2023/10/biden-polling-israel-palestine-gaza-hamas-war-youth.html.
Sanger, David E. and Peter Baker. "Biden Is 'Outraged.' But Is He Willing to Use America's Leverage With Israel?" *The New York Times*, April 3, 2024. https://www.nytimes.com/2024/04/03/us/politics/biden-israel-gaza.html.
Santner, Eric L. "Miracles Happen: Benjamin, Rosenzweig, Freud, and the Matter of the Neighbor." In *The Neighbor: Three Inquiries in Political Theology*, with a New Preface, edited by Slavoj Žižek, Eric L. Santner, and Kenneth Reinhard, 76–133. Chicago: University of Chicago Press, 2013.
Santos, Boaventura de Sousa. "Epistemologies of the South and the Future." *From the European South* 1 (2016): 17–29.
Sartre, Jean-Paul. *Being and Nothingness*. Translated by Hazel E. Barnes. New York: Philosophical Library, 1956.
Sartre, Jean-Paul. "Preface." In *The Wretched of the Earth*, translated by Richard Philcox, xliii–lxii. New York: Grove Press, 2004.
Sayegh, Fayez. *Zionist Colonization in Palestine*. Beirut: Research Center, Palestine Liberation Organization, 1965.
Sazzad, Rehnuma. *Edward Said's Concept of Exile: Identity and Cultural Migration in the Middle East*. New York: I.B.Tauris & Co. Ltd., 2017.
Scahill, Jeremy. "Netanyahu's War on Truth: Israel's Ruthless Propaganda Campaign to Dehumanize Palestinians." *The Intercept*, February 7, 2024. https://theintercept.com/2024/02/07/gaza-israel-netanyahu-propaganda-lies-palestinians/.
Schwarz, Alon. "How to Cover Up a Massacre." *Haaretz*, August 12, 2022. https://www.haaretz.com/israel-news/2022-08-12/ty-article-magazine/how-to-cover-up-a-massacre/00000182-9271-d9bc-affb-f3ff387f0000.

Scott, David. "Preface: Soul Captives are Free." *Small Axe* 11, no. 2 (2007): v–x.
Sebald, W. G. "Against the Irreversible. On Jean Améry." In *On the Natural History of Destruction*, 143–67. Toronto: Alfred A. Knopf, 2003.
Segal, Raz. "A Textbook Case of Genocide." *Jewish Currents*, October 13, 2023. https://jewishcurrents.org/a-textbook-case-of-genocide.
Seidel, Timothy. "'Occupied Territory Is Occupied Territory': James Baldwin, Palestine and the Possibilities of Transnational Solidarity." *Third World Quarterly* 37, no. 9 (2016): 1644–60.
Sekyi-Out, Ato. "Dialectics in Dispute, with Aristotle as Witness." In *Violence, Slavery and Freedom between Hegel and Fanon*, edited by Ulrike Kistner and Philippe Van Hauteix, 1–24. Johannesburg: Wits University Press, 2020.
Sekyi-Out, Ato. *Fanon's Dialectic of Experience*. Cambridge, MA: Harvard University Press, 1996.
Sekyi-Out, Ato. *Homestead, Homeland, Home: Critical Reflections*. Ottawa: Dajara Press, 2023.
Sen, Somdeep. "There is Nothing Surprising About Hamas's Operation." *Al Jazeera*, October 8, 2023. https://www.aljazeera.com/opinions/2023/10/8/there-is-nothing-surprising-about-hamass-operation.
Sexton, Jared. "Affirmation in the Dark: Racial Slavery and Philosophical Pessimism." *The Comparatist* 43 (2019): 90–111.
Sexton, Jared. "African American Studies." In *A Concise Companion to American Studies*, edited by John Carlos Rowe, 210–28. Malden: Wiley-Blackwell, 2010.
Sexton, Jared. "The Social Life of Social Death: On Afro-Pessimism and Black Optimism." *In Tensions* 5 (2011): 1–47.
Sexton, Jared. "Unbearable Blackness." *Cultural Critique* 90 (2015): 159–78.
Sexton, Jared and Daniel Colucciello Barber. "On Black Negativity, or the Affirmation of Nothing." *Society and Space*, September 18, 2017. https://www.societyandspace.org/articles/on-black-negativity-or-the-affirmation-of-nothing.
Shafer, Ellise. "Joaquin Phoenix, Elliott Gould, Chloe Fineman and More Jewish Creatives Support Jonathan Glazer's Oscars Speech in Open Letter." *Variety*, April 5, 2024. https://variety.com/2024/film/global/jonathan-glazer-oscars-speech-support-jewish-creatives-open-letter-1235960158/.
Sharpe, Christina. "Black Studies: In the Wake." *The Black Scholar* 44, no. 2 (2014): 59–69.
Sharpe, Christina. *In the Wake: On Blackness and Being*. Durham: Duke University Press, 2016.
Shatz, Adam. "Israel's Descent." *London Review of Books*, June 20, 2024. https://www.lrb.co.uk/the-paper/v46/n12/adam-shatz/israel-s-descent.
Shatz, Adam. *The Rebel's Clinic: The Revolutionary Lives of Frantz Fanon*. New York: Farrar, Straus and Giroux, 2024.
Sheehi, Lara and Stephen Sheehi. *Psychoanalysis Under Occupation: Practicing Resistance in Palestine*. New York: Routledge, 2022.
Shoard, Catherine. "Jonathan Glazer: More than 450 Jewish Creatives Denounce Oscars Speech in Open Letter." *The Guardian*, March 19. https://www.theguardian.com/film/2024/mar/19/jonathan-glazer-more-than-450-jewish-creatives-denounce-oscars-speech-in-open-letter-zone-of-interest.
Shohat, Ella. "Sephardim in Israel: Zionism from the Standpoint of Its Jewish Victims." *Social Text* 19/20 (Fall 1988): 1–35.
Siddiqui, Usaid. "Israel's War on Gaza Updates: UN to Add Israeli Army to Child Harm List." *Al Jazeera*, June 7, 2024. https://www.aljazeera.com/news/liveblog/2024/6/7/israels-war-on-gaza-live-hospital-barely-coping-with-dead-and-wounded.

Simek, Nicole. *Alchemies of Blood and Afro-Diasporic Fiction: Race, Kinship, and the Passion for Ontology*. New York: Bloomsbury, 2024.

Singh, Kanishka. "US Criticizes ICJ Opinion on Israeli Occupation of Palestinian Territories." *Reuters*, July 20, 2024. https://www.reuters.com/world/us-criticizes-icj-opinion-israeli-occupation-palestinian-territories-2024-07-20/.

Skinner, Jordan. "Thought is the Courage of Hopelessness: An Interview with Philosopher Giorgio Agamben." Interview by Jordan Skinner. *Verso Books*, June 17, 2014. https://www.versobooks.com/blogs/1612-thought-is-the-courage-of-hopelessness-an-interview-with-philosopher-giorgio-agamben.

Smerconish, Michael. *CNN Transcripts*, May 11, 2024. https://transcripts.cnn.com/show/smer/date/2024-05-11/segment/01.

Smith, Mitch and Tim Arango. "'We Need Policemen': Even in Liberal Cities, Voters Reject Scaled-Back Policing." *The New York Times*, November 3, 2021. https://www.nytimes.com/2021/11/03/us/police-reform-minneapolis-election.html.

Spaulding, Daniel. "On Hating Students." *e-flux*, May 28, 2024. https://www.e-flux.com/education/features/610182/on-hating-students.

Speri, Alice. "Israel Responds to Hamas Crimes by Ordering Mass War Crimes in Gaza." *The Intercept*, October 9, 2023. https://theintercept.com/2023/10/09/israel-hamas-war-crimes-palestinians/.

Spillers, Hortense J. "Mama's Baby, Papa's Maybe: An American Grammar Book." *Diacritics* 17, no. 2 (1987): 64–81.

Spivak, Chakravorty Gayatri. *Critique of Postcolonial Reason: Toward A History of the Vanishing Present*. Cambridge, MA: Harvard University Press, 1999.

Spivak, Chakravorty Gayatri. *Outside the Teaching Machine*. New York: Routledge, 1993.

Spivak, Chakravorty Gayatri. *The Post-Colonial Critic: Interviews, Strategies, Dialogues*. Edited by Sarah Harasym. New York: Routledge, 1990.

Standing Together. "Where There is Struggle There is HOPE." https://www.standing-together.org/en.

Stawarska, Beata. "Struggle and Violence: Entering the Dialectic with Frantz Fanon and Simone de Beauvoir." In *Violence, Slavery and Freedom between Hegel and Fanon*, edited by Ulrike Kistner and Philippe Van Hauteix, 93–115. Johannesburg: Wits University Press, 2020.

Stockman, Farah. "What Happens When Palestinians Tell Their Stories Directly to the World?" *The New York Times*, November 12, 2023. https://www.nytimes.com/2023/11/12/opinion/gaza-family-killed-war.html.

Strub, Whitney. "Palestine Is the Single Most Urgent Free Speech Crisis in the U.S. Today." *Mondoweiss*, November 12, 2023. https://mondoweiss.net/2023/11/palestine-is-the-single-most-urgent-free-speech-crisis-in-the-u-s-today/.

Sullivan, Shannon. "White Priority." *Critical Philosophy of Race* 5, no. 2 (2017): 171–82.

Syal, Rajeev, Dan Sabbagh, and Kiran Stacey. "Suella Braverman Calls Pro-Palestine Demos 'Hate Marches.'" *The Guardian*, October 30. https://www.theguardian.com/politics/2023/oct/30/uk-ministers-cobra-meeting-terrorism-threat-israel-hamas-conflict-suella-braverman.

Táíwò, Olúfẹ́mi O. *Against Decolonisation: Taking African Agency Seriously*. London: C. Hurst & Company, 2022.

Taylor, Charles. "The Politics of Recognition." In *Multiculturalism: Examining the Politics of Recognition*, edited by Amy Gutmann, 25–74. Princeton: Princeton University Press, 1994.

Taylor, Keeanga-Yamahtta. "The Enduring Power of 'Scenes of Subjection.'" *The New Yorker*, October 17, 2022. https://www.newyorker.com/books/second-read/the-enduring-power-of-scenes-of-subjection-saidiya-hartman.

Taylor, Keeanga-Yamahtta. "Forward" to Hartman's 2022 edition of *Scenes of Subjection*. xiii–xxviii. New York: W.W. Norton & Co, 2022.

Taylor, Keeanga-Yamahtta. *From #BlackLivesMatter to Black Liberation*. Chicago: Haymarket Books, 2016.

Thobani, Sunera. "Empire, Bare Life and the Constitution of Whiteness: Sovereignty in the Age of Terror." *Borderlands* 11, no. 1 (May 2012): 1–30.

Thomas, Greg. "Afro-Blue Notes: The Death of Afro-Pessimism (2.0)?" *Theory & Event* 21, no. 1 (2018): 282–317.

Thomas, Greg. "PROUD FLESH Inter/Views: Sylvia Wynter." *ProudFlesh: New Afrikan Journal of Culture, Politics, and Consciousness* 4 (2006): 1–35.

Tondo, Lorenzo and Quique Kierszenbaum. "'Solidarity over Hatred': The Small Band of Israelis Stopping Settlers Obstructing Aid Trucks." *The Guardian*, May 31, 2024. https://www.theguardian.com/world/article/2024/may/31/solidarity-over-hatred-the-small-band-of-israelis-stopping-settlers-obstructing-aid-trucks.

Too Black. "Unburdened by Palestine: Shedding Black Liberalism for Anti-imperialism." *Mondoweiss*, August 22, 2024. https://mondoweiss.net/2024/08/unburdened-by-palestine-shedding-black-liberalism-for-anti-imperialism/.

Tuck, Eve and K. Wayne Yang. "Decolonization Is Not a Metaphor." *Decolonization: Indigeneity, Education, and Society* 1, no. 1 (2012): 1–40.

Turki, Fawas. *The Disinherited: Journal of a Palestinian Exile, With an Epilogue 1974*. New York: Monthly Review Press, 1974.

Turki, Fawas. "Meaning in Palestinian History: Text and Context." *Arab Studies Quarterly* 3, no. 4 (1981): 371–83.

"Ukrainian Letter of Solidarity with Palestinian people." *Commons*, November 2, 2023. https://commons.com.ua/en/ukrayinskij-list-solidarnosti/.

The United Nations, "Demand for Ceasefire in Gaza Report of the Secretary-General." *The United Nations*, January 30, 2025. https://www.un.org/unispal/document/demand-for-ceasefire-in-gaza-needs-assessment-for-gaza-humanitarian-and-socioeconomic-impact-of-gaza-war-un-response-secretary-general-report-a-79-739/.

The United Nations Human Rights Office. "Detention in the Context of the Escalation of Hostilities in Gaza." The United Nations Human Rights, July 31, 2024. https://www.ohchr.org/en/documents/reports/detention-context-escalation-hostilities-gaza.

Upfront. "Angela Davis: 'Palestine is a Moral Litmus Test for the World.'" *Al Jazeera*, October 27, 2023. https://www.aljazeera.com/program/upfront/2023/10/27/angela-davis-palestine-is-a-moral-litmus-test-for-the-world.

U.S. Department of Defense. "Secretary of Defense Lloyd J. Austin III Joint Press Conference With Israeli Defense Minister Yoav Gallant in Tel Aviv, Israel." *Transcript*, December 18, 2023. https://www.defense.gov/News/Transcripts/Transcript/Article/3621107/secretary-of-defense-lloyd-j-austin-iii-joint-press-conference-with-israeli-def/.

Vance, JD *Hillbilly Elegy*. New York: HarperCollins Publishers, 2016.

Varoufakis, Yanis. "The Speech That Got Me Banned From Germany." *Jacobin*, April 13, 2024. https://jacobin.com/2024/04/yanis-varoufakis-germany-banned-palestine-gaza?mc_cid=d49beb4b8d&mc_eid=0317ccf9ee.

Veracini, Lorenzo. *The Settler Colonial Present*. New York: Palgrave Macmillan, 2015.

Vergès, Françoise. "Chains of Madness, Chains of Colonialism: Fanon and Freedom." In *The Fact of Blackness: Frantz Fanon and Visual Representation*, edited by Alan Read, 46–75. Seattle: Bay Press, 1996.

Vogt, Erik. "Žižek and Fanon: On Violence and Related Matters." In *Žižek Now: Cultural Perspectives in Žižek Studies*, edited by Jamil Khader and Molly Anne Rothenberg, 140–58. Cambridge: Polity Press, 2013.
Warren, Calvin L. "The Karen Call: Emergency, Destiny, and Surveillance." *Critical Philosophy of Race* 10, no. 2 (2022): 141–57.
Warren, Calvin L. *Ontological Terror: Blackness, Nihilism, and Emancipation*. Durham: Duke University Press, 2018.
Warschawski, Michel. *Toward an Open Tomb: The Crisis of Israeli Society*. Translated by Peter Drucker. New York: Monthly Review Press, 2004.
Warschawski, Michel. "We Have Gone Beyond War Crimes in Gaza." *Verso Books*, November 6, 2023. https://www.versobooks.com/blogs/news/michel-warschawski-we-have-gone-beyond-war-crimes-in-gaza.
Waziyatawin. "Malice Enough in their Hearts and Courage Enough in Ours: Reflections on US Indigenous and Palestinian Experiences under Occupation." *Settler Colonial Studies* 2, no. 1 (2012): 172–89.
Weheliye, Alexander. *Habeas Viscus: Racializing Assemblages, Biopolitics, and Black Feminist Theories of the Human*. Durham: Duke University Press, 2014.
Weill, Nicolas. "Levinas trahi? La réponse de Judith Butler." *Le Monde*, March 21, 2013. https://www.lemonde.fr/idees/article/2013/03/21/levinas-trahi-la-reponse-de-judith-butler_5994702_3232.html.
West, Cornel. "Truth." In *Examined Life: Excursions with Contemporary Thinkers*, edited by Astra Taylor, 1–24. New York: The New Press, 2009.
Westfall, Sammy and Joe Snell. "Netanyahu's History of Clashing With U.S. Presidents Spans Decades." *The Washington Post*, July 24, 2024.
Wilderson, Frank B. III. *Afropessimism*. New York: Liveright, 2020.
Wilderson, Frank B. III. "Afro-Pessimism and the End of Redemption." *Humanities Futures. Franklin Humanities Institute: Duke University*, October 20, 2015. https://humanitiesfutures.org/papers/afro-pessimism-end-redemption/.
Wilderson, Frank B. III. "Biko and the Problematic of Presence." In *Biko Lives! Contesting the Legacies of Steve Biko*, edited by Andile Mngxitama, Amanda Alexander, and Nigel C. Gibson, 95–114. New York: Palgrave, 2008.
Wilderson, Frank B. III. "Gramsci's Black Marx: Whither the Slave in Civil Society?" *Social Identities* 9, no. 2 (2003): 225–40.
Wilderson, Frank B. III. *Red, White & Black: Cinema and the Structure of U.S. Antagonisms*. Durham: Duke University Press, 2010.
Wolfe, Patrick. "Recuperating Binarism: A Heretical Introduction." *Settler Colonial Studies* 3, no. 3–4 (2013):257–79.
Wolfe, Patrick. "Settler Colonialism and the Elimination of the Native." *Journal of Genocide Research* 8, no. 4 (2006): 387–409.
Wynter, Sylvia. "A Black Studies Manifesto." *Forum N.H.I. Knowledge for the 21st Century* 1, no. 1 (1994): 3–11.
Wynter, Sylvia. "No Humans Involved: An Open Letter to My Colleagues." *Forum N.H.I. Knowledge for the 21st Century* 1, no. 1 (1994): 42–73.
Wynter, Sylvia. "Unsettling the Coloniality of Being/Power/Truth/Freedom: Towards the Human, After Man, Its Overrepresentation—An Argument." *CR: The New Centennial Review* 3, no. 3 (2003): 257–337.
Yancy, George. "Afropessimism Forces Us to Rethink Our Most Basic Assumptions About Society." *Truthhout*, September 14, 2022. https://truthout.org/articles/afropessimism-forces-us-to-rethink-our-most-basic-assumptions-about-society/.

Yancy, George. *Black Bodies, White Gazes: The Continuing Significance of Race in America*. Lanham: Rowman & Littlefield, 2017.

Young, Robert J. C. "Frantz Fanon and Hannah Arendt: Anger and Racism." *The Comparatist* 48 (2024): 164–76.

Zalloua, Zahi. *Being Posthuman: Ontologies of the Future*. New York: Bloomsbury, 2021.

Zalloua, Zahi. *Continental Philosophy and the Palestinian Question: Beyond the Jew and the Greek*. New York: Bloomsbury 2017.

Zalloua, Zahi. "The Left and (New) Antisemitism: The Palestinian Question and the Politics of *Ressentiment*." *Crisis and Critique* 9, no. 2 (2022): 390–413.

Zalloua, Zahi. *The Politics of the Wretched: Race, Reason, and Ressentiment*. New York: Bloomsbury, 2024.

Zalloua, Zahi. *Solidarity and the Palestinian Cause: Indigeneity, Blackness, and the Promise of Universality*. New York: Bloomsbury, 2023.

Zalloua, Zahi. *Žižek on Race: Toward an Anti-Racist Future*, with Preface by Slavoj Žižek. New York: Bloomsbury, 2020.

Zeavin, Hannah. "Diagnosing Resistance: What Aaron Bushnell's Death Says About Power, Protest, and Pathology." *Bookforum*, Spring 2024. https://www.bookforum.com/print/3004/what-aaron-bushnell-s-death-says-about-power-protest-and-pathology-25343.

Zenun Almada, Flavio. "The Particular Lived Experience of the Black in Portugal." In *Fanon Today: Reason and Revolt of The Wretched of the Earth*, edited by Nigel Gibson, 27–49. Québec: Daraja Press, 2021.

Zhang, Sharon. "Israel 'Systematically' Uses Gaza Children as Human Shields, Rights Group Finds." *Truthout*, August 21, 2024. https://truthout.org/articles/israel-systematically-uses-gaza-children-as-human-shields-rights-group-finds/.

Zirin, Dave. "The Left Is Not 'Anti-Jewish.'" *The Nation*, November 6, 2023. https://www.thenation.com/article/world/jewish-left-israel-protests/.

Ziv, Oren. "'I'm Bored, So I Shoot': The Israeli Army's Approval of Free-For-All Violence in Gaza." *+972 Magazine*, July 8, 2024. https://www.972mag.com/israeli-soldiers-gaza-firing-regulations/.

Ziv, Oren. "A Riot for Impunity Shows Israel's Proud Embrace of Its Crimes." *+972 Magazine*, August 1, 2024. https://www.972mag.com/sde-teiman-beit-lid-protests-detainees/.

Žižek, Slavoj. *Absolute Recoil: Towards a New Foundation of Dialectical Materialism*. New York: Verso, 2014.

Žižek, Slavoj. "Afterword: Objects, Objects Everywhere." In *Slavoj Žižek and Dialectical Materialism*, edited by Agon Hamza and Frank Ruda, 177–92. New York: Palgrave Macmillan, 2016.

Žižek, Slavoj. "Afterword: With Defenders Like These, Who Needs Attackers?" In *The Truth of Žižek*, edited by Paul Bowman and Richard Stamp, 197–255. New York: Continuum, 2007.

Žižek, Slavoj. *Against the Double Blackmail: Refugees, Terror and Other Troubles with the Neighbours*. London: Penguin Random House, 2016.

Žižek, Slavoj. "Against the Game of Total War." *Substack: Žižek Goads and Prods*, August 10, 2024. https://slavoj.substack.com/p/against-the-game-of-total-war?utm_source=publication-search.

Žižek, Slavoj. "Anti-Semitism and Its Transformations." In *Deconstructing Zionism: A Critique of Political Metaphysics*, edited by Gianni Vattimo and Michael Marder, 1–13. New York: Bloomsbury, 2014.

Žižek, Slavoj. "Assange Is Free, But Are We?" *Project Syndicate*, June 27, 2024. https://www.project-syndicate.org/commentary/julian-assange-freed-but-media-still-carrying-water-for-the-powerful-by-slavoj-zizek-2024-06.

Žižek, Slavoj. "Change Things So That Nothing Will Really Change!" *Substack: Žižek Goads and Prods*, July 6, 2024. https://slavoj.substack.com/p/change-things-so-that-nothing-will.

Žižek, Slavoj. *Christian Atheism: How to Be a Real Materialist*. New York: Bloomsbury, 2024.

Žižek, Slavoj. "Class Struggle Against Classism." *The Philosophical Salon*, May 10, 2023. https://thephilosophicalsalon.com/class-struggle-against-classism/.

Žižek, Slavoj. "Class Struggle or Postmodernism? Yes, Please!" In *Contingency, Hegemony, Universality: Contemporary Dialogues on the Left*, edited by Judith Butler, Ernesto Laclau, and Slavoj Žižek, 90–135. New York: Verso, 2000.

Žižek, Slavoj. *The Courage of Hopelessness: Chronicles of a Year of Acting Dangerously*. New York: Allen Lane, 2017.

Žižek, Slavoj. *Demanding the Impossible*. Edited by Yong-June Park. Cambridge: Polity Press, 2013.

Žižek, Slavoj. *Disparities*. New York: Bloomsbury, 2016.

Žižek, Slavoj. "Disputations: Who Are You Calling Anti-Semitic?" *The New Republic*, January 6, 2009. https://newrepublic.com/article/62376/disputations-who-are-you-calling-anti-semitic.

Žižek, Slavoj. *Event: Philosophy in Transit*. London: Penguin Books, 2014.

Žižek, Slavoj. *First As Tragedy, Then As Farce*. New York: Verso, 2009.

Žižek, Slavoj. *For They Know Not What They Do*. New York: Verso, 2008.

Žižek, Slavoj. "Forward: The Importance of Theory." In *Žižek on Race: Toward an Antiracist Future*, by Zahi Zalloua, x–xiii. New York: Bloomsbury, 2020.

Žižek, Slavoj. *The Fragile Absolute, or, Why Is the Christian Legacy Worth Fighting For?* New York: Verso, 2000.

Žižek, Slavoj. *Freedom: A Disease Without Cure*. New York: Bloomsbury, 2023.

Žižek, Slavoj. *Heaven in Disorder*. New York: OR Books, 2021.

Žižek, Slavoj. "Hegel: The Spirit of Distrust." In *Reading Hegel*, edited by Slavoj Žižek, Frank Ruda, and Agon Hamza, 13–100. Cambridge: Polity Press, 2022.

Žižek, Slavoj. "Holding the Place." In *Contingency, Hegemony, Universality: Contemporary Dialogues on the Left*, edited by Judith Butler, Ernesto Laclau, and Slavoj Žižek, 308–29, New York: Verso, 2000.

Žižek, Slavoj. "How to Begin from the Beginning." *New Left Review* 57 (2009): 43–55.

Žižek, Slavoj. *How to Read Lacan*. New York: Norton, 2006.

Žižek, Slavoj. "Human Rights and Its Discontents." Lecture at Bard College, November 15, 1999. http://www.lacan.com/zizek-human.htm.

Žižek, Slavoj. *In Defense of Lost Causes*. New York: Verso, 2008.

Žižek, Slavoj. "Introduction: Cogito as a Shibboleth." In *Cogito and the Unconscious*, edited by Slavoj Žižek, 1–8. Durham: Duke University Press, 1998.

Žižek, Slavoj. "The Jacobin Spirit." *Jacobin*, May 26, 2011. https://jacobin.com/2011/05/the-jacobin-spirit.

Žižek, Slavoj. "Jews Between Assimilation and Zionism." *Substack: Žižek Goads and Prods*, April 27, 2024. https://slavoj.substack.com/p/jewsbetween-assimilationism-and/comments.

Žižek, "Language, Violence and Non-Violence," *International Journal of Žižek Studies* 2, no. 3 (2008): 1–12.

Žižek, Slavoj. *A Left That Dares to Speak Its Name*. Cambridge: Polity Press, 2020.

Žižek, Slavoj. "A Leftist Plea for 'Eurocentrism.'" *Critical Inquiry* 24, no. 4 (1998): 988–1009.

Žižek, Slavoj. "Lenin's Lesson for Israel and Ukraine." *Syndicate*, February 6, 2024. https://www.project-syndicate.org/commentary/lenin-principled-pragmatism-fidelity-to-cause-requires-changing-position-by-slavoj-zizek-2024-02#:~:text=If%20there%20is%20one%20element,blind%20dogmatism%20and%20cynical%20opportunism.

Žižek, Slavoj. *Less Than Nothing: Hegel and the Shadow of Dialectical Materialism*. New York: Verso, 2012.

Žižek, Slavoj. *Like a Thief in Broad Daylight: Power in the Era of Post-Humanity*. New York: Allen Lane, 2018.

Žižek, Slavoj. *Mad World: War, Movies, Sex*. New York: OR Books, 2023.

Žižek, Slavoj. "Neighbors and Other Monsters." In *The Neighbor: Three Inquiries in Political Theology*. With a New Preface, edited by Slavoj Žižek, Eric L. Santner, and Kenneth Reinhard, 134–90. Chicago: University of Chicago Press, 2013.

Žižek, Slavoj. *Organs without Bodies: On Deleuze and Consequences*. New York: Routledge, 2004.

Žižek, Slavoj. *Pandemic! 2: Chronicles of a Lost Time*. New York: OR Books, 2020.

Žižek, Slavoj. *The Parallax View*. Cambridge, MA: MIT Press, 2006.

Žižek, Slavoj. *The Plague of Fantasies*. New York: Verso, 1997.

Žižek, Slavoj. *The Puppet and the Dwarf: The Perverse Core of Christianity*. Cambridge, MA: MIT Press, 2003.

Žižek, Slavoj. "The Real of Sexual Difference." In *Reading Seminar XX: Lacan's Major Work on Love, Knowledge, and Feminine Sexuality*, edited by Suzanne Barnard and Bruce Fink, 57–76. New York: State University of New York Press, 2002.

Žižek, Slavoj. *The Relevance of the Communist Manifesto*. Cambridge: Polity Press, 2019.

Žižek, Slavoj. "The Shooting of Trump." *Substack: Žižek Goads and Prods*, July 17, 2024. https://slavoj.substack.com/p/the-shooting-of-trump.

Žižek, Slavoj. "A Soft Focus on War." *In These Times*, April 21, 2010. http://www.inthesetimes.com/article/5864/a_soft_focus_on_war/.

Žižek, Slavoj. "Some Concluding Notes on Violence, Ideology and Communist Culture." *Subjectivity* 3, no. 1 (2010): 101–16.

Žižek, Slavoj. *Surplus-Enjoyment: A Guide for The Non-Perplexed*. New York: Bloomsbury, 2022.

Žižek, Slavoj. *Too Late to Awaken: What Lies Ahead When There is No Future?* London: Allen Lane, 2024.

Žižek, Slavoj. *Trouble in Paradise: From the End of History to the End of Capitalism*. Brooklyn: Melville House, 2014.

Žižek, Slavoj. *The Ticklish Subject: The Absent Center of Political Ontology*. New York: Verso, 1999.

Žižek, Slavoj. "Truth Has the Structure of a Fiction: An Imagined Phone Call." *The Philosophical Salon*, November 20. https://thephilosophicalsalon.com/truth-has-the-structure-of-a-fiction-an-imagined-phone-call/.

Žižek, Slavoj. *The Universal Exception*, ed. Rex Butler and Scott Stephens (New York: Continuum, 2006).

Žižek, Slavoj. *Violence: Six Sideways Reflections*. New York: Picador, 2008.

Žižek, Slavoj. *Welcome to the Desert of the Real! Five Essays on September 11 and Related Dates*. New York: Verso, 2002.

Žižek, Slavoj and Glyn Daly. *Conversations with Žižek*. Cambridge: Polity Press, 2004.

Zuber, Maria T. "How to Declare War on Coal's Emissions Without Declaring War on Coal Communities." *The Washington Post*, February 24, 2017. https://www.washingtonpost.com/opinions/how-to-declare-war-on-coals-emissions-without-declaring-war-on-coal-communities/2017/02/24/610c7da2-f864-11e6-bf01-d47f8cf9b643_story.html.

Zupančič, Alenka. "Desire, Hysteria and the Indirectness of Truth." Unpublished manuscript.

Zupančič, Alenka. "Love Thy Neighbor as Thyself?!" *Problemi International* 3, no. 2 (2019): 89–108.

Zupančič, Alenka. "A Perfect Place to Die: Theatre in Hitchcock's Films." In *Everything You Always Wanted to Know About Lacan, But Were Afraid to Ask Hitchcock*, edited by Slavoj Žižek, 73–105. New York: Verso, 1992.

Index

Note: Page reference for note numbers are indicated by 'n'.

1993 Oslo Accords   33, 92, 147, 150, 158–9
1994 Crime Bill   71

Abbas, Mahmoud   109, 116, 229 n.73
abolition of sovereignty   115, 230 n.103
Abu El-Haj, Nadia   92–4, 150, 215 n.44
Abunimah, Ali   32, 108, 110, 232 n.29
Ackerman, Seth   89
Afropessimism   1, 42, 44, 49–50, 52–3, 55, 57–9, 61, 111, 115, 151–2, 164–6, 168, 170, 176–7, 183, 210 n.108, 230 n.103
Agamben, Giorgio   147, 152, 244 n.3
Alexander, Gil   234 n.153
Alexander, Michelle   69, 214 n.34
"All Lives Matter"   34, 73
Althoff, Sebastian   67
alt-right movement   1
Améry, Jean   13, 16, 194 n.71
Anderson, Patrick D.   139–40
animalization/animality   22, 37, 45, 59, 61, 140
antagonism   1, 14, 31, 38, 53, 61, 68, 70, 75, 86, 93–4, 99–100, 106–10, 112, 158, 166, 183, 218 n.68, 225 n.150
anti-Blackness   2, 6, 12, 21, 38, 39, 42, 48–9, 52–3, 55, 57, 60, 67–76, 130–2, 139, 143, 151–2, 164–9, 171, 174–6, 184, 204 n.7, 215 n.43, 216 n.47
anti-Black futurology 37, 44

anti-Black gaze   10
anti-Black libidinal economy   42–3, 53, 75, 108, 132
anti-Black structures of privilege   117
anti-Black violence   12, 16, 53
anti-Black world   12, 14, 37, 45, 50, 52, 54–5, 67, 76, 98, 104–5, 118, 164, 169, 171, 238 n.72
anti-colonial reason   83, 94, 159, 179, 181–4
Anti-Defamation League   152
anti-hermeneutic   97
anti-identitarianism   41, 104–5
anti-Semitism   16, 33–4, 36, 39, 71, 78–80, 82, 83, 85, 88, 91, 93–4, 116, 122, 125, 137–8, 139, 145, 150, 152, 154, 155–7, 159, 162, 166–9, 175, 178, 184, 202 n.169, 219 n.77, 220 n.88, 236 n.45, 242 n.116
anti-Zionism   67, 94, 120, 122, 234 n.153
anti-Zionist hermeneutic   159–60, 163
apartheid   19, 24, 32, 36, 66, 69, 70–1, 84, 87, 119, 124, 142, 148–50, 154, 179, 218 n.69, 233 n.131, 238 n.65, 245 n.11, 246 n.23, 246 n.27
apocalyptic language   120–2
Appadurai, Arjun   112
Arab Slave Trade   165
Arendt, Hannah   196–7 n.110
Armée de Libération Nationale (ALN)   112–13
Armstrong, Jason P.   202 n.175

asymmetry   16, 92, 128, 147, 166, 195 n.83, 249 n.45
Austin, Lloyd   160–1
Ayalon, Ami   147

Baby Suggs (*Beloved*)   51–2
Baldwin, James   1, 202 n.172
Balibar, Étienne   177
band-aid solutions   70
Barghouti, Marwan   147
Bartleby ("Bartleby, the Scrivener")   70–1
Bartov, Omer   162, 232–3 n.131, 236 n.45
The Battle for Justice in Palestine (Abunimah)   32
Beauvoir, Simone de   48–9, 106
Begin, Menachem   85–7, 136
Being   6, 41, 46
being-in-the-world   115, 121
Bell, Derrick   72
Beloved (Morrison)   37, 42, 45, 50–2, 69, 71, 152, 245 n.6
Ben-Gurion, David   88–9, 223 n.140
Benhabib, Seyla   28, 30–1
Benjamin, Walter   138
Berardi, Franco   22, 183
Berger, Elisabeth   103, 227 n.33
Bernasconi, Robert   113
Biden, Joe   23, 26, 33, 67, 73, 154, 212 n.6, 246 n.27, 254 n.14
Bildung   113
binationalism   31, 91, 124, 149
Bisharat, Odeh   81, 94
Black abjection   39, 127, 129–32
Black imago   42–4, 59, 74, 132, 205 n.11, 210 n.104, 215 n.43
Black Lives Matter (BLM)   6–7, 21, 23, 34, 67, 69–73, 76, 131, 144, 173, 175, 205 n.7
   BLM Global Network   70
   BLM Inland Empire   70
Blackness   2, 9, 14, 42–3, 49, 53–6, 59–60, 74, 105, 127, 129–30, 132, 139, 168
Black Panther Party   38, 99, 110, 197 n.112
Black radical tradition   70

Black Skin, White Masks (Fanon)   2, 14, 18, 102, 105, 128–9, 151, 170–1
Blakeley, Grace   62
Blinken, Antony   241 n.112
Block, Niko   150
Bou Ali, Nadia   104, 212 n.10
Boycott, Divest, and Sanctions (BDS) movement   31–2, 34, 66–7, 71, 76, 83, 92, 94, 121, 124, 148, 162, 216 n.56
Braverman, Suella   156
BREATHE Act   74
Bresheeth-Zabner, Haim   33
Bryant, Rodney   203 n.175
B'Tselem   32
Bushnell, Aaron   119, 232 n.129
Butler, Judith   9, 28, 30, 78, 82–3, 86, 122, 132, 136–7, 149, 154, 157, 169, 182, 216 n.59, 220 n.88, 220 n.97
Byrd, Jodi   15, 250 n.57

Callamard, Agnès   212 n.4
cancel culture   32–3, 154
Cartesian *cogito*/subjectivity   37, 41, 45, 46
Cartesianism   45, 206 n.30
catastrophe   22–3, 28, 57, 74, 121, 147, 149–52, 162, 185
Catlin, Samuel P.   198–9 n.127
Césaire, Aimé   18, 81, 99, 138–40, 156, 194 n.68, 228 n.52
Chamoiseau, Patrick   44
Chandler, Nahum   174
Chaouat, Bruno   176, 252 nn.104–5
Civil Rights Movement   59, 73, 148
class struggle   1, 18, 58, 61, 69–70, 108, 110, 112, 172–3, 175–7, 210 n.106, 251 n.88
Clinton, Bill   248 n.41
Clinton, Hillary   71
CNN   22, 72
cogito   37, 41–2, 45–8, 63–4
Cohen, Eli   156
colonialism   2, 8, 10–12, 17, 19–20, 87, 99–100, 103, 106–7, 113–14, 138–9, 151, 156, 165, 182, 233 n.131

colonial ideology   21
Colonial Matrix of Power
    (CMP)   101–2, 107
colonial violence   19–20, 66, 87,
    156, 162
Cook-Lynn, Elizabeth   224 n.140
Cotton, Tom   215–16 n.47, 224 n.140
Coulthard, Glen   15, 115
counter-reactional behavior   13
counter-violence   2, 3, 8, 13, 17–18,
    20, 31, 39, 53, 61–2, 82–3,
    99, 113, 125, 182, 184–5, 223
    n.127
courage of hopelessness   146–7,
    149–50, 172
Critical Black Studies   42, 131
Critical Race Theory (CRT)   66–7, 71,
    75–6, 134
Critique of Dialectical Reason
    (Sartre)   112
Crouch, Stanley   245 n.6
cruel optimism   146
cultural imaginary 5, 37, 41, 44, 60, 73,
    144, 151, 162

Dalet Plan   89–90
Dalits   106–8
Danon, Danny   115–17, 120
Davidson, Miri   227 n.40
Davis, Angela   178, 231 n.121
death drive   64, 205 n.8, 211 n.126
decolonization   11, 38, 71, 85,
    90–2, 95, 98–100, 103–5, 108,
    110–15, 125, 139, 227 n.40,
    230 n.101
  decolonial analytics   101
  decolonial future   99, 205 n.7
  decoloniality   1, 38, 100–2, 105,
    107, 110, 111–12, 114, 126,
    181, 227 n.40
  decolonization of the mind   38,
    100, 105, 111
de-development   26
defund the police   21, 23, 73,
    198 n.123
dehumanization   112, 131, 157,
    163, 175, 181–3, 242 n.120,
    246 n.23
Deleuze, Gilles   85, 178, 241 n.108

Delport, Terblanche   116–17,
    231 n.111
Democratic National Committee   70
de-Nazification   139
Derrida, Jacques   135, 137, 141
Descartes, René   45–6
de-Zionization   120, 122
disalienation   105–6
Discourse on Colonialism
    (Césaire)   81, 138
Discourse on Method (Descartes)   45
double colonization   110
Du Bois, W. E. B.   47, 157, 237 n.52
Dussel, Enrique   134, 141

econocide   26, 100
Edelman, Lee   41–2, 63, 198 n.127,
    204 n.7, 205 n.8
empathy   27, 82, 122–4, 130, 131,
    140, 141, 143–4, 157–8, 166–7,
    169, 179
epistemicide   100–1, 112, 114, 163,
    226 n.13
equality   2, 16, 31, 35, 49, 70, 107,
    122, 131, 147–8, 150, 162, 178,
    244 n.5
equi-sapiens (*Sorry to Bother
    You*)   45, 59–64, 118,
    210 n.108
Erakat, Noura   184
Erikson, Erik   110
Estes, Nick   224 n.140
ethical petrification   141
ethical Zionism   137, 145, 234 n.153
Eurocentric knowing   101
Eurocentrism   108
exceptionalism   17, 67, 104, 151–2,
    170, 175, 178–9

facelessness   39, 127–9, 140, 143
fake recognition   15
Fanon, Frantz   1–4, 7–12, 14, 16–20,
    23, 25, 35, 37–9, 42–3, 47–8,
    53, 55, 58, 64, 66, 68, 77, 91–2,
    94, 98–108, 111–16, 118–19,
    125, 127–30, 138–40, 145, 151,
    153, 156, 169–75, 177, 181–3,
    194 n.68, 196–7 n.110, 197
    n.112, 210 n.104, 227 n.38,

227 n.40, 227 n.46, 228 n.60, 230 n.101, 242 n.120, 251 n.82
far Right   28, 33–4, 37–8, 66–8, 71, 74–6, 81, 85–6, 89–90, 94, 154, 218 n.68, 227 n.40
Feiglin, Moshe   34
feminine logic   5–6
Ferreira da Silva, Denise   59
fetishist disavowal   30, 38, 65–6, 68, 72–4, 76, 84, 93–4, 119, 146, 184, 216 n.47
Finkelstein, Norman   77
Finkielkraut, Alain   133, 136, 144, 252 n.105
The Florida Board of Education   215 n.47
Floyd, George   21, 55, 73, 74
The Fragile Absolute (Žižek)   50
freedom   2, 8, 10, 12, 16, 25, 31, 36, 49, 51, 64, 70, 82, 85–7, 109, 122, 144, 147, 150, 157–9, 165, 171–2, 178, 191 n.9, 208 n.58, 229 n.71, 230 n.103, 244 n.5
Freud, Sigmund   5, 43, 46, 68, 101, 110, 226 n.16
Friedman, Thomas   22–3, 146
Fugitive Slave Law of 1850   50, 52

Gallant, Yoav   160–1, 163
Gaza   3, 17, 20, 22–3, 26–8, 30, 32, 34, 65–7, 82, 94, 109, 121–4, 133, 144–6, 150, 154, 156–7, 159–62, 177, 179, 183, 197 n.110, 198 n.123, 200 n.141, 212 n.4, 212 n.10, 214 n.34, 224 n.140, 231 n.125, 233 n.131, 237 n.45, 237 n.55, 237 n.58, 239–40 n.85, 241 n.109, 243 n.120, 247 n.27
genocidal self-defense   28
genocide   16, 20–1, 28, 32, 53, 66–7, 81, 84, 87, 92–3, 95, 124, 142, 145–6, 150, 155, 157, 160, 177, 184, 194 n.71, 198 n.123, 200 n.141, 218 n.69, 219 n.77, 224 n.140, 226 n.13, 237 n.58, 239 n.85, 241 n.109, 244 n.5, 246 n.27, 247 n.37

Georgia International Law Enforcement Exchange (GILEE)   202 n.175
Gessen, M.   231 n.125, 254 n.14
Gibson, Nigel C.   17
Glazer, Jonathan   80, 218 n.69
Glynos, Jason   98
Gordon, Lewis   9, 250 n.76
gratuitous violence   52, 168, 174
Great Arab revolt of 1936–9   20
greater violence   19, 31–2
Green, Alon-Lee   123

Haddad, Toufic   109
Hamas   3, 20, 22, 24, 26–8, 30, 32, 77–83, 86–7, 93–4, 121, 123, 133, 156, 161–3, 175, 184, 195 n.94, 198 n.116, 216 n.56, 225 n.150, 229 n.71, 233 n.131, 244 n.5, 248 n.44
Hartman, Saidiya   37, 39, 127, 130–2, 137, 143, 145, 158, 247 n.33
Hegel, G. W. F.   8–11, 34, 46, 48, 104, 113, 143
Heidegger, Martin   46
Hillbilly Elegy (Vance)   213–14 n.29
Hitler, Adolf   34, 80, 82, 138–9, 201 n.160, 218 n.70
Holocaust   13, 80, 138, 151–7, 162, 166, 168, 170, 175–6, 218 n.69, 220 n.88, 250 n.69
Hook, Derek   117, 231 n.111
hopelessness   129, 146–7, 149–50
Horkheimer, Max   184, 254 n.19
human animal   82, 129, 140, 160–1, 163, 183, 233 n.131
humanism   6, 44, 45, 46, 59, 64, 127, 128, 129–32, 138, 142, 143, 182–3
al-Husseini, Haj Amin   79–80
hyperbolic doubt   46–7

identity politics   1, 14–15, 17, 35, 39, 69–70, 103, 108, 116–17, 125, 152, 173, 254 n.14
idiopathic identification   131, 143–4
IfNotNow   66, 71, 162
Illouz, Eva   77–80, 87–8, 91, 93–4, 201 n.167, 216 n.56, 216 n.59, 218 n.70, 220 n.97, 221 n.109

Indigenous sovereignty 15, 115, 147
"The Instance of the Letter in the Unconscious, or Reason since Freud" (Lacan) 46
International Court of Justice 81, 147, 247 n.37
international law 24, 65
In the Wake: On Blackness and Being (Sharpe) 166
Israeli Defense Forces (IDF) 25–6, 32–4, 161
Israeli manifesto 178
Israeli Occupation Forces (IOF) 34, 110, 121, 123, 157, 160, 164–6, 174, 232 n.131, 248 n.44
Israeli paranoia 30
Is Theory Good For Jews? (Chaouat) 176

Jabotinsky, Vladimir "Ze'ev" 20, 88–9, 197 n.115
Jabr, Samah 103
Jacobson, Howard 88, 90, 93
Jerusalem 76, 79–80
Jones, Van 72
Judea and Samaria 122
justice 2, 8, 16, 21, 23–5, 35, 38, 49, 60–1, 68, 70, 72, 118–19, 126, 133, 135, 141, 143, 145, 147, 150, 178–9, 184, 214 n.34, 243 n.120, 254 n.14

Kallner, Ariel 28
Kanafani, Ghassan 183
Kant, Immanuel 7, 13, 47, 143
Kapoor, Ilan 105, 112
Kashani, Maryam 33
Kattoura, Nicki 20
Kelley, Robin D. G. 60, 62, 74
Khader, Jamil 144
Khalidi, Rashid 20, 31, 81, 148, 244 n.5
King, Martin Luther 59, 73, 214 n.34
King, Rodney 54
King, Tiffany Lethabo 204–5 n.7
Kleinberg, Aviad 78–9, 91
Kojève, Alexandre 10
Kristeva, Julia 105

Lacan, Jacques 4, 5, 41, 43, 46, 105, 189, 192 n.16, 206 n.30, 211 n.126, 212 n.10
Laclau, Ernesto 45
Lamont Hill, Marc 191 n.9
Lanzmann, Claude 167
Laruelle, François 41
law and order 67, 73–5, 238 n.65
law of castration 5
Leahy Law 76, 216 n.50
Leifer, Joshua 28
Levi, Emanuel Yitzhak 123
Levi, Primo 141, 152
Levinas, Emmanuel 39, 127–8, 133–41, 144–5, 151, 252 n.104
LeVine, Mark 19
Levy, Daniel 160
liberal Left 38, 66–8, 71, 73, 75–6, 116, 184, 254 n.14
liberal Zionism 38, 65, 91, 94–5
Livni, Tzpi 239 n.85
Lorde, Audre 81, 122–4

Maafa 39, 50, 151–3, 164, 169–70, 245 n.6
Mações, Bruno 24
Maher, Geo 10, 20
McCarthyism 34, 71, 93
McGowan, Todd 44, 51
"Make America anti-Palestinian Again" 66
"Make America Great Again" (MAGA) 66, 72, 74–6
"Make America White Again" 72
Malcolm X 117, 120, 125, 221 n.109
Malka, Shlomo 133–4
Manichean logic 18, 78, 92
Mannoni, Octave 65
Markmann, Charles Lam 171
Marriott, David 118
Marx, Karl 124, 173
Marxism 1, 38, 98, 102, 176
masculine logic 5–6
master-slave dialectic 8, 10
Mbembe, Achille 7, 27, 61, 156, 177, 217 n.59, 246 n.23
Meir, Golda 221 n.109
Melville, Herman 70

Middle Passage   50, 131, 151–2, 168, 206 n.25
Mignolo, Walter   101–2, 104, 108, 111–13, 227 n.46
Mohanty, Chandra Talpade   35
Morgan, Michael L.   135–6
Morris, Benny   223–4 n.140
Morrison, Toni   37, 42, 45, 50–2, 68–9, 71, 152, 245 n.6
Moses, Dirk   21, 154
Moten, Fred   230 n.103
Movement for Black Lives (M4BL)   16, 23, 36, 67, 69, 72–4
Mufti of Jerusalem   80, 218 n.70
multicultural liberal states   15
multidirectional memory   168
Muselmann   141, 152, 164, 174, 233 n.131, 244 n.3
mutual recognition   8–11, 18, 142

Nafar, Tamer   82
Nakba   20, 28, 74, 90, 92, 94, 100, 137, 152, 169–70, 223–4 n.140, 236 n.45, 243 n.120
naked violence   19, 31–2
Nanibush, Wanda   115
Nassar, Tamara   109
National Liberation Front (FLN)   112, 227 n.40
Nechin, Etan   86–7
Négritude movement   105, 117, 228 n.50, 228 n.52
negrophilia   130
negrophobia   9, 12, 72, 130, 132, 165, 172
Nelson, Cary   83, 220 n.88
neoliberal conflict resolution model   109
Netanyahu, Benjamin   26, 31, 65–6, 77, 80–1, 84, 89, 93–4, 121, 146–9, 158, 218 n.70, 220 n.88, 247 n.37, 248 n.41
"Never Again"   154, 220 n.88
"New Jim Crow"   69, 74
Newton, Huey P.   38, 99, 110–11, 113, 117–20, 197 n.112
Nguyen, Hoai-An   177
Nietzsche   12–13, 14

No Humans Involved (N.H.I.)   54, 56, 62–3
nonrecognition studies   10
non-violence   3, 18
normative horizon   10
not-all   4–7, 35, 64, 144, 172

Obama, Barack   69, 72, 232 n.130, 248 n.41
objective violence   25–7, 30, 32, 34, 68, 86, 98, 125, 145
Occupation   26–7, 38, 65, 77, 80–3, 86, 93–4, 103–4, 109, 124, 145–6, 148, 162–3, 179, 219 n.77, 248 n.41
one-state solution   31, 89. 91, 92, 147, 148, 149, 150
ontology   1–2, 4, 6–7, 41–3, 46–7, 55, 57, 84, 98, 107, 127–8, 130, 132, 139–40, 164, 174, 225 n.150
Operation Al-Aqsa Flood   3
Operation Iron Swords   3, 32, 100, 121, 232 n.131, 236 n.45, 239 n.85
Oppression Olympics   152, 169, 177
Otherwise than Being (Levinas)   138
overrepresentation   36, 163, 174
Oz, Amos   125, 158

Palestine-Israel conflict   103
Palestinian Authority (PA)   108–10, 149, 229 n.71, 229 n.73, 232 n.130
Palestinian Lives Matter   23, 67, 157
Palestinian Ministry of Health   103
Palestinian violence   20, 22, 82, 125
Palestinophobia   19, 34
Pappé, Ilan   89–90, 223 n.140
Parting Ways: Jewishness and the Critique of Zionism (Butler)   28
The Passions of the Soul (Descartes)   45
Peace Camp   31, 75, 146
Pelosi, Nancy   73
Phenomenology of Spirit (Hegel)   8, 10
Philcox, Richard   171, 207 n.43, 251 n.81
Philip, NourbeSe   206 n.25

"Philosophy for Palestine"   30, 133
Pluth, Ed   46
Polgreen, Lydia   91
politics of recognition   9, 14–16, 143
Posnock, Ross   105
Progressives Except for Palestine (PEP)   67
Pro-Human Camp Network   181
proletarian position   6, 172–6
provincialization   104, 151, 168, 176, 217 n.59
psychoanalysis   1, 38, 41, 45, 97–8, 101–8, 189, 206 n.30, 226 n.16
Psychoanalysis Under Occupation (Sheehi and Sheehi)   103
public use of *ressentiment*   13–14, 16, 36, 119, 232 n.131
The Question of Palestine (Said)   157

racial elimination   81, 92
Rancière, Jacques   6, 14
Rankin, John   130–1, 144
the Real   6, 37, 41, 52, 59, 128, 142, 205 n.8
reconciliation   31, 84, 90–1, 243 n.120
Red Skin, White Masks (Coulthard)   15
refusal   1, 13, 16, 22, 28, 36, 87, 94, 100, 119, 124, 142, 189, 194 n.71, 205 n.7, 224 n.140, 242 n.120
refuseniks   122
RegalView   56, 58, 60–1
reparations   90, 92, 148, 242–3 n.120
reproductive futurism   198 n.127
ressentiment   12–17, 31, 36, 100, 119, 185, 194 n.71, 232 n.131, 238 n.65
revolutionary suicide   39, 117–20, 124, 126, 231 n.123, 232 n.131
Revolutionary Suicide (Newton)   118
Riley, Boots   37, 42, 45, 63–4, 209 n.88
Robinson, William I.   177
Rose, Jacqueline   80, 253 n.124
Rothberg, Michael   156, 168, 250 n.69
Roy, Sara   26

Rufo, Christopher   71

Sacco, Joe   28, 237 n.55
Said, Edward   33, 36, 79, 91–2, 120–2, 125–6, 147, 149–50, 157–9, 169–70, 177–9, 217 n.59, 250 n.78, 252 n.116
Sammon, Alexander   246 n.27
Sanbar, Elias   178, 241 n.108
Sartre, Jean-Paul   18, 49, 104, 112–13, 172, 196 n.103
Sayegh, Fayez   80, 82, 85
Scahill, Jeremy   160
Scenes of Subjection (Hartman)   130, 158, 253 n.121
Schwarz, Alon   90–3, 223–4 n.140
Scott, David   151
Sebald, W. G.   16
The Second Sex (Beauvoir)   48
Segal, Raz   28
Segev, Tom   197 n.114
Sekyi-Otu, Ato   8, 17, 24, 182
self-defense   21–2, 135–6, 148, 159
self-immolation   119
self-violence   4, 39, 99–100, 113–15, 120
settler-colonial framework   28, 31, 86–7
settler colonialism   17, 20, 22, 28, 30–2, 37–8, 68, 79–81, 85, 88, 91–2, 94, 98–9, 116, 125, 139–40, 144–5, 147, 150, 156–7, 159, 165–6, 194 n.71, 221 n.109, 224 n.140, 243 n.120
Settler Orientalism   163
Sexton, Jared   53
Sharpe, Christina   51, 127, 166–9, 206 n.25
Shatz, Adam   18, 112, 194 n.67, 195 n.94, 198 n.123
Sheehi, Lara   93, 103, 106, 116, 144, 219 n.73
Sheehi, Stephen   93, 103, 106, 116, 144, 219 n.73
Shoah   13, 39, 80, 94, 138–9, 151–6, 162–4, 166–70, 176, 218 n.69, 245 n.6, 250 n.69, 252 n.104
Simek, Nicole   116

Simpson, Leanne   115
Sixty Million and more (Morrison)   52, 152
skepticism   6, 9, 16, 97, 78, 97, 100, 104–5, 205 n.7
slavery 2.0   57
Smerconish, Michael   22
Smotrich, Bezalel   146, 149, 158, 222 n.121
social death   10, 42, 53, 118, 145
social violence   37, 42, 172
Sorry to Bother You (Riley)   37, 42, 45, 54, 57, 61–3, 118
Spillers, Hortense   99, 131
Spivak, Gayatri Chakravorty   79, 144, 217 n.59, 217 n.64, 230 n.105
Srebnik, Simon   167–9
Standing Together   122–4
Stephanopoulos, George   73
Stewart, Patrick   187
Stolypin, Pyotr Arkadyevich   188
subjective violence   25, 27, 32
the Symbolic   4–6, 63, 109, 117
symbolic violence   25, 27, 48, 116
systemic violence   25, 30, 61–2

Táíwò, Olúfẹmi   35
Tantura (Schwarz)   90
Taylor, Charles   9
Taylor, Keeanga-Yamahtta   60, 210 n.106
A Tempest (Césaire)   99
Thakur, Gautum Basu   2
Third World politics   110
Thobani, Sunera   244 n.3
three-dimensional violence   17
To Die for the People (Newton)   118
Too Late To Awaken (Žižek)   149
Totality and Infinity (Levinas)   127
tragic entanglement   131, 137
Trump, Donald   16, 66, 72, 74–6, 94, 138, 184, 212 n.6, 213 n.29, 254 n.14
Truth   188–9
Tuck, Eve   30, 38, 86, 98
Turki, Fawaz   25, 222 n.126
Turner, Nat   77
two-state solution   23, 31, 75, 84, 91, 109, 146–9, 158, 246 n.27

ultranationalism   68, 94
"The Uses of Anger" (Lorde)   81, 123–4

Vance, JD   213–14 n.29
Varoufakis, Yanis   219 n.77
Veracini, Lorenzo   165
Vergès, Françoise   104
violence. *See also individual entries*
    anti-Black   12, 53
    colonial   19–20, 66, 87, 156, 162
    counter-violence   2, 3, 8, 13, 17–18, 20, 31, 39, 53, 61–2, 82–3, 99, 113, 125, 182, 184–5, 223 n.127
    ethical   99
    gratuitous   52, 168, 174
    greater   19, 31–2
    naked   19, 31–2
    vs. non-violence   3, 18
    objective   25–7, 30, 32, 34, 68, 86, 98, 125, 145
    social   37, 42, 172
    subjective   25, 27, 32
    symbolic   25, 27, 48, 116
    systemic   25, 30, 61–2
Vogt, Erik   113

Wahnich, Sophie   188
Wall Street Democrat   71
Warren, Calvin   42
warrior of the imaginary   44, 63, 99
Warschawski, Michel   109, 231 n.123
Waziyatawin   178
West, Cornel   69, 128, 210 n.106
West Bank   26, 30, 33, 65, 90, 93, 108–9, 123–4, 133, 144, 146, 148–9, 159–60, 174, 241 n.109
white voice   54–6, 59–60, 62, 209 n.88
Wilderson III, Frank B.   42–3, 50, 52, 55, 151–2, 164–6, 168, 174, 176
Wolfe, Patrick   30, 86
World Central Kitchen   26
wretched   1, 6, 10, 14–15, 17–18, 98, 104–5, 107–8, 114–16, 128, 130, 143, 153, 169–70, 172–3, 175, 177, 181, 183–4

The Wretched of the Earth
 (Fanon) 11, 13, 18, 38, 98,
 102, 108, 112–13, 196 n.110,
 230 n.101, 251 n.82
Wynter, Sylvia 36, 54–5, 84, 102

Yancy, George 132–3
Yang, K. Wayne 30, 38, 86, 98, 132
Young, Robert J. C. 196–7 n.110
Youngkin, Glenn 71–2

Zalloua, Zahi 187, 189
Zeavin, Hannah 119
Zelensky, Volodymyr 24
Zenun Almada, Flavio 17
Zimmerman, George 69
Zionism 16, 19–20, 30–1, 33, 36–8,
 65, 79–82, 85–93, 95, 110,
 120, 122, 125–6, 135–7, 140,
 145–6, 149, 152, 154, 157–8,
 183, 194 n.71, 195 n.94, 218
 n.69, 219 n.77, 220 n.88, 221
 n.109, 233 n.131, 234 n.153

Zionist anti-Semitism 34, 125,
 220 n.88
Žižek, Slavoj 1–7, 9–11, 13, 17, 21,
 23–5, 27, 31–5, 37–9, 41–3,
 45–8, 50–1, 57, 63, 65, 67–8,
 71, 78, 84, 93, 95, 97, 99–100,
 103–7, 111, 113, 116–17, 119,
 122, 125, 128, 140–3, 146–9,
 153, 171–6, 181, 183–4, 201
 n.160, 205 n.8, 207 n.44, 213
 n.29, 216 n.59, 220 n.88, 225
 n.150, 231 n.120, 242 n.116,
 242 n.120, 249 n.45, 251 n.82
Žižekian *cogito* 42, 45–6
zone of being 140
Zone of Interest (Glazer) 80
zone of nonbeing 9, 26, 37, 42–4,
 47, 49–50, 58, 60, 63–4, 84, 98,
 103, 115, 118, 127, 131, 134,
 139–40, 142, 145, 153, 170–6,
 182, 184
"Zong #15" (Philip) 206 n.25
Zupančič, Alenka 49, 64, 114, 143